Big Dreams

Big Dreams

The Science of Dreaming and the Origins of Religion

KELLY BULKELEY

OXFORD
UNIVERSITY PRESS

OXFORD
UNIVERSITY PRESS

Oxford University Press is a department of the University of Oxford. It furthers
the University's objective of excellence in research, scholarship, and education
by publishing worldwide. Oxford is a registered trade mark of Oxford University
Press in the UK and certain other countries.

Published in the United States of America by Oxford University Press
198 Madison Avenue, New York, NY 10016, United States of America.

© Oxford University Press 2016

Library of Congress Cataloging-in-Publication Data
Names: Bulkeley, Kelly, 1962–
Title: Big dreams : the science of dreaming and the origins of religion / Kelly Bulkeley.
Description: New York : Oxford University Press, 2016. |
Includes bibliographical references and index.
Identifiers: LCCN 2015034057 | ISBN 978–0–19–935153–4 (cloth : alk. paper)
Subjects: LCSH: Dreams. | Experience (Religion)
Classification: LCC BF1078 .B779 2016 | DDC 154.6/3—dc23 LC record available at
http://lccn.loc.gov/2015034057

3 5 7 9 8 6 4 2
Printed by Sheridan, USA

For Hilary

Lately I've been rereading psychology books,
and I have felt singularly defrauded.
All of them discuss the mechanisms of dreams
or the subjects of dreams, but they do not mention,
as I had hoped, that which is so astonishing,
so strange—the fact of dreaming.

JORGE LUIS BORGES, "Nightmares"

Contents

List of Tables   ix

Introduction   1

PART I: *Sleep*

1. Evolution   15
2. The Brain   27
3. Health   44
4. Culture   56

PART II: *Dreaming*

5. Recall   77
6. Content   95
7. Continuities   112
8. Discontinuities   128

PART III: *Big Dreams*

9. Aggressive   145
10. Sexual   160

11. Gravitational   177

12. Mystical   195

PART IV: *Religious Experience*

13. Demonic Seduction   213

14. Prophetic Vision   228

15. Ritual Healing   242

16. Contemplative Practice   257

Conclusion   271

Acknowledgments   275

Notes   277

Bibliography   307

Index   325

Tables

4 .1 Frequency of Insomnia in the 2007
      Demographic Survey   66

4.2   Frequency of Insomnia in the 2010
      Demographic Survey   67

4.3   Frequency of Insomnia in the 2015
      Demographic Survey   71

5.1   Frequency of Dream Recall in the 2015
      Demographic Survey   87

6.1   SDDb Baseline Dreams   103

6.2   Emotions in the Baselines   107

6.3   Elements in the Baselines   109

6.4   Colors in the Baselines   110

9.1   Frequency of Nightmare Recall in the 2010
      Demographic Survey   148

9.2   Typical Dreams: Being Chased or Attacked   150

10.1 Typical Dreams: Sexual   162

10.2 2010 Demographic Survey Responses to Typical
      Dreams: Sexual   165

10.3 Frequencies of Sexually Related Words in the
      Baselines   167

10.4 Frequencies of Sexually Related Words in
      Individual Dream Series   168

10.5 Sexual Dreams before Sexual Activity in the 2010
      Demographic Survey   173

11.1 Typical Dreams: Falling   179

11.2 2010 Demographic Survey Responses to Typical
      Dreams: Falling   181

11.3 Frequencies of Falling-Related Words in the
      Baselines   183

11.4 Frequencies of Falling-Related Words
      in Individual Series   184
12.1 Typical Dreams: Flying and Visitation   197
12.2 Frequencies of Flying-Related Words in the
      Baselines and Individual Series   199

Big Dreams

Introduction

(Romeo): Peace, peace, Mercutio, peace!
Thou talk'st of nothing.
(Mercutio): True, I talk of dreams,
Which are the children of an idle brain,
Begot of nothing but vain fantasy,
Which are as thin of substance as the air
And more inconstant than the wind . . .

WILLIAM SHAKESPEARE, *Romeo and Juliet*

THE VAST MAJORITY of dreams are forgotten. Wispy and amorphous, they evaporate quickly in the light of morning. Gone without a trace, as if they never happened.

A few of them, however, do not flee with the dawn. These unusual dreams possess a special vividness and intensity that makes them difficult if not impossible to forget. They burst across the threshold of waking awareness and seize conscious attention, imprinting themselves so deeply into memory they can be clearly recalled weeks, months, or even years later.

This book starts with the simple observation that a majority of dreams are immediately forgotten, while a few are highly memorable. A reasonable theory of dreaming should be able to account for both aspects of this observation, the tendency to forget most dreams and the tendency to intensely remember a few of them.

The conventional scientific approach has been to pay attention to just one side of the equation, focusing on recent dreams gathered from surveys or sleep laboratory experiments. These are mostly trivial dreams that would have been forgotten if someone had not prompted their recollection. Many researchers have built their theories using only these kinds of dreams, ignoring the more unusual and memorable types that tend not to appear in sleep laboratories or surveys. The result is a shallow and rather bland view of dreaming that excludes precisely those types of dreams people have always found most interesting and meaningful.

An alternative scientific approach is to reverse the order of significance. Instead of treating highly memorable dreams as marginal, make them the center of inquiry. Look at them not as trivial exceptions to the general rule of ordinary dreaming but as singular expressions of the tremendous potential of the dreaming mind.

This can be considered a "Black Swan" approach because it emphasizes the pivotal impact of rare phenomena on scientific theorizing. The basic idea goes back to the eighteenth-century Scottish philosopher David Hume and his concerns about the logical fallacy of overgeneralizing from limited experiences (also known as the problem of inductive reasoning).[1] Philosophers since Hume have frequently used the example of white swans and black swans to illustrate this fallacy: if you observed thousands upon thousands of white swans, you might easily assume that all swans are white, but your conclusion could be quickly and decisively disproven by the appearance of just one *non*-white swan. The Black Swan is a metaphor for the fragility of conventional knowledge and the surprising importance of rare events. It is about overestimating the significance of ordinary phenomena, and underestimating the significance of extraordinary phenomena. Black Swans do not appear often, but when they do they can dramatically change our long-held beliefs and assumptions. Nicholas Nassim Taleb has written about the failure to appreciate Black Swan events in recent economic history,[2] and I believe researchers who study dreams are in danger of falling into the same intellectual trap: too much focus on the White Swans of average, ordinary, forgettable dreaming, and not enough attention to the Black Swans of anomalous, extraordinary, highly memorable dreaming.

If we take this alternative approach of striving for better scientific knowledge of unusually intensified dreams—what Carl Jung called *big dreams*[3]—at least two important benefits will emerge.

First, we gain a much more comprehensive and integrated view of the nature of dreaming. More than 100 years after Sigmund Freud's monumental *The Interpretation of Dreams*, and more than 50 years after the breakthrough discovery of rapid eye movement (REM) sleep, scientists still do not have a consensus theory about why people dream and what their dreams mean. One of the biggest obstacles to progress has been the failure to appreciate the significance of rare but extremely impactful dreams. When we take into account the latest research on both ordinary and extraordinary types of dreams, a much clearer picture emerges of the nature of dreaming in its full range and potentiality.

Second, an improved scientific understanding of dreaming has surprisingly important implications for the study of religion. In a previous book, *Dreaming in the World's Religions*, I analyzed sacred texts, historical records, and anthropological reports to highlight the recurrent roles that dreams have played in religious and cultural traditions through history and around the world: communicating with divine beings, foreseeing future events, healing illnesses, and protecting against attack from evil powers, among others. From a conventional scientific perspective, based only on the study of ordinary dreams, these cross-cultural religious teachings appear bizarre and unintelligible. But once we take new research findings on highly memorable dreams into account, the cross-cultural religious teachings no longer seem so alien. In fact, we find that religious traditions through history have accurately described several types of big dreams that modern-day researchers have analyzed and explained in terms of their naturalistic roots in the human brain. The more we know about the science of big dreams, the more we can learn about the experiential origins of religious beliefs and practices.

I hasten to point out that this thesis is not original to me. It has a long and venerable history in the Western intellectual tradition, as the following quotes on pages 4–5 make clear.

These thinkers share the vital insight that *dreaming has something to do with the way religious ideas and feelings get started in people's minds.* All of them agree, whether they used the language of philosophy, theology, psychology, or anthropology, that dreams are a key to understanding the experiential origins of religious symbols, behaviors, beliefs, and practices.

My goal is to add more empirical substance to the discussion. I want to put this classic thesis to the scientific test by clarifying and improving it with better data, sharper analysis, and a broader evolutionary framework. This means gathering evidence from multiple sources, looking for patterns of similarity and difference, questioning prior assumptions, and building predictive models that can be applied to new sets of data. The notion of a connection between dreaming and religion has always been intuitively compelling as a philosophical aphorism. By the end of this book I hope to have transformed it into a solid premise of religious studies and brain/mind science.

Dreaming and the Origins of Myth and Religion

LUCRETIUS

How the idea of gods spread to all nations, stocking their cities with altars and making men tremble to undertake the solemn rites . . . is not hard to explain in a few words. In those days mortal men saw while awake the excellent countenances of the gods, or rather in dreams they gasped at their vast size. . . . [I]n dreams they saw them do miraculous things, and many, without an effort.

On the Nature of Things, first century C.E.

THOMAS HOBBES

And for the matter, or substance of the invisible agents, so fancied [in religions]; they could not by natural cogitation, fall upon any other conceit, but that it was the same with that of the soul of man; and that the soul of man, was of the same substance, with that which appeareth in a dream, to one that sleepeth.

Leviathan, 1651

EDWARD B. TYLOR

The evidence of visions corresponds with the evidence of dreams in their bearing on primitive theories of the soul, and the two classes of phenomena substantiate and supplement one another. . . . That this soul should be looked on as surviving beyond death is a matter scarcely needing elaborate argument. Plain experience is there to teach it to every savage; his friend or his enemy is dead, yet still in dream or open vision he sees the spectral form which is to his philosophy a real objective being, carrying personality as it carries likeness.

Primitive Culture, 1873

FRIEDRICH NIETZSCHE

Misunderstanding of the dream.—The man of the ages of barbarous primordial culture believed that in the dream he was getting to know a second real world: here is the origin of all metaphysics. Without the dream one would have had no occasion to divide the world into two. The dissection into soul and body is also connected with the oldest idea of the dream, likewise the postulation of a life of the soul, thus the origin of all belief in spirits, and probably also of the belief in gods. "The dead live on, for they appear to the living in dreams": that was the conclusion one formerly drew, throughout many millennia.

Human, All Too Human, 1880

SIGMUND FREUD

[D]reaming is on the whole an example of regression to the dreamer's earliest condition, a revival of his childhood, of the instinctual impulses which were then available to him. Behind this childhood of the individual we are promised a picture of a phylogenetic childhood—a picture of the development of the human race. . . . [W]e may expect that the analysis of dreams will lead us to a knowledge of man's archaic heritage, of what is psychically innate in him.

The Interpretation of Dreams, 1899

MIRCEA ELIADE

For there is no mythic motive or scenario of initiation which is not also presented, in one way or another, in dreams and in the working of the imagination. In the oneiric universe we find again and again the symbols, the images, the figures and the events of which the mythologies are constituted.

Myths, Dreams, and Mysteries, 1956

PAUL RICOEUR

It is in dreams that one can catch sight of the most fundamental and stable symbolisms of humanity passing from the "cosmic" function to the "psychic" function.

The Symbolism of Evil, 1967

WENDY DONIGER O'FLAHERTY

Both dreams and myths draw their vocabularies from certain intense moments in actual human experience, but it is art that transforms those moments, bringing them from the private realm of the dream into the public realm of the myth.

Dreams, Illusion, and Other Realities, 1984

Dreams and the Cognitive Science of Religion

The chapters to come will frequently draw upon concepts and findings from the cognitive science of religion, a new field of scholarship using the latest findings in brain/mind research to shed light on the study of religion. "Cognitive science" refers to an alliance of six disciplines—psychology, linguistics, philosophy, computer science, neurology, and anthropology—that first banded together in the 1970s to push for a better understanding of how the mind works. They were seeking new ideas beyond the confines of psychoanalysis and behaviorism, the two theories that dominated academic psychology in the twentieth century. It was clear from the start that cognitive science had important implications for religious studies, and in recent years many books and articles have been written using its findings to analyze a variety of religious phenomena like rituals, myths, belief systems, prayer, and moral codes.[4]

Some have suggested cognitive science offers a revolutionary new approach to religious studies, but that claim seems too strong. The cognitive science of religion (hereinafter CSR) is better understood as an extension of earlier traditions in the psychology of religion, a lineage that includes Freud, Jung, William James, and many others whose work remains relevant today. If we take a longer historical view, CSR can be appreciated as a continuation and expansion of their efforts, offering new technologies and interdisciplinary models that can improve our understanding of topics having a long history of prior study and research. The value and significance of CSR derives not from its radical originality but from the advanced scientific methods it can apply to the exploration of interesting ideas about religion that have been around for quite a while.

Although a few attempts have been made to study dreams from a CSR perspective, the nocturnal imagination remains largely unexplored territory for this still-young field.[5] I see that as an opportunity to offer a model of how cognitive scientific tools can be put into practice in a new research context. Big dreams are a perfect subject for CSR analysis. They are deeply rooted in the evolved nature of our brain/mind system and they are venerated as a source of religious inspiration by cultural traditions all over the world. If ever a topic invited the use of analytic resources from both cognitive science and religious studies, this would seem to be it.

The present book does not, however, try to explain the nature or essence of religion as a whole. The focus here is much more limited. I examine a specific aspect of human experience, namely dreaming, and try to explain in cognitive scientific terms why it has always been so closely associated with special beliefs and practices found throughout the history of religions, often in their original stages of development. A targeted CSR approach like this seems more likely to lead to valid and useful findings that other researchers can build on.[6]

The Sleep and Dream Database

Much of the evidence presented here comes from the Sleep and Dream Database (SDDb[7]), a digital archive and search engine I began developing in 2009 to promote the scientific study of dreams. The SDDb holds a collection of more than 20,000 dream reports from a variety of sources, including personal diaries, opinion surveys, cultural texts, and psychological experiments. It is an open-access resource for studying dreams using a number of simple but powerful and highly flexible tools of analysis. For a project like this one, the biggest benefit is giving readers a direct means of evaluating my evidence. When I make a claim using material in the SDDb, you do not have to take my word for it; you can go to the SDDb yourself, find the information I am using to support that claim, and form your own conclusions about it. My hope is that the transparency of this process will encourage readers not only to follow my ideas but go beyond them, exploring new insights they have discovered while directly engaging with the data.

The SDDb is, and perhaps will always be, a work in progress. I am continually uploading new material, tweaking the analytic functions, and changing features of the user interface to make the system easier to navigate. The material contained in the SDDb comes from several different sources, including demographic surveys, individual diaries, thematic collections, experimental studies, and cultural texts. Each source has its own advantages and disadvantages.

Demographic surveys provide information from large numbers of people, enabling statistical comparisons on a variety of social variables (gender, age, education, race, income, religious behavior, political beliefs, etc.). However, these surveys are relatively shallow, lacking depth of personal information.

Individual diaries give valuable insight into personal meanings and long-term developmental trends, although it can be hard to make claims about bigger research questions based on the experiences of a single dreamer.

Thematic sets offer the ability to study many people's dreams about one particularly interesting theme, but these reports often come from idiosyncratic and unverifiable sources.

Experimental studies provide high-quality dream reports and other data gathered in controlled circumstances by trained academic researchers. The methodological rigor of these studies adds confidence to their findings, but their narrow academic focus can offset this advantage and limit their relevance.

Cultural texts (such as historical, anthropological, literary, or cinematic sources) enable a broader study of dream patterns from various life circumstances. But it can be difficult if not impossible to verify the authenticity of the dreams as reported.

Each of these sources is useful in some ways and not in others, which underscores the importance of analyzing multiple collections of data to produce more balanced research results.

An Outline of the Argument

The book has four parts, each of which develops a thesis that paves the way to the next part. In their simplest form, the four theses represent the core ideas of the book:

Sleep is active and adaptive.
Dreaming is imaginative play in sleep.
Big dreams provoke greater consciousness.
Dreaming is a primal wellspring of religious experience.

Part I starts by describing current knowledge about sleep, since sleep is the basic physiological substrate of dreaming. Long assumed to be a mental desert devoid of cognitive activity, sleep turns out to involve a remarkably complex and energetic state of brain/mind functioning with deep roots in the evolutionary history of terrestrial life. A basic premise of CSR research is that explanations of religion should be grounded in current knowledge about evolution. Part I makes good on this premise by introducing readers to the evolutionary context of sleep and dreaming. By studying the key features of sleep—its variability among different animal species (chapter 1), its cycles of electrical, chemical, and anatomical arousal in the brain (chapter 2), its influence on health and development (chapter 3), and its cultural elaboration through history and around the world (chapter 4)—we begin to see the contours of a scientifically informed approach to religiously meaningful dreams.

Next, Part II presents the best available evidence about the characteristic patterns of ordinary or "little" dreams (i.e., the relatively forgettable dreams that come during an average night's sleep). These findings will clarify what exactly makes big dreams so unusual. To fully appreciate the extraordinary, we need to know what counts as ordinary. Included in this part are chapters on dream recall frequencies among various groups of people (chapter 5); the major patterns in the content of people's dreams, such as perceptions, emotions, and characters (chapter 6); the meaningful continuities between dream content and waking life (chapter 7); and the meaningful discontinuities between dreaming and waking (chapter 8).

This material prepares the way for a detailed analysis in Part III of what I call the four *prototypes* of big dreaming: aggressive (chapter 9), sexual (chapter 10), gravitational (chapter 11), and mystical (chapter 12). Each of these four prototypes is associated with a distinct kind of emotional and physiological arousal—a fight/flight response in a chasing nightmare, an actual orgasm in a "wet" dream, a startled sensation of vertigo in a falling dream, and a joyous feeling of freedom and power in a flying dream. For each prototype I explain its recurrent features of form and content, its foundations in various brain/mind processes, and the reasons for its long-lasting psychological impact on the dreamer.

As a preview, here are four brief examples of big dreams with prototypical features, drawn from people who responded to SDDb surveys in 2010 and 2011 about their most memorable dreams:

(Aggressive) I was being chased by a man with hideously deformed features; no matter how fast I ran, he was always right behind me.[8]

(Sexual) I've never watched or read any *Twilight* [films or novels], but I had a dream I had sex with Edward [the handsome vampire hero] and it was the best sex I've ever had![9]

(Gravitational) I dreamed I was falling off a cliff. I kept turning and turning. I had a great feeling of fear in my stomach and woke up just before hitting the ground.[10]

(Mystical) At about age 14 I had dreams of flying (just me, no plane) over and around my parents' large yard and small orchard area. It was a beautiful spring day, sunny and green, blue sky in the dream.

I felt free and exhilarated and amazed with the sensation of flying. The joy I felt during the dream has rarely been matched.[11]

After a close study of unusually vivid dreams like these, all the pieces will be in place to advance the book's principal thesis that dreaming is a primal wellspring of religious experience. Part IV shows how this idea plays out in four different spheres of religious activity: demonic seduction (chapter 13), prophetic vision (chapter 14), ritual healing (chapter 15), and contemplative practice (chapter 16). In each of these chapters I connect the best available scientific evidence about dreaming with specific cross-cultural themes in religious history. These connections will lead, by the end of the book, to a better understanding of the time-honored idea that religious beliefs are psychologically rooted in experiences of intensified, highly memorable dreaming.

To organize each individual chapter I have drawn upon what might seem like an unlikely source: Thomas Aquinas and his thirteenth-century work *Summa Theologica*, a magisterial synthesis of Christian theology and Aristotelian science. The contents of Aquinas's work interest me less than the structure and flow of his arguments. The *Summa*'s basic unit is the *article*, which consists of five elements: (1) a title posed as a question, (2) an initial statement of an answer opposite to the one Aquinas will eventually give, (3) a short response to the opposition, (4) a longer analysis and discussion of the question, and (5) a final reply to the initial statement, leading to the next question. I have always admired Aquinas's willingness to confront head-on the strongest critical challenges to his ideas. He built within his reasoning process a meaningful place for dissenting points of view, in recognition of their value in clarifying and sharpening everyone's understanding of the question at hand.

With the *Summa* article as a model, each chapter in this book starts with an opening question from the perspective of a skeptical thinker who disputes the answer I will be proposing. Like Aquinas, I want these critical, challenging voices to be part of the discussion from the outset. Then I give a brief response to the skeptic's question, mapping out an alternative approach. The main body of the chapter provides data and discussion, with an extended analysis of the various kinds of evidence that can help us effectively address the opening question. This leads to an empirically grounded answer that responds to the skeptical perspective (and circles back to shed new light on the epigraph that heads the chapter). The concluding response is presented as a working hypothesis, meaning it can be changed as new evidence arises, but it can serve for now as a reasonable principle for moving forward. Each chapter's concluding response sets up the initial question for the following chapter. The solution of one puzzle begets another.

This Aquinas-inspired approach is meant to emphasize the importance of the critical questions that people naturally ask about dreams and religion. We are in a better position than ever to give solid, data-driven answers to those questions.

And in the end, we may find the skeptics were right all along.

PART I

Sleep

I

Evolution

Night bore hateful Doom and black Fate and Death,
And she bore Sleep and the tribe of Dreams.

HESIOD, *Theogony*

Opening Question

Must we sleep?

Thomas Edison, the genius inventor of electric lights, phonographs, and many other modern technologies, claimed in a 1908 interview with the *New York Times* that sleep is superfluous and unnecessary, a behavioral relic due to the dullness of our ancestors. As he saw it, people have merely fallen into the habit of sleeping at night. "Men first learned to sleep," Edison declared, "because when darkness came they had nothing else to do. Through the ages their descendants, doing likewise, made sleep a custom—a matter of course. But if men had always lived in a land of perpetual light and sunshine, I don't suppose we would sleep at all."[1]

Was Edison right? Is sleep just a habit that humans picked up because they have nothing else to occupy themselves in the dark of night? Do we have no fundamental need for sleep?

Initial Response

Yes, we do need to sleep. Sleep is a biological imperative built into the evolved structure of our brains and bodies.

Even Edison yielded to slumber for 4 or 5 hours a night, and he was famous for taking daily naps at his office and in his study at home (in both places he always had a cot, blankets, and pillows at the ready).

Data and Discussion
The Earliest Ancestral Environment

A basic idea in the cognitive science of religion is that the human mind has been shaped by evolutionary forces originating long ago in the prehistory of our species. According to this notion, the psychological abilities that characterize the human mind were originally formed to meet the challenges of survival on the savannas of Africa hundreds of thousands of years ago.[2] This means that any attempt to understand the evolved nature of human psychology requires attention to the conditions of our early ancestral environment. We cannot build our psychological theories based solely on what human minds are doing today, in the modern civilized world, because these are not the circumstances in which the cognitive architecture of our minds originally developed. We need to go back in time to our African progenitors and the environmental situation they were facing, as a primate species of hunter-gatherers living in the forests and grasslands.

In the case of sleep, though, we need to go farther back than that. Much farther. Edison hinted at the reason why when he imagined a "land of perpetual light and sunshine." If those were indeed the conditions of the early ancestral environment of our species, then Edison might be right, and humans could have evolved without a need for sleep. But in reality, humans do not live in a land of perpetual light and sunshine. We live, and have always lived, on a planet that cycles between light and darkness, day and night, heat and cold, activity and rest. Rather than fantasizing about a sleepless existence, we should look more closely at this primordial rhythm of terrestrial life.

It ultimately goes back to the Big Bang. Of course, in scientific terms everything goes back to the Big Bang. Approximately 13.8 billion years ago the universe emerged from a singular point of infinite density and temperature that exploded with unimaginable heat and energy, bursting outwards and expanding rapidly in all directions. Over time the universe, though still expanding, cooled enough for subatomic particles to form (such as protons, neutrons, and electrons), which then constellated into the simplest of elements like hydrogen, helium, and lithium. These elements gathered in massive clouds where the effects of gravity began pulling them together to form stars. As the stars grew they eventually exploded into supernovae, in the process creating new, heavier elements with more complex atomic structures. These heavier elements gradually coalesced into rocky chunks of matter forming rings, disks, and planetary spheres orbiting the stars—such as our earth orbiting its star, the sun.

From the very beginning of earth's formation about 4.5 billion years ago, its surface has been exposed to a recurrent cycle of light and darkness. This, I propose, is the earliest ancestral environment of the human need to sleep. Everything on earth and all its forms of life have been fundamentally shaped in response to this basic planetary reality. Our biological cycle of waking and sleeping is ultimately rooted in an ancient orbital cycle of the earth spinning toward, then away from, the light of the sun.

The theory of the Big Bang is the best model yet devised to explain our cosmological origins. It is not, however, a perfect or complete theory. In fact, several questions about the physical nature of the universe remain unanswered. What if anything happened before the Big Bang? Is there just one universe, or many? Why is there more matter than anti-matter? How do the paradoxes of quantum physics interact with the laws of ordinary Newtonian physics? Why does the speed of cosmic expansion seem to be increasing, despite the decreasing density and temperature of the universe? Are we being driven to a "Big Rip," a cataclysmic tearing apart of the physical fabric of the cosmos? Open questions like these should be kept in mind whenever we use scientific research to build up our knowledge. They help us stay humble and aware of the horizons of uncertainty that surround all of our ideas and beliefs, including the best of our cosmological theories.

Circadian Rhythms and Sleep Behaviors

The *orbital periodicity* of a planet is the amount of time it takes to make one complete rotation around its axis. The orbital periodicity of the earth was originally shorter than it is now, closer to 22 hours. Since then the earth has slowed down somewhat, and for the past billion years its orbital periodicity has been 24 hours, give or take a few seconds. This simple astrophysical fact has been inscribed into the deepest biological code of virtually every living creature on earth in the form of *circadian rhythms*. The term "circadian" combines the Latin words for "around" (*circa*) and "day" (*diem*), and biologists have found evidence of innate 24-hour rhythms in everything from bacteria and plants to insects and mammals.[3] Although we still do not know how life first emerged on earth (another horizon of scientific uncertainty), it appears that some of the earliest forms of single-cell life quickly developed the ability to detect the presence or absence of sunlight so they could self-regulate the timing of their metabolic activities. All plants have circadian clocks that enable them to maximize photosynthesis, drawing energy from the sun during the day and storing it in starches that fuel the plant's growth during the night. In animals, circadian rhythms are associated with energy conservation, cell regeneration, hormone release, and strategies for seeking prey and avoiding predators.

Circadian rhythms are not merely reflexive responses to the external presence or absence of light. That was Edison's mistake—we do not sleep simply because the sun has gone down. As numerous experiments have shown, a creature's internal 24-hour clock continues to operate even when it is totally deprived of external light.[4] Circadian rhythms are genetically programmed patterns of healthy biological functioning that keep our bodies finely attuned to the earth's 24-hour orbital period. Sleep can thus be conceived as that portion of the circadian rhythm, usually occurring at night, when outward behavioral activity is maximally reduced and certain inward-focused metabolic processes become more active.

Setting aside the question of whether plants can be said to sleep on a nightly or seasonal basis, the conventional definition of sleep applies chiefly to animals, and it includes these major criteria: physical quiescence in a typical place and posture, reduced muscle tone, less sensitivity to outside stimulus, lower overall expenditure of metabolic energy, and an ability to reverse states and wake up rapidly if necessary (unlike hibernation or a coma). For all animals, sleep has *homeostatic* qualities, meaning each creature needs a certain baseline amount of sleep for healthy survival. If an animal is deprived of its usual amount and then allowed to sleep normally again, it will experience a "rebound" of extra sleep, apparently in an effort to restore the prior balance.[5]

It is possible that some animals never sleep. Certain species of deep ocean fish may live in eternally dark caves or swim continuously in the sunless depths. Research is scant on such creatures. But we know that many other species of fish definitely do sleep, in terms of becoming physically inactive and unresponsive to external stimuli for extended periods of time at night. For example, the sleep of the zebra fish (*Danio rerio*), a member of the minnow family native to the rivers of northeast India, has been studied especially closely.[6] From their larval stages through adulthood, zebra fish follow a circadian rhythm of physical activity during the day and quiescence during the night, accompanied by lower respiration, less external sensitivity, and motionless body postures in the water. In experiments where zebra fish have been deprived of their normal amount of sleep, they respond with increased sleep and higher arousal thresholds on the following nights.

In all these ways, zebra fish have circadian sleep patterns that are very similar to other animals like ourselves. A huge gap of evolutionary time and development separates the zebra fish from humans, yet the same basic biological system—sleep—has been preserved throughout.

The total amount of sleep in a 24-hour period needed by the average member of a species can vary widely. At one end of the spectrum, the big brown bat (*Eptesicus fuscus*), a flying mammal from North and Central America weighing about half an ounce, sleeps up to 20 hours a day. At the other end of the spectrum, African bush elephants (*Loxodonta africana*) are the largest land mammals on earth, weighing up to 13,000 pounds, yet they only sleep around 4 hours per night, half of it standing and half lying on their sides.

This kind of variation raises the question of whether the benefits of sleep depend purely on the total hourly amount. If that were true, it would seem the bats are getting five times more of the alleged benefits than the elephants. Perhaps extreme amounts of slumber are required given the unusual demands on bat brains from using an echo-location system to fly through the environment? A more likely explanation is that the drastically different amounts of sleep between bats and elephants reflect their different places in the local food chain. The big brown bat is a dominant predator in its environment, whereas elephants are grazing animals constantly threatened by meat-eating predators. As documented by Jerome Siegel and other researchers, the amount of time animals spend sleeping correlates to a considerable degree with each animal's position vis-à-vis the predators and prey in their ecosystem: "carnivores sleep more than omnivores, which in turn sleep more than herbivores."[7] This makes a rough kind of evolutionary sense. Creatures at the lower end of the food chain need to stay awake and vigilant as much as possible to protect against predators, whereas creatures at the higher end have the leisure to sleep for many hours each day and focus their waking activities on those times most advantageous for hunting their prey.

The picture becomes more complex when we take marine mammals like dolphins and whales into account. Their evolutionary challenge has been to accommodate the needs for sleep and safety from predators and the additional need to keep breathing while continuously swimming in the water. Bottlenose dolphins (*Tursiops truncatus*) have developed the ability to sleep with one half of their brain at a time, while the other half remains awake and moderately alert. The eye on the opposite side of the awake hemisphere stays open to scan the environment for predators and obstacles, while the dolphin's body floats quietly at the surface so its blow-hole always has access to air for breathing. After an hour or two the brain hemispheres switch sides so the second half can sleep while the first half keeps watch. Dolphins sleep mostly at night, for 8 or 9 hours total, often in the company of other dolphins in their pod. This half-off, half-on system of sleep seems to be present in all cetacean species (whales, dolphins, and porpoises) that live in the water and confront the ecological need to balance sleep, safety from predators, and breathing.[8]

An intriguing variation in the sleep patterns of bottlenose dolphins occurs immediately after birth, when mothers and their calves stay awake and in constant visual contact for more than two straight months. Whatever sleep they get during this time is extremely brief and fragmentary.[9] This is the exact opposite of the sleep patterns of all terrestrial mammals, whose total sleep time is the highest at birth and in the first stages of development. Another curious variation comes from the northern fur seal (*Callorhinus ursinus*), a native to the northern Pacific Ocean whose biggest bull males weigh up to 600 pounds. Fur seals sleep just like other marine mammals when they are out in the water on hunting journeys, with one half of their brain asleep and the other half alert and attentive to the environment. When they come ashore, however, fur seals behave like other terrestrial mammals, with both sides of their brain sleeping simultaneously (i.e., bilaterally).[10]

The unusual sleep patterns of dolphins and fur seals indicate that sleep, though necessary, can be remarkably flexible in relation to other basic survival activities and environmental circumstances.

Among birds a similar flexibility in satisfying the need for sleep can be seen in species that take long migratory journeys. Birds like the Arctic tern (*Sterna paradisaea*) and the American golden plover (*Pluvialis dominica*) travel more than 10,000 miles from one seasonal home to another. During their long flight these birds manage to function well for extended periods of time with drastically less sleep than usual. More than half of all bird species migrate according to seasonal changes, and their sleep patterns are clearly able to adapt to these times of increased need for waking activity, and thus reduced time for sleep. Swainson's thrush (*Catharus ustulatus*), for example, an olive-brown bird weighing about an ounce, migrates 3,000 miles from Canada to southern Mexico. They travel mostly by night, flying for many hours at a stretch, stopping only for brief rests in unfamiliar places filled with unknown dangers—not great places for deep, restful sleep. Researchers have found the thrush manages the sharp curtailment of normal, safe sleep by alternating between numerous micro-naps, periods of semi-alert drowsiness, and a kind of unilateral sleep in which one eye stays open while the other is closed and resting. When the thrush flocks finally reach the end of their long journey, they revert to their normal pattern of wakefulness during the day and sleeping at night.[11]

In warm-blooded creatures with sufficiently complex central nervous systems, the occurrence of sleep can be measured by variations in electrical activity in their brains. This typically involves a neurological shift from low-voltage fast waves during waking, to high-voltage slow waves in the phase known as *slow wave sleep* (SWS), and then again to low-voltage fast waves during the phase known as *paradoxical sleep* (PS), so named because the brain is definitely asleep yet also extremely active as if it were awake. One of the most easily observed signs of PS is the erratic twitching of the eyes under their closed lids. Hence, this phase of sleep is also referred to as *rapid eye movement* (REM) sleep, with the companion term *non-rapid eye movement* (NREM) sleep for the slow wave phases.

These two pairs of terms—SWS and PS, NREM and REM—are referring to the same basic cycle of brain activity during sleep, and they will be used interchangeably in this book.[12] Researchers are uncertain if some variation of this pattern occurs with cold-blooded creatures like fish and reptiles; the evidence so far suggests their brains generate some elements of NREM sleep, but none of the neurological features of REM sleep as found in mammals and birds.[13] Water-dwelling mammals like dolphins and whales, with their unilateral brain patterns in sleep, seem to have no REM sleep, only NREM. Intriguingly, the fur seal has unilateral NREM sleep and no REM sleep during its long journeys in the water, but when it sleeps on land it has bilateral NREM and REM sleep. More discussion of the brain's role in sleep will come in the next chapter. For now, it is enough to know that this is another way researchers study and measure sleep in various animal species.

Even though the evolutionary lineages of birds and mammals diverged hundreds of millions of years ago, they share several features of sleep that distinguish them from reptiles and fish. Most important, birds and mammals both experience alternating neurological cycles of quiet, slow wave sleep and active, fast wave paradoxical sleep. Reptiles and fish have no clear signs of PS, and only some of the features of SWS. Researchers do not know if this means birds and mammals inherited the same dual-phase sleep cycle from an ancient common ancestor, or if they each separately evolved this kind of sleep cycle in response to similar biological needs.[14] We know, for example, that birds and mammals are both warm-blooded, and it thus seems likely their sleep behaviors are closely related to their need to maintain a steady body temperature and conserve energy through the night.

A big advantage of being warm-blooded is that it has enabled birds and mammals to develop more complex brains and a much wider range of cognitive abilities than found in fish or reptiles. Birds, like many mammals, show signs of referential language, abstract reasoning, theory of mind, and working memory. This seems to be the case with the zebra finch (*Taeniopygia guttata*) (not to be confused with the zebra fish mentioned earlier), a red-beaked songbird common to the dry woodlands of Australia whose males learn elaborate mating songs from their fathers. Eventually each male teaches the same songs to its sons. The ability to learn and then transmit these rhythmically complex musical compositions indicates a high degree of cognitive functioning, and researchers are exploring a possible connection with their sleep, which so closely resembles mammalian patterns. Zebra finches generally sleep at night in nesting pairs, and they have both SWS and PS, with more PS later in the night toward waking.[15] As Niels Rattenborg and Charles Amlaner commented in their review of the literature on avian sleep, "it is conceivable that birds also evolved mammalian-like sleep states to maintain their heavily interconnected brains and advanced cognition."[16]

We should not overstate the similarities, however. Birds may have some degree of genuine PS, but the amount is much less than mammals have as a proportion of their overall sleep. As intelligent as some birds may be, their brains are not nearly as anatomically complex as the brains of most mammals, and this neurological difference seems to be reflected in the relatively short bursts of PS they experience, compared to the longer phases of PS typical in mammalian species.

During the 65-million-year lineage of our closest evolutionary kin, the primates, there has been a dramatic shift of behavior that moved them/us in the direction of greater sleep consolidation. The oldest of our primate ancestors were nocturnal tree-dwellers in the forests of Africa, and several primate species alive today such as the owl monkey (*Aotus trivirgatus*) and mouse lemur (*Microcebus murinus*) still live a nocturnal life. Other primates, however, changed at some point from a nocturnal to a diurnal pattern of activity. Instead of sleeping during the day and foraging through the tree canopies at night, these primates began sleeping at night and exploring food resources on the ground by daylight. This shift exposed them to a host of new predators (large cats, hyenas, snakes, etc.), and it seems likely that at least three new cognitive abilities developed as a result of this heightened vulnerability.

First, these primates began relying less on a sense of smell and more on visual perception to quickly and accurately scan wide swaths of the surrounding environment for the presence of possible attackers and possible food. Second, they devoted much more attention to social cohesion as a powerful defense network against predators. This meant that increased amounts of mental energy and attention became focused on daily social interactions supporting kinship intimacy, safe child-rearing, and group bonding.[17] The third cognitive innovation among these newly diurnal, land-dwelling primates was a move toward shorter, deeper, monophasic sleep. In hourly terms, some of the longest sleeping mammals are the nocturnal tree-dwellers like the owl monkey at 17 hours and the mouse lemur at 15 hours. These and other early primates engage in *polyphasic* sleep, meaning they have several periods of sleep throughout the 24-hour cycle.[18] For diurnal primates like monkeys, apes, and humans, their sleep has shifted toward a shorter *monophasic* cycle of one long sleep period at night. For example, the common chimpanzee (*Pan troglodytes*) of west and central Africa sleeps between 9 and 10 hours a night. Humans, with an estimated species-wide average of 7 to 8 hours of sleep per night, are at the low end of primate sleep totals.

The shift to shorter monophasic sleep seems to have had several benefits: increasing wake time for food gathering, more carefully regulating body temperature during the night, and improving the efficiency of their sleep. *Sleep efficiency* can be measured in terms of the ratio of NREM and REM sleep, with a higher proportion of REM equaling greater efficiency. Primates who lead a nocturnal life have many total hours of sleep, but it is not efficient sleep; a relatively small proportion of it occurs in the REM phase. The shorter sleep of diurnal primates comes from a reduced amount of NREM sleep, but not a comparable reduction in REM sleep, leading to a higher proportion of REM in their overall sleep cycles. Humans have the highest amount of REM sleep per night, which, when combined with our relatively short amount of total sleep, gives us the highest sleep efficiency—the most REM-intensive sleep—among all primate species.

The Functions of Sleep

In 1971 Allan Rechtschaffen, one of the pioneering sleep laboratory researchers at the University of Chicago, observed, "If sleep does not serve an absolute vital function, then it is the biggest mistake the evolutionary process ever made."[19] Something that is so pervasive throughout the animal kingdom cannot be a pointless waste of time—can it? More than 40 years later researchers are still reluctant to say what precisely the function of sleep might be.

This scholarly hesitation is due in part to the amazing variability of sleep. Earth's creatures have found so many different ways of sleeping that it seems impossible to conceive a single comprehensive theory of its function. Added to that is the dynamic nature of evolution—species can change over time, and so can the functions of their bodies and neural systems, generating new species and novel forms of biodiversity. A feature that provided adaptive benefits to an earlier species might not be adaptive to a species that evolved later. Conversely, a feature that had no benefits to earlier species might develop new beneficial functions in later species. The endlessly tinkering process of natural selection has generated such kaleidoscopic variability in animal sleep patterns that researchers struggle to devise a theory that definitively identifies an essential, one-size-fits-all function of sleep.

Fortunately, we do not need a settled answer to that question to make use of the basic findings in this field. We can follow the scientific evidence about the nature of sleep as far as it leads, to its own horizon of uncertainty, and then we can pause to consider what we have learned. It seems reasonably clear that sleep is pervasive in the animal kingdom, with evolutionary roots in the ancient circadian rhythms of plants and microbial life. As just noted, sleep can take many forms in terms of how much a creature needs, where and when it sleeps, what parts of its brain are active and inactive, polyphasic vs. monophasic, and so on. Sleep is tolerant of long stretches of wakefulness, as seen in migrating birds and dolphin mothers and calves (the human record for staying awake, by the way, is 264 hours[20]). But no terrestrial creature can completely give up on sleep. The "rebound" effect found across nearly all species indicates a strong homeostatic need for a baseline amount of sleep. Sleep is profoundly necessary for our biological welfare, and also remarkably generous and flexible in how we can satisfy its basic requirements.

For many creatures one of sleep's most important functions is helping them manage their energy consumption and core body temperature. This function has a well-documented connection to the evolution of activity and rest cycles in plants and earlier forms of microbial life.[21] Sleep is a state of restful immobility and lowered energy use that helps each animal synchronize its metabolism with the circadian cycle of warmer temperatures in the day and colder temperatures at night. The thermoregulatory function of sleep seems to be especially important in warm-blooded creatures like birds and mammals, whose sleeping brains develop more complex and intensified forms of neural activity than those found in fish and reptiles.

Another one of sleep's functions seems to relate to the survival value of being immobile for long periods of time. As formulated by Jerome Siegel, this notion of *adaptive inactivity* explains animal sleep patterns as the product of sophisticated evolutionary calculations determining the best times for minimizing vulnerability to predators and maximizing opportunities to find prey.[22] The "carnivores-sleep-more-than-omnivores-who-sleep-more-than-herbivores" tendency illustrates this idea, showing the impact that survival pressures can have on each creature's distinctive calculus for when it is most and least advantageous to be awake.

Both of these ways of explaining sleep—as thermoregulation and as adaptive inactivity—touch on truly "vital" biological needs of the sort Rechtschaffen was seeking. Yet neither fully can explain why creatures sleep rather than just rest quietly. Of special significance for our project, neither of these ideas can explain the evolutionary changes toward more complex and intense forms of PS for birds and mammals. This development seems puzzling and even counterproductive from a thermoregulation perspective. During PS the energy usage of avian and mammalian brains increases dramatically, to levels that are comparable to waking awareness. This is inconsistent with the claim that sleep's function is to diminish metabolic activity. It appears that, for birds and mammals at least, more is going on in sleep than simply reducing energy usage.

The adaptive inactivity theory faces a similar difficulty. The supposed function of sleep—enforcing strategic periods of inactivity—does not help us understand why birds and mammals have developed a complex sleep cycle with periods of internally focused neurological activation and dramatically less responsiveness to external stimuli. Sleep may indeed help creatures avoid predators, but it is not inactive, at least not in an absolute sense. Sleep is active—sometimes extremely so—with metabolic processes that are timed specifically for those phases in the circadian cycle when a creature is safely disengaged from the external environment.

To understand the evolutionary functions of sleep, we need to look in more detail at the brain's activities during sleep. That is the topic of the next chapter.

Concluding Response

Humans, like virtually every other life form on our planet, have innate circadian cycles of activity and rest. In our species this cycle takes the form of waking and sleeping, the latter for a single nocturnal period of about 7 to 8 hours on average. As in other species, human sleep is remarkably flexible in length and frequency. Most people tend to be monophasic sleepers, although some, like Thomas Edison, can easily adopt polyphasic sleep patterns.

2
_____

The Brain

This is how he dreams.
He takes materials from the entire world and,
taking them apart on his own and
then on his own putting them back together,
he dreams with his own radiance, with his own light.
In that place this person becomes his own light.

Brihadaranyaka Upanishad

Opening Question

Does the brain shut down its most important functions during sleep?

The brain does not completely deactivate when sleeping. It is not like a light switch going on and off. But many neural systems do shut down in sleep, or at least drastically diminish their activities. Perhaps a better analogy for the sleeping brain would be a lamp with a dimmer switch turned to a very low setting—the power is still on, but just barely. That was the general view conveyed by Antonio Damasio, a pioneering neuroscientist and author of several best-selling books about the nature of consciousness, including *Descartes' Error* (1995) and *The Feeling of What Happens* (2000). At the end of the latter book Damasio summarized his key notion of "stepping into the light" as a metaphor for consciousness: "When self first comes to mind and forevermore after that, two-thirds of each living day without pause, we step into the light of mind and we become known to ourselves."[1] This eloquent appraisal of the waking two-thirds of life implies, of course, that the other one-third spent in the sleep state is less significant and less worthy of scientific attention. Like many other neuroscientists, Damasio is simply not interested in exploring the darker realms of the sleeping brain. Compared to the bright, quick intelligence of waking consciousness, sleep seems to be a murky, cognitively barren realm of lethargic unconsciousness.

Damasio's view poses a skeptical challenge to the goals of this book: Why should scarce scientific resources be devoted to the study of a brain state defined by its lack of "the light of mind"? Is not the sleeping brain devoid of all the interesting, sophisticated, high-level functions that are most important for waking consciousness?

Initial Response

There is more high-level neurological activation, more "light of mind," in the sleeping brain than is generally recognized.

The brain during sleep engages in a variety of complex, dynamically interacting cycles of activity that involve many of the same neural systems considered essential to waking consciousness. It no longer makes sense to think of waking and sleeping as polar opposites, nor to treat one as more valuable or important than the other. Rather, they are different yet complimentary modes of brain activity with many layers of similarity and difference, all revolving around the basic evolutionary needs of our species.

Data and Discussion
The Emergence of the Human Brain

Around 6 million years ago a female ape in Africa bore children who split into two separate family lines. One of these lines led to modern apes, chimpanzees, and gorillas. The other led to us.

During that 6-million-year period, the brains of our ancestors went through major changes in size and function. Brains do not leave fossils, but skulls do, and archeological evidence suggests there were at least two major bursts of brain growth in our evolutionary past. When the fossil evidence is combined with information about climate patterns, social behaviors, and predator/prey relations, it becomes possible to identify with a fair degree of confidence the distinctive mental abilities that have been inscribed into our brains by evolutionary pressures over millions of years. This background will give us a deeper biological context for understanding the brain's activities during sleep, before we start talking in detail about cerebral anatomy, neurotransmitters, EEG readings, and other findings of current brain research.

The key point to remember going forward is this: the cognitive challenges facing our ancestors were not just challenges for *waking consciousness* but challenges for the *whole brain*. The special mental abilities humans developed to successfully overcome these survival problems were rooted in the integrated and harmonious functioning of the brain through all its varying modes of activation.

Let us start by considering more closely that pivotal moment 6 million years ago when the hominids (i.e., our immediate genetic family) split off from the other primates. What behaviors and attributes did we bring with us from our primate cousins? We can get a rough idea by looking at the lives of our closest non-hominid relative, the common chimpanzee (*Pan troglodytes*), with whom we share 98.4% of our genetic background. The typical brain size of *P. troglodytes* is 280–500 cubic centiliters (cc.). Common chimps live in groups ranging from two dozen to more than one hundred members, sleeping in trees by night and foraging on the ground by day. Their diet is mostly herbivorous and heavy with fruit, although they do eat some meat. They use simple tools to help in gathering food, and they employ a variety of vocal sounds to communicate with each other, but there is no evidence of any greater sophistication in their technology or language abilities. Their social structures, however, are enormously complex, with every individual keenly aware of its place in a dynamic group hierarchy. As Frans de Waal has showed in *Chimpanzee Politics* (1982), chimps have cognitively advanced abilities for interacting with other members of their social group. Most important, they have a capacity for "theory of mind," a term we will discuss later which means the ability to recognize other living beings as having their own inner thoughts and feelings.

This portrait of the common chimpanzee gives a sense of the mental resources already built into our neurological system when the hominid lineage began its separate path of development.[2]

The best fossil yet discovered from our early family ancestry is "Lucy," the nickname for an adult female of the species *Australopithecus afarensis*. Lucy lived about 3.2 million years ago in what is today Ethiopia, and she stood and walked upright on two legs (bipedalism), with a probable height of 3 feet, 7 inches (1.1 m) and weight of 64 pounds (29 kg). Her cranial capacity is hard to determine exactly, given the remaining fragments of her skull, but it seems to indicate a brain size in the range of 375–500 cc. This is consistent with the 400–500 cc. brain sizes of other *A. afarensis* fossils that have also been found in eastern Africa. These findings make it clear that for millions of years after our departure from the evolutionary line of other primates, the hominid brain remained about the size of a large chimp's.

The first major change in the brain came about 2 million years ago, with the appearance of two new hominid species, *Homo habilis* and *Homo erectus*. The skulls of these species are considerably larger than those of Lucy and her *A. aferensis* kin, with brain size estimates of 500–800 cc. for *H. habilis* and 750–1,250 cc. for *H. erectus*. This anatomical change marked a decisive turning point in our evolutionary history. Hominids suddenly had brains two to three times bigger than those of their primate cousins, with the potential for exponentially more neural processing power.

We have to be careful here with causal explanations, since the archeological evidence is so fragmentary and there were so many other factors involved in these early stages of hominid evolution. Nevertheless, it is clear that several new, cognitively advanced abilities and behaviors appeared simultaneously with these larger brained species, strongly suggesting a connection between their increased brain power and better survival-enhancing abilities. Fossil records indicate that both *H. habilis* and *H. erectus* began designing their tools more intentionally and using them more effectively to expand and improve their diet, eating more meat from hunting and scavenging. Their posture became more fully upright, with much more mobility, greater visual range, and the freedom to use their hands for fine motor-skill tasks. Leaving the safety of the trees behind, they began a fully terrestrial, ground-level life, exploring new territories and settling in a variety of different ecosystems. *H. erectus* first appeared in Africa and quickly spread through many parts of Asia, finding ways to travel over remarkably long distances and successfully adapt to previously unknown environments.

We have no direct evidence about the social relations of these hominids, but it seems likely that the growth in brain capacity at this time coincided with the beginnings of spoken language, which would give them a powerful new means of communicating, planning, rearing children, and strengthening group cohesion. Archeological findings show their food-gathering practices improving and benefiting from a more refined mental capacity to observe, analyze, and remember information about the environment, including the ability to anticipate approaching weather, seasonal changes, and the movements of prey and predators. The increased role of meat in their diet fueled their physical growth, but it also put them in direct competition with other carnivores, requiring more sophisticated defense strategies and heightened awareness of potential threats. The rapid and apparently very successful expansion of *H. erectus* into Asia must have required tremendous amounts of cooperation, flexibility, and ingenuity in devising new ways to live and prosper.

All of this evidence suggests that the sudden spurt of brain growth in *H. habilis* and *H. erectus* had something to do with several important behaviors and skills that appeared around the same time and dramatically enhanced their ability to survive. Unfortunately we do not know exactly what was cause and what was effect—did the bigger brains prompt the development of these new behaviors, or did the new behaviors prompt the development of bigger brains? That question marks one of the horizons of uncertainty in this field of study.

A second large expansion of brain size occurred sometime between 500,000 and 200,000 years ago, with the arrival of *Homo heidelbergensis*, *Homo neanderthalis*, and archaic *Homo sapiens*. These species were the first hominids to migrate into Europe, and their fossil remains indicate they had considerably larger skulls than their predecessors, with estimated brain sizes of 1,100–1,400 cc. for archaic *H. sapiens* and 1,200–1,750 cc. for the Neanderthals. It may be surprising that this additional leap in brain size—now three to four times the size of a chimp's brain—was not followed by any radical transformation in tool making or material culture. Archaic *H. sapiens* and the Neanderthals were definitely more advanced technologically than any other primates, and their language abilities were surely growing rapidly, but their bigger brains did not immediately spark any dramatic changes in their manipulation of the physical world.

It should be remembered, however, that this was an era of cataclysmic changes in global climate, with massive ice sheets sweeping back and forth across the continents and sudden alterations in sea level, temperature, rainfall, and vegetation. The fact that these hominids survived at all through such extreme and inclement conditions is impressive in itself, suggesting they were endowed with unusual powers of adaptability. Their bigger brains seem to have given them an advantage over other creatures in responding to abrupt shifts in weather, climate, and terrain. They found ways not merely to survive through environmental changes that wiped out countless other species, but to thrive and spread to new, previously inaccessible areas.

Anatomically modern humans, *Homo sapiens sapiens*, appeared around 200,000 years ago, during this environmentally turbulent period of repeated ice ages and global thaws. Their skull fossils indicate a brain size of 1,200–1,700 cc., which is essentially the size of our brains today.

The evolutionary story of the hominid family is one of *encephalization*, meaning a progressive growth and expansion of the brain. Many other physical changes have separated us from the primates, but the quadrupling of brain size is by far the most consequential. Its importance can be measured not only in terms of its survival advantages but also in terms of its survival *costs*. A bigger brain is very costly—it has significant disadvantages for survival—in at least two ways.

First, the brain uses a tremendous amount of energy, much more than any other part of the body. In humans the brain constitutes 2% of our body mass, yet it consumes 20% of the body's energy.[3] The brain also requires a very consistent internal temperature to function properly. A rise or drop of just a few degrees can lead to severe and potentially fatal neurological problems. This adds extra urgency to the perpetual, year-round need to find a steady supply of high-calorie food.

Second, a larger brain is costly in putting acute strain on pregnant females whose pelvic bones become the limiting factor in how big the skull can grow before birth. The skull size of hominid fetuses seems to have developed to a point where the physical process of delivery is just barely survivable. The evolutionary pressure to push pregnant females to such extremes is directly related to the need for as much neurological development within the womb as possible. Even after nine full months of gestation, which is on the long side of pregnancy length for mammals, human newborns enter the world in a very immature condition. Their brains are still so underdeveloped they are incapable of caring for themselves for several years, requiring an extensive investment of time and energy from their kin (in contrast, newborn horses are able to get up and run on their own within a few minutes of birth).

These are the high costs of encephalization. Bigger brains require an abundant, steady supply of energy and careful temperature maintenance, and they put enormous stress on pregnant females. The fact that brain size has increased despite these costs implies this trait must provide some kind of compensating advantage. In terms of evolutionary logic, the higher the cost of a trait for an organism, the more it must contribute to that organism's survival and reproductive success; otherwise it would have been weeded out by natural selection. If we knew nothing else about the enlarged hominid brain, we would have to infer that it serves some extremely important survival functions to justify the expense of such disadvantages.

Our species, *H. sapiens sapiens*, most likely descended from archaic *H. sapiens* in Africa. Anatomically modern humans spread into Asia 100,000 years ago and made a sea journey to colonize Australia about 60,000 years ago. They entered Europe 40,000 years ago, and by 30,000 years ago they were the only remaining hominid species in the world. Ten thousand years ago, they invented agriculture and spread through the Americas. During this era a "creative explosion" occurred— for the first time in history there is unambiguous evidence of decorative art, religious ideas, and technological innovation in design, materials, and functions. The Neanderthals also had some elements of true culture, particularly in their funeral rites, but they produced nothing like the spectacular proliferation of new tools, weapons, seafaring technologies, languages, symbolic expressions, and cultural traditions that began to be generated by *H. sapiens sapiens* around 45,000 years ago (the time when archeologists have found the first instances of elaborate cave paintings and "Venus" figurines of curvaceous females—other changes and innovations may have come earlier).

What exactly sparked this explosion of creativity? It could not have been brain size alone, since archaic *H. sapiens* and the Neanderthals had similarly large cranial capacities. Rather, it must have been something our species began *doing* with our bigger brains. In this new, specifically human stage of neurological evolution the changes have occurred not in the brain's physical size but in the ways it grows, learns, organizes itself, and channels its processing power.

Cycles of Activity in the Sleeping Brain

Now we can turn from skull fossils to study the actual brains of *H. sapiens sapiens*, whose brains are our brains. The neurological capacities we humans have today are approximately the same as those of the first members of our species 200,000+ years ago. This means that current neuroscientific research can give us a window into the evolutionary changes that sent our species hurtling down the path of heightened cultural creativity. Most important for this book, recent findings about the sleeping brain can be applied to early *H. sapiens sapiens* as well. We may not know exactly how long they slept or in what kinds of conditions, but we do have a pretty good idea what was going on in their brains during sleep.

There are three basic ways to measure the sleeping brain: electrically, chemically, and anatomically. All three dimensions of neural activity are vital to sleep, all of them are incredibly complex, and no one has a clear understanding of how they interact with each other. To put it mildly, many uncertainties remain in the neuroscience of sleep. However, researchers do know enough to help us answer the question posed at the outset of this chapter about the brain shutting down its most important conscious functions during sleep. Three separate sources of neuroscientific evidence enable us to reject that idea and develop a more accurate portrait of the dynamic cycles of activity in the sleeping brain of *H. sapiens sapiens*.[4]

Electrical

Neural activities throughout the brain generate complex patterns of electricity with varying frequencies, intensities, and amplitudes. These patterns can be measured by the electroencephalograph (EEG), a device that works by placing a web of electrodes across the individual's scalp to detect rates of electrical discharge within the brain. Researchers are still unclear about the underlying processes that are being measured by the EEG, but the results do correlate with other measures that gauge the overall state of neural activation.

As discussed briefly in the previous chapter, a widely used system for analyzing the brain's electrical activity during sleep divides it into two major stages, REM and NREM, with three sub-stages of NREM sleep. In a state of relaxed wakefulness, the brain generates alpha rhythms occurring at a frequency of 8–12 cycles per second (cps). When a person is focusing attention on a specific task, visual perception, or bodily movement, faster beta waves of 12–30 cps come to the fore. When a person becomes drowsy and drifts off to sleep, the alpha rhythms return. Sleep onset leads to stage 1 NREM sleep, with both alpha waves and theta waves at 5–8 cps. This initial stage of sleep lasts for several minutes before the appearance of "spindles" (i.e., sudden spikes of electrical activation from various parts of the brain, occurring at a sigma frequency of 14–15 cps). In addition to these spindles, "K-complexes" begin to show up on the EEG. These are especially strong flares of internally generated electricity with sharp negative drops in amplitude. The appearance of spindles and K-complexes marks the beginning of stage 2 NREM sleep.

Next comes a dramatic change. Electrical activities diminish significantly, and the brain is now dominated by delta waves at a very low frequency of 0.5–2.0 cps. This is the slow wave sleep of stage 3 NREM, also known as "deep sleep." Brain waves at this point have their highest amplitude and slowest speed, and they are broadly synchronized, meaning they reflect the simultaneous, coordinated firing of many neural systems all over the brain.

Then comes an equally dramatic change in the opposite direction. New excitatory bursts of electrical energy known as PGO spikes suddenly appear. These spikes signal the onset of REM sleep. A few seconds later the overall electrical discharges in the brain surge and intensify to a level that is equal to, and in some cases greater than, the brain's activities in the waking state. The slow waves of deep sleep are replaced by theta waves, with some beta waves at 12–30 cps and spontaneous gamma waves at frequencies of 30–80 cps.[5] The PGO spikes continue, and the overall pattern of brain activity becomes desynchronized (as it does in the waking state), although many specific neural systems become more synchronized in local clusters.

During an average night's sleep for an adult human, one whole cycle of NREM and REM sleep takes about 90 minutes. The first REM phase of the night is the shortest, perhaps 10 or 15 minutes in length. After a phase of REM sleep ends, the activation level of the brain returns to stage 2 NREM, and then back to the deep sleep of stage 3 NREM, followed by another, longer period of REM. This pattern continues for the first two or three cycles of the night, after which deep sleep mostly disappears, and the brain oscillates between longer phases of REM and stage 2 NREM sleep.

In short: the first half of the night emphasizes deep sleep, the second half of the night emphasizes REM sleep, and stage 2 NREM sleep goes on throughout the night. In terms of EEG measurements, REM sleep and the waking state are virtually indistinguishable:

> The paradox that a similar EEG activity characterizes two states of vigilance that are commonly regarded as extreme poles of the sleeping-waking cycle suggests that, with regard to brain cellular activities, waking and REM sleep are closer than is usually believed, and both are opposed to NREM sleep, which is characterized by widely synchronized activities.[6]

One of the most important clues to the potential function of PS regards its connection with early brain development, as Howard Roffwarg pointed out many years ago.[7] A great deal of research by Roffwarg and others has shown that "in all species, PS, defined by several of its behavioral components, is at its height in early life, either in the fetus or in the neonate. It is initially the predominant state—for example, occupying 90% of the kitten's first days of life and perhaps even more time in the infant rat."[8] This high proportion of PS appears especially in animals whose newborns are *altricial*, meaning immature and underdeveloped (such as baby cats, rats, and humans). They have more PS in infancy than do species that are born more mature and cognitively developed (i.e., *precocial* species like horses). Human newborns spend between 50% and 80% of their sleep in PS. The amount of PS tapers off in later childhood and adolescence, and by adulthood most people have an average of 20% to 25% of their sleep in PS. In advanced adulthood and old age the proportion of PS seems to diminish further, and deep sleep becomes much shorter and more tenuous, disappearing entirely for many people.

This well-documented pattern of more PS in the newborns of immature species like humans indicates a close relationship between this stage of sleep and the early growth of the brain. Again, we have to be careful about overly simplistic causal explanations. For instance, more PS cannot be directly equated with higher intelligence, since dolphins, whales, and other ocean-dwelling mammals—all species with advanced cognitive abilities—have little or no PS. But in *H. sapiens sapiens* the extremely high level of internally generated electrical activity in PS, particularly in early life, has evolved in tandem with a much larger brain that requires a great deal of postnatal development and neural self-wiring. Indeed, there is good reason to suggest that human evolution has favored increasing prominence for this mode of sleep. As discussed in the previous chapter, the historical shift from polyphasic to monophasic sleeping behaviors among our primate ancestors led to a shortening and intensification of their sleep patterns. We saw that compared to other primate species, humans have developed the shortest overall sleep time and the most overall time in PS, making our sleep unusually intensive in the PS mode. We can add to that the fact that human newborns spend more time in PS than do the infants of other primate species. Taken together, these strands of evidence point to a strong evolutionary connection between the paradoxical stage of sleep and the early development of the human brain.

Chemical

When neurons in the brain "fire," they release neurotransmitters, special chemicals that interact with the receptors of other neurons to stimulate or inhibit the release of still other neurotransmitters. We are far from understanding the full range and complexity of these fast, densely interconnected chemical reactions (more than 80 neurotransmitters have been identified so far, with more likely to be discovered in the future). Researchers have found it hard to study neurotransmitters directly in the human brain without causing harmful and unethical damage, so most of our knowledge in this area has come from invasive experiments on animal brains and observations of the indirect effects of various medications on human mental and physical abilities.

Several neurotransmitters have been identified that have their highest rates of production during the waking state. These include *acetylcholine, noradrenaline, dopamine, histamine, glutamate,* and *orexin.* Generally speaking, medications that inhibit the functioning of these neurotransmitters make people distracted, drowsy, or unconscious. Medications that stimulate these neurotransmitters tend to increase alertness and attention.

At sleep onset all of these neurotransmitters lower their levels of production, while other neurotransmitters become more active. *Serotonin* increases as sleep approaches, probably to help calm the mind (medications that boost serotonin in the brain are effective treatments for phobias, anxiety, and depression). To fall asleep, we need to detach our attention from external perceptions, and serotonin seems to play a role in that process. So does *adenosine,* a neurotransmitter that suppresses arousal and causes drowsiness at elevated levels (caffeine works by blocking adenosine). An important neurotransmitter known as *GABA* is released in its greatest amounts during deep sleep. GABA generally has inhibitory effects on other neurons, slowing down their overall activities. Many generations of sleep medications, including barbiturates, Valium, Halcion, and now zolpidem (marketed as Ambien) have been designed to increase GABA's effects on the brain at sleep onset. Other chemical substances and compounds appear in greater amounts in the brain during sleep (these are collectively known as *sleep factors*), but their precise roles in the sleep/wake cycle are not well understood.

The chemistry of the brain changes considerably during the shift from NREM to REM sleep. The production of GABA diminishes, so there is no longer a general dampening of neural activity. Serotonin diminishes to its lowest levels, so the mind is no longer neurochemically pacified. Acetylcholine increases during REM sleep to levels comparable to the waking state. Given that higher acetylcholine has the effect in waking consciousness of stimulating arousal and attention, it is a remarkable fact that this same neurotransmitter appears at such elevated levels in the midst of sleep. Similarly, REM sleep also depends on brain activities involving *dopamine*, another neurotransmitter associated in the waking state with arousal, desire, and curiosity. Animals that have been deprived of dopamine experience a complete suppression of REM sleep.[9]

A crucial neurotransmitter for the human sleep process is *glycine*, which increases during REM sleep. Glycine has the effect of inhibiting brain systems for motor actions such as the physical movements of our arms and legs. This neurotransmitter helps make sure our bodies do not physically act out whatever is happening in the sleeping brain. According to research from Michael H. Chase and Francisco R. Morales, the level of brain activation of REM sleep becomes so intense that glycine has to counter it by rendering the neurons for physical movement "extraordinarily unexcitable. This results in a kind of muscle paralysis, also called *atonia*, that is a primary characteristic of REM sleep."[10] The internal tension between these sharply opposing forces "produce(s) muscle contractions and subsequent movements unlike those that occur during any other state. It is like applying pressure to the brakes of a car and at the same time to the accelerator."[11]

Finally, it should be noted that many other neurotransmitters besides the ones mentioned are active in various ways throughout the wake/sleep cycle, maintaining basic levels of brain functioning across all states of consciousness.[12]

These findings support the idea that the waking state and REM sleep have many important similarities in terms of brain activities. They are not identical, of course, but neither can they be conceived as sharply opposed to each other. The best evidence to date indicates that some of the neurotransmitters most vital to the waking state are also vital to REM sleep.

Anatomical

This approach to the brain focuses on its physical parts and regions. Two basic methods have helped scientists map out the functional anatomy of the brain during various states of consciousness. One method uses observations of people or animals suffering specific kinds of neurological illness or damage (*lesions*) to make inferences about the functions of different areas of the brain. For example, if damage to brain region A consistently leads to people having problems with cognitive ability B, then it seems reasonable to infer that A is anatomically necessary for B.

The second method uses powerful new imaging technologies like fMRI, PET, SPECT, and others to identify which parts of the brain are active or inactive during certain kinds of mental processes. If scanners show the A part of the brain is consistently active when people are using the B cognitive ability, we can fairly hypothesize that A is anatomically necessary for B.

If both methods lead to the same conclusion about A and B, we can build on the results with much more confidence because of this dual confirmation. Our confidence will rise even further if these anatomical results also correlate with the EEG and neurotransmitter findings mentioned earlier. The study of sleep and dreams is fortunate to have several instances where the results of these different methods of measuring neural activity match up to a high degree.

In studying the anatomy of the brain, several limiting factors should be noted. The cognitive problems caused by brain lesions are often temporary, and the lifelong flexibility of the brain (its *neuroplasticity*, a term to be discussed in more detail in coming chapters) makes it difficult to precisely locate any one cognitive function in any one fixed place in the brain. With imaging studies, the activation of a neural region can mean it is being excited *or* inhibited; these opposing effects show similar patterns of energy usage. In addition to that source of ambiguity, brain scanners usually require participants to remain perfectly still; otherwise the machines cannot make their subtle measurements. Thus, imaging technologies can reveal a lot about brain functioning while the body remains motionless, but not as much about what happens when people are engaged in physical movements of various kinds.

Sleep seems to be just immobile enough to enable the effective use of these tools. By combining results of imaging technologies with those of lesion studies, we can get as clear a view as current evidence allows of the functional anatomy of the sleeping brain.

The simplest way to start is with the division of the brain into two hemispheres, left and right.[13] In humans some of our cognitive functions show a preference for one hemisphere over another (such as certain aspects of language), but for the most part all high-order cognitive processing is *bilateral*, meaning it relies on systems located in both hemispheres. Imaging and lesion studies alike indicate that sleep in humans is fully bilateral, although damage to portions of the left or right hemisphere can disrupt sleep in various ways.

After the easily observed feature of its two hemispheres, the human brain's anatomy becomes much more difficult to describe in brief, non-technical language. I find it helpful to think of the brain's physical structure in terms of three stages of evolution. The oldest part is the *brainstem*, which is basically a bulbous extension of the spine and central nervous system. The anatomy of the human brainstem has changed very little from that of reptiles, which goes back hundreds of millions of years. More recent in evolutionary terms is the part of the brain surrounding the brainstem known as the *limbic system*, comprising several specific neural structures (such as the *amygdala* and *hippocampus*) that humans share with other mammals. The newest part of the brain, and the one that seems to have grown so dramatically during hominid encephalization, is called the *cerebral cortex*. This is the outer layer of the brain, the size and density of which is greater among humans than any other species.

All of these regions, the old and the new, work very closely together throughout our lives. This should make us cautious about brain-based explanations of mental functions that focus too narrowly on any one specific anatomical region. To extend the earlier example, brain region A may be anatomically *necessary* for cognitive function B, but it is probably not anatomically *sufficient*. Brain regions C, D, E, and F may also be anatomically necessary for A. Virtually any kind of brain function depends on multiple networks and feedback loops of neural connectivity between all three of these broadly defined regions—the brainstem, the limbic system, and the cerebral cortex.

This is especially true in sleep. Compared to the waking state, the brain has less activity in several areas during the early phases of SWS. These include the *locus coeruleus* in the brainstem, which makes sense given that this part of the brain produces the neurotransmitter noradrenaline, already known to decrease during sleep. Parts of the *prefrontal cortex* diminish in activity, too, in areas associated with focused attention and short-term memory. However, other parts of the brain become more active during SWS, such as the *cerebellum* near the brainstem and the *parahippocampal gyrus* in the limbic system.[14] Based on a study of neural activity during SWS using both EEG and fMRI devices, Thien Thanh Dan-Vu and his colleagues concluded that "SWS is not a state of brain quiescence, but rather is an active state during which brain activity is consistently synchronized to the slow oscillation in specific cerebral regions."[15]

When the brain shifts to REM sleep, several other neural regions increase their energy consumption and become highly engaged with each other. In the brainstem, a network known as the *reticular activating system* begins sending signals that stimulate various parts of the cortex, just as it does in the waking state. The *thalamus*, which helps connect the brainstem to the cortex, becomes more active in REM sleep, and so does the *basal forebrain*, another structure connecting brainstem and cortex. The basal forebrain is a source of the neurotransmitter acetylcholine that is so crucial to both waking and REM sleep.

Another highly active part of the brainstem region during REM sleep is the *pontine tegmentum*, a key source of the neuroelectrical PGO waves that start just before the onset of each phase of REM sleep and continue till its end. Lesions to the pontine tegmentum lead to a loss of REM sleep. In the waking state this part of the brain is key to orienting responses to novel stimuli—it becomes very active when a person is faced with an unknown environment.[16]

Many elements of the limbic system, especially the amygdala and hippocampus, become extremely active in REM sleep. In the waking state the limbic system is central to emotions, memories, and instinctual responses to survival-related situations (fight/flight, sexual arousal, etc.). Portions of the cerebral cortex also increase their activities in REM sleep. They include the *occipital* and *temporal* regions associated with visual and auditory processing, and the *anterior cingulate*, a key part of the executive cognitive system of waking consciousness that connects emotional arousal from the amygdala with the attention and orienting systems of the prefrontal cortex.

From a dream research perspective, one of the most important anatomical shifts in REM sleep involves the reactivation of the *medial temporal lobe* and the *fusiform gyrus*, both of which are directly involved in visual imagination, internal imagery, and social cognition. At the same time, activity in the *primary visual cortex* (also known as *V1*), the part of the brain that receives sensory input from the eyes, decreases considerably. This means that during REM sleep there is no primary visual information coming in from the external environment, yet the secondary visual processing parts of the brain are extremely active.[17]

G. William Domhoff and others have argued that a good way to interpret the neural activities of REM sleep is to compare them to the "default network," a kind of baseline brain system that operates in "mind wandering," when the mind is not focused on an external task. In a study

Domhoff performed with Kieran Fox and colleagues, they compared the neural evidence on REM sleep and the default network, and found "large overlaps in activation patterns of cortical regions." This led them to offer the provocative proposal that "dreaming can be understood as an 'intensified' version of waking MW [mind wandering]. . . . We suggest, then, that dreaming amplifies the same features that distinguish MW from goal-directed waking thought."[18]

The Neural Correlates of Sleep

Readers may feel a justified sense of relief upon nearing the end of this chapter, which has covered a great deal of dense technical research from many different scientific sources. Some readers may even have begun to wonder if we have drifted rather far from the study of religion. Understandably so! But to pursue a cognitive scientific approach to religion means we should begin any project by paying close, critical attention to this kind of technical research so we can develop hypotheses grounded in the best available evidence about how the brain/mind system actually works.

The findings discussed in this chapter can be summarized as follows.

- The human species has evolved with an unusually big brain and an unusually REM-intensive sleep cycle.
- Human newborns spend an extremely high proportion of their sleep in REM, indicating it plays an important role in early brain development.
- In deep sleep (stage 3 NREM), the brain has lower overall energy use and slow, synchronized EEG waves in the delta frequency.
- In REM or PS the brain shifts to a high energy, high activation mode with faster EEG waves in the theta, beta, and gamma frequencies. Parts of the brain devoted to short-term memory and focused attention are relatively quiet, and the paths to motor action are blocked, while neural systems involved in arousal, emotion, long-term memory, instinct, curiosity, orienting, and visual imagination are highly active.

These findings give us a good sense of the neural correlates of sleep. They show why the term "paradoxical sleep" is not just a poetic turn of phrase. It aptly describes the strange way the brain has aspects of both waking and sleeping during this time.

The more we learn about PS, the less it seems we can rely on theories claiming the general function of sleep is to conserve energy during the night. That may be true in some phases of sleep, but certainly not in PS, when the brain uses as much or more energy as it does in the waking state. As we have already seen, the human brain is a very expensive part of the body in terms of its high metabolic requirements. By the same token, we can now recognize that PS is very expensive sleep. It most definitely does not conserve energy. On the contrary, it uses abundant amounts of metabolic fuel for internally focused purposes that do not require active sensory engagement with the external environment.

The next chapter considers in more detail what those purposes might be.

Concluding Response

During the one-third of life that humans spend asleep, our brains are alight with brilliant bursts and powerful waves of electrical, chemical, and anatomical excitation. These dynamic patterns of neural activity overlap in many significant ways with the brain's conscious functioning during the waking state.

3

Health

No small art is it to sleep; it is necessary
for that purpose to keep awake all day.
FRIEDRICH NIETZSCHE, *Thus Spoke Zarathustra*

Opening Question

Is too much sleep dangerous?

Long before Antonio Damasio and the rise of modern neuroscience, and long before Thomas Edison and the invention of electric lights, people from ancient cultures also viewed sleep with a skeptical eye. One expression of this dubious attitude came in The Book of Proverbs, a Jewish sacred text written nearly 3,000 years ago. Proverbs contains numerous short maxims of wisdom attributed to the great King Solomon, ruler of the Israelite monarchy at the height of its wealth and prosperity (970–931 B.C.E.). In verse 13 of chapter 20 it reads, "Love not sleep, lest thou come to poverty; open thine eyes, and thou shalt be satisfied with bread."[1] This passage echoes other verses in Proverbs that emphasize a moral contrast between wakeful activity and slothful indolence.[2] It reflects an idea common in early Jewish and Greek thought that sleep may be necessary, but too much of it will cause problems, both materially (economic impoverishment) and spiritually (ignorance of the divine).

Should we accept this wary, guarded attitude toward sleep? Is it true that too much of it is potentially dangerous to human welfare? If yes, then perhaps we should refrain from attaching any special value to dreams, since they come during this somnolent, unproductive phase of mental life when our eyes are physically and spiritually closed.

Initial Response

In some cases too much sleep may cause problems, but far more common in modern society are problems with too little sleep.

The mental and physical health of every human being depends upon getting an adequate amount of slumber. A better understanding of normal, natural, healthy sleep will help us determine what counts as an "excessive" amount of it, enabling a more realistic assessment of the possible dangers. This will open the way for new insights later in the book when discussing the interactions between dreaming, the body, and religious rituals of healing.

Data and Discussion
The Sleeping Body

When night falls, the *pineal gland* in the brainstem releases greater amounts of the hormone *melatonin* into the bloodstream, where it spreads through the body and induces a general sense of drowsiness that usually leads to sleep. The pineal gland is a fascinating piece of human physiology, and not only because seventeenth-century philosopher René Descartes called it "the seat of the soul" (i.e., the point of physical contact between one's divine essence and material body). Located in a central position deep within the brain, the pineal gland processes information about light and darkness, and it plays a vital role in regulating the body's behavior through the circadian cycle. The evolutionary history of the pineal gland goes back hundreds of millions of years, with ancestral connections to the "third eye" photoreceptors of extremely primitive vertebrates like the lamprey (*Petromyzontiformes*). Melatonin, the hormone produced by the pineal gland, also has a long historical lineage as "a phylogenetically ancient molecule that is present in unicellular organisms."[3] Its exact mechanisms remain unknown, but according to current research, "melatonin appears to be involved in the translation of light-dark information into a hormonal message."[4] The centrality of the pineal gland and melatonin in the sleep cycle is further evidence that the rhythms of human sleep have their roots in the deepest biological processes of our evolutionary predecessors.

Along with melatonin, several other hormones and chemical substances are naturally released into the body during sleep, including *human growth hormone, interleukin-1,* and *tumor necrosis factor.* Human growth hormone, as its name indicates, has the effect of stimulating cell growth and tissue repair throughout the body, and its biggest burst of activity comes during the first phase of SWS. Interleukin-1 and tumor necrosis factor both help the immune system respond to inflammation and infection, and they both have their largest release in the early stages of sleep. When researchers give people experimental doses of these chemicals, the common effect is to induce drowsiness and sleep. Multiple sources of evidence indicate that these substances are crucial for the immune system's response to damage and disease, and they depend on a regular sleep cycle for their normal functioning. These facts have led eminent researcher William Dement to declare, "In this complex and roiling symphony of interaction, it is impossible to separate cause and effect. . . . Does the immune system govern sleep, or does sleep govern the immune system? The more we study sleep, the more it emerges as an integral and inseparable part of the body's vital cycles."[5]

Now let us consider the sleeping body at a larger scale. At sleep onset the eyes close and begin to drift slowly under the lids. The other senses—hearing, smell, taste, touch—withdraw from the world, becoming much less responsive to external stimulation. During the slow wave phase of deep sleep, muscle activity relaxes all over the body. Breathing slows down, and so does the heartbeat. With less metabolic activity, "there is a lowering of the regulated temperature during [NREM] sleep, a change analogous to lowering the setting on the thermostat of a building heating system during the night."[6]

By now, you might guess that much of this will change with the onset of REM sleep, and indeed it does. The eyes suddenly become very active, twitching and jerking "rapidly" under the lids. Respiration and heartbeat become faster and irregular. Greater blood flow to the genitals leads to penile erections in males and clitoral swelling in females.[7] The sharp rise in internally generated metabolic activity (especially in the brain) leads to an increase in the overall body temperature. Strangely, however, REM sleep also has the effect of nearly eliminating the capacity for thermoregulation, so the body's temperature floats up and down depending on the balance of internal heat production and external conditions. We become like reptiles during REM sleep, briefly transforming into creatures whose body temperature fluctuates freely with the ambient surroundings.[8]

The body remains generally motionless during REM sleep, but only because various brain systems (including the thalamus) have paralyzed it by actively blocking the pathways to direct physical action. This leads to the brakes-and-accelerator quality of atonia in REM sleep, with a body that is almost completely immobilized yet still subject to brief, erratic muscle spasms and contractions.

Toward the end of the night melatonin production from the pineal gland slows down, then effectively ceases. Other hormones and substances diminish their production, too (with the exceptions of *prolactin*, a hormone associated with reproduction, and *cortisol*, an energy-boosting substance, both of which rise to their peak levels at the end of the night). SWS disappears, and for the final few hours of the night there is nothing but an alternation between REM and stage 2 NREM. During this most neurologically active phase of the human sleep cycle, internal heat generation increases in the brain and throughout the body. This makes it easier to shift into waking consciousness when morning finally comes.

Sleep Deprivation

A classic scientific strategy for trying to understand the function(s) of a certain feature within a bigger system is to eliminate that feature and then observe what happens to the system. This is the logic behind sleep deprivation experiments, which researchers began to conduct on animals and humans in the late 1800s. What happens to a creature when it is prevented from sleeping for a prolonged period of time? What functions are lost or impaired?

These experiments seem to have the virtue of conceptual simplicity, but their results are clouded by several limitations.[9] In animal studies, the effort to prevent a creature from sleeping inevitably requires some kind of forceful, aggressive treatment (e.g., electric shocks, water immersion, or constant handling), making it unclear if the resulting impairments come from sleep deprivation or from acute anxiety and stress. Published studies of humans have not pushed the deprivation process to these extremes, but the same problem arises of how to disentangle the effects of sleep deprivation from the effects of the stressful experimental procedures.

Many researchers have tried to selectively deprive animals and humans from NREM sleep while allowing them to have REM sleep, or conversely deprive them of REM sleep but allow them to have NREM sleep. Again, the disruptive effects of the experimental interventions make it difficult to draw more than a few tentative conclusions. The dynamically interconnected nature of the sleep cycle means that any experimental change to one of its elements will ripple throughout the whole system, affecting the timing, duration, and intensity of many other processes.

That fact accounts for the main finding of this body of research: Prolonged sleep deprivation will eventually kill a creature. Various behavioral impairments accumulate along the way as the deprivation continues, but if the experiment is pushed far enough the final result is always a widespread physiological failure leading to death. The cumulative effects of sleep deprivation go beyond the loss of this or that specific function to a precipitous and ultimately fatal decline in all functions.

For humans the first signs of sleep deprivation are unpleasant feelings of fatigue, irritability, and difficulties concentrating. Then come problems with reading and speaking clearly, poor judgment, lower body temperature, and a considerable increase in appetite. If the deprivation continues, the worsening effects include disorientation, visual misperceptions, apathy, severe lethargy, and social withdrawal.

Surprisingly, even with these worsening deficits, sleep-deprived humans can still perform remarkably well on tests for certain kinds of repetitive motor and cognitive skills. These abilities remain functional even when people no longer have any imaginative spark or feel actively engaged with the world. According to sleep researcher Michael H. Bonnet, "responses [to performance tests] during sleep loss may occur as rapidly as before, but those responses tend to be more stereotyped and less creative."[10] Another researcher, Jim Horne, put it like this: "in effect, progressive sleep loss turns us into automatons and, in losing the ability to think independently, conscious awareness of ourselves is impaired and we are no longer prescient. Nevertheless, we can still run on 'auto-pilot' and perform routine behavior and other well-rehearsed tasks and procedures."[11]

The numerous problems arising from sleep deprivation add more evidence to the idea that sleep, however we may define its specific functions, is clearly indispensable for human health and survival.

And yet, sleep is quite flexible. It grants wide latitude in how and when we satisfy its needs. As discussed in chapter 1, many animal species have modified their sleep cycles to accommodate other survival-related needs and activities (e.g., migrating birds or dolphin mothers). Humans can modify their sleep cycles, too, and rather easily at that. Partial or total sleep deprivation can be tolerated for several days, especially if one or more arousal factors are present: noise, light, exercise/movement, drugs (caffeine and amphetamines have especially strong effects on sleep-deprived people), and most important, motivation. If people are intrinsically driven to stay awake for some purpose (e.g., studying, partying, or taking care of a sick child), they can rally the cognitive wherewithal to temporarily override the accumulating negative effects of sleep deprivation.[12] This factor undoubtedly helped Randy Gardner, the California teenager who stayed awake for 264 hours as part of a high school science experiment in 1965. During the experiment Gardner became the focus of national media attention and active efforts by researchers like William Dement to help him prolong his wakefulness.[13] The abundance of positive reinforcement surely boosted Gardner's motivation to remain awake for as long as possible.

In all species, human included, the deprivation of sleep is followed by a *rebound effect* of increased amounts of sleep when the deprivation ends. If we lose sleep one night, we try to make up for it the next night. This indicates some degree of homeostatic regulation of sleeping and waking, a general balance toward which we naturally gravitate.[14] However, the rebound effect usually does not compensate for all the deprived sleep, just a portion of it. When Gardner finally ended his eleven straight days of wakefulness, he slept for about 15 hours, and then slept normally again after that. Fifteen hours is a long time to sleep, but it is just a small fraction of what Gardner lost during his experiment. This highlights the fact that the longer and more severe the deprivation, the lower the percentage of sleep that can be potentially regained during the rebound phase.

Neuroplasticity

In addition to examining the functional losses when people are deprived of sleep, scientists have also tried to illuminate the functional gains when people are able to sleep normally. Over the past several decades a great deal of research has focused on the interaction of sleep, memory, and learning. Many studies of animals and humans have shown that sleep helps the mind process information from waking experiences, consolidate memories, and learn new skills.[15] These results seem to support a view of sleep as essential to healthy mental functioning. However, many other studies have produced conflicting results that cast doubt on the alleged linkages between specific stages of sleep and specific types of memory.[16]

The best way to make sense of this contentious area of research is to view it in light of *neuroplasticity*, which means the capacity of the brain to change, adapt, and reorganize itself in response to experience. This concept will play a big role through the rest of this book, and it comes up now because learning and memory can be seen as small-scale instances of neuroplasticity.[17] Whenever we learn something new or form a memory of something that happened to us, our brains physically change. The microcircuitry of synaptic connections is altered, and new neural networks are created. The strength of these networks, as measured by the intensity and consistency of their neural firing patterns, reflects the strength of the new knowledge or memory. A common expression for this idea is, "cells that fire together, wire together."

Thinking about sleep in these terms diminishes the need to focus on particular sleep stages or types or memory. Instead, sleep's function can be conceived more globally as providing a good environment for the brain to work on these highly adaptive, neurally transformative processes of network-building. Pierre Maquet and his colleagues have put this idea most succinctly: *"Sleep is favorable for brain plasticity."*[18] An experiment showing what this means was conducted in 2001 by Matthew Walker, who trained rats to run through mazes and monitored their sleep during the learning process. Walker performed brain scans of the rats during the maze-running and during their sleep, and he found the same sequences of neural firings from the maze were also occurring in PS.[19] In effect, the rats' brains were replaying in sleep the same neural networks that were activated when they were awake and learning how to run the maze. Whether or not this means the rats were dreaming (a question to be discussed later), it certainly illustrates the brain's plasticity in sleep (i.e., its adaptive responsiveness to the neural impact of waking experience). Learning experiences change the way the brain works, and sleep helps to process and consolidate those changes.

Perhaps, as some researchers claim, REM sleep is especially good at boosting the strength of *procedural* or *implicit* memories (e.g., how to tie a shoe lace, play a musical instrument, or run through a maze) while NREM sleep is most important for strengthening *declarative* or *explicit* memories (e.g., the name of the US president, your home address, or what you had for breakfast this morning).[20] Whether or not those hypotheses are confirmed by future research, the important point is the broader one: Sleep as a whole plays a role in forming, organizing, and maintaining all kinds of memory and knowledge. As Maquet and his colleagues say, sleep creates an excellent set of conditions for neuroplasticity. It temporarily suspends external attention so the brain can do the complicated, detailed work of adapting to new experiences and flexibly integrating them into ongoing neural operations.

Research on neuroplasticity is still relatively new, so we have to be careful not to overemphasize this aspect of brain functioning or exaggerate its importance. At the same time, we should not forget that mainstream scientific opinion on this topic was, until recently, quite wrong. Through most of the twentieth century, medical textbooks taught that neural circuitry takes shape during a brief window of time in early childhood, and after that the brain remains essentially static and unchanging for the rest of life. Pioneering neuroscientist Santiago Ramon y Cajal, who won the Nobel Prize in Medicine in 1906, asserted that "in the adult centers [of the brain] the nerve paths are something fixed, ended and immutable."[21] Because neurons do not divide like other cells, Ramon y Cajal and others assumed they had no other way of reproducing or regenerating themselves. This seemed to imply that human brains, once formed in childhood, were fated to a one-way decline through the rest of life as their neurons slowly died, never to be replaced.

Eventually researchers realized that, even though neural cells do not divide, the brain has a large stock of neural stem cells with the ability to grow into various kinds of neurons when called upon at later times of life. And it turns out the pathways between neurons not only can change, they do change, continuously in all modes of functioning. A few scientists had early insights into these features of the brain, including psychologist and philosopher William James, who first used the term "plasticity" in his 1890 work *Principles of Psychology:* "Organic matter, especially nervous tissue, seems endowed with a very extraordinary degree of plasticity."[22] And in 1917 neuroscientist Charles S. Sherrington compared the brain's ever-changing activities to "an enchanted loom, where millions of flashing shuttles weave a dissolving pattern, always a meaningful pattern, though never an abiding one."[23] Only in recent years have empirical researchers caught up with these prescient ideas to recognize the brain's wide-ranging flexibility and open-ended dynamism.

To be clear, the brain is not infinitely elastic or malleable. But neither is it fixed in concrete. The current trend in neuroscience, and in sleep research, is toward recognizing more and more plasticity in the brain in a greater variety of its functions.

Pathological Sleep

The best scientific evidence to support the opening verse from Proverbs about the dangers of excessive sleep comes from a 2002 study by Daniel

Kripke and his colleagues. They analyzed survey data from 1.1 million American adults asking them questions about their health and sleep, and found the best survival rates were for people who slept an average of 7 hours a night. People who slept more than 8, or fewer than 6, hours a night tended to have shorter life spans. Higher mortality did not correlate with insomnia, but death rates rose with increased use of prescription sleeping pills. The study controlled for demographics and health factors, and its results are broadly consistent with other studies showing more pathology among people who sleep for extremely short or extremely long periods of time.[24]

The work of Kripke and his colleagues revealed a kind of Goldilocks zone for sleep and health. The amount of sleep associated with the longest lifespan was neither too short nor too long but right in the middle, and problems and pathologies appeared more often at both extremes. Much of the commentary on Kripke et al.'s findings emphasized the unexpected finding of higher mortality of people who slept the most. Other studies had already shown problems with excessively short sleep—that was old news. But Kripke and his colleagues found that people who reported unusually long amounts of sleep also had higher mortality rates. This result seems to confirm the general idea from Proverbs 20:13 that too much sleep can be a bad thing.

However, the numerous studies of excessively short sleep that have been conducted over the years have identified specific physiological mechanisms that lead to people dying at earlier ages. We have good explanations for why too little sleep is harmful. But no such mechanisms have been found with people who sleep longer than average. Kripke et al.'s finding on this point is purely correlational, without the support of any experimental evidence or causal explanation. There are no "sleep gluttonization" studies to compare with sleep deprivation studies. This means the higher mortality of long sleepers may not have the same underlying causes as the higher mortality of short sleepers. Perhaps people who sleep an unusually long amount of time do so because their immune systems have detected the health problems and have begun mobilizing the body's sleep-dependent resources to protect against those dangers. Their additional sleep may be an adaptive response to the health danger, not the cause of it.

Looking more broadly now at the field of sleep medicine, researchers have identified numerous pathological syndromes, almost all of them involving problems that limit or disrupt sleep. The one that might seem an obvious disorder of too much sleep, namely *narcolepsy*, turns out to be a strange form of sleep deprivation. Narcolepsy means "sleep seizure," and its primary symptom is extreme daytime sleepiness, which is often misdiagnosed as laziness and indolence. Human and animal narcoleptics seem to be lacking proper amounts of the neurotransmitter orexin. As mentioned in the previous chapter, orexin helps to regulate the normal cycle of waking and sleeping. Without orexin, this vital cycle breaks down: "The polysomnographic data available to date indicate that patients with narcolepsy have difficulty maintaining a given neural state, whether sleep or wake. Thus, these patients tend to fall asleep during their waking hours and to wake up more frequently during their sleeping period."[25] In addition to daytime sleepiness, narcoleptics are subject to *cataplexy*, a sudden muscular weakness at moments of high emotional arousal (laughing, anger, surprise, or sexual excitement) leading to a temporary physical collapse. Cataplexy seems to be an intrusion of REM sleep atonia into the waking state. When the brain is in the highly aroused state of REM sleep, it sends signals that block bodily movement and relax the muscles; in narcoleptics these paralyzing signals appear in waking, too. Narcoleptics also suffer disturbing *hypnogogic hallucinations* at sleep onset and episodes of *sleep paralysis* (discussed later), and when they do sleep they shoot directly into REM, with very little time in NREM sleep.

All in all, narcoleptics can hardly be accused of loving sleep, even though they seem to overindulge in it. The health problems of narcolepsy accrue from a loss of normal sleep, not from an excessive amount of it.

More common pathologies like *apnea* (obstructed breathing) and *restless limb syndrome* involve physiological disruptions of the sleep cycle. Rare but dramatic disorders like *REM behavior disorder* (REMBD) stem from a malfunction in the neural mechanism that blocks physical activity during REM. Instead of becoming atonic, the muscles become quite tonic, and the individual begins to engage in physically "complex and violent behaviors."[26] REMBD is different from *sleepwalking*, which almost always occurs during NREM sleep in the first few hours of the night. In sleepwalking the brain has aspects of both waking and NREM sleep. Without the paralyzing atonia of REM sleep, the individual's body is free to open its eyes, move around, and have mumbling conversations.

The occurrence of sleepwalking in NREM sleep connects it to another "disorder of arousal": *night terrors* (the pre-modern medical term for this affliction was *pavor nocturnus*). As most parents know, night terrors are especially prevalent in children. They occur during NREM sleep in the

first few hours of the night, and their features are distressingly consistent: The afflicted people sit up in bed, eyes wide open, and scream in
terror. Sweating, breathing fast, their hearts pounding, they appear to be
reacting to something of an intensely frightening nature. Yet they do not
respond to external efforts to calm them down, much to the dismay of the
people around them. The victims are strangely inconsolable and oblivious
to their immediate surroundings, even though they otherwise behave as
if awake. As noted by researcher Mark W. Mahowald, "These phenomena demonstrate a curious paradox: profound internal arousal immune to
external arousal."[27] And yet, despite all outward appearances, night terrors
are generally benign and do no lasting harm. They usually last only a few
minutes, then the person goes back to sleep and retains no memory of
what happened upon awakening the next morning. By all accounts, the
worst effects of night terrors are on those who witness someone else having the experience.

Yet another disorder of arousal, *sleep paralysis*, involves a mixing of
waking consciousness and REM sleep.[28] Episodes of sleep paralysis usually occur at the beginning or end of the night, during the transitional
phases leading from the waking state into sleep (*hypnogogic*), and from
sleep back into waking (*hypnopompic*). The typical sensations include fear,
disorientation, physical immobility, constricted breathing, pressure on
the chest, an inability to speak or cry out, and the sense of a menacing
presence nearby. Most researchers agree that the core problem has to do
with the mechanisms of atonia in REM sleep, which paralyze the body
either too soon, before the brain has fully fallen asleep, or for too long,
when the brain has already started to wake up. Sleep paralysis occurs
more frequently in people who have shorter REM *latency*, meaning their
brains enter the first phase of REM sleep more quickly than normal. This
is why narcoleptics so often experience sleep paralysis, because they have
very short REM latencies and their sleep is made up almost entirely of
abrupt, fragmented bursts of REM. This is also why sleep-deprived people
are more vulnerable to sleep paralysis, because the deprivation shortens
their REM latencies and builds up pressure for faster, more intense phases
of REM when they finally do get to sleep.

We could, of course, go even further with this exploration of the
phantasmagoria of sleep pathology. Enough has been covered, however,
to highlight an important but unappreciated aspect of neuroplasticity in
sleep. Several of the disorders just mentioned, such as sleepwalking, night
terrors, and sleep paralysis, involve unusual mixtures of the core elements

of sleep. Different parts of the brain are shifting into waking, REM, or NREM, different parts of the body are highly active or completely paralyzed, different cognitive functions are fully engaged or totally offline— it is as if every possible combination of these elements has been tested through human history and given a chance to show what it can do. These *parasomnias* (a general term for abnormalities of sleep) occur in people with various medical problems, but they can also appear spontaneously in normal, healthy people.

It turns out that the basic components of sleep are not locked in place but have some degree of flexibility in their interactions with each other. The fact that parasomnias like sleepwalking, night terrors, and sleep paralysis rarely do any lasting harm suggests that it might be better not to conceive of them as medical disorders at all but rather as somewhat common, usually benign variations in the normal course of the human sleep cycle.

Concluding Response

Too much sleep is not dangerous, and there is no health-related reason not to "love sleep." People differ in how many hours constitute a personally optimal amount of sleep, but there is no health risk for anyone in stretching it out on the longer side, and many well-documented health risks in constraining it too much on the shorter side.

4

Culture

There's our secret sign, I tell you, our life story!
Does the bed, my lady, still stand planted firm?

HOMER, *The Odyssey*

Opening Question

Is sleep a purely individual experience?

It would seem the functions of sleep, however we define them, pertain only to the individual. As the ancient Greek philosopher Heraclitus said, "The waking have one common world, but the sleeping turn aside each into a world of his own."[1] In this view sleep can be explained as pure solipsism, a detachment and withdrawal from the community leading into a state of total self-absorption. A sleeping person checks out of social reality, shuts down the external senses, and remains silent, immobile, and unresponsive for many hours at a stretch. Sleep appears to be the antithesis of waking sociability, the polar opposite of interpersonal relations. This suggests that whatever benefits we might attribute to sleep (including possible benefits involving dreaming) apply exclusively to the sleeping individual.

The apparent solipsism of sleep poses a challenge for this book's attempt to investigate how religions originate in dreaming. Religions always have social as well as personal dimensions. At least as far back as Émile Durkheim's *The Elementary Forms of Religious Life* (1906), scholars have recognized that religious beliefs and practices are interwoven with social realities. If sleep is indeed a fundamentally non-social behavior, then it becomes harder to argue that dreaming, which occurs during sleep, has any special relevance for understanding human religiosity.

Initial Response

Human sleep is culturally influenced and socially contextualized at many levels.

The solipsistic aspects of sleep should not overshadow the multiple ways in which cultures shape each individual's sleeping experiences. Every cultural tradition has its own distinctive practices revolving around sleep and its role in the ongoing life of the community. These practices involve when people sleep, where, with whom, on what, and for how long. Every culture has time-honored teachings about the conditions for optimally healthy sleep, and also about the shadowy dangers that may be lurking in slumber. When viewed in this light, it becomes evident that sleep is not a purely solitary experience. Current research suggests it would be more accurate to say that *sleep is social behavior in a different mode*, a quieter and more yielding mode that depends on, and contributes to, intimate and trusting relationships with others.

Data and Discussion
Group Sleeping

A proper answer to this question requires that we expand the scope of research to include new sources of evidence from anthropology and history. These disciplines study human beings not only as discrete biological organisms but also as members of social groups and cultural traditions who actively participate in multiple webs of interpersonal relations. The wider lens of social scientific research reveals the cultural influences on sleep that individual-focused perspectives tend to overlook.

Recall the discussion in chapter 1 about the sleep patterns of primates and early hominids. Millions of years ago when our evolutionary ancestors came down from the trees and began expanding into a wider range of ecosystems, they developed the practice of sleeping together in small groups. Co-sleeping provided the thermoregulatory benefits of shared body heat, plus better protection against predators during the night. The vulnerability of sleeping on the ground could be diminished by staying in close physical proximity to a group of others who could raise the alarm if needed and help defend against external attack.

Here it should be emphasized that the sensory detachment of sleep is not absolute. Certain kinds of outside stimuli do register in the sleeping mind, potentially triggering an immediate awakening. Parents, for example, can sleep through any number of loud sounds but will spring awake at a soft whimper from their child. Faint odors or subtle changes in temperature, ambient light, or air flow—a sleeping person remains capable of perceiving these and many other kinds of stimuli, primed to wake up rapidly if the perceptions seem to indicate danger. When several people sleep near each other, their low-level perceptual sensitivities overlap and effectively form a protective network that maintains a high degree of vigilance toward possible threats from the external environment. Add to that the frequency during a normal night's sleep of micro-awakenings in which people wake up for a few moments (usually when a REM phase has just ended), check their surroundings, change body positions, and then fall back asleep. In a group of people sleeping together, all of their individual micro-awakenings contribute to a kind of collective early warning system that scans the environment for potential dangers at brief, irregular intervals throughout the night. Group sleep has enormous survival advantages over solitary sleep. That evolutionary fact has made a lasting imprint on the history of human social life.

This is not the place for a detailed, globe-spanning historical analysis of sleep. The main concern in this chapter is to highlight some of the most important cultural practices and social forces that influence sleep, in order to set up later discussions about the collective dimensions of dreaming.[2] Traditional community beliefs about sleep can have a big impact on people's interest in dreams and motivation to remember them. To study dreams without including this cultural material about sleep would be like studying a forest without considering the soil out of which the trees are growing.

Who sleeps with whom? In most social groups this question has multiple answers that can change over time.[3] A common principle in nearly all cultures is that parents sleep close to their children, especially in the first few years of life. This practice has many obvious benefits. First and foremost, children represent the procreative future of the group. By protecting them through the night, the group is protecting its own survival prospects in the years to come. The extreme immaturity of newborn humans makes them more vulnerable than anyone else to nocturnal dangers; they need extra safeguarding during sleep, exactly the service provided by their parents and other family members.

In many cultures sexual mates sleep with each other, a practice found among other primates as well. Many human cultures also practice sleep in single-gender groups, with the adult males sleeping together in one place and the females and young children sleeping in another. But even in these more segregated cultures, people in the various subgroups are still sleeping together in a bigger community context, regardless of the physical distance between them. What varies is an individual's sleeping position relative to others in the social sphere; what does not vary is the sphere itself, the broader social network in which each individual's sleep is located.

Group sleeping seems to have started in a family/reproductive context, but the practice is not exclusive to immediate blood relatives. For example, research from anthropologist Roger Lohmann shows that the Asabano people of New Guinea sleep with each other in various combinations of family, friends, adults, children, guests (an Asabano host considers it a proper act of hospitality to sleep with a visitor), and gender (males have their own sleeping house, and females have both a regular sleeping house with the children and a separate house for sleeping during menstruation). Lohmann says the Asabano ideal of sleep "is a kind of freedom of movement, day and night, that contrasts with European fixity of residence.... [N]o one always sleeps in the same house.... [A]dults, as well as children, might easily move back and forth among different potential sleeping houses, reflecting current relations, activities, and convenience."[4]

This kind of fluidity of sleeping appears not only among tribal cultures but also in highly modernized societies. For example, commuters on subway trains in present-day Japan engage in short, light naps known as *inemuri*, a word combining "to be present" and "sleep."[5] During *inemuri* people are genuinely asleep, but they maintain the ability to awaken at the precise moment when the train reaches their stop. These Japanese commuters have cultivated a special kind of slumber that is perfectly adapted to the circumstances of their social environment. They take advantage of an otherwise inactive period of time by sleeping as deeply as they can, for as long as they can, while preserving just enough perceptual vigilance and cognitive awareness to wake up when external action is required. The widespread practice of *inemuri* depends on people feeling a high degree of trust in their social surroundings when they sleep, a trust that likely grows out of early experiences with *soine*, the Japanese term for parent and child co-sleeping.[6]

A similar practice appears in other parts of the modern Western world where people feel comfortable enough with their immediate social environment to lower their personal guard and drift off into a light slumber. The number of people in movie theaters, libraries, airplanes, and various forms of public transportation who are asleep sometimes exceeds the number of people who are awake. English does not have a specific term for this phenomenon (maybe "catnap"?), but it seems to be at least as prevalent in places like the United States, Canada, and Britain as *inemuri* is in Japan.[7]

New cultural attitudes toward group sleeping emerged in Europe during the early industrial age (the 1600s onward), as people from traditional agrarian communities were transformed into assembly-line factory workers, while factory owners, merchants, and financiers prospered as never before. The rapid rise of industrial capitalism generated enormous wealth for the upper classes of society, leading to the development of new cultural norms of behavior that reflected their tastes, aspirations, and elevated status. Foremost among these new values was personal privacy. The upper classes could afford to physically separate themselves from other people, whereas the lower classes could not. This key cultural ideal of early modern capitalism had a radical impact on the sleeping behaviors of people across Europe. According to historian Roger Ekirch, "new norms of civility in Western society extended to slumber.... By the eighteenth century, communal sleep inspired widespread disdain among the gentle classes.... In no other sphere of preindustrial life did a mounting appreciation for personal privacy among the upper ranks of society manifest itself more plainly. Many religious leaders added their voice, condemning the morality of families in common beds."[8]

This cultural shift toward more private, solitary sleeping was a reflection, Ekirch says, of broader changes in the basic organization of Western society. These changes went beyond industrialization to include the rise of rational science, global commerce, colonial conquest, and missionary Christianity. People in this new era put greater cultural emphasis on the individual as a free, autonomous agent, and less emphasis on people's interdependent roles in broader social networks.

Without questioning the significance of this historical shift toward greater individualism and privacy, I want to caution against making sharp categorical distinctions between "communal" and "individualistic" cultures. At least in the case of sleep, every culture has both communal and individualistic features. Indigenous tribal groups like the Asabano have collective sleep patterns with a great deal of interpersonal intimacy, and yet at certain stages of life they sleep at greater distances from each other, with more individual freedom of movement. Modern societies in North America and Western Europe put more emphasis on personal privacy in sleep, but they still value the broader interpersonal network in which each individual sleeps. Everyone in a present-day US household may sleep in his or her own room, but the family as a whole still sleeps under one roof. The point is that trying to separate "individualistic" from "communal" cultures is not a useful exercise. It can be useful, however, to study the various strands of individualism and communalism woven together in different cultures. We will do much more of that kind of cultural-psychological analysis in the chapters to come.

Bedtime

Few archeological records remain to indicate the exact locations and material conditions of sleep among the earliest humans. However, based on indirect evidence from primate sleep behaviors and the practices of present-day tribal cultures, it seems likely the original "beds" were ground-level nests of grasses, leaves, and animal hides. At least some early humans slept in caves, and other groups must have found or built comparably sheltered places in which to lie down each night. The first architectural impulses in our species may have arisen from this basic need to sleep in a safe, warm, dry place.

Several thousand years ago the rulers of the great kingdoms of Mesopotamia (such as the Egyptians, Assyrians, and Babylonians) began sleeping on ornately carved structures that elevated them above the floor. The common people still slept on the ground on mats or piles of straw, but the monarchs had the privilege of sleeping apart from the earth. These royal sleep contrivances had large wooden frames, decorated headboards and footboards, and tightly woven lattices of palm reeds and leather thongs in the center. From the ancient Egyptians onward, an elaborately gilded and bejeweled bed became a symbol of a ruler's power and majesty. Over time these special pieces of furniture grew in cultural prominence as members of the nobility, the aristocracy, and the wealthier classes also acquired finely wrought beds raised up on wooden frames.

By the time of the Industrial Revolution in Europe, elevated bed frames were produced using iron and brass in addition to wood, and they became more accessible to the general population. The improved comfort and safety of these beds helped to spur their growing popular appeal, and so did their time-honored symbolic meaning as prized possessions of the wealthy and powerful. In the early modern period of England, Ekirch said that "[b]eds were among the first items bequeathed in wills to favored heirs as well as the first possessions purchased by newlyweds. In modest homes, beds sometimes represented over one-third the value of all domestic assets. Although humble families often made their own frames, a bed was usually the piece of furniture first acquired upon entering the 'world of goods.' "[9]

The word "mattress" comes from the Arabic *matrah*, meaning "to throw down." The earliest ones consisted of sacks filled with straw, cotton, or feathers. The big innovation occurred in the early twentieth century with the appearance of box spring and innerspring mattresses, which used rows of small metal coils to provide stronger and more consistent support. Other types of modern mattresses use either foam or some kind of floatation medium (such as waterbeds and airbeds). As different as these materials may be, they all involve a wooden and/or metal frame that holds the mattress at a certain height above the floor. The kind of sleeping arrangement that was once a special privilege of the Pharaohs is now a common feature of the modern Western household.

Not all cultures have taken this path with the design and construction of their bedding. The Japanese, for example, generally sleep on *futons*— supple pads, several inches thick, filled with cotton, wool, or other soft materials that people roll out on the floor when it is time to sleep. In the morning, the futon is rolled up again and set aside, leaving the room open for other uses (a practical advantage in Japan's densely populated residential areas). Futons have been used for many centuries by people all across the social spectrum, rich and poor alike. Despite many variations in style, design, and quality, Japanese bedding has not developed in the direction of greater structural size and height as it has in Western cultures.

Perhaps the biggest shift between traditional and modern sleep practices regards pillows. Fluffy softness has not been a top priority in all cultures. The oldest known pillows were rocks and logs positioned to support a sleeping person's head and neck. An early mention of this practice comes in the book of Genesis, when the Jewish patriarch Jacob is said to have slept one night in a remote wilderness location: "[A]nd he took of the stones of that place, and put them for his pillows, and lay down in that place to sleep."[10] Many cultures in Africa have traditionally used beautifully carved wooden headrests of varying sizes and shapes, some of which are specially designed to preserve the sleeping person's hair arrangements and body paint. The ancient Chinese created ceramic pillows of hollow porcelain that could be filled with ice in the summer or hot water in the winter to keep the sleeping person's head at a comfortable temperature.[11] By contrast, pillows in modern Western society tend to be shaped like small versions of old-fashioned mattresses (i.e., sacks of soft material like cotton, feathers, or foam).

The cultural significance of beds, mattresses, and pillows reflects their central place in some of the most meaningful moments of the human life cycle. The bed is not only the place where people sleep; it is also where they make love, recuperate from illness, tell stories, bear children, and eventually die. It is a place of sanctuary and repose, where people wear less clothing than usual, or no clothing at all. Beds are lively social arenas for a host of intimate interpersonal activities.

Demographic Trends

The duration and quality of sleep depends on more than the physical conditions of one's bedding. It also depends on a variety of sociological factors that deeply influence people's waking and sleeping lives. These factors include gender, nationality, ethnicity, marital status, education, and economic status. We already know that people at different ages have different sleep patterns—children tend to sleep the most, and the elderly sleep the least. Do sleeping patterns also vary for people from different social groups?

Research on these kinds of demographic categories generally makes use of surveys, questionnaires, and interviews with groups of people who are supposed to represent the experiences of a larger population. We discussed one of these studies in the previous chapter, with Kripke's analysis of how many hours per night American adults tend to sleep. We also discussed some of the limits of quantitative approaches like this, such as the uncertain honesty and accuracy of the answers, the limited diversity of the sample groups, and the difficulty of distinguishing causal connections from statistical coincidences. These methodological limits are not necessarily fatal, but they do have to be openly acknowledged before trying to draw any conclusions from this kind of research.

In 2013 the National Sleep Foundation (NSF) released the results of an international survey of 1,500 adults between the ages of 25 and 55 in six different countries: the United States, Canada, Mexico, the United Kingdom, Germany, and Japan.[12] These are some of the most developed and economically advanced countries in the world, and the participants were adults in the prime ages of their working lives. The results of this survey offer a good picture of the sleep practices of people who are highly active in the modern economy.

First, the most prominent similarity: people in all six countries reported sleeping an average of 45 minutes longer on weekend nights than they did on nights during the work week. This finding suggests a mild but chronic cycle of sleep deprivation and rebound, with sleep debt building up during each week and then extra sleep on the weekends to make up for some, but probably not all, of what was lost. Such a sleep pattern is "unnatural" in the sense of not being rooted in the deeper biological functioning of our species. Instead, it reflects Western cultural traditions about the structure of time going back to the Book of Genesis in the Bible. This distinctively Western cycle of sleep shows how cultural beliefs and practices can shape the physiological functioning of people's bodies.

In addition to that shared phenomenon, the NSF survey results revealed several differences in national sleep behaviors. The Japanese and Americans reported sleeping the fewest hours (between 6.5 and 7), Mexicans and Canadians the most (between 7.5 and 8). Mexicans and Americans were the most likely to pray or meditate before going to bed. British people were most likely to sleep naked.

An earlier study by the NSF in 2010 focused on sleep, ethnicity, and racial differences in the United States. The survey involved a group of 1,007 people between the ages of 25 and 60 who identified themselves either as White, Black/African American, Asian, or Hispanic. Of course, these are quite broad categories that oversimplify the social complexities of ethnic and racial identity. The results of the survey do, however, highlight a number of variations in each group's sleep behaviors that seem likely to have a cultural component. For example, Asians were the most likely to say they slept well, with little insomnia, the least nighttime worrying, and least use of sleep medications. Blacks/African Americans reported the least amount of total sleep and the most time in bed without sleeping. Whites had the most insomnia, the highest use of sleep medications, and were least likely to sleep in the same room as their children. Much higher proportions of Blacks/African Americans and Hispanics said they prayed every night before bed. Those two groups also reported far more nighttime worries about jobs, finances, and health than did the Asians or Whites.

Neither of these studies took gender into account, but other surveys have found considerable differences in male and female sleep behaviors.[13] Most significantly, women of all ages are more likely than men to have insomnia and other sleep problems. The worst difficulties with women's sleep occur, not surprisingly, during pregnancy and the months immediately following delivery. Men's sleep quality declines with age; women's sleep quality declines even more as they get older and pass through menopause. These differences in sleep are related in some measure to the biology of human reproduction and the different roles of male and female bodies in the process. But there may be additional reasons why men tend to sleep better than women, reasons having to do with cultural practices of childrearing, domestic labor, caregiving for the sick and elderly, and sexual availability. In many cases these practices make the bed a less restful, more stressful place for women than it is for men.

Research by Sara Arber and her colleagues at the Center for the Sociology of Sleep at the University of Surrey has found clear connections between socioeconomic status and sleep quality.[14] In a study based on interviews with 8,578 British men and women between the ages of 16 and 74, Arber and her colleagues identified several social and economic factors associated with lower quality sleep: unemployment, low household income, low educational achievement, and living in rented or public housing. Women had worse sleep problems than men, and divorced or widowed people had worse sleep problems than married people. Intriguingly, women with higher socioeconomic status had fewer sleep problems, a finding that underscores the importance of cultural as well as biological influences on women's sleep. Overall, their study found that disadvantages in social and economic life were strongly correlated with poor quality sleep. Noting the negative health consequences of sleep deprivation, Arber and her colleagues suggested that "disrupted sleep may potentially be one of the mechanisms through which low socioeconomic status leads to increased morbidity and mortality."[15]

Some of the material in the Sleep and Dream Database has relevance to this topic. In recent years I have conducted several large demographic surveys among American adults 18 years and older. One of the questions in these surveys asked the participants to estimate how many nights per week they have insomnia or trouble sleeping. For this discussion I have condensed their answers into three groups: 0 nights per week, 1–2 nights per week, and 3 or more nights per week.

The first survey, in 2007, used telephone interviews with 705 American adults (table 4.1).[16]

The gender difference in sleep quality found by other researchers also appeared in this survey: men were more likely than women to have 0 nights of insomnia, and women were twice as likely as men to have 3 or more nights of insomnia per week. Consistent with Arber et al.'s research, higher education and higher annual income correlated with less insomnia. The poorest participants were twice as likely as the wealthiest participants to have 3 or more nights of insomnia per week. An additional question about political ideology revealed an intriguing result: conservatives slept better than liberals. Conservative men reported the least insomnia and liberal men the most.

The second survey, in 2010, was administered online to 2,992 American adults (table 4.2).[17]

Again, women had more insomnia than men, and poorer, less educated people tended to have more insomnia than wealthier and better

Table 4.1 Frequency of Insomnia in the 2007 Demographic Survey (N = 705)

	Nights of insomnia per week			Total responses
	0	1 to 2	3 or more	
	Percent	Percent	Percent	
Gender				
Females	56	16	26	338
Males	63	21	13	367
Gender/education				
College+ females	64	16	16	92
Non-college females	54	16	28	273
College+ males	69	17	12	83
Non-college males	61	23	14	254
Gender/age (younger or older than 50)				
Young women	58	14	26	197
Older women	54	18	25	165
Young men	62	24	14	223
Older men	65	17	13	110
Gender/political ideology				
Liberal men	44	28	27	64
Liberal women	61	10	29	88
Moderate men	65	24	12	100
Moderate women	57	23	18	114
Conservative men	70	18	9	139
Conservative women	57	17	23	132
Race				
White	60	18	20	486
Black	65	15	15	71
Hispanic	55	28	17	85

Table 4.1 Continued

	Nights of insomnia per week			Total responses
	0	1 to 2	3 or more	
	Percent	Percent	Percent	
Annual Income				
<$30,000	50	20	29	173
$30,000–$50,000	63	19	17	133
$50,000–$100,000	63	18	17	192
$100,000+	63	21	14	87

Note: For Gender/education, "College+" meant completed a college degree, "Non-college" meant did not complete a college degree. For Gender/age, "Young" meant younger than 50, "Older" meant 50 or older. For the other questions, the participants were given options and asked to self-identify.

Table 4.2 Frequency of Insomnia in the 2010 Demographic Survey (N = 2,992)

	Nights of insomnia per week			Total number of responses
	0	1 to 2	3 or more	
	Percent	Percent	Percent	
Females				
18–29	45	30	25	56
30–49	34	38	27	229
50–64	31	37	32	454
65+	40	39	22	282
Males				
18–29	52	31	17	139
30–49	42	38	19	426
50–64	50	33	16	782
65+	53	27	19	506

(continued)

Table 4.2 Continued

	Nights of insomnia per week			Total number of responses
	0	1 to 2	3 or more	
	Percent	Percent	Percent	
Marital status, females				
Married	34	39	27	636
Divorced/separated	30	43	27	157
Single, never married	39	32	29	107
Civil union/domestic partnership	48	19	32	31
Widowed	45	29	26	86
Marital status, males				
Married	50	33	17	1,309
Divorced/separated	52	25	23	178
Single, never married	48	34	18	247
Civil union/domestic partnership	39	37	24	75
Widowed	46	33	21	39
Education, female				
No college degree	34	34	32	411
College degree +	36	39	24	617
Education, male				
No college degree	49	29	22	579
College degree +	50	34	16	1,270
Race/ethnicity, female				
White	35	38	26	806
African American	36	34	30	64
Hispanic	33	31	36	61
Asian	47	40	13	15

Table 4.2 Continued

	Nights of insomnia per week			Total number of responses
	0	1 to 2	3 or more	
	Percent	Percent	Percent	
Race/ethnicity, male				
White	49	33	18	1,393
African American	57	24	19	79
Hispanic	37	41	22	139
Asian	57	26	17	47
Annual income, female				
<$25,000	33	24	43	83
$25,000–$35,000	46	35	19	94
$35,000–$50,000	28	44	28	110
$50,000–$75,000	32	39	30	176
$75,000–$100,000	38	31	30	128
$100,000	36	39	25	244
Annual income, male				
<$25,000	47	31	22	87
$25,000–$35,000	44	32	25	110
$35,000–$50,000	53	35	12	178
$50,000–$75,000	46	29	25	342
$75,000–$100,000	52	29	19	315
$100K+	47	38	15	583
Religious worship, female				
Weekly+	42	36	21	85
Weekly	35	41	25	195
1 or 2 times a month	30	41	29	100
Holidays	30	45	25	67
Rarely	35	36	30	347
Never	38	32	30	213

(continued)

Table 4.2 Continued

	Nights of insomnia per week			Total number of responses
	0	1 to 2	3 or more	
	Percent	Percent	Percent	
Religious worship, male				
Weekly+	56	29	15	212
Weekly	49	36	15	352
1 or 2 times a month	49	36	15	191
Holidays	47	40	13	122
Rarely	49	28	23	586
Never	47	36	17	362
Political ideology, female				
Progressive	39	35	26	173
Liberal	30	41	28	217
Moderate	39	30	31	193
Libertarian	41	31	29	49
Conservative	34	41	25	251
Very conservative	37	41	21	121
Political ideology, male				
Progressive	47	31	22	201
Liberal	47	35	18	190
Moderate	49	32	19	326
Libertarian	48	34	18	204
Conservative	50	33	17	599
Very conservative	54	30	15	317

Note: These answers have been adjusted ("Not Sure" responses removed from the totals) and consolidated (the participants selected a number from 0 to 7, and their responses were grouped into three categories). The percentages have been rounded to the nearest whole number, so the three columns may not always add up to 100.

educated people. On the political ideology question, people on the Left side of the spectrum reported more insomnia than people on the Right.

This survey also asked participants to estimate how often they attended religious worship services. This is a frequently used survey question that helps to gauge the importance of religion in a person's life. In this case, the results showed that people who were more religiously observant reported somewhat less insomnia than people who were not as religiously observant. The similar results on the politics and religion questions may stem from the same social reality in contemporary America: people who are politically right-of-center are also likely to have strong religious beliefs, while people who are politically left-of-center often have little or no interest in religion.

A third survey, conducted in 2015, was administered online to 2,303 American adults (table 4.3).[18]

The results here correspond very closely to those of the previous studies. Women have more insomnia than men, poor people have more insomnia than wealthy people, less educated people have more insomnia than better educated people, and political liberals have more insomnia than political conservatives.

Table 4.3 Frequency of Insomnia in the 2015 Demographic Survey (N = 2,303)

	Nights of insomnia per week			Total number of responses
	0	1 to 2	3 or more	
	Percent	Percent	Percent	
Gender				
Females	22	35	43	1,145
Males	37	31	32	1,132
Age				
18 to 34	25	34	39	710
35 to 54	27	34	38	670
55+	34	32	34	898
Religious worship				
Weekly+	30	32	38	198
Weekly	29	34	35	336
1 or 2 times a month	25	41	33	182
A few times a year	31	31	38	306
Seldom	29	31	39	532
Never	30	32	39	680

(continued)

Table 4.3 Continued

	Nights of insomnia per week			Total number of responses
	0	1 to 2	3 or more	
	Percent	Percent	Percent	
Annual income				
Under $40K	25	30	44	910
$40K to $80K	31	33	36	639
$80K+	36	34	29	401
Education				
High school or less	30	31	39	939
Some college	25	32	43	722
4-Year college graduate	34	35	31	395
Post-graduate	32	38	31	221
Political ideology				
Very liberal	25	34	41	259
Liberal	26	35	40	355
Moderate	29	34	38	692
Conservative	32	33	35	487
Very conservative	31	36	32	259

Note: These answers have been consolidated (the participants selected a number from 0 to 7, and their responses were grouped into three categories). All figures are from YouGov Plc. Total sample size was 2,303 adults. Fieldwork was undertaken between July 15 and 17, 2015. The survey was carried out online. The figures have been weighted and are representative of all US adults (aged 18+). The percentages have been rounded to the nearest whole number, so the three columns may not always add up to 100.

The limitations of survey research, while considerable, may be partially overcome by combining the results of multiple surveys that use comparable methods, questions, and groups of participants. If the quantitative results of many different surveys all point in the same direction, we can be more confident the findings are not just statistical flukes. Viewed in that light, these sociological surveys of sleep certainly point in the same direction. Quality of sleep appears directly proportional to socioeconomic status. People who have greater cultural, social, and financial power tend to sleep better than people who do not have such power.[19]

Modern Comforts

Do people today sleep better, or worse, than in times past? After four chapters discussing the nature and functions of sleep across the course of human history, we have reached a point where we should be able to offer a well-informed response to that question.

Modern Western society has created a historically unique set of living conditions that puts extremely negative pressures on the quality and duration of sleep. Thanks to early twentieth-century engineers like Thomas Edison, electric lights have turned night into day, extending the possibility of wakefulness and thus shortening time for sleep. After World War II, the mass production of inexpensive mechanical alarm clocks gave everyone in society the ability to forcibly awaken themselves at a predetermined time, putting individual sleep more firmly in the sphere of social and economic control. Newer technologies like televisions, computers, mobile phones, and the Internet have dramatically transformed all aspects of life, especially during people's evening and bedtime activities (the NSF international survey found that large majorities [66% to 80%] of people in all six countries used some kind of electronic device in the hour before sleep). These technologies have helped generate a fast-moving and extremely disruptive global economy in which many people struggle to maintain stable employment and some degree of financial security. These uncertain conditions stir up enormous anxieties that feed into worse insomnia and shorter sleep times. Not coincidentally, the widespread use of caffeine and other powerful stimulants, both legal and illegal, fuels a cultural striving for near-constant wakefulness and externally focused activity, seducing people into living by the motto, "I'll sleep when I die."

This is our brave and sleepless new world. None of these modern developments has any real historical or evolutionary precedent. People today are living in an environment radically different from those of all our human ancestors. The cumulative effect of these changes has taken a heavy toll on the length and quality of people's sleep.[20]

Not everything has been for the worse, however. Far from it. Modern advances in hygiene, heating, and building materials have created vastly safer and healthier sleeping conditions. Compared to humans living in premodern times, people today sleep in dwellings with much better protection against noise, fire, and inclement weather. Modern sleepers are less exposed to insects and larger predators, and they have many kinds of comfortable, easily accessible bedding options to choose from (better options than rocks and logs, in any case).

We should not romanticize the past and overlook the physical hardships our ancestors endured, hardships that have been minimized or completely eliminated in modern society. People today enjoy better sleep than ever before in many, many ways. But it is more fragile and constrained sleep, vulnerable to painful disruptions from a variety of distinctively modern behaviors and activities.

Concluding Response

Heraclitus was right about many things. But on the solipsism of sleep, the philosopher had it wrong. In sleep each person goes into a world that remains profoundly social, with ongoing connections to interpersonal relationships, collective realities, and cultural systems of meaning and value. Sleep involves a lowering of sensory awareness, but not a total withdrawal, and sleep almost always occurs within the familiar context of a broader community. A social dimension of sleep has deep roots in the evolution of our species. From the earliest times through the modern era, humans have naturally preferred sleeping together.

Heraclitus's poetic predecessor, Homer, was closer to right in his portrayal of Queen Penelope's "bed trick." The epigraph to this chapter comes from the very end of the *Odyssey*, after Odysseus had journeyed home, defeated the suitors, and reclaimed his kingdom. To the hero's dismay, Penelope still would not accept that this man who had suddenly reappeared after 20 years was truly her husband. She treated him as an honored stranger, and to thank him for liberating her from the suitors she ordered her maids to move the royal bed from its private chamber to the guest quarters. Odysseus reacted to this command with shock and anger—he knew the truth about this bed, that it had been carved into a living tree, specially designed on the occasion of their marriage, and it had always been an intimate secret hidden from the rest of the world, known only to the two of them. Odysseus feared that if their royal bed could be moved, it meant their special place for co-sleeping had been cut down and destroyed forever. When Penelope heard his response, she finally had definitive proof that her husband had returned. Their bed was their bond; it was the deepest secret shared between them, the culminating symbol of their marital devotion, and the physical arena for their most intimate time together, sleeping side by side.

PART II

Dreaming

5

Recall

On awakening he appeared to himself to have a distinct
recollection of the whole, and taking his pen, ink, and
paper, instantly and eagerly wrote down the lines that
are here preserved. At this moment he was unfortunately
called out by a person on business from Porlock . . .

SAMUEL TAYLOR COLERIDGE, PREFACE TO "KUBLA KHAN,
OR A VISION IN A DREAM. A FRAGMENT"

Opening Question

Are dreams a legitimate subject for scientific research?

Sleep may be necessary, active, adaptive, and healthy, but none of that necessarily means that scientists ought to take dreams seriously. Everything
we discussed about sleep in the preceding part may be true, and yet
dreaming could still be a pointless thing to study. Some contemporary
scientists regard the insignificance and triviality of dreaming as a self-
evident fact. "Dreams are not a legitimate subject of scientific research."
That is a quote from an anonymous reader of a manuscript I submitted
several years ago to an academic journal; the quote is the entirety of the
review. I have always remembered that terse, ultra-skeptical evaluation
and thought about what the reviewer might have said if he or she had
taken the time to lay out the case against dream research. What are the
biggest obstacles to a legitimately scientific study of dreams?

An obvious problem is the tenuous and fragmentary nature of dream
memories, which can disappear in an instant upon awakening. People
often have great difficulty remembering the details of their dreams, and
what they do manage to remember is often vague, patchy, and disjointed.
The skeptic's case would likely begin by arguing that dream reports are

such messy and unreliable data that no valid scientific conclusions can be drawn from them.

Added to that is the problem of a seemingly unbridgeable gap between the dream as *dreamt* and the dream as *reported*. We never have direct access to dreams; we only have indirect access to people's subjective reports of their dream memories, some period of time after the dreams themselves originally occurred. There is no objective way to verify the accuracy of these reports, no way to tell if people have added or removed details, no way to be sure it really is a report of a dream and not just a made-up fantasy.

And besides, some people claim they never remember any dreams at all, and they appear to lead normal, intelligent, healthy lives. What about these non-dreamers? Their prevalence in the general population seems to contradict any claim that dreaming is psychologically necessary or universally valuable.

In its most concentrated form, the ultra-skeptical case against the study of dreams amounts to this: There is nothing *there* for science to investigate.

Initial Response

Dreams are difficult, but not impossible, to study scientifically.

It seems rather cowardly to reject a phenomenon because it cannot be easily analyzed using conventional methods. Why don't scientists look at these difficulties instead as exciting opportunities for new discovery? As bracing challenges that call for greater research ingenuity and scholarly innovation?

Actual research, rather than personal opinion, shows that dreams can be reliably remembered and reported, virtually everyone does indeed dream at some point in their lives, and there are a number of consistent demographic patterns in people's dream recall frequencies. The key to a scientific approach to the study of dreaming is to gather large, diverse collections of high-quality data, with as much transparency as possible about their sources and limitations. There is no denying the subjectivity of individual dream reports, but that hardly casts them beyond the pale of scientific analysis. The neuroscientist Antonio Damasio, whose attitude toward sleep I questioned in chapter 2, opposes extreme skepticism toward the value of introspective reports, and on this point I think he gets it right: "Whether one likes it or not, *all* the contents in our minds are subjective, and the power of science comes from its ability to verify objectively the consistency of many individual subjectivities."[1]

Data and Discussion
What Is a Dream?

The first piece of evidence in favor of taking dreams seriously in scientific research comes from etymology, the study of word origins. By tracing the linguistic roots of the words that people have used to talk about their dreams, we find the earliest historical indications of the nature and functions of dreaming in human life.

The closest relatives to the Modern English word *dream* are *traum* in German and *droom* in Dutch. All three words stem from the older Proto-Germanic word *draugmaz*, which had the meanings of dream, deception, delusion, hallucination, festivity, and ghost.[2] This word in turn seems to have arisen from the older base word *draug* or *dreug*—to deceive, injure, or damage—in the Proto-Indo-European language. Proto-Indo-European culture emerged more than 5,000 years ago among the horse-riding people of the temperate grasslands of Western Asia, and it later spread into both Europe and India. Prior to the Proto-Indo-Europeans, we do not know what languages humans spoke. This is where the study of linguistics reaches its horizon of uncertainty.

So the deepest roots of *dream* lead straight to an ancient word for *deception*. Not a ringing endorsement of its scientific respectability! However, there is more to the etymological story than that. The Proto-German word *draugmaz* also referred to ghosts and festivities, suggesting that delusional departures from ordinary reality could take either frightening or pleasurable forms. In Old English, spoken between the fifth and twelfth centuries C.E., the word *dream* referred to music, mirth, joy, and minstrel singing. The same was true with the Old Norse *draumr* and the Old Saxon *drom*, both of which meant noisy merriment. Some etymologists have argued that the musical *dream* is a completely different word from the sleep *dream* because in the Old English time period another term, *swefn*, was used when speaking of nocturnal visionary experiences. (*Swefn* goes back to the Proto-Indo-European *swepno*, a word meaning *sleep* that gave rise to dream terms in many languages: *hypnos* in Greek, *svapna* in Sanskrit, *somnium* in Latin, *sueno* in Spanish, and *songe* in French.) By the time of Middle English, between the twelfth and fifteenth centuries, *swefn* was replaced by *dream*, which from that point forward was no longer used to refer to music, only to visions of the night.

The word *dream* that we use today has thus arrived with a curiously polysemic prehistory. As one linguistic researcher has said, "the two groups of cognates with the meaning of 1) deceive, phantom, ghost, and 2) joy, music, dream represent a double development of meaning."[3]

In Modern English we speak of *having* a dream, whereas in many languages around the world people speak of *seeing* a dream. In ancient Egypt, for example, there were two hieroglyphic figures for dream, *resut* and *qed*. According to Egyptologist Kasia Szpakowska, "*resut* is most often determined [pictured in its hieroglyph] by an open eye, which is also used for words related to visual perception. . . . The other term meaning dream was *qed*, which derived from the word 'sleep.' When this word meant 'sleep,' it was followed by the sign of a bed, but when it meant 'dream,' it used the same open eye sign as *resut*."[4] Similarly with the ancient Greeks, who used the word *oneiros* (from Proto-Indo-European *oner*) to speak of both dreams and the figures who appear in them (often standing at the head of the sleeping person's bed). Classicist E. R. Dodds said, "[T]he Greeks never spoke as we do of *having* a dream, but always of *seeing* a dream."[5] The same custom is found in Sanskrit and Tibetan languages, as noted by religious studies scholar Serinity Young: "South Asians consistently use the verb 'seeing' a dream rather than 'having' a dream."[6] The Chinese term, *meng*, is rendered by an ideograph whose top part indicates "confused vision" or "bad eyesight," and the bottom part "evening."[7] The Zulu people of South Africa employ the same word, *iphupho*, to refer to both sleeping dreams and waking visions. When the Melpa people of the New Guinea highlands speak of dreaming, they say, "*Ur kumb etepa koni*," meaning "to make a sleep-likeness and see something."[8]

This list could go on. The cross-cultural emphasis on dreams as visual experiences in sleep is a remarkable fact that any theory of human nature should acknowledge and take into account. For thousands of years the language practices of people all over the world have recognized a closely intertwined relationship between sleep, dreams, and visions.

The effort to define dreaming, to go beyond common linguistic usage and establish a rationally grounded explanation, began in the Western tradition at least 2,300 years ago with the Greek philosopher Aristotle (384–322 B.C.E.). Aristotle talked about dreams in his short treatise *De Somniis*, one of his many writings about the human mind and body. A dream, in Aristotle's view, could be defined as a *presentation* in sleep: "for a presentation which occurs in sleep—whether simply or in some particular way—is what we call a dream."[9] A presentation is a series of internal images that reflect the residual effects of sense perceptions from the daytime. When people go to sleep, they no longer perceive objects in the external world. However, impressions from those objects are still echoing within the mind while it sleeps, and those echoes become new objects of internal perception. These objects are "presented" to the mind as images that seem highly realistic because they do in fact derive from external sense perceptions. As these images emerge within the sleeping mind, they stimulate additional thoughts, feelings, and desires that become woven into the overall dream experience.

Aristotle's analysis of dreaming is no historical relic; it is perhaps more widely accepted today than it was during his own time. Most contemporary dream researchers endorse some version of his basic definition, which has been enshrined in the Oxford English Dictionary, the most authoritative source of Modern English: "Dream (noun): a train of thoughts, images, or fancies passing through the mind during sleep; a vision during sleep; the state in which this occurs. Dream (verb): to have visions and imaginary sense-impressions in sleep."[10]

As Aristotle himself acknowledged, this definition does not restrict dreaming to humans. The same process may occur in the minds of other animals while they sleep, too: "For sleep does not pertain to one organ in animals and dreaming to another; both pertain to the same organ."[11] Contemporary researchers have found evidence to support the idea that at least some animals do have the capacity to dream, according to the Aristotelian definition of the term. In chapter 3 we discussed Matthew Walker's finding that the brain activities of rats during REM sleep closely correspond to their brain activities when running a maze while awake. This seems very much in line with Aristotle's notion that dreaming can be stimulated by residual sense-impressions from waking activities. We also discussed earlier the pioneering French sleep scientist Michel Jouvet, whose research focused on cats. Jouvet and his colleagues have shown that if the part of the brainstem responsible for physical paralysis during REM sleep is surgically removed, cats will act out a variety of instinctual behaviors while they are sleeping, as if they were attacking, exploring, or fleeing. Jouvet has written, "We can be sure that human subjects dream during paradoxical sleep, for they can describe their recalled dreams, but how can we wake a cat during paradoxical sleep and ask it questions? We cannot, but the discovery and analysis of oneiric behavior would lead us to believe that cats do dream."[12]

None of this directly answers the questions raised at the outset about fragmentary memories, subjective reports, non-dreamers, and so on. But this deep linguistic context should give the skeptics pause. Maybe we should not be so quick to dismiss something that every historical language has a word for, that serious minds have been studying for thousands of years, and that non-human animal species also seem to experience.

The First Dream Recallers

Of the six core disciplines of cognitive science—neurology, computer science, psychology, linguistics, philosophy, and anthropology—the most unexpected member might be anthropology, since it studies things like rituals, customs, and symbol systems that do not seem amenable to precise scientific analysis. In fact, professionals in the field of anthropology today are sharply split over this very issue. Some anthropologists view their discipline as having its own interpretive, qualitative methods that are distinct from, and critically suspicious of, those used in the natural sciences. Other anthropologists, however, emphasize the benefits of building bridges with other scientific fields on topics of common interest, such as the nature and functions of the human mind.

In debates like this I find it best to take a pragmatic approach. Where do these ideas work? Where are they most helpful in developing our knowledge, and where do they become counterproductive? In several places later in the book I draw on the research of interpretive anthropologists to clarify aspects of big dreams and religious experience. Here, though, I follow the bridge-builders who have contributed so much to cognitive science already. They have shown that anthropology provides a powerful means of testing claims about the basic functions of the mind. The test is simple: any cognitive trait found in present-day people should also be observable in people from many other cultures and periods of history. If the trait is indeed observed in a wide variety of places and times, that counts as evidence in favor of its being a genuine part of the evolved architecture of the human mind. If the trait is not observed cross-culturally, the likelihood diminishes that it is a fundamental, hard-wired part of human nature. Anthropology and its allies in ethnography, history, and archeology offer an invaluable source of data to support or undermine theories about the universality of specific cognitive functions.

Judging by this test, dreaming surely appears to be a universal experience in our species. In a previous book, *Dreaming in the World's Religions: A Comparative History*, I discussed the various roles of dreaming in Hinduism, Chinese religions, Buddhism, religions of the Fertile Crescent (Egypt, Mesopotamia, etc.), ancient Greek and Roman religions, Christianity, Islam, and the indigenous religions of Africa, Oceania, and the Americas.

The conclusion of that book serves as a prologue to this one: "Dreams and dreaming have been a widely recognized and highly valued part of human life—particularly in relation to people's religious beliefs and practices—in virtually every cultural community known to have populated the planet."[13]

The strength of all this evidence, reflecting more than a century's worth of data from researchers studying and working in cultures all over the world, suggests a hypothesis that may never be proven but seems impossible to ignore. It goes back to our discussion in chapter 1 of the "creative explosion" of culture in our species during the Upper Paleolithic period about 60,000 years ago. What if the artists who painted the magnificent caves of Lascaux and Corvet were history's first dream recallers, and the paintings on the cave walls were their dream journals? What if the cognitive spark that lit the explosion of Paleolithic creativity was shamanic dreaming?

In recent years archeologists who study Paleolithic art have drawn upon the findings of neuropsychology to advance new explanations for the astonishingly skillful images in these caves. David Lewis-Williams, David S. Whitley, and others have shown that new findings in brain science enable a much better understanding of why the ancient cave paintings were created and what functions they served in Paleolithic society. They start with the fact, which we noted in chapter 2, that the basic size and shape of the *H. sapien sapiens* brain has remained the same for at least 200,000 years. Paleolithic humans had brains essentially just like those of people today, and that means we can use research on the functioning of our brains to make inferences about the functioning of their brains. Lewis-Williams, Whitley, and others who use the neuropsychological approach try to reconstruct the trancelike effects that these vibrantly painted caves would have produced in Paleolithic people's minds: "[P]hysical entry into the subterranean passages was probably seen as equivalent to psychic entry into deeply altered states of consciousness."[14] Several factors seem to have contributed to these mind-altering effects: the long and arduous journey down into the earth (many of the best paintings are located in chambers hundreds of feet beyond the cave entrance); the flickering firelight that provided the only illumination, casting dancing shadows into the darkness; and then the sudden encounter with the majesty of the paintings themselves—vivid renderings of powerful animals and strange creatures of half-animal, half-human form, along with the overlapping imprints of people's hands and a host of recurrent geometric shapes and figures. Some of the animals and creatures were obviously dead, others were running or leaping, and still others were in a state of sexual excitement.

The placement of these dramatic images was not random, nor was it determined by the location of the easiest places to paint (e.g., the flattest, smoothest surfaces). Instead, the images seem to have been positioned to maximize visual impressions of movement, depth, and vitality. Some of the paintings used special outcroppings of rock as parts of the animals' bodies; other creatures appear to be coming out of crevices in the cave walls, creating a sense of porous, permeable boundaries. Acoustical dynamics were another factor in determining where to position the paintings. Archeologists have found that some of the Paleolithic cave paintings were located within one meter of resonance points for specific musical notes.[15] The areas with the most powerful musical resonance were always marked with some kind of painting or coloring, even when the physical conditions of the cave wall made it difficult to create any full-sized figures.

Descending into the caves was an extraordinary neuropsychological experience of both visual and auditory stimulation. Archeologist Chris Scarre has tried to reconstruct some of the musical practices that were likely part of the creative environment incubated within these cave complexes: "Drums, flutes, and whistles may have been used in cave rituals— bone flutes have been found at several Paleolithic sites in Europe of roughly the same age as the paintings. The potential of cave resonance would, however, be elicited only by the much greater range of the human voice. The image of the cave artists chanting incantations in front of their paintings may not be too fanciful."[16]

Who were these musically attuned cave artists? Most archeologists refer to them as *shamans*. The word *shaman* means "one who knows" in the language of the Tungus people of Siberia. A shaman is a ritual specialist who serves his or her social group as a healer, prophet, historian, and mediator between the living and the dead. Shamanic practices have been found among the earliest human communities in every continent on earth, from Africa and Asia to the Americas and Australia.[17] The Paleolithic cave paintings of southern Europe give us a window into the mental world of these highly creative people who generated the first known works of civilization.

Unfortunately we have no direct evidence showing that Paleolithic shamans or anyone else in their communities actually slept in the caves and dreamed there. We do not know for sure if any of the rock art represents dream experiences, nor do we know if people had any unusual dreams after spending time in the caves. The horizon of uncertainty on this topic is close enough to touch.

However, as later chapters will show, there is evidence from later periods of history indicating that shamans and other people have purposefully gone into caves to sleep and dream. We also know that many of the themes depicted in the Paleolithic cave paintings are prominent themes in dream content. And modern researchers have found that various kinds of pre-sleep stimulation can have a tangible impact on people's dreams. The lack of direct evidence should not obscure the abundance of indirect evidence that the earliest records of human dream experience are painted on the walls of these shamanically designed Paleolithic caves.

Patterns of Dream Recall Frequency

Now we can begin to answer the questions raised at the outset about the scientific quality of dream data. As anthropologists and archeologists have shown, the experience of dreaming is familiar to people all over the world, in every culture and in every historical period, as far back as we have evidence of human culture. Even though dreams can be fragmentary and ephemeral, people do remember at least some of them.

A few dreams are neither fragmentary nor ephemeral; these are the highly memorable "big dreams" to be discussed in more detail in Part III. The cross-cultural occurrence of big dreams refutes the most extreme version of the skeptic's case (i.e., that no coherent data can ever be derived from dreaming). Big dreams are often quite coherent, highly structured, and easily remembered. Just because some dreams are easily forgotten does not mean that all dreams are nonsense.

The gap between the dream as *experienced* and the dream as *reported* may seem daunting, but the problematic consequences of this gap should not be exaggerated. Many aspects of people's dream reports are plausibly grounded in actual dreaming experiences. For example, the prevalence of visual imagery in people's dream reports (a fact embedded in the words of many languages) makes perfect sense in relation to the high levels of activation during REM sleep of parts of the brain involved in visual imagination. REM sleep also involves high levels of activation in the limbic parts of the brain associated with emotional arousal, which seems consistent with dream reports involving strong emotions and passionate feelings. This does not mean that everything in people's dreams can be reduced to a specific function in their brains; it is obviously much more complex than that. These kinds of correlations do, however, make it harder to accept the skeptical notion that dream reports have nothing whatsoever to do with dream experiences. When people report their dreams, they may not be able to convey everything they experienced, but they can convey a great deal of it, and we have good reasons to believe they are accurately describing something that actually happened within their minds during sleep.

These questions about the quality of dream data can be asked of any other field of research that relies on people's subjective, self-reported descriptions of their lives. The issue is ultimately one of trust: How can an investigator be sure that people are not misrepresenting their experiences, either intentionally or unintentionally? The truth is that we cannot be sure. There will always be the possibility of revisions, alterations, and embellishments in people's reports of their dreams, and in their subjective reports of anything else. However, even as we acknowledge that basic uncertainty, we should be careful not to let this concern lead to a complete rejection of all personal, introspective data. That would surely be an overreaction. Excessive skepticism can too easily become a kind of quasi-autistic inability to accept that other people really do have minds and subjective experiences of their own.

It may be difficult for investigators to gain reliable knowledge about those inner experiences, but it is not impossible. Recall Antonio Damasio's comment, quoted in the initial response to this chapter, about trying to "verify objectively the consistency of many individual subjectivities." This means that the problems with subjective data can be overcome, to a degree, by gathering large numbers of high-quality reports from a wide variety of people and sources, and then looking for consistent patterns in the subjective experiences described by all these people. Following such a methodological path does not eliminate the possibility that some of the participants are editing or even fabricating their accounts, but it lowers the chances that such extraneous elements are going to obscure the bigger patterns in the data set as a whole. These bigger patterns can give us a relatively clear view of the consistent features in people's inner psychological experiences.

We can now apply this approach to one of the fundamental questions of dream research, namely how often people remember their dreams. Table 5.1 contains findings from the 2015 Demographic Survey discussed in chapter 4, this time showing people's answers to a question about dream recall frequency. As noted before, this survey comes from demographically diverse samples of contemporary American adults.[18]

The results in table 5.1 indicate that for both genders and in every demographic group, about half the population remembers a dream at least once a week. These broadly distributed results are compatible with earlier studies like Stepansky et al.'s 1998 study of 1,000 demographically

Table 5.1 Frequency of Dream Recall in the 2015 Demographic Survey (N = 2,303)

| | Dreams recalled per week | | | | | | Total number of responses |
| | Almost every morning or more often | Several times a week | Once a week | 1 to 3 times a month | Less often than once a month | Never | |
	Percent	Percent	Percent	Percent	Percent	Percent	
Gender							
Females	14	27	15	19	21	3	1145
Males	10	27	16	18	23	6	1132
Age							
18 to 34	16	29	19	18	14	5	710
35–54	12	25	16	19	23	5	670
55+	9	27	13	19	28	4	898
Religious worship							
Weekly+	18	25	13	20	21	2	198
Weekly	11	28	16	22	22	2	336
1 or 2 times a month	11	29	28	10	18	4	182

(continued)

Table 5.1 Continued

	Dreams recalled per week						Total number of responses
	Almost every morning or more often	Several times a week	Once a week	1 to 3 times a month	Less often than once a month	Never	
	Percent	Percent	Percent	Percent	Percent	Percent	
Religious worship							
A few times a year	12	29	15	18	17	9	306
Seldom	10	25	15	20	27	3	532
Never	12	28	13	18	23	5	680
Annual income							
Under $40K	13	27	13	19	23	4	910
$40K to $80K	12	27	16	18	23	4	639
$80K+	8	27	21	20	21	3	401
Education							
High school or less	12	24	13	18	26	6	939
Some college	12	27	18	19	20	4	722
4-year college graduate	11	32	18	18	19	2	395
Post-graduate	12	34	15	22	16	2	221

Political ideology							
Very liberal	14	32	14	21	19	0	259
Liberal	9	30	16	19	24	2	355
Moderate	13	25	17	19	22	5	692
Conservative	8	28	18	19	23	3	487
Very conservative	12	27	12	18	26	4	259

Note: The six categories of dream recall in the columns of this table follow the approach used by Michael Schredl in "Dream Recall: Models and Empirical Data." All figures are from YouGov Plc. Total sample size was 2,303 adults. Fieldwork was undertaken between July 15 and 17, 2015. The survey was carried out online. The figures have been weighted and are representative of all US adults (aged 18+). The percentages have been rounded to the nearest whole number, so the three columns may not always add up to 100.

representative Austrians, which used a slightly different question (how often do you dream per month?) but generated a similar profile: 31% of the respondents were high dream recallers (more than 10 dreams recalled per month), 37% were moderate recallers (1–9 per month), and 32% were low recallers (less than 1 per month or never).[19]

Belicki's 1986 study of 828 Canadian college students, which used another variation on the basic question (how many dreams do you typically recall per week?), found that 58% of the students were high recallers (2 or more dreams per week), 25% were moderate recallers (1 dream per week), and 16% were low recallers (less than once a week or never).[20] The large proportion of high recallers in Belicki's study may be due to the younger age of her college student participants.

My survey and Stepansky et al.'s study found that younger people are more likely to be high recallers and older people are more likely to be low recallers. However, in Yu's 2010 and 2012 studies of Chinese college students, age seemed to be less of a factor. Yu's 2010 survey of 608 people with an average age of 19 found that 18% were high recallers, 63% were moderate recallers, and 20% were low recallers. The comparable figures for his 2012 survey of 1,186 people, also with an average age of 19, were 28% high recallers, 45% moderate recallers, and 28% low recallers.[21]

Stepansky et al. did not find any gender differences in dream recall frequencies among their Austrian sample, and Belicki and Yu did not analyze their Canadian and Chinese results in terms of gender. My 2015 survey indicated that women are somewhat more likely than men to be very high recallers, and other demographic surveys in the SDDb have pointed in the same direction. Most other researchers have found a similar gender imbalance. In a review by Schredl of the literature on gender and dream recall, he cited a dozen studies that found higher frequencies among women than men (the Stepansky et al. study of Austrian adults was the only one that did not find any gender difference). Schredl said, "to summarize, there is a solid database showing that women report recalling their dreams more often than men."[22]

Overall, two fairly consistent themes emerge from the research data. Dream recall frequency tends to be higher among (1) women than men and (2) younger than older people. The differences are not absolute—some older men have high recall and some younger women have low recall—but the same patterns have appeared in so many studies that they do seem to reflect broader realities about human dreaming experience.

Other demographic variables seem to have modest relevance to dream recall frequencies. In the results of the 2015 Demographic Survey shown in table 5.1, there are only slight differences in relation to religious worship, annual income, education, and poltical ideology.

These results point to a broader consistency. In every demographic group there are some people who remember their dreams very frequently, and some people who rarely or never remember their dreams. The majority of people are somewhere in between, with an average recall frequency of about one or two dreams a week.

Why We Forget

The epigraph to this chapter describes what happened when Samuel Taylor Coleridge, the English Romantic poet and philosopher, awoke one morning in the summer of 1797 from an opium-induced sleep with a fantastically vivid dream fresh in his mind. He started writing a description of his experience, and in just a few moments he had composed the opening lines of "Kubla Khan," one of the most famous poems in the English language. Then came a knock at the door—a person on business from Porlock (a nearby town) unexpectedly appeared for a visit, and by the time the man left Coleridge could no longer remember his dream. The poem remained unfinished, a fragmentary vision from Coleridge's sleeping imagination that he kept private for 20 years, publishing it only toward the end of his life at the urging of his friends.

Coleridge's experience illustrates the vulnerability of dream recall to disruption by external circumstances. Researchers have found that many different factors can impede people's ability to remember their dreams, including pathologies of sleep (e.g., apnea or insomnia), stressful problems in waking life, use of alcohol and drugs (many of which have the side effect of diminished dream recall), the sleep behavior of bedtime partners (e.g., spouses, children, or pets), and adverse conditions during the process of awakening.[23] The single biggest obstacle to dream recall in contemporary times may be the alarm clock, a fixture of the modern bedside table that functions like our own special "person on business from Porlock." Countless millions of people in countries all over the world wake up each morning to the jarring sound of an alarm that abruptly terminates their sleep, jolts them into waking consciousness, and focuses their attention on the time-structured demands of the day. Conditions of awakening like these make dream recall difficult if not impossible.

A student once told me that when he was a child he assumed that dreams only occurred on weekends, because he never remembered any dreams during the regular week when he had to get up early for school. Eventually he realized that he remembered dreams on weekends because those were the only mornings when he could sleep as long as he wanted, without setting an alarm. His experience is one example of how cultural practices can directly influence people's frequency of dream recall, in this case for the worse. Alarm clocks can have a kind of oneirocidal effect that lowers people's dream recall to a level below what it would be if they were able to wake up naturally.

The puzzle remains of non-dreamers, who claim they never remember dreaming in any circumstances, whether or not alarm clocks, alcohol, stressful problems, or other factors are involved. Non-dreamers apparently forget all their dreams, which could also be a way of saying they never dream to begin with. This is why skeptics so often emphasize their existence: non-dreamers seem to represent living proof against the idea that dreaming is necessary or valuable for everyone. But in research specifically focused on people who say they never remember their dreams, sleep medicine expert James Pagel has found that true non-dreamers are few and far between. For two years Pagel and his colleagues asked patients at their sleep laboratory to fill out a survey about their dreams. A total of 598 patients completed the survey, and of those people 93% reported dreaming and 7% reported never having a dream or nightmare. In follow-up interviews with the non-dreamers, Pagel found that many of them said they did in fact remember dreams—they either misspoke on the survey, or they could remember some dreams from childhood, or they started dreaming following their treatment at the laboratory. After accounting for these patients, the percentage of non-dreamers dropped below 1%. Pagel said, "This result suggested that true non-dreaming was very rare in our sleep lab population."[24]

In another study with 16 non-dreamers in which they slept in his laboratory and were awoken frequently during REM and NREM sleep, Pagel found the people still remembered no dreams, even when awakened from stages of sleep most closely associated with dream recall. He concluded that, although their numbers seem to be very small, "there is a group of individuals without obvious brain trauma or illness who do not experience dreaming."[25] In terms of their personalities and backgrounds, "the two most glaring demographic characteristics in our non-dreamers are a lower level of employment . . . and a much lower level of creative interest" as compared to the general patient population.[26] While noting the small number of participants in his study as reason for caution in interpreting the results, Pagel suggested that for "non-dreamers, those individuals who have never ever experienced a dream, involvement in creative processes may be unusual."[27]

We still have no solution to the puzzle of non-dreamers, but in light of Pagel's research it now seems a smaller and less significant puzzle than previously assumed. His work casts into sharp relief a more significant fact, one that we have seen emerge from numerous studies involving many different social and cultural groups: the vast majority of the human population consists of dreamers, not non-dreamers. Most people do remember their dreams and nightmares, at least some of the time.

The variability of dream recall depends not only on external factors like the conditions of awakening but also on internal factors like interest and motivation. Researchers like Schredl have found that giving people even a slight amount of encouragement to remember their dreams leads to an actual increase in their recall frequency, especially for people who are low recallers. Several studies have shown "how sensitive DRF [dream recall frequency] is to comments of the experimenter; simple encouraging comments produced a marked increase in DRF. Even the completion of a short dream questionnaire yielded a higher DRF after four weeks."[28] These findings might be doubted because of the possible influence of "demand effects" that bias people into giving answers they believe will be pleasing to the researchers. But in a way, that is exactly what these studies have tried to determine. Is a person's dream recall frequency a fixed quantity that never changes, or does it have some degree of flexibility depending on personal interest and motivation? The research suggests that when people want to remember more of their dreams, they can usually do so.[29]

The negative impact of low interest in dreaming has been demonstrated by Dominic Beaulieu-Prevost and Antonio Zadra, who have performed two studies comparing people's estimates of their dream recall frequency with their actual recall as measured by home diaries.[30] It turns out that people with negative attitudes toward dreaming consistently underestimate how often they remember their dreams. According to Beaulieu-Prevost and Zadra, "a negative attitude toward dreams appears to bias one's estimate of dream recall frequency. . . . In comparison to individuals with a positive attitude toward dreams, individuals with a negative attitude pay less attention to the dreams they recall and this, in turn, impedes their encoding into long-term memory. . . . Individuals with a relatively negative attitude towards dreams show a clear pattern of dream recall frequency underestimation."[31]

If you don't build it, they won't come.

Concluding Response

The scientific study of dreams has its fair share of methodological challenges, but none of them are insurmountable. The evidence gathered so far indicates that *humans are a dreaming species*. Some degree of dream recall is a natural, normal part of our lives. Most people recall one or two dreams a week on average, although the memories may not last long. A few people have much higher recall frequencies, as many as several dreams per night. At the other end of the spectrum, a few people remember their dreams much less frequently and a very few people remember no dreams at all. Women tend to recall their dreams more often than men do, and younger people more often than older people. One's attitude toward dreams seems to have a big impact on dream recall frequency, with a positive attitude leading to higher recall and a negative attitude contributing to lower recall.

6

Content

Opening Question

Are dreams merely the random side effects of the brain's activities in sleep?

Even if people do remember some of their dreams, it can still be argued that the contents of those dreams are nothing but chaotic noise, the arbitrary byproducts of automatic physical processes that occur in the brain while we slumber. The idea that dreaming is epiphenomenal to sleep has a long and distinguished history, going back at least as far as Thomas Nashe, the sixteenth-century English author of *The Terrors of the Night*, who said, "A dream is nothing else but a scum or froth of the fancy, which the day hath left undigested; or an after-feast made of the fragments of idle imaginations."[1]

In modern times this same dismissive notion has been proposed by leading researchers like Nathaniel Kleitman, who compared dreaming to a kind of mental vomiting;[2] Francis Crick and Graeme Mitchison, who defined dreams as neural parasites that the brain is actively trying to expel;[3] J. Allan Hobson, who claimed dreams are merely side effects of neurochemical changes in the brainstem;[4] and Owen Flanagan, who called dreams "free-riders" that take advantage of the functions of sleep to fill our minds with nonsense.[5] The academic prominence of these researchers (Kleitman was co-founder of REM sleep; Crick won a Nobel Prize; and

Hobson runs a laboratory at Harvard) has added weight to their argument that dreaming is nothing but random noise from the sleeping brain.

Initial Response

Dreams have consistent, recurrent patterns of content that can be objectively observed and measured in various populations.

Those who emphasize the randomness of dreaming tend to be surprisingly unfamiliar with the actual scientific literature on dream content. Quantitative research in this area goes back more than 100 years, and the results have repeatedly shown that dream content is characterized by far more structure, coherence, and consistency than would be expected of a purely random process. These studies have revealed a number of recurrent patterns in dream content that appear in many different groups of people. The skeptical claim that dreams are essentially random nonsense cannot account for such evidence.

Data and Discussion
REM Sleep ≠ Dreaming

The modern versions of the "dreams are epiphenomenal" argument usually claim there is a total identity, an *isomorphism*, between dreaming and REM sleep. In this view, everything that happens in dreams can be explained in terms of the brain's functioning in REM sleep. Once you understand REM sleep, you therefore understand dreaming. Hobson and McCarley's Activation-Synthesis model is the best-known example of this approach, which G. William Domhoff has critically but fairly termed "brainstem reductionism."[6]

If brainstem reductionism were true, then it would make sense to view dreams as essentially nothing more than parasites, free-riders, mental vomit, and so on. However, a great deal of evidence indicates that brainstem reductionism is false. The problem with theories based on REM-dreaming isomorphism is their failure to account for several decades' worth of research showing various ways that dreaming is independent of REM sleep.

When Aserinsky and Kleitman performed their pioneering study of REM sleep in 1953, they found that people awakened from REM sleep remembered a dream 74% of the time (20 out of 27 awakenings), while people awakened from a NREM phase of sleep remembered a dream only

17% of the time (4 out of 23 awakenings).[7] Those initial findings made NREM sleep seem almost incidental to dream research, in contrast to dream-rich REM, which some researchers briefly dubbed "D-Sleep." Then David Foulkes, a colleague of Aserinsky and Kleitman's at the University of Chicago, performed a study using a more open-ended question (instead of asking the participants, "Do you remember a dream?" he asked them, "Was anything going through your mind?"), and he found more than 60% of NREM awakenings included reports of mental activity that could properly be called dreams.[8] Many other researchers have found varying levels of REM versus NREM dream recall, with results showing more recall in REM but far from trivial amounts of recall in NREM. Nielsen's meta-analysis of research on this topic yielded an overall estimate of 80% dream recall for REM sleep awakenings and 40% dream recall for NREM sleep awakenings.[9]

No one doubts that REM sleep and dreaming are closely related. The question is whether dreaming occurs apart from REM sleep, and the answer seems to be yes. A great deal of evidence shows that dreaming also occurs in NREM sleep—not as much as in REM sleep, but far more than brainstem reductionism would allow. Some research has suggested that NREM dreams are more thought-like, less vivid, and less aggressive than REM dreams. There may be varying proportions of certain types of content in REM versus NREM dreams, but the differences are not absolute. Some REM dreams are thought-like, unemotional, and non-aggressive, and some NREM dreams are vivid, emotional, and action-packed. As Domhoff said in his review of this literature, "more than enough NREM reports contain full-blown dream content to contradict the strict equation of REM sleep and dreaming."[10]

It now seems more scientifically accurate to say that dreaming depends not on REM sleep per se but rather on the brain reaching a certain threshold of activation in several different neural systems.[11] REM sleep may be a reliable trigger of dreaming, but genuine dreams can also occur outside of REM sleep any time the brain is sufficiently stimulated. This broader view accounts for dreams at the hypnogogic transition between waking and dreaming (long before the first REM phase of the night) and for dreams during NREM stage 2 toward the end of night, when the brain's overall metabolism rises to its highest level of the sleep cycle. Cognitive psychologist Tracey Kahan has highlighted the well-documented findings of numerous researchers showing that "Stage 1 sleep at sleep onset, late-night Stage 2, and occasionally Stage 3 sleep, are associated with vivid dreaming that *cannot* be distinguished from vivid REM dreaming."[12]

Kahan also points out that in actual practice, sleep laboratory research does not always yield the clear-cut distinctions cited by brainstem reductionists: "sleep staging can be difficult and sometimes results in 'mixed' states not clearly identifiable as REM or NREM."[13] These considerations undercut the idea that an exclusive focus on REM sleep is the most scientific way to study dreams.[14]

Some of the strongest evidence against REM-dreaming isomorphism comes from Mark Solms, a neuropsychologist who performed a landmark study of 332 patients suffering from a variety of brain injuries and lesions.[15] During their treatment he asked each of the patients about their dreams, and he found that 200 of the patients reported no changes in their dreaming. These people had damage to various parts of the brain crucial for waking thought, awareness, and eyesight (e.g., the dorsolateral prefrontal cortex, the sensorimotor cortex, and the primary visual cortex), but they continued to dream just as they had before their neurological problems. This is important negative evidence. As vital as these particular regions of the brain are for waking cognition, they do not seem necessary for the process of dreaming.

The patients who did report changes in dreaming were divided by Solms into four syndromes: (1) *global anoneira*, a total loss of dreaming, (2) *visual anoneira*, cessation or restriction of visual dream imagery, (3) *anoneirognosis*, increased frequency and vivacity of dreaming, with confusion between dreaming and reality, and (4) *recurring nightmares*, an increase in the frequency and intensity of emotionally disturbing dreams. By comparing these effects on dreaming with the various types of brain damage, Solms identified several brain regions involved in dreaming:[16]

1. Basal forebrain pathways: associated with appetitive interests, seeking behaviors, curiosity, exploration, and expectation.
2. Medial occipito-temporal structures: important for visual associations, symbolic representations, and complex imagery.
3. Inferior parietal region: involved in spatial cognition.
4. Frontal-limbic region: supporting mental selectivity, reality monitoring, and the separation of dreaming from waking.
5. Temporal-limbic structures: involved in emotional arousal, instinctual behaviors, and seizure-like behavior.

The simplest observation about this list may also be the most significant: there are many brain regions contributing to the experience of dreaming, not just one single generating center. Damage to any one of these areas can disrupt or completely eliminate the capacity to dream. This evidence indicates that dreaming is a widely distributed and non-modular process, much like other complex mental faculties that depend on the harmonious interaction of neural systems all over the brain. Solms found that strictly unilateral damage on either the left or the right side of the brain could lead to global anoneira, a total loss of dreaming. This showed that both cerebral hemispheres are necessary for normal dreaming. And, as will be discussed in more detail in chapter 14, Solms found a "double dissociation" between visual imagery in dreams and visual perception in waking. Patients with damage to their primary visual cortex had severe problems with waking eyesight, but they still had normal dreaming; and patients with damage to their brain's visual association cortex lost visual dreaming, but their eyesight in waking life was unaffected. The brain's process of seeing while awake is apparently different from its process of seeing in a dream.

None of these neuropsychological findings makes sense in a framework of brainstem reductionism. I agree with Solms that his results contradict the basic premise of REM-dreaming isomorphism:

> [T]he neural mechanisms that produce REM are neither necessary nor sufficient for the conscious experience of dreaming. . . . [N]ormal dreaming is impossible without the active contribution of some of the highest regulatory and inhibitory mechanisms of the mind. These conclusions cast doubt on the prevalent notion—based on simple generalizations from the mechanism of REM sleep—that the primary motivating force of dreaming is not psychological but physiological.[17]

The point of reviewing this evidence is not to depreciate REM sleep, but to assign it a more fact-based role in the dreaming process. REM sleep consistently generates levels of brain activity that are highly conducive to dreaming, but, as Solms says, REM is neither necessary nor sufficient for dreaming. People can experience genuine dreaming in NREM stages of sleep, and they can have perfectly healthy REM sleep but no capacity to dream.

Why has REM-dreaming isomorphism appealed to so many researchers, despite such an abundance of contradictory evidence? It may have to do with the theory's kinship with philosophical materialism and the idea that all of consciousness, not just dreaming, is ultimately an epiphenomenal byproduct of physical activities in the brain. To make my own bias clear, I confess to a deep agnosticism about the relationship of mind and body. Classical dualism of the type often attributed to René Descartes does not help to explain the many ways that physical changes in the brain can impact the conscious experiences of the mind. But materialist efforts to explain consciousness in purely physical terms never seem to get very far. This is especially evident in the field of dream research, where brainstem reductionists have been unable to give anything close to a convincing explanation of how all the different dimensions of brain activity during sleep—including electrical, chemical, anatomical, and cognitive factors, along with the influences of gender, age, interpersonal relations, and cultural context—add up to the multisensory experience of a dream. Perhaps one day a satisfying materialist explanation of consciousness and dreaming will emerge, but researchers today should not take credit for discoveries they hope will appear in the future. The philosopher of science Karl Popper once admitted that his position amounted to a "promissory materialism," its truth dependent on facts yet to be discovered. If we entertain that kind of thinking, we might as well consider "promissory dualism," too. Who knows what discoveries the future will bring?

The debate over the mind–body relationship should not become a distraction from the pragmatic task of gathering large and diverse collections of data so we can test and refine our explanatory models. Instead of assuming we know how the brain produces dreams and then looking for evidence to fit that theory, we should concentrate on gathering as much dream data from as many different sources as possible, and then build up our models based on the strongest, most consistent patterns that can be objectively identified in the evidence.

The Scientific Study of Dream Content

For more than 100 years, psychologists and other social scientists have been using quantitative methods to study the content of dreams. Some of the researchers who took early steps in this direction were Mary Calkins, whose 1893 article "Statistics of Dreams" described how she systematically gathered 375 dream reports and analyzed several elements of their content; Lydiard Horton, whose 1925 book *The Dream Problem and the Mechanism of Thought* focused on recurrent themes in his collection of more than 1,000 dream reports; and Dorothy Eggan, who wrote a series of articles in the 1940s and 1950s using quantitative methods to study hundreds of dream reports from Hopi Native Americans. A turning point came with the work of Calvin Hall and Robert Van de Castle in the 1960s, when they developed a large-scale coding system to analyze many common facets of dream content.[18] Along with the Hall and Van de Castle (hereinafter HVDC) system, many other researchers have presented innovative ways of measuring dream content, as in Fred Snyder's 1968 article "Phenomenology of REM Dreaming," Carolyn Winget and Milton Kramer's book *The Dimensions of Dreaming* (1979), David Foulkes's *A Grammar of Dreams* (1982), Inge Strauch and Barbara Meier's *In Search of Dreams* (1996), Ernest Hartmann's *Dreams and Nightmares* (1999), and G. William Domhoff's *Finding Meaning in Dreams* (1996) and *The Scientific Study of Dreams* (2003).

The driving idea behind the work of these investigators has been a shared conviction that dream content contains a great deal of psychological information that can be observed, measured, and verified using carefully constructed methods of analysis.

Nevertheless, progress in this area has been slow. One problem has been the proliferation of competing coding systems, a concern that Winget and Kramer long ago termed "the chaos of the manifold ways of scoring dream content."[19] A bigger problem has been that nearly all of these analytic methods rely on "hand-coding" (i.e., one or more investigators reading each dream report and counting the appearance of various elements of dream content). These hand-coding methods are labor-intensive, time-consuming, and limited by difficulties with inter-coder reliability. The results can be difficult to replicate and compare with other data sets, especially if idiosyncratic scales of measurement have been used.

New digital technologies have removed some of these obstacles to faster progress. Initially I thought these technologies were more likely to harm dream research than help it. I worried that a computer-driven quantitative approach would lead researchers to atomize dreams into tiny, decontextualized bits of information that could never tell us anything meaningful about dreams as whole, integrated experiences. But at a certain point I began wondering about the potentially positive uses, not just the dangerous abuses. What if we could create a system that uses digital technologies to do what they are best at—analyzing large amounts of data quickly, easily, and precisely—in order to enhance the abilities of human analysts to do what they are best at—evaluating the patterns for meaning, significance, and relevance? In science-fiction terms, my attitude shifted away from "Blade Runner" anxiety about the dystopic, dehumanizing aspects of new technologies, and more toward "Star Trek" curiosity about their liberating, horizon-expanding possibilities.

For several years I have been experimenting with computerized word search methods to study dream content. I started with Domhoff and

Schneider's Dreambank.net website, which is distinguished by a large
and well-curated collection of dream reports, an easy-to-use word search
function, and a statistical package (DreamSAT) for the HVDC coding system.[20] Inspired by Domhoff and Schneider's work, I began developing the
Sleep and Dream Database (SDDb) so I could test other possible uses of
digital technology beyond the scope of the Dreambank. One goal was to
gather and analyze empirical data on sleep, in recognition of the importance of sleep for the study of dreams. Some of that material has already
been presented in chapters 3 and 4.

Another goal of the SDDb was to find a way of streamlining the word
search process, so the results of different analyses could be easily compared
with each other. This is why I built into the SDDb a word search template, now
in its 2.0 version, to provide a reliable way of pursuing comparative analyses
of dream content. The 2.0 template has 40 categories of words, grouped into
8 classes. These classes and categories are grounded in the work of previous
generations of researchers like Calkins, Eggan, and Hall and Van de Castle,
to encourage the backwards compatibility of new word search analyses with
the findings of earlier studies. Just because we have new technologies, we
should not ignore the enduring value of older sources of information.

Table 6.1 presents the results from using the 2.0 template to analyze a
large collection of dream reports I am calling the *SDDb Baseline Dreams*,
or just *the baselines*. They represent a large, diverse, and high-quality
collection of dream reports. The results show the percentage of dream
reports containing at least one instance of a word in each of the 40 categories, separated by gender. The patterns of word usage in the baselines, as
identified by the 2.0 template, can provide a useful empirical foundation
for making comparisons with other sets of dreams.

The baselines consist of 5,208 total dreams (3,095 female and 2,113
male) from five different sources: the *Demographic Surveys*, 1,004 female
and 665 male dreams I gathered from American adults in 2010 and 2013;
the *HVDC Norms*, a collection of 490 female and 491 male dreams gathered
from American college students by Calvin Hall in the late 1940s and early
1950s; the *International Survey*, 790 female and 645 male dreams collected
by Stanley Krippner in the 1990s from people in seven different countries
(Argentina, Brazil, Japan, England, Ukraine, Russia, and the United States);
the *Santa Clara Dreams*, a total of 811 dreams gathered by Tracey Kahan
in 2008 from female American college students; and the *Miami Home/
Lab Dreams*, 312 dreams collected by Calvin Hall from a group of young
American men in both home and laboratory settings in the early 1960s.

Table 6.1 SDDb Baseline Dreams (N = 5,208)

	Female		Male	
	N = 3,095		N = 2,113	
	Average word length: 101		Average word length: 106	
	Percent	4 most used words	Percent	4 most used words
Perception				
Vision	37	see, saw, watching, seeing	34	see, saw, watching, seeing
Hearing	10	hear, heard, noise, listening	9	heard, hear, noise, sound
Touch	12	hand, hands, holding, held	12	hand, hands, hold, holding
Smell and taste	2	nose, sweet, taste, smell	1	smell, nose, smelled, taste
Color	18	white, black, red, green	13	white, red, black, blue
Emotion				
Fear	23	scared, upset, afraid, frightened	15	afraid, scared, fear, frightened
Anger	7	angry, mad, annoyed, anger	5	angry, mad, irritated, anger
Sadness	5	sad, lonely, disappointed, depressed	3	sad, disappointed, depressed, unhappy
Wonder and confusion	18	suddenly, sudden, surprised, confused	18	suddenly, surprised, sudden, surprise
Happiness	9	happy, relieved, glad, relaxed	6	happy, pleased, relieved, glad
Characters				
Family	40	family, mother, husband, sister	27	wife, mother, father, brother
Animals	13	dog, cat, animals, dogs	12	dog, animal, bird, fish
Fantastic beings	2	spirit, fairy, witch, monster	2	monster, spirit, alien, devil

(continued)

Table 6.1 Continued

	Female		Male	
	N = 3,095		N = 2,113	
	Average word length: 101		Average word length: 106	
	Percent	4 most used words	Percent	4 most used words
Characters				
Male references	47	he, him, his, man	40	he, him, his, man
Female references	44	she, her, girl, mother	35	she, her, girl, woman
Social interactions				
Friendliness	46	friend, friends, boy-friend, help	34	friend, friends, girl-friend, help
Physical aggression	14	hit, kill, chasing, killed	21	hit, shot, fight, kill
Sexuality	4	kiss, sex, naked, kissed	6	sex, sexual, inter-course, kissed
Movement				
Walking and running	27	walking, running, walked, ran	27	walking, running, walked, run
Flying	4	flying, fly, floating, flew	6	flying, fly, floating, flew
Falling	8	fall, fell, falling, dropped	8	fell, fall, falling, falls
Death	9	died, dead, deceased, die	7	dead, died, death, die
Cognition				
Thinking	39	think, thought, decided, thinking	38	think, thought, real-ized, noticed
Speaking	35	said, talking, say, called	32	said, talking, say, saying
Reading and writing	6	read, books, book, write	4	book, reading, read, books
Culture				
Architecture	47	house, room, home, door	42	house, room, home, door

Table 6.1 Continued

	Female		Male	
	N = 3,095		N = 2,113	
	Average word length: 101		Average word length: 106	
	Percent	4 most used words	Percent	4 most used words
Food and drink	14	food, eating, dinner, eat	12	eating, eat, food, drinking
Clothing	14	wearing, dressed, clothes, dress	11	clothes, wearing, dressed, shirt
School	17	school, teacher, college, students	13	school, teacher, college, students
Transportation	24	car, street, road, stairs	31	car, street, road, cars
Money and work	18	work, working, buy, job	22	work, working, money, job
Technology and science	7	phone, computer, telephone, machine	9	machine, phone, television, radio
Weapons	3	knife, gun, bomb, guns	5	gun, rifle, knife, sword
Sports	4	gym, basketball, sports, tennis	4	football, baseball, golf, sports
Art	10	movie, dance, dancing, singing	7	movie, music, dancing, dance
Religion	7	church, Christmas, spiritual, god	6	church, spiritual, Christmas, god
		Elements		
Fire	4	sun, fire, star, burning	4	fire, sun, star, stars
Air	4	air, breathing, wind, breath	5	air, wind, blowing, breath
Water	13	water, lake, river, ocean	12	water, river, lake, sea
Earth	10	hill, dirty, land, mountain	10	hill, mountain, land, stone

In each of these five collections the investigators used standard academic procedures to gather one or more reports of "most recent dreams" from participants who had been recruited specifically for research purposes. Each collection represents a rigorous and systematic effort to collect high-quality evidence for use in the analysis of basic patterns in dreaming.

Blending data from multiple sources has the advantage of protecting us from overreliance on any one source and its inevitable limitations and idiosyncrasies. By combining these particular collections of dreams I wanted to create a data set with these features:

- *Dreams of varying lengths.* To make the baselines comparable to the widest variety of dreams, they include sources of relatively short dreams (the Demographic Surveys, with an average of 58 words per report), medium-length dreams (the HVDC Norms, 124 words per report), and longer dreams (the Miami Home/Lab Dreams, 218 words per report).
- *Large numbers of both male and female participants.* Men are often underrepresented in dream research. The baselines still have a 3:2 imbalance of females to males, but the total of 2,113 male reports is large enough to serve as a basis for general comparison.
- *Large numbers of people older than college students.* The baselines have three sources from college student or young adult participants (the HVDC Norms, Santa Clara Dreams, and Miami Home/Lab Dreams) and two sources (the Demographic Surveys and the International Survey) that include adult participants from a much wider age range, with many people in their fifties, sixties, and seventies.
- *Geographic diversity.* The International Survey adds a non-American element to the baselines, with at least 100 male and 100 female dreams from each of six countries outside the United States.
- *Historical diversity.* The baselines include dream reports gathered in the 1940s and 1950s (HVDC Norms), the 1960s (Miami Home/Lab), the 1990s (International Survey), the 2000s (Santa Clara Dreams), and the 2010s (Demographic Surveys).

Of course, even in their broadly balanced and aggregated form, the SDDb baselines are limited and idiosyncratic, too. They do not represent a perfect map of human dream content. Nevertheless, the baselines have some practical value insofar as they offer a better map than perhaps any other yet developed—a bigger, more diverse map that takes its point of departure from some of the best evidence of dreaming currently available, using new digital technologies to illuminate recurrent patterns in the data.

Signals in the Noise

The next two chapters are devoted to unpacking the implications of the SDDb baseline findings for our understanding of waking–dreaming continuities (chapter 7) and the metaphorical dimensions of dreaming (chapter 8). In this chapter the specific focus is responding to the question of whether or not dreams are random nonsense, and that is the lens I want to use in this initial engagement with the information presented in table 6.1.

If dreaming were a purely chaotic process, then we would expect the content of dreams to contain an unpredictable, arbitrary mish-mash of any and every possible kind of thing. There should be no rhyme or reason to it, just senseless noise, like static on a radio. But when we look at large collections of dreams like the SDDb baselines, we find remarkable consistency in the frequencies of various elements of content. As an example, let us look at the baseline findings on the five categories of emotion, which are shown

Table 6.2 Emotions in the Baselines

	Female SDDb Baselines				
	Baselines Total	Demographic Surveys	HVDC Norms	Santa Clara Dreams	International Survey
Emotion	Percent	Percent	Percent	Percent	Percent
Fear	23	22	28	23	23
Anger	7	6	10	12	4
Sadness	5	5	5	5	4
Wonder	18	9	29	20	20
Happiness	9	8	11	7	9

	Male SDDb Baselines				
	Baselines Total	Demographic Surveys	HVDC Norms	Miami Home/ Lab Dreams	International Survey
Emotion	Percent	Percent	Percent	Percent	Percent
Fear	15	12	16	14	18
Anger	5	3	7	12	3
Sadness	3	3	3	3	2
Wonder	18	8	29	13	23
Happiness	6	6	7	6	6

in table 6.2, broken down into their respective sources. This table shows how the variations within each category stay within a fairly narrow range.

The use of words related to fear ranged between 22% and 28% for the female participants and 12% to 18% for the male participants. There was more variation in the use of anger-related words, with a range of 4% to 12% for the females and 3% to 12% for the males. References to sadness and happiness were very close and consistent across all sources, for both genders. The use of wonder and confusion words varied somewhat from one source to another, from 9% to 29% for the females and from 8% to 29% for the males, although the results for each gender were mostly consistent within each source (e.g., the lowest frequency of wonder and confusion words among both males and females [9% and 8%] was in the Demographic Surveys, and the highest frequencies among both genders [29%] were in the HVDC Norm Dreams).

These frequencies of word usage display much more structure and coherence than would be anticipated by a "dreams are epiphenomenal" theory. In every one of the baseline sources there are more references to fear than to happiness, more references to wonder and confusion than to anger, and fewer references to sadness than to any other emotion. That does not look like a mish-mash of random content; it starts to look like a fairly stable pattern of emotional expression in dreaming.

Another good example regards the class of Elements. Table 6.3 shows how many references to the elements of fire, air, water, and earth appeared in each of the baseline sources.

Here, too, the results vary only slightly among the different sources, with the same basic proportions among all of them. In all the sources, the percentages of dreams with a reference to fire or air were in the low to mid-single digits. In all the sources but the Demographic Surveys, the percentages of dreams with a reference to water or earth were in the low to mid-teens, two to three times higher than the corresponding results for fire and air. The percentages of water and earth references were not quite that high in the Demographic Surveys, but they were still about twice as high as the references to fire and air.

Admittedly, some of the other classes besides emotions and elements have more variability than this. I do not want to overstate the consistency of the results. But many of the variations in the baseline sources can be easily explained in terms of the different average word lengths of the dream reports. Shorter reports, like those in the Demographic Surveys, tend to have lower frequencies of word usage across all categories. Longer reports, like those from the Miami Home/Lab study, tend to have higher frequencies of all categories. That is a predictable kind of variation, not a sign of randomness.

Table 6.3 Elements in the Baselines

Female SDDb Baselines

Elements	Baselines Total	Demographic Surveys	HVDC Norms	Santa Clara Dreams	International Survey
	Percent	Percent	Percent	Percent	Percent
Fire	4	2	3	4	7
Air	4	3	3	3	6
Water	13	8	17	15	17
Earth	10	5	12	12	14

Male SDDb Baselines

Elements	Baselines Total	Demographic Surveys	HVDC Norms	Miami Home/ Lab Dreams	International Survey
	Percent	Percent	Percent	Percent	Percent
Fire	4	3	6	4	5
Air	5	4	4	7	5
Water	12	5	14	14	15
Earth	10	6	12	13	12

Many of the other variations among the baseline sources can be explained as reflections of meaningful continuities between the content of people's dreams and their waking life concerns. These kinds of differences in word usage frequencies can be valuable clues to deeper patterns and consistencies in the data.

As a final example for this chapter, consider the category for colors. Table 6.4 shows the four most used words for color among the baseline sources.

White, black, and red are three of the top four most used color words in every one of the sources. Blue was also in the top four for all of the male sources and two of the female sources. If the distribution of colors in dream content were truly random, we would expect any number of possible combinations of top four colors—yellow, purple, orange, and gray, for example. But that is not what we find in the data. Each time the word search results yield the same basic color profile: white, black, red, and usually blue. Although much more research will have to be done to elaborate on these findings, the results certainly seem relevant to the work of Brent Berlin

Table 6.4 Colors in the Baselines

Female SDDb Baselines

	Demographic Surveys		HVDC Norms		Santa Clara Dreams		International Survey	
	Percent	4 most used words	Percent	4 most used words	Percent	4 most used words	Percent	4 most used words
Colors	7	white, black, blue, red	27	white, black, red, green	19	white, red, black, blue	24	white, black, green, red

Male SDDb Baselines

	Demographic Surveys		HVDC Norms		Miami Home/ Lab Dreams		International Survey	
	Percent	4 most used words	Percent	4 most used words	Percent	4 most used words	Percent	4 most used words
Colors	4	white, red, blue, black	14	red, white, blue, black	26	white, black, blue, red	15	white, black, blue, red

and Paul Kay in their 1969 study *Basic Color Terms: Their Universality and Evolution.*[21] Using linguistic and anthropological evidence, Berlin and Kay argued that all cultures have at least two color words, one for white and one for black; and if a culture has a third color word, it is for red.[22] Apparently these three colors are the "basic colors" of dreaming experience as well.

The observation of a consistent pattern like this, a genuine signal in the noise, does not necessarily reveal any immediate insight into the cause, meaning, or significance of that signal. But the more patterns like this we find, the harder it becomes to hold onto the idea that dream content is purely and entirely nonsensical.

Concluding Response

The evidence from the scientific study of dream content does not support the claim that dreaming is nothing but neural nonsense. Such a claim is inconsistent with the best available information about the actual patterns of dream content, information that comes not only from the SDDb baselines but also from many other researchers going back more than a century. As Dilbert found in his "Tour of Accounting," something the experts have told us is a generator of randomness turns out to produce content with an unexpectedly high degree of consistency and structure.

7

Continuities

How many times has it occurred that the
quiet of the night Made me dream of my usual habits:
that I was here, Clothed in a dressing gown, and sitting by
the fire, Although I was in fact lying undressed in bed!
RENÉ DESCARTES, *The Meditations Concerning First Philosophy*

Opening Question

Do dreams have any intrinsic meaning?

Dream content may have some degree of recurrent structure, but that does not necessarily imply it has any significance beyond what we read into it. A more likely explanation is that people attribute meanings to their dreams, just as people imagine they see faces and shapes in the clouds (another idea that goes back to Aristotle). A great deal of research in evolutionary psychology has shown that our minds are highly primed to notice other living beings—so highly primed, in fact, that we often make the mistake of thinking we see something alive when nothing animate is actually there. Cognitive scientists have called this the "hyperactive agency detection" module in the human mind.[1] The extreme sensitivity of this module has a plausible evolutionary function in terms of promoting our long-term survival. Better to have a bias toward over-interpreting our surroundings than under-interpreting them. The consequences of a perceptual false positive are trivial (thinking you see a snake, when it is actually a stick) compared to the potentially fatal consequences of a false negative (thinking you see a stick, when it is actually a snake). In the same way, humans throughout history seem to have had a bias toward over-interpreting their dreams, claiming to find in them special messages from supernatural beings. Those messages could, in fact, be imposed after waking and have nothing to do with the dreams themselves, which may be entirely devoid of meaning.

Initial Response

The patterns of dream content offer an accurate reflection of meaningful activities, concerns, and relationships in a person's waking life.

For more than a century, researchers have been gathering evidence in support of the idea that certain patterns in dream content are meaningfully connected to people's waking life concerns. The *continuities* between waking and dreaming are so strong and numerous that they can often be accurately identified without any input from the dreamer, "blindly" as it were. Many more continuities can be identified with the help of additional information from the dreamer, but a blind analysis that initially brackets out such information provides an especially convincing means of identifying waking–dreaming continuities. These meaningful connections are not something we read into the dreams, but rather something that emerges out of the objectively verifiable patterns of dream content.

Data and Discussion
Pioneers

As many studies have shown, humans have a "faces in the clouds" tendency to attribute meanings to phenomena that are actually random and meaningless.[2] But before we can apply this idea to the study of dreams, we need to be clear about the ways in which dreams are not like clouds in the sky. Everyone can agree, I trust, that dreams are not amorphous assemblies of airborne gases. Rather, dreams are produced by complex cycles of activation within an individual's mind, brain, and body during sleep. They weave together the individual's intimate memories, experiences, fears, and desires, all embedded in a dynamic cultural matrix of symbols, traditions, and interpersonal relations. The connection you have to your dreams is vastly closer—and vastly more meaningful—than your connection to a passing cloud. Your dreams are an integral part of you in a way a cloud is not. Whatever additional ideas people may project onto dreams, researchers have found strong evidence of meaningful patterns in the dreams themselves, patterns that accurately reflect some of the most personally significant aspects of an individual's life.

Sigmund Freud is often considered the first modern scientist of dreaming, but there were many other psychologists in the late nineteenth and early twentieth centuries besides Freud who were using scientific methods to investigate dream content. Four articles published between 1888 and 1915 in the *American Journal of Psychology* can be highlighted as representatives of those pioneering researchers, showing how pre-digital quantitative methods were used to identify significant connections between dream content and waking life concerns and activities.

The first of these articles, "A Study of Dreams" by Julius Nelson, appeared in one of the earliest issues of the journal, which was founded in 1887 by the eminent American psychologist G. Stanley Hall. Starting with the premise that "every psychological inquiry should as far as possible be based upon and connected with so much of physiological knowledge as we can command," Nelson used the principles of cell biology to guide his analysis of thousands of his own dreams that he had meticulously recorded over the course of many years.[3] He organized the dreams into several groups depending on the time of night they occurred, their length, and their complexity, and he tried to find meaningful connections between the dreams and the physiological processes of his body. Twenty pages into the article Nelson finally revealed, using very circumspect language, that his primary focus was sexually arousing "wet" dreams. Noting the 28-day periodicity of the female reproductive cycle, he wondered if male physiology had a similar kind of cycle, which might be observed and measured in terms of the frequency of seminal emissions during sleep. This was the clearest statement of his hypothesis:

> The presence of the reproductive elements exerts a constant stimulus upon the brain cells, which causes them to generate characteristic dreams that in turn react to produce expulsion of the gametal cells. This *gonekbole* will be more frequent at periods when the psychic cells are most irritable, and therefore furnishes data for plotting the sexual curve in the case of the male.[4]

A *gonekbole*, or *ekbole* (from the Greek word for throwing cargo overboard) as he later termed it, is equivalent to a wet dream. Unfortunately, Nelson's idiosyncratic language and methods of analysis made it difficult to compare his results with later studies. However, Nelson had a legitimate hypothesis about dreaming–waking continuity that was worth testing: Do physiological processes of sexual excitation manifest themselves in dream content? According to his findings, the answer was yes: "[I]n the monthly period the variation in the dream curve is parallel to that of the sexual curve."[5]

A more broadly conceived research method was employed by Mary Calkins in her 1893 article "Statistics of Dreams." She and a male colleague recorded their dreams over a period of 8 weeks, producing a total set of 375 dream reports. Her method, she said, "was very simple: to record each night, immediately after waking from a dream, every remembered feature of it. For this purpose, paper, pencil, candle, and matches were placed close at hand."[6] Despite her small sample size and rudimentary tools, Calkins identified many of the basic patterns of dream content that later researchers have confirmed with much larger groups of participants and much more sophisticated analytic methods. Here are some of her most prescient observations:

- The most vivid dreams come later in the night, toward morning.
- A few dreams directly reflect external stimuli, but not many.
- "The preponderance of visual images is very striking,"[7] much more than hearing or the other senses.
- Emotions vary in dreams, and are mostly negative or painful, although some dreams have no emotions.
- Some dreams have a great deal of drama and narrative continuity.
- The faculties of attention and volition tend to be weaker in dreams than in waking.
- Many dreams have high-order mental activities that function just as well as they do in waking; "not only imagination, but real thought occurs in dreams, though the fact is often denied."[8]
- Dreams have a prominent social dimension, usually containing multiple characters with whom the dreamer interacts in a variety of ways; "The dream world is well-peopled."[9]
- Most of the characters, places, and activities in dreams are familiar from current waking life.

This is a remarkable list of valid insights about the empirical patterns of dream content. Although Calkins has received scant attention from later generations of researchers, many of her claims have stood the test of time. Most significantly for our purposes here, she analyzed the dreams in terms of their relations with recent experiences in waking life, and she found that only 11% of the dreams had no such relations; "the most obvious conclusion ... is the close connection between the dream-life and the waking-life."[10] She suggested that emotions might be one of the motivating causes of these continuities: "the persistence of some feeling of the waking life seems to determine the character of the associated dream features."[11]

James Ralph Jewell published "The Psychology of Dreams" in 1905, building his analysis on a collection of more than 2,000 dream reports from surveys distributed to approximately 800 participants. The participants were students, mostly young women, in American teaching colleges. Although he had a large number of dreams and survey responses to work with, Jewell provided no statistical measures of dream recall frequency or patterns of content. Nevertheless, his study of these dreams led him to advance several conclusions about the general content of dreams, including these:

- "There seems to be an age of dreams about the time of puberty and dawning adolescence."
- "Dreams differ markedly with respect to age and locality, and probably with respect to nationality as well."
- "While the judgment usually does not work logically, during sleep, it may do so."
- "One may, while sound asleep, know that he is dreaming."
- "The influence of dreams upon real life is vastly greater than is usually thought, as has been seen in many ways."
- "There is no mode of functioning of the mind in the waking state that may not take place during sleep."[12]

As with Calkins, many of Jewell's claims hold up well in light of current research. His study has the advantage of using a much larger pool of participants, although each participant provided a much smaller number of dreams than did the participants in the studies by Nelson and Calkins.

Madison Bentley's "The Study of Dreams: A Method Applied to the Seminary," was published in 1915, and it reported an experiment Bentley conducted with five residents of a seminary. No further details are given about the participants or their seminary, so we are left to assume they were probably male, educated, unmarried, and Protestant Christians. They may have been familiar with introspective practices of prayer and contemplation, which would explain why Bentley recruited them and why they were willing to participate in a study involving a lengthy period of systematic self-observation. They apparently lived in the same residential facility, and this made it easy for Bentley to awaken them at precisely scheduled times of night to ask for dream reports. Bentley's first conclusion was that dreaming is much more frequent in the later hours of the sleep cycle. Regarding dream content, he found that realistic visual and auditory perceptions appear more often than any other senses; most emotions in dreams are negative or unpleasant; and many characters appear in dreams, most of them known to the dreamer. Although he found some dreams lacking in logic and judgment, this was not a general characteristic of dreaming: "We are told that 'people' do not think in dreams, that dreams are wholly irrational, that incongruities are not recognized, that dreams do not pursue a given topic, and what not. In our own introspections we found not one of these generalizations to hold."[13]

The most intriguing comment in Bentley's article was a direct anticipation of the continuity hypothesis: "In spite of this strange conglomeration of items drawn from many sources, however, the dream not infrequently reflects the 'personality' of the dreamer; that is to say, his temperament, traits, persistent interests, ethical and social principles, color and temper the dream."[14] A little later Bentley described the patterns of dreams as running "in old grooves" formed over the course of the individual's life. Bentley did not provide any biographical information about the participants, so it remains unclear what specific dreaming–waking continuities he identified. But his claims of continuity go beyond recent activities to consider long-term, deeply rooted aspects of a person's life—"temperament, traits, persistent interests, ethical and social principles."

These four authors—Nelson, Calkins, Jewell, and Bentley—never again wrote anything of substance about dreams, and their works are rarely cited in contemporary studies. *But they had the right idea.* This is an instance of what psychologist of religion Jeremy Carrette calls "disciplinary amnesia," whereby later researchers forget the work of previous pioneers in their field.[15] Those of us studying dreams in the twenty-first century would do well to remember these pioneering authors, and others like them, who developed scientifically rigorous methodological principles that guided their discovery of many of the same meaningful patterns of dreaming–waking continuity identified by researchers today.

Where does Freud fit into this history of the early days of empirical dream science? His first and arguably greatest work, *The Interpretation of Dreams*, was published in the fall of 1899 but given the publication date of 1900, so it would belong to the new century. He knew of Calkins's research and favorably mentioned it in a few places,[16] although his psychoanalytic approach led in a very different direction. Freud distinguished the *manifest* contents of a dream from its *latent* contents. The manifest content is the dream's outer appearance, the strange, disjointed images we remember upon awakening. The latent content is the true inner meaning, the unconscious wishes and desires that gave rise to the dream. Freud claimed that the latent content is deliberately distorted and disguised by a part of the mind that is trying to protect the individual's need for restful sleep. In Freud's view, the manifest dream is not supposed to be understood—it is designed to be incomprehensible so the sleeping person will not be disturbed by any unvarnished expressions of our baser instincts. This led Freud to a version of the "faces in the clouds" theory: dreams at the manifest level are meaningless, with no rhyme or reason to their contents. Any attempt to derive meaning from the intentionally garbled images of the manifest dream is doomed to failure. Only with the personal associations of the dreamer could the nonsensical façade of the manifest content be broken down to reveal the dream's underlying latent content.

Freud's psychoanalytic theory dominated research on dreams for most of the twentieth century. But a few dissenters continued to argue that better analytic methods could help us identify the truly meaningful aspects of the "manifest" content of dreaming. Dorothy Eggan, an anthropologist at the University of Chicago, was one of the first to make the case for a scientific approach to quantitative patterns in large collections of dreams. In a 1952 article in *American Anthropologist* titled "The Manifest Content of Dreams: A Challenge to Social Science," Eggan accepted Freud's notion that understanding the latent content of dreams requires personal associations from the dreamer. But she argued that a great deal of meaning could be identified in the manifest content of dreams by using quantitative methods of analysis, without personal associations from the dreamer. To support the argument she cited her collection of more than 600 dream reports gathered over several years from Hopi Native Americans in the southwest region of the United States. She introduced her analysis with a future vision of dream research that resonates strongly with my own aspirations:

> However, dreams, even at the manifest level, are exceedingly complex, and if they are to be used in numbers adequate for the eventual formulation of hypotheses of value in the social sciences, methods must be devised to organize the materials in readily comprehensible form. Thus further problems are more clearly indicated and both individual and cultural data are more easily examined, when dream elements are arranged on a chart.[17]

Eggan began her first dream-coding "chart" in 1939, an elaborate spreadsheet in which she carefully recorded each dream told to her by a male Hopi informant over a 6-year period. She analyzed 254 of this man's dreams and coded them for various elements and themes. She found, for example, that 67% of his dreams had at least one reference to persecution and conflict, consistent with his troubled relationships in waking life with other people in his community. In 40% of his dreams there was some reference to religion or ceremonial activities, and 73% of them included a supernatural character (e.g., a ghost or dead person). This, too, was consistent with his frequent participation in Hopi healing rites.

As an anthropologist, Eggan combined this quantitative approach with the standard tools of her discipline—ethnographic fieldwork, in-depth personal interviews, cultural history—to gain new insights into the personalities of the Hopi dreamers and their dynamic interactions with the traditions, symbols, and ideals of their culture. One of her cultural insights had to do with "the superficiality of Hopi conversion to Christianity." She found that Hopi dreams were filled with traditional religious activities and characters, reflecting the true character of their spiritual life despite their apparent affiliation with the Christian faith brought by Anglo missionaries. Eggan said, "[A] survey may show that 30% of a village is Christian in that they attend a missionary church; but their dreams indicate that the majority of the old Hopi who list themselves as Christian have as much respect for *Masau'u*, and many other Hopi deities, as they ever had."[18]

In a later writing titled "Dream Analysis," Eggan described how she learned an important methodological lesson in the course of her analysis of the Hopi man's long series of dreams. She found that the more of his dreams she gathered, the more clearly she understood his personal concerns and cultural conflicts, and the more easily she could correct her mistaken inferences about his life based on a smaller sample of his dreaming. Increasing the number of dreams in the analysis enabled her to identify his dreaming–waking continuities with greater accuracy and precision. Eggan realized this had implications not only for anthropology, but for the study of dreams in general:

> From such a chart one sees clearly the consistency of individual patterns of dreaming over periods of months and years. . . . The chart does not constitute, in itself, an 'analysis' of any dream. It merely illustrates a technique for the arrangement of manifest dream data which enables analysis of materials to proceed more effectively. . . . [I]t

is precisely these *patterns* in dreaming—and this tendency to correct previous distortions in successive dreams—which are most useful to any researcher who works with dreams.[19]

Dimensions of Continuity

The notion of "continuity" took more precise form in the work of Calvin Hall, a psychologist at Case Western University who was the first to formulate it as a hypothesis: "This may be called the *continuity hypothesis* because it assumes there is a continuity between dreams and waking life."[20] Starting with a 1947 article titled "Diagnosing Personality by the Analysis of Dreams," Hall made a prolific career of studying the various connections between dreaming and waking. His major contention was that dreams reflect an individual's "conceptions and concerns" in waking life. These conceptions include how we look at ourselves, our relationships, and our personal conflicts. One of Hall's major insights came after much trial-and-error research when he realized that dream content could be continuous with people's waking activities or their waking thoughts *about* their activities. For example, in a study he did of more than 1,000 dreams from an engineer named Karl, Hall noticed a high number of dreams with references to football, and so he inferred that Karl was very involved with that sport. However, Karl said that in fact he had quit playing football years ago. But after further discussion, Karl acknowledged that he did still think about football, and indeed he frequently imagined what it would be like to play with a professional team. The patterns in his dreaming reflected not just his waking behavior but also his waking thoughts, concerns, and desires.[21]

After moving to the University of Miami, Hall began working with psychologist Robert Van de Castle on a coding system to streamline the process of quantitative analysis of dream content. Their 1966 book *The Content Analysis of Dreams* presented the most sophisticated method yet devised for coding dreams in terms of categories for characters, emotions, social interactions, settings, misfortunes, objects, and several other types of content. The Hall and Van de Castle (HVDC) system has been used in hundreds of studies over the past half century, and it is one of the main inspirations for my word search approach.

When Hall moved to California in 1966, he and G. William Domhoff, a social psychologist at the University of California, Santa Cruz, became colleagues in dream research until Hall's death in 1985. Domhoff refined the HVDC system and made it much more accessible to researchers from various backgrounds. His biggest study focused on the dream series of "Barb Sanders," a woman who kept a dream journal for more than 25 years, recording a total of 3,116 dream reports. Domhoff analyzed a representative subset of her dreams using the HVDC system and found several easily identifiable continuities between her dream content and her waking life. For example, her mother was the most frequently appearing character in Sanders's dreams, and their interactions were often aggressive. This pattern accurately reflected the importance of her mother and their troubled relationship in waking life. Of Sanders's three children, she dreamed most frequently about her middle daughter, with even more aggressive interactions than in the dreams with her mother. This was continuous with Sanders's emotionally intense and problematic relationship with that particular child. These and other findings led Domhoff to conclude, "[T]here was strong continuity when it came to characters and her conceptions of them."[22]

The HVDC approach has produced a great deal of empirically based knowledge about the connections between people's dream content and their waking life concerns, conflicts, and preoccupations. Other psychologists have highlighted further dimensions of dreaming–waking continuity by looking at the formal properties of thought and perception in dreams. Rather than studying the *content* of dreams, as the HVDC system does, these researchers have analyzed the *form* of dreams as multifaceted cognitive experiences. Not *what* we dream about, but *how* our minds work while we are dreaming. In a 2007 study, Richard Wolman and Miloslava Kozmova carefully examined a set of 40 dream reports from 10 American adult participants for evidence of rational thought processes within the dreaming experience.[23] They found numerous instances of sophisticated mental activities like planning, evaluating, recognizing, deciding, and problem-solving. These forms of thought seem to operate in dreaming much as they do in waking, suggesting a high degree of cognitive continuity between the two. Wolman and Kozmova's findings suggest that "however bizarre and hallucination-like a dream may appear to the dreamer, the thought processes that support these cognitions and percepts are, in themselves, rational."[24]

A similar conclusion was reached in 2011 by Tracey Kahan and Stephen LaBerge in their research on *metacognition*, or "thinking about thinking," in dreams.[25] Metacognition involves self-reflection and awareness of ongoing thoughts and perceptions. Kahan and LaBerge provided new evidence to show that complex cognitive abilities are not restricted to waking thought but also occur in dreaming as well. A fully "lucid" dream is the best example of this (i.e., a dream in which the individual is consciously aware of being in a dream state). It is hard to argue that lucid dreams are lacking in high-level cognitive activities comparable to those in waking. But Kahan and LaBerge went beyond lucid dreaming to study metacognitive abilities in non-lucid dreams, and here too they found an abundance of sophisticated thought processes, such as choice, planning, focused attention, and reflective awareness. Their results led them to claim, "high-order cognition is much more common in dreams than has been assumed, so any theory of dreaming that does not take this into account is out-of-date. The continuity theory now has evidence for not only the similarities of mental content throughout states, but also similarities at the process levels of cognition."[26]

Let us pause and summarize the dimensions of dreaming–waking continuity that have been proposed by this lineage of empirically minded researchers over the past 100+ years. Patterns of dream content seem to accurately reflect these aspects of waking life experience:

- Sexuality
- Visual perception
- Social relationships
- Language abilities
- Daily activities and routines
- Long-term interests, conceptions, and concerns
- Personality and temperament
- Cultural ideals and conflicts
- Religious outlook
- Cognitive processing

We do not know how far these continuities extend or how stable they are over time or across different populations. As the next chapter will show, many aspects of dream content are clearly not continuous with waking life, so we have to be careful not to overstate the case.[27] But enough evidence has accumulated from many different sources to give us reasonable confidence about these basic areas of dreaming–waking continuity, all of which tend to revolve around especially meaningful activities and concerns in people's lives.

Blind Analysis

A good way of testing the continuity hypothesis is to perform a "blind analysis" with a series of dreams. Blind analysis means studying the dreams and making inferences about what they mean based exclusively on empirical patterns in the dream data, without knowing anything about the dreamer's waking life identity or personal associations to the dreams. This method tries to overcome a valid criticism of the continuity hypothesis, which harkens back to the initial question at the opening of the chapter. The criticism goes like this: If you already know personal details about the dreamer's waking life, how can you be sure the continuities you claim to find in the dreams do not actually reflect your prior knowledge of the individual, rather than anything intrinsically meaningful in the dreams? Blind analysis controls for that kind of influence by giving the researcher as little information as possible about the dreamer, so the inferences can be developed directly from the content patterns of the dreams.

Since 2009 I have performed several experiments of blind analysis with the help of Domhoff, Schneider, and the resources of their highly useful website Dreambank.net. My initial interest was exploring the possibility that a blind analysis could identify continuities between people's dreams and their religious beliefs and practices in waking life. Domhoff recruited one of the Dreambank's participants, "Merri," for a project in which I would study her series of 316 dream reports, make inferences about her waking life, and then ask her to confirm or disconfirm my predictions. All I knew about Merri was that she was a female, an artist, and an avid dream journaler. Using the Dreambank's word search function, I looked for dreams with religion-related words, and I read those dreams for clues to the role of religion in her waking life. Based on those dreams I inferred that Merri was raised as a Christian, specifically a Baptist, but she was no longer a member of that tradition. Although not an atheist, she had very negative feelings about the harmful, coercive forces of some religious groups. When Domhoff relayed my inferences about her religious background to Merri, she confirmed them as accurate.

However, I also predicted that she would not consider herself an especially "spiritual" person, and Merri said this was incorrect. She said she had become quite a spiritual person after the unexpected death of her sister, which had prompted a great deal of reflection about life after death. After our exchange I went back and looked at all of Merri's dreams with death-related words, and I found them to be more illuminating about her religious and spiritual perspectives than the ones I found using spe-cifically religion-related words. This was the first of many instances in blind analysis where a mistaken inference led to a helpful new insight.

Along with Merri, I made a parallel analysis of the Barb Sanders series of 3,116 dreams. I knew a lot about Sanders from Domhoff's prior work, but I did not know her religious background or spiritual views, so I was "blind" on this topic when the analysis began. I used the same process of searching for religion-related words, reading the dreams that included those words, then making inferences about Sanders's waking life, after which she confirmed or disconfirmed the inferences, with Domhoff again serving as our intermediary. I predicted that she was not raised in a distinctly religious family, does not consider herself Christian, but does consider herself a spiritual person who is open to the existence of divine beings and powers. Sanders confirmed this as accurate. These results, combined with those from the Merri series, showed that a blind analysis of a person's dreams could reveal meaningful continuities with his or her conceptions and concerns about religion.

In the ensuing dialogue with Sanders about her dreams, I had a moment of puzzlement when she mentioned that earlier in life she had converted to the Episcopalian Church when she had gotten married. I had seen no evidence of anything like a religious conversion in her dreams, so I immediately thought this might indicate a limit in the continuity hypoth-esis. But when I asked Sanders about the conversion, she said it was just a formality and had no real significance for her. Seen in this way, the lack of dream references to the conversion was in fact an accurate reflection of its lack of meaning in her waking life. This echoes Dorothy Eggan's observa-tion about the Hopi people's superficial conversions to Christianity and the value of dreams as a relatively honest gauge of people's true religiosity.

The success of these studies made me realize several things. First, it would help to have a more general system for word searching dreams, covering other areas of content besides religious themes. Second, it would really help to have some baseline frequencies about the expectable pat-terns of dream content, to use as a measuring stick in these kinds of stud-ies. When I was analyzing Merri's and Barb Sanders's dreams, I had no idea if their frequencies of religion-related words were unusually high or low. I had nothing to compare them to.

Soon after this I began developing a set of 40 broad categories for word searching dreams, which I now refer to as the 1.0 template. I tested these categories on the HVDC Male and Female Norm dreams (N = 981), long considered the most useful baselines in dream research. I also tested the template on the dream series (N = 136) of Paul, an 80-year-old man whose dreams had already been content analyzed using traditional HVDC hand-coding methods. The results of these tests, published in 2010, showed that word searches could identify many of the same patterns of dream content as the hand-coding method, in a fraction of the time and with no question of inter-coder reliability. This study was not a blind analysis, but it aimed at making it easier to perform blind analyses in the future by establishing a clear link between the solid findings of traditional content analysis and the new potentials of systematic word searching.

A third realization arising from the study of Merri and Barb Sanders was that I knew I could push the process of blind analysis one step further. What if, in addition to knowing nothing about the dreamer's personal life or associations, I never even read the dream reports and only focused on the numerical frequencies of word usage to make my inferences? That would be an extra-blind mode of analysis, and a much stricter test of the continuity hypothesis. My results with Merri and Barb Sanders could be questioned because of my prior knowledge about dream narratives in general. When I read through their dreams, I was able to identify the continuities without much trouble, but perhaps that was only because I have experience with these kinds of texts and I know what to look for. A more objective approach, and a more convincing way of proving the point, would be to identify dreaming–waking continuities based on numbers alone, without any reference to the dream narratives. This was the challenge: Are there any continuities so strong and clear they can be observed by anyone (not just experts) simply by looking at the quantitative patterns of word usage?

In a study published in 2010, Domhoff forwarded to me a series of 192 dream reports from "Van." I only knew that Van was a young man, nothing else.[28] I analyzed his dreams using the 40 categories of the 1.0 template, and I recorded the word usage frequencies without ever looking at or reading the dreams themselves. Then I compared Van's frequencies to those of the HVDC Male Norms and made several inferences about his waking life. Domhoff conveyed the inferences to Van, who confirmed most of them (12 of 14) as accurate. These included the predictions that Van is an even-tempered extrovert who does lots of reading and writing, works for a newspaper, is sexually active, has little interest in religion, likes dogs better than cats, and has closer relationships with his two older brothers than his sister or younger brother.

One of the incorrect inferences led to a valuable insight. I had predicted that Van is a frequent nightmare sufferer, given the relatively high
frequencies of words relating to fear, physical aggression, falling, and
death in his dreams. But he said that was untrue. Some of his dreams
were nightmares, but mostly they were enjoyable to him, even though they
involved all sorts of violent danger and frightening mayhem. It turned
out that Van was an avid player of video games, and he regarded these
"adventure" dreams as comparable to the excitement and stimulation he
felt when immersed in playing a great video game. I belatedly realized his
unusually high frequency of words relating to fantastic beings (still the
highest frequency on that category I have ever seen) would have been a
good clue to his interest in video gaming.

The next test of this extra-blind mode of analysis, published in
a 2012 article, had a new feature.[29] The dreamer, "Bea," provided
Domhoff with two series of dreams, which he forwarded to me. I knew
nothing beyond the facts that Bea was a young woman and the first
series (N = 183) came before the second series (N = 40). Using the same
process as with Van's dreams, I calculated Bea's word usage frequencies in the two series, compared them to the HVDC Female Norms,
and made a number of inferences about her waking life in the two
time periods. Via Domhoff, Bea confirmed most of the inferences (11
of 15) as correct. She was a student who had moved from high school
(series 1) to college (series 2), and I could tell she had become more aca-
demically challenged, was playing more field hockey and less soccer,
had a boyfriend, was more sexually active, felt more concerned about
her family (parents and one brother), and had experienced a negative
emotional downturn between the times of series 1 to series 2. In a
follow-up conversation Bea said that during her first year of college
she sought counseling for recurrent bouts of anxiety, with persistent
fantasies about threats to her family. Later in college she became a
resident assistant, which involved extensive training in how to respond
to various problems and dangers that might arise in the dormitories.
Bea asked us why she had so many negative dreams in series 2, since
nothing truly "bad" had actually happened to her during that time.
Our best answer was that her dreams seemed to reflect not the actual
events of her life, but rather her thoughts, feelings, and concerns during that time, particularly the "worst case scenarios" that might afflict
her family or friends at school. That is what was on her mind during
the day, and that is what she dreamed about at night.

These experiments in blind analysis have shown how to identify dreaming–waking continuities in a *series* of dreams from one individual. Meaningful continuities can also be found in *sets* of dreams from many different people. I first learned this, appropriately enough, when I was studying a set of dream reports from blind people. I was doing the initial tests of the 1.0 word search template, starting with categories of words relating to perception. I applied these categories to more than 20 series and sets of dreams in the Dreambank, and right away I noticed that in every case, words relating to vision were much higher than for any other sense—except for the blind people. They were the only ones with hearing references higher than their vision references. They also had higher references to smell and taste than anyone else did. It made me realize that if you knew nothing about these people besides these unusual frequencies of word usage in their dreams, you would be able to accurately guess they were blind. This showed that a significant feature of waking life—being sighted or not—was accurately reflected in sets of dreams gathered from a large number of people.

Concluding Response

Many aspects of dream content are meaningfully connected to the important concerns of a person's waking life. Empirical patterns in dream content have been found to accurately reflect the individual's social relationships, emotional temperament, sexual desires, daily activities and routines, long-term interests, cultural ideals, religious outlook, and metacognitive skills. The blind analysis method provides an objectively verifiable means of identifying these continuities in the patterns of the dreams themselves, without any other information about the dreamer. These findings refute the skeptic's claim that dreams have no intrinsic meaning beyond what we project onto them.

I imagine that many of the pioneering researchers mentioned earlier in this chapter would have been fascinated by these new digital technologies for the study of dreams. They would have enjoyed using such tools to boost the power and speed of their investigations. And I expect that eventually they would have thought about taking the next step, going beyond the continuities to explore the potentially meaningful discontinuities between dream content and waking life.

8

Discontinuities

(Bottom): I have had a most rare vision.
I have had a dream, past the wit of man
to say what dream it was. Man is but an ass
if he go about to expound this dream.

WILLIAM SHAKESPEARE, *A Midsummer Night's Dream*

Opening Question

Does everything in dreams have a meaning?

Some aspects of dream content are continuous with waking life, but many others are not. Indeed, many dreams are filled with bizarre images and outlandish activities that have no connection to the individual's waking reality. This makes it absurd to claim, as Freud did, that every element of a dream is not only meaningful but contains multiple meanings. In *The Interpretation of Dreams*, Freud said,

> a dream never tells us whether its elements are to be interpreted literally or in a figurative sense or whether they are to be connected with the material of the dream-thoughts directly or through the intermediary of some interpolated phraseology. In interpreting any dream-element it is in general doubtful a) whether it is to be taken in a positive or negative sense (as an antithetic relation), b) whether it is to be interpreted historically (as a recollection), c) whether it is to be interpreted symbolically, or d) whether its interpretation is to depend on its wording. . . . [I]t is in fact never possible to be sure that a dream has been completely interpreted. Even if the solution seems satisfactory and without gaps, the possibility always remains that the dream may have yet another meaning.[1]

An indeterminate, open-ended approach like this violates the basic tenets of scientific reasoning. Freud's interpretations cannot be falsified. There is no conceivable evidence that could refute his claims because he can always shift the focus to other putative layers of meaning. Frederick Crews, a contemporary critic of psychoanalysis, has denounced these unbridled interpretive excesses: "When Freud tells you that, in principle, every last detail of a dream can be explained in terms of unconscious conflict, you would do well to regard the claim as a warning flag. As is so often said, a theory that explains everything explains nothing."[2]

Dream researchers remain on solid scientific ground when they concentrate on direct, literal continuities between dream content and waking life. Any other aspects of dreaming should be set aside as unsuitable for scientific investigation.

Initial Response

Many of the discontinuities between dreaming and waking are genuinely meaningful.

We cannot prove that all aspects of dreaming are meaningful, any more than we can prove all dreams are nonsense. But current research strongly supports the idea that dreams are genuinely meaningful in a variety of ways, and not just in cases of obvious continuities between dreaming and waking. The discontinuities between dreaming and waking can also reflect meaningful dimensions of an individual's life. Some of these discontinuities involve the mind's capacity to generate metaphors, a powerful aspect of human creativity that operates in sleeping as well as in waking. The best way to understand these aspects of dreaming is to view them in a broader evolutionary framework of mammalian play. Both the continuities and discontinuities of dreaming are manifestations of play behavior within the human mind. Seen in this light, dreaming can be defined as *imaginative play in sleep.*

Data and Discussion
Dimensions of Discontinuity

The previous chapter laid out evidence showing that most dream content is fairly mundane and reality-based. We tend to dream about familiar people, in familiar places, doing familiar things. Systematic studies of dream content have repeatedly reached this conclusion. For example, Frederick Snyder and his colleagues published an article in 1968 titled "Phenomenology of REMS Dreaming" in which they analyzed 635 dream reports from 58 healthy participants, gathered in a laboratory setting while they were in REM sleep. Snyder et al. found these dreams "generally involved clear, coherent accounts of realistic situations in which the self was involved in mundane activities and preoccupations. 90% would have been considered credible descriptions of everyday waking experience."[3] More recently, I conducted two surveys (in 2007 and 2010) involving 3,675 American adults (1,436 women and 2,239 men) who were asked if they had ever experienced a dream exactly like waking life. Fifty-nine percent of both the men and women answered yes, indicating that a majority of the participants were able to remember a dream that simulated, with a high degree of realism, the conditions of their current waking lives.

Evidence like this makes it hard to argue that dream content is completely bizarre, incoherent, and detached from reality. The dreaming imagination clearly has the ability to create realistic portrayals of regular daily life. This is a key point, because it means that when bizarre elements do appear in dreaming, they may not stem from failures or deficiencies of cognitive functioning. They may represent a different, but not necessarily defective, kind of output from the mind in sleep. "Bizarreness" in dreaming may occur by design, not by accident.

What exactly constitutes bizarreness in dreams, and how often does it occur? For decades researchers have struggled with the difficulty of devising reliable tools of measurement to help answer this question. Allan Hobson and his colleagues have developed coding scales for three different categories of bizarreness: discontinuities, incongruities, and uncertainties.[4] Richard Bonato and his colleagues created the "Carleton University Scale of Impossibility and Improbability," which they used in tandem with a "Global Realism Scale."[5] Antti Revonsuo and Christina Salmivalli produced a system of 14 categories of dream content, each of which could be coded as "bizarre" or "non-bizarre."[6] Several other methods of measuring bizarreness in dreams have been generated over the years, but none of them have been widely replicated. Most suffer from limited inter-coder reliability, and their categories are usually incompatible with those used by other researchers.

The main problem with all these coding systems is the difficulty of defining the central term. As Bonato et al. point out, the only common theme in these various systems is that bizarre dream content somehow "differs from reality." Unfortunately, no one can agree on how "different" the content has to be from reality to qualify as bizarre. Must it be something that is physically impossible, or highly improbable, or just unlikely? What about things that are possible but socially improper, or weird combinations of people or objects, or unexpected shifts of setting or time? Do those count as bizarre, too? In the actual practice of dream content analysis, it can be devilishly difficult to code a group of dreams using such ambiguous and nonspecific categories.

A bigger problem with these bizarreness studies has to do with something most of the researchers agree about, namely their implicit definition of the "reality" against which dream content is measured. Their notion of reality is anchored in ordinary waking behaviors and the laws of the physical world. But as we found in the previous chapter, people dream not only about their daily activities but also about their daily thoughts, feelings, and concerns. These personal preoccupations often include fantasies and speculations about impossible, improbable, or outlandish things. Furthermore, every individual lives in a cultural environment filled with otherworldly fictions and mythic stories. If someone reads a book about a vampire and then dreams about a vampire, is that bizarre? Does it count as bizarre if a person sees a movie about ancient Greece and then has a dream that combines ancient Greece with present life? Yes, if the standard of reality is current physical existence. But no, not if reality includes psychological factors such as what people think about, feel, remember, and imagine during the day.

These problems raise the possibility that focusing on bizarreness in dreaming is simply a dead end. Once we recognize that dream content accurately reflects the psychological reality of people's waking thoughts, emotions, and cultural experiences, it becomes more difficult, and less interesting, to try labeling one or another kind of content as "bizarre."

Metaphors

A more promising approach looks at discontinuities in dreaming as expressions of metaphorical thinking in sleep. Recent work by cognitive linguist George Lakoff and his colleagues has investigated the role of metaphors in the waking mind. As Lakoff and Mark Johnson defined the term in their 1980 book *Metaphors We Live By*, "the essence of metaphor is understanding and experiencing one kind of thing in terms of another."[7] Metaphors are tools of thought that help us make sense of the world by using what we know to understand what we do not know. For example, to understand the abstract concept of time, we often speak of it as a moving object (e.g., "time flies," "the afternoon passed slowly"). The metaphor "time is a moving object" uses our concrete experiences with moving objects to make it easier to grasp the abstract qualities of time. Putting it in Lakoff's terminology, the *target* of this metaphor is time, and the *source* of the metaphor is moving objects. Generally speaking, metaphors use our tangible interactions with a source to make better sense of the more abstract qualities of a target. Sources can be drawn from experiences with our bodies, the physical world, and our cultural communities. Targets can be any abstract concept in human thought.

Lakoff and his colleagues have emphasized the limits of metaphors. A metaphor is always partial and imperfect. It highlights some aspects of a target, but obscures others. This is why people use multiple metaphors, so they can better grasp complex realities and avoid getting trapped in narrow conceptualizations of the world. For example, in addition to "time is a moving object," people also use the metaphor "time is a limited resource" (e.g., "a lost year," "budgeting your time"). According to Lakoff and Johnson, "successful functioning in our daily lives seems to require a constant shifting of metaphors. The use of many metaphors that are inconsistent with one another seems necessary for us if we are to comprehend the details of our daily existence."[8]

In a 1993 article "How Metaphor Structures Dreams: The Theory of Conceptual Metaphor Applied to Dream Analysis," Lakoff argued that metaphorical thought processes are also active in sleep and play a generative role in dream formation, providing "a natural mechanism for relating concrete images to abstract meanings."[9] He analyzed several dreams to illustrate their metaphorical structures, showing how seemingly bizarre images could be explained in terms of the normal processes of thinking metaphorically.

Lakoff's general proposition seems solid, but difficulties emerge when we try to identify specific metaphors in dreams. As Lakoff's colleagues pointed out in the 2014 book *The Power of Metaphor*, the same source can be metaphorically mapped onto multiple targets, and the same target can be mapped by multiple sources.[10] Basically, anything can be a metaphor for anything else. This seems to allow the kind of unscientific free-for-all that Frederick Crews criticized in Freudian psychoanalysis. To be fair, Lakoff's theory does provide a scientific account of how metaphors function in the mind, and there is a growing body of empirical research to support its basic principles.[11] But conceptual metaphor theory offers little practical guidance in finding specific instances of metaphors in dreams and sorting through the multiplicity of their possible meanings.

To get a better sense of the advantages and disadvantages of Lakoff's approach, let us consider an example of a metaphorically rich dream. The following report was shared with me several years ago by a former student, "Rose," a 24-year-old woman who was married with a 2-year-old daughter.[12]

In the dream I can see myself asleep in bed next to my husband. It is as if I am looking down from the ceiling watching us sleep. As I watch myself sleep, an angel or spirit comes to me and takes me up through the ceiling into the starry sky. I cannot see this spirit, but I can feel her presence. As we soar through space, I feel totally exhilarated. It seems there is some sort of static electricity surging through my body. The spirit asks me if I want to see Heaven. I ecstatically agree. Just then I look ahead and I can see where the sky and stars end and Heaven begins. It is similar to the view from the beach where the water ends and the horizon begins. It is a bright, beautiful, and misty place. I feel an overwhelming sense of peacefulness and happiness. Just as we are about to cross over into Heaven, I feel an urge to share this with my husband. I reach down with my arm and somehow am able to reach all the way back through the ceiling into our bedroom. I grab hold of his hand and "telepathically" tell him to come with me to see this beautiful place. But instead of floating up to meet me, he pulls me back into our bedroom. The ceiling closes up and I do not get to see Heaven. I am extremely disappointed.

This dream came to Rose at a time when her daughter was old enough to attend a local childcare center, and Rose had returned to work. Her husband became upset about this, leading to serious marital problems.

By any measure, Rose's dream was filled with fantastic images and impossible abilities that had no apparent connection to ordinary physical reality. And yet we can easily identify, using Lakoff's work, at least two conceptual metaphors that shape the overall narrative. Rose's experience of flying through space embodied the common metaphor "up is good," and the opposing metaphor "down is bad" framed the disappointing ending, with her husband pulling her back into the bedroom. The dream's imagery may have been physically impossible, but the basic structure of these two metaphors accurately represented the emotional reality of her waking life. Rose had career aspirations that made her want to "reach for the stars." She experienced these desires as good, strong, and inspiring, and she was willing to follow them as far they led her. She wanted to include her husband in her upward journey, but unfortunately he was not willing to join her. He pulled her back down, back into the conjugal confines of their bedroom. That downward movement was accompanied by an intensely negative emotional reaction, which mirrored her feelings in waking life about her husband's reaction to her plans.

Interestingly, in discussing her dream, Rose acknowledged it might have a more self-critical meaning, too. Perhaps by pursuing her lofty ambitions and out-of-home activities, Rose had been "drifting away" from her family. The metaphor "physical closeness is intimacy" may have been at work here, too, as the farther up into the heavens she went, the more distant she became from her family. According to that metaphorical mapping of her emotional experiences, Rose's husband could be seen as trying to bring her "back to earth," restoring their physical closeness by "grounding" her in the needs of their family. As Lakoff said, we need more than one metaphor to make sense of life's complex realities.

The dream did not tell Rose what to do. Rather, it presented her with a new perspective ("seeing is knowing") on her marriage, her life, and her hopes for the future. The dream had personal value for Rose insofar as it played a role in her difficult decision to get a divorce and move to a new home with her daughter. The dream's value derived in large measure from the conceptual clarity and emotional honesty of the metaphorical images.

The study of an individual case like Rose's can show that specific types of metaphors are present in a particular dream. But does that mean all dreams are filled with metaphors? Can all dreaming–waking discontinuities be explained as instances of metaphorical thinking? It is hard to build a compelling scientific argument one case study at a time, no matter how good a job the researcher does in probing and analyzing the individual's dream.

An alternative method of identifying metaphors in dreams emerged rather serendipitously during a blind analysis project I performed with Domhoff and Sandu Iordache, a psychologist in New Zealand.[13] Iordache sent a set of 100 most recent dream reports (one each from 67 women and 33 men) to Domhoff, who forwarded them to me with no additional information about the dreamers other than their location in New Zealand. Previously I had only tried the blind analysis method on individual dream series, so here was an opportunity to see if I could identify the characteristics of a group of people based exclusively on the word usage frequencies in a set of their dreams. Using the 1.0 version of the SDDb template of word search categories, I analyzed the dreams and compared the results to the HVDC norms.

I checked and double-checked the numbers, trying to be extra careful because I was worried that one of my research interests, namely end-of-life dreams, was overly influencing my analysis. When I looked at the statistical frequencies of these dreams, I had a very strong and immediate feeling these were end-of-life patients, and so I had to make sure to consider all other possibilities before settling on any conclusions. Eventually I sent Domhoff my inferences that these people were older, disengaged from the social world, and concerned with death. Domhoff forwarded the inferences to Iordache, who confirmed them as correct: the dreamers were patients in a palliative care program for people with terminal illnesses.

If I made a mistake with this study, it was not having the courage of my convictions and making the specific prediction that the dreamers were hospice patients. I was definitely thinking that, but I did not want to risk an overly specific inference based on evidence that included a metaphorical interpretation of the word search results. One of the main reasons I felt sure these were end-of-life patients was their high frequency of transportation words. Overall, this set of 100 dreams had relatively low frequencies in all the other word categories, but a much higher transportation frequency (24% for both women and men). This caught my attention because in 2006 my mother Patricia M. Bulkley and I wrote a book about pre-death dreams in which we talked about the metaphor "death is a journey." One of the chapters was about transportation metaphors in people's dreams prior to death, with examples of dreams of riding in cars, or sailing in ships, or walking down paths, moving some place far beyond where they are now. I noticed the unusually high transportation frequency in this set of dreams, and I could not help thinking it was connected with the other results pointing at end-of-life patients (e.g., low school and high death references). But in no previous blind analysis project had I made an inference based on a *metaphorical* continuity between dreaming and waking. I had been intentionally focusing on *literal* continuities, to keep the early development of the word search method as simple and straight-forward as possible. Yet after the successful results of this study I real-ized I had a good piece of evidence, more trustworthy because I was not initially looking for it, that word searches can be used to identify unusual features of dream content with metaphorical significance.

To follow up on that study (and test the possibility that it was just a fluke) would require a specific metaphor, a group of participants likely to dream of that metaphor, and a sufficient number of their dreams to perform a quantitative analysis. These are difficult conditions to meet, but not impossible. If more research projects like this were performed, their results might reveal systematic, predictable patterns of metaphori-cal meaning in dreams beyond what can be found with the case study method.

Until then, we are left with the rather unsatisfying conclusion that dreams almost surely have the capacity to engage in metaphorical think-ing, but we know very little about how that capacity actually works, which metaphors are more or less likely to appear, what they mean, or how they relate to other aspects of dream content.

Dreaming Is Play

Beyond the metaphors we identify in particular dreams, there is a broader way to account for the discontinuities between dream content and waking life. Dreaming, I propose, is a kind of *play*, the play of the mind during sleep. A great deal of research on the evolution of play and its role in ani-mal development has been published in recent years, along with studies of play in various human cultures.[14] Pioneering psychologists from the mid-twentieth century like Jean Piaget, Erik Erikson, and D. W. Winnicott argued that human health and creativity fundamentally depend on the ability to play. More recent investigations by Marc Bekoff, John A. Byers, Brian Sutton-Smith, Gordon M. Burghardt, and others have shown how play in humans and other animal species are related to a host of survival-enhancing behaviors, indicating a high degree of evolutionary value. It would take a book-length treatment to do justice to all this material, but a brief overview will be enough to show the relevance of play to an under-standing of the discontinuities of dreaming.

Play behavior has been found in many species of birds and mammals, with some evidence that reptiles like turtles also engage in rudimentary forms of play. In all species, the proportion of time devoted to play is highest in the younger phases of life. Animals with more complex central nervous systems, such as horses, cats, dolphins, and chimpanzees, display especially elaborate and exuberant play behaviors in youth. Humans seem to engage in greater amounts of play, and more varied kinds of play, than any other species.[15]

Researchers have found several recurrent features that characterize play behaviors across species. Play often revolves around activities that will become important for survival in adulthood, such as grooming, finding food, resolving conflicts, defending against attack, and courting mates. Play occurs in an "unreal" space in which play actions do not have the same consequences that similar acts would have outside of play (e.g., in a play fight no one actually gets hurt). This makes it a safe arena in which to experiment with a wide variety of possible actions and responses to different situations. Play often takes exaggerated and extravagant forms, making it appear frivolous and nonsensical. But a special kind of concentration and focus is generated in play activities, a paradoxical combination of deep absorption and openness to surprise and unpredictability. Play is physically and cognitive stimulating, and it seems to have a very strong intrinsic appeal—it is enjoyable, it makes one happy. Even when play involves darker themes of aggression, sadness, loss, or misfortune, it still gives free reign to curiosity and the desire to explore.

Play serves no one single function, but it contributes to healthy development in many ways. It enables practice with the survival skills of adulthood, rehearses instinctual responses to novel situations, and promotes general flexibility in both mind and body. Play increases a creature's adaptive readiness for the typical challenges of life faced by a member of its species. In humans, play provides a space to experiment with different social roles, cultivate a deeper capacity for empathy, and build interpersonal trust.

If you reread the preceding three paragraphs and substitute "dreaming" for "play," you will find that nearly all of the research findings remain true.[16] As the previous chapters have shown, sleep and dreaming have a long evolutionary history, a history we can now see is profoundly intertwined with the evolution of play.

Thinking of dreaming as imaginative play in sleep has many benefits, the first of which is reorienting our approach to discontinuities in dream content. Consider a kitten stalking a leaf, or a foal spontaneously leaping and kicking in the air, or a group of human children setting up a miniature house for a family of dolls. Do these activities reflect malfunctioning brains? Are they evidence of cognitive deficiencies or diminished mental capacities? Not at all. These are natural play behaviors that engage the creature's brain/mind system in a mode of functioning different from, but not inferior to, its ordinary waking condition. Exactly the same can be said of dreaming. Both play and dreaming are innate behaviors of our species that have the adaptive, survival-enhancing effect of stretching our minds beyond what is to imagine what might be. Discontinuities in dream content are evidence of how far our minds can be stretched, how widely our imaginations can range across multiple possible realities.

A second benefit of this approach is how well it accounts for instances when the playful qualities of dreaming are damaged or disrupted. For example, people with post-traumatic stress disorder (PTSD) often suffer from repetitive nightmares that graphically replay the traumatizing experience (e.g., an accident, assault, or natural disaster) in vividly realistic detail. Therapists who work with PTSD victims find these persistent and repetitive nightmares to be symptomatic of the overwhelming shock of the trauma. From the perspective I am advocating, PTSD nightmares represent the antithesis of playful dreaming. They are fixed in content, unchanging in form, and utterly devoid of freedom or creativity.

The same play-stunting dynamics also appear in recurrent anxiety dreams about work, school, or other highly stressful activities in waking life. In these dreams people find themselves trapped in repetitive loops of frustrating activities from the waking world, struggling vainly against the same problems that plague them during the day. Such dreams are like mini-PTSD nightmares, with precious little room for playful discontinuities or fanciful departures from the status quo.

It seems that when pressures and dangers from the external world reach a certain critical threshold, the capacity for ordinary playful dreaming can falter and lose its imaginative flexibility. In some cases the loss may be permanent, as seems to have happened with the Holocaust survivors in psychiatrist Peretz Lavie and Hanna Kaminer's 1991 study, "Dreams That Poison Sleep."[17] Lavie and Kaminer found that the Holocaust survivors who were most psychologically healthy were the ones who dreamed the least: "the suppression of dream recall in the well-adjusted survivors has served an adaptive protective function."[18]

In most PTSD cases, however, the disruptions to healthy dreaming are temporary, and playful energies eventually reassert themselves. Clinical research has found that over time, and with the help of therapeutic treatment, PTSD nightmares tend to change—they become *dreamier.*[19] The traumatizing experience no longer dominates all awareness, as other thoughts, feelings, and memories gradually enter the dream space. The psychic wounds from the trauma may never entirely disappear, but in time they are subsumed into the ongoing flow of the individual's normally weird dream life. For PTSD victims, the increasing playfulness of their dreams provides a clinically useful indicator of their recovering health and emotional balance. Psychoanalyst D. W. Winnicott once spoke of therapy as "bringing the patient from a state of not being able to play into a state of being able to play. . . . [P]laying is itself a form of therapy."[20] For people who have suffered a trauma or some other kind of severe psychological stress, the appearance of playful discontinuities in dream content may represent "green shoots" of potential healing and growth.

The third benefit of the dreaming-is-play approach is that it fits very well with neuroscientific research on brain activities in waking and sleeping, and specifically with the notion that dreaming can be understood as a subsystem of the brain's "default mode network."[21] This network governs how the brain operates "at rest," when it is not focused on an external task or problem. Marcus Raichle and his colleagues were the first to perform experiments showing that a closely interconnected set of neural regions (including portions of the temporal, parietal, and frontal lobes) remains remarkably active even when the brain is seemingly not doing anything in particular, just quietly idling.[22] Other researchers have connected the default network to similar brain activity patterns in daydreaming, mind wandering, and meditation. In all these phenomena, certain regions of the brain become highly activated when there is a pause in cognitively demanding, externally oriented tasks. According to psychologist Randy Buckner and colleagues, "the default network is a specific, anatomically defined brain system preferentially active when individuals are not focused on the external environment. . . . [T]he default network is active when individuals are engaged in internally focused tasks including autobiographical memory retrieval, envisioning the future, and conceiving the perspectives of others."[23]

Further research has shown that aspects of the default network are active in REM sleep and in deep or slow wave sleep.[24] Domhoff has made the strongest case that dreaming can be explained as a neurological subsystem of the default network: "[D]reams can be seen as a unique and more fully developed form of mind wandering, and therefore as the quintessential cognitive simulation."[25]

The language used by researchers to describe the default mode network is essentially the language of play. When no external tasks are requiring attention, the mind contents itself with an easy flow of loosely associated thoughts, images, feelings, and ideas. As Domhoff and others have argued, this is exactly what happens during sleep when external stimuli are screened out and the brain becomes sufficiently energized: the default network activates, the mind begins to wander, and the imagination is free to simulate anything and everything from the individual's past, present, or future. Dreaming, one could say, is the brain's default network at its most playful.

Concluding Response

The discontinuities between dreaming and waking are not necessarily breakdowns in mental functioning. In many cases, such as those involving metaphorical thinking, the discontinuities reflect meaningful aspects of the individual's waking thoughts and concerns. It is normal and healthy for humans to have bizarre, unrealistic, playful dreams. As a consequence, the answer to the opening question is yes, *everything* in a dream has potential meaning. More than that, *everything* in a dream has *many* potential meanings, an astonishing superabundance of possible connections with and beyond the individual's waking life. This is the most honest and evidence-based answer to the question, even though it may scandalize those who insist that scientific research must always lead to clear, singular, unambiguous results (and who think Freud must have been wrong about everything). To study the multiplicities of dreaming beyond this point will require a more sophisticated and innovative approach than that.

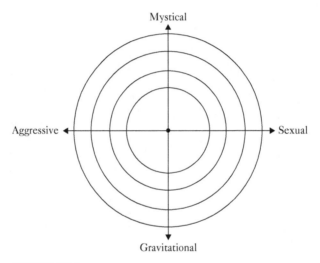

FIGURE III.I

PART III

Big Dreams

9

Aggressive

(Pertelote:) O dearest heart,
What's ailing you? Why do you groan and start?
Fie, what a sleeper! What a noise to make!
(Chanticleer:) Madam, I beg you not to take
Offence, but by the Lord I had a dream
So terrible just now I had to scream;
I can still feel my heart racing from fear.
God turn my dream to good and guard all here.

GEOFFREY CHAUCER, *The Nun's Priest's Tale*

Opening Question

Should people try to eliminate their nightmares?

All creatures, humans included, instinctively avoid that which appears harmful or threatening. This is a natural self-protective reaction, and it explains why most people pay little or no attention to nightmares of being chased or violently attacked. These upsetting dreams are filled with extremely disturbing images, distressing emotions, and painful physical sensations. It seems the most sensible approach a person could take would be to shun such nightmares in every way possible, and ideally to find a way of blocking them from happening in the first place.

The eighteenth-century Scottish philosopher Thomas Reid did exactly that when he trained himself to awaken every time his dreaming took a nightmarish turn. As an adolescent, Reid suffered recurrent dreams of being attacked by aggressive assailants, giving rise to painful emotions that carried into his waking awareness and troubled him through the day. So Reid decided that each night before going to sleep he would focus as intently as possible on the idea that his dreams were not real and he could stop them if wanted to. Eventually he succeeded in taming and then banishing the nightmares: "The effect of this commonly was, that

I immediately awoke. But I awoke calm and intrepid, which I thought a great acquisition. After this, my dreams were never very uneasy; and, in a short time, I dreamed not at all."[1]

Initial Response

Intense nightmares of aggression orient people's awareness toward potential threats in waking life.

Extremely vivid nightmares of being chased or attacked are fairly widespread among the general population, even though they rarely appear in the normal course of most people's dream lives. In this way they fit the definition of *big dreams*: infrequent, but highly memorable and impactful when they do occur. These kinds of nightmares have characteristic patterns of content (literal and metaphorical) that distinguish them from other dreams. Neuroscientists have made great progress in identifying the brain systems most likely to be active while such frightening experiences are happening. Intensely aggressive dreams have the psychological effect of stimulating people's waking awareness, preparing them for evolutionarily probable threats, and priming their mental and physical abilities to respond should such threats ever appear in waking reality.

Data and Discussion
Prototypical Patterns of Dreaming

The next four chapters expand on the idea that more scientific attention should be focused on the "black swans" of the dream world, namely big dreams. Studies of normal, ordinary dreams can only tell us so much. To understand the full range and potential of human dreaming, we must explore rare, unusual, and extraordinary types of oneiric experience.

These chapters build on the findings of the previous two parts: sleep is active and adaptive (Part I) and dreaming is imaginative play in sleep (Part II). The first part emphasized the dimensions of neuroplasticity in sleep, and the second part highlighted the innately playful creativity of dreaming. This third part looks at what happens when the evolved capacities for sleep and dreaming are pushed to their most extreme levels of intensification.

No typology can ever do justice to the boundless diversity of human dream experience. But enough good evidence already exists to identify several recurrent patterns in the form and content of big dreams. I have found it most useful to think of four *prototypes* of big dreaming experience: *aggressive, sexual, gravitational,* and *mystical*.[2] In figure III.1, these prototypes are mapped out along two axes. The horizontal line is the *relational* axis, expressing the quality of the dreamer's social interactions with other characters. The vertical line represents the *elemental* axis, reflecting the dreamer's experiences with gravity, mass, entropy, and other aspects of physical reality.

The concentric circles indicate a dream's intensity, memorability, and impact on the individual. At the center are dreams that possess insufficient strength to cross the memory threshold, dreams that never rise to the level of waking awareness. Most of what passes through the mind during each night's sleep is forgotten in this sense. Closer to the center are "little dreams" relating to the ordinary concerns of daily life. Farther out from the center are more intense dreams with greater likelihood of being remembered. The widest circle represents the boundary of sleep itself, which some dreams overleap with vivid and long-lasting effects on the dreamer's mind and body in waking life.[3]

Part III starts with the aggressive prototype of big dreaming, and not only because these kinds of dreams were influential in my own development. More important, such nightmares are often the first dreams people can remember, and sometimes the only dreams they can ever remember experiencing. The extremely negative emotions generated by big dreams like these immediately raise the question of how they could possibly have any valuable meaning or purpose in waking life. The strongest skeptical case against paying attention to big dreams would likely start with horrendously violent nightmares. These dreams may indeed be highly intensified and unusually memorable, but that just means their harmful effects are all the worse. Why should people pay any attention to emotionally damaging dreams like these?

Nightmare Frequencies

The Modern English word *nightmare* derives from the Old English *mare*, which was drawn from proto-Germanic legends and folk tales about *maron*, a female goblin who tormented people in their sleep. Some of the symptoms of an attack by *maron*, such as constricted breathing and feelings of extreme pressure on the chest, sound more like what researchers today would call an episode of sleep paralysis rather than a nightmare.[4] But the core meaning of the ancient word *nightmare* remains in common usage today: a vivid and intensely frightening dream of malevolent assault.

How often do nightmares occur? In the 2010 Demographic Survey I asked the participants (2,970 American adults) a question about how often they remembered a nightmare. The results appear in table 9.1.

These data confirm the idea that nightmares are an infrequent occurrence for most people. A large majority of the participants said they had nightmares less than once a month, or never. However, younger people reported higher nightmare frequencies than did the older people, especially the younger women (although there were relatively few of them in this survey).

The findings of the 2010 study agree with Tore Nielsen and Ross Levin's two observations in their 2007 article "Nightmares: A New Neurocognitive Model." First, "nightmares are known to be less frequent in elderly populations," and second, "females at all ages consistently report nightmares

Table 9.1 Frequency of Nightmare Recall in the 2010 Demographic Survey (N = 2,970)

	Almost every morning	Several times a week	Once a week	2 or 3 times a month	Less often than once a month	Never	Total number of responses
	Percent	Percent	Percent	Percent	Percent	Percent	
Gender							
Female	2	3	6	11	61	18	1,009
Male	1	3	6	9	56	25	1,831
Gender/Age							
Female 18–29	4	9	14	12	54	7	57
Female 30–49	2	6	8	16	57	11	222
Female 50–64	2	2	6	10	65	17	448
Female 65+	1	3	4	8	57	27	275
Male 18–29	1	4	11	18	51	16	134
Male 30–49	0	2	8	10	63	17	420
Male 50–64	1	2	4	9	59	25	783
Male 65+	1	4	5	7	48	34	491

Note: These six categories of nightmare recall follow the approach used by Michael Schredl in "Dream Recall: Models and Empirical Data." The answers have been adjusted, meaning "not sure" responses have been removed from the totals. The percentages have been rounded to the nearest whole number, so the sum of all the columns for each row may not equal exactly 100.

more often than do males."[5] The 2010 survey found that older people had lower nightmare recall than younger people, for both women and men. The biggest gender difference appeared in the earlier age groups, with more nightmares for the young women. The gender difference was much smaller in the later age groups, with the older men somewhat more likely to say they never remembered any nightmares.

Surveys that ask about nightmares in general usually receive answers that include both of the prototypes I refer to as *aggressive* and *gravitational*. To get a better sense of the frequency of nightmares with specifically aggressive content, we can look at research using the "Typical Dreams Questionnaire," or TDQ. This approach grew out of the work of early twentieth-century anthropologists like C. G. Seligman, who asked people in indigenous cultures around the world if they had recurrent dream scenarios like those experienced by people in modern Western societies.[6] One of the "types" of dreams Seligman found in all cultures was the dream of being chased or attacked. In 1958 Griffith and his colleagues developed a typical dreams survey asking questions about 53 different kinds of dreams, which they used with groups of American and Japanese college students. Since then, several other researchers have used versions of Griffith et al.'s TDQ survey with many different populations. The result is a multicultural collection of high-quality data that can be used to gauge the general frequency of various types of dreams.

One of the standard TDQ questions asks if the participant has ever experienced a dream of "being chased or attacked." Table 9.2 shows the results for eight different groups of participants: the Japanese and American college students from Griffith et al.'s 1958 study; Israeli Jewish and Arab students from Giora et al.'s 1972 study; Canadian college students from Nielsen et al.'s 2001 study; German college students from Schredl et al.'s 2004 study; Jordanian college students from Nasser and Bulkeley's 2009 study; and American adults from the 2007 and 2010 Demographic Surveys.[7]

The TDQ has its limits, of course. A "yes" answer could indicate the person has experienced that type of dream only once, or every single night of his or her life. It is impossible to know if the participants have correctly understood the question or if they have honestly answered it. A single TDQ study by itself would not be very persuasive. But in our case, the results of these multiple TDQ studies correspond closely with each other and with the results of other methods of measuring nightmare frequency, giving us more confidence in the basic patterns emerging from the data.

Table 9.2 Typical Dreams: Being Chased or Attacked

Survey	Number of participants	Percent answering "yes"
Griffith et al. 1958		
American male	134	77
American female	116	78
Japanese male	132	90
Japanese female	91	92
Giora et al. 1972		
Kibbutz female	114	70
Kibbutz male	102	69
Arab female	101	51
Arab male	308	66
Nielsen et al. 2001		
Canadian female	840	83
Canadian male	341	78
Schredl et al. 2004		
German female	376	89
German male	68	87
Nasser and Bulkeley 2009		
Jordanian total	279 f, 47 m	48
Demographic Surveys 2007 and 2010 combined		
American female	1,436	53
American male	2,239	49
Demographic Survey 2010 by gender and age		
American female 18–29	58	76
American female 30–49	233	65
American female 50–64	471	57
American female 65+	288	44

Table 9.2 Continued

Survey	Number of participants	Percent answering "yes"
American male 18–29	144	62
American male 30–49	436	61
American male 50–64	809	50
American male 65+	517	39

In every one of these studies, the "chasing or attacked" question had one of the highest frequencies of affirmative answers of all the questions asked. This is clearly a familiar type of dream for people all across the world, even if they actually experience nightmares like this only rarely. Most of the TDQ studies involved college student participants, so the sample inevitably had a younger bias. But looking at the results for the 2010 Demographic Survey, which included many older people, we find the same pattern noted a moment ago: higher frequencies of chasing/attacked dreams for younger people, especially younger women, and lower frequencies for both men and women in the oldest age group.[8]

Motifs

Numbers alone cannot tell the story of how these kinds of dreams feel to the afflicted individual. Even a long, detailed narrative is incapable of fully conveying the experiential qualities of a terrifying nightmare. The Argentinian author Jorge Luis Borges wrote a wonderfully erudite essay on "Nightmares" (part of his 1980 collection *Seven Nights*) in which he emphasized this point by describing "the most terrible" nightmare of his life, about a sightless "King of the North" standing at the foot of his bed. The dream had a distinct carry-over effect on Borges: "Then I awoke. But I continued to see the king for a while, because he had made such a strong impression on me."[9] Borges knew the ghastly horror of his dream would be difficult to appreciate from an outsider's perspective: "Retold, my dream is nothing; dreamt, it was terrible."[10] Certain aspects of dreaming experience remain forever inaccessible to anyone but the dreamer.

Still, if we listen to the retellings of many different nightmares from many different people, we begin to notice a few motifs that recur especially frequently. A *motif* can be defined as a basic theme or scenario, a narrative pattern that shapes the plot of the dream. A brief look at some of the most common motifs in aggressive nightmares will give us a better understanding of the emotional experiences they generate.[11]

Borges's dream of the King of the North embodied one such motif, namely an *invasion of intimate personal space*. The king appeared inside Borges's room, standing at the foot of his bed, close enough to touch. The extreme terror of this dream was generated not by anything the king did—he just stood there, gazing blindly upwards—but by his sheer presence in what should be the safest, most private place in a person's life.[12] Many nightmares feature this motif of a menacing intruder who enters the dreamer's bedroom with ominous intent. The high frequency of bedrooms as a setting for nightmares can be illustrated via word search analysis. The 2010 Demographic Survey gathered reports of most recent dreams and worst nightmares, and the nightmares had many more references to beds and bedrooms (9% for the women, 13% for the men) than did the most recent dreams (4% and 1%, respectively).[13] Here is one example from that survey, from a 59-year-old man from Pennsylvania: "I dreamed that aliens had emerged from a wall by my bed and were dragging me away, back with them. I woke shaking with fear and silently screaming. It was weeks before I was free of the dread and shock. Even though this dream occurred nearly 15 years ago, I can still feel the shock and horror of it."[14]

Another common nightmare motif has to do with a sense of *being trapped in an inescapable fight*, unable to stop, overcome, or get away from the attack. A classical expression of this scenario comes in Book 22 of the *Iliad*, when Homer used relentless chasing dreams as a metaphorical source to describe the climactic battle between Achilles and Hektor: "as in a dream a man is not able to follow one who runs from him, nor can the runner escape, nor the other pursue him, so he [Achilles] could not run him [Hektor] down in his speed, nor the other get clear."[15] A special kind of horror seems to be aroused by this motif of being trapped in an eternal conflict, whether it involves endless chasing, fighting, or some other kind of aggressive struggle.

Sometimes the nonstop violence takes an ideological form, as found in several reports in Charlotte Beradt's remarkable 1966 book *The Third Reich of Dreams*, which presented a large collection of dreams gathered from people living in Germany in 1933–1939, during the rise of Adolph Hitler and the Nazis. Many of the dreams reflected a nightmarish sense of totalitarian mind control. One of Beradt's participants dreamed repeatedly that his radio was blaring over and over, "In the name of the Fuhrer, in the name of the Fuhrer ... ," while a girl told her she dreamed of seeing the slogan "Public Interest Comes before Self-Interest" printed in endless repetition on a banner.[16]

Many nightmares feature aggressive animals and threats to the individual's family. But these themes are also found in normal, non-nightmarish dreams. A more distinctive motif regarding the characters in nightmares is the threatening presence of a *monstrous alien*. The dreamer is being chased or attacked by an inhuman creature or creatures from some unknown, otherworldly realm. Word search results support the distinctiveness of this motif: the worst nightmares in the 2010 Demographic Survey had many more references to fantastic beings like monsters, aliens, and demons (10% for the women, 11% for the men) than were found in the most recent dreams (2% and 1%, respectively).

In some nightmares the frightening antagonists have vaguely human forms, but they are so overwhelmingly numerous and weirdly impersonal that they assume monstrous proportions. As a cross-cultural example, anthropologist Marie Reay wrote about her research on the dreams of the Kuma people from New Guinea's Central Highlands. She found that all the men periodically had a nightmare they referred to as "The Dream Struggle." Reay said the nightmare always began with the dreamer "alone fighting a vast crowd of men whose faces he can see but dimly. They are nearly overpowering him when he manages, with a colossal effort, to brush them all aside with a single gesture and knock them down. But they spring up and rush against him again."[17] This was a terrifying and otherworldly nightmare that haunted the waking lives of these otherwise brave and fearless Kuma warriors.

One final motif of aggressive dreaming is worth mentioning: nightmares in which *the dreamer is the aggressor*, violently striking out at others. Some of the TDQ studies mentioned earlier included a question about dreams of killing someone else, and the results indicated about a quarter of the population in various cultures had experienced this nightmarish theme.[18] Fear may be involved in these upsetting dreams, but so are feelings of shock at one's own aggressive behavior. As an example, one of the respondents to a "most memorable dream" survey in 2011 among American adults was a 65-year-old woman from Montana who reported the following: "I helped my husband kill an IRS agent that was after us for unpaid taxes. We buried his or her body in the woods and never spoke of it again. This dream recurred for several years and seemed extremely real. I finally asked my husband if it was real. He laughed and said no, and I never had the dream again."[19]

An ancient instance of this motif involved King Shabaka, an Ethiopian monarch of the eighth century B.C.E. whose empire reached as far north as Egypt. According to the Greek historian Herodotus, King Shabaka "had seen in his sleep a vision, in which it seemed to him that a man came and stood by him and counseled him to gather together all the priests in Egypt and cut them asunder in the midst."[20] The king interpreted this murderous dream as a temptation to do something so evil that the gods would be justified in destroying him as punishment. Sorely disturbed by the dream, he voluntarily withdrew his forces from Egypt and returned to his homeland.

Many other motifs could be considered and explored in greater detail, but these four give us enough to begin an empirical analysis of the experiential qualities of aggressively nightmarish dreams. An invasion of intimate personal space, being trapped in an endless struggle, fighting against a monstrous alien, violently attacking someone else—these motifs consistently evoke strong emotional reactions of fear, dread, shock, and horror, and they have long-lasting effects on waking awareness. The frequency of their recurrence in various cultural and historical settings suggests they are grounded in deeply rooted networks of brain/mind functioning.

Reverse Engineering

There is no neuroscientific research directly bearing on the activities of the brain during these extraordinary kinds of nightmares. True, a great deal of study has been devoted to the nightmares of people suffering PTSD, and some of the results are relevant to non-traumatic nightmares. But we should be cautious about relying too heavily on PTSD research for understanding nightmares in general. A malfunctioning brain is not always a good model for understanding the brain's activities in normal, healthy conditions. The fact that PTSD includes recurrent nightmares as one of its prominent symptoms does not necessarily mean that all nightmares are the product of neuropathology. Many people who are healthy and non-traumatized occasionally have extremely frightening nightmares of aggressive interactions with other characters. Those kinds of dreams have not been directly studied from a neurological perspective, and they are the ones I believe are most in need of better scientific explanation.

The principle of *reverse engineering* is drawn from the industrial and military practice of analyzing a device (such as a competitor's product or an enemy's weapon) in terms of the mechanisms that were most likely involved in its creation.[21] Reverse engineering provides a framework for indirect reasoning about processes for which we do not have direct evidence. In our case the reverse engineering question is this: Which brain systems are most likely to be involved in the production of extremely intense nightmares? Aggressive dreams of being chased or attacked happen to so many people, in so many cultures and periods of history, that it seems very likely they arise from well-established capacities of the brain that are innate in our species. What might those capacities be?

To start, they must have something to do with creating an all-consuming sense of vivid realism. Many of these nightmares involve states of acute visual, tactile, and kinetic awareness, and they strike the dreamer as no less real than anything he or she experiences in waking life. The pervasive feelings of intense fear and stress point to the influence of brain systems responsible for fast, instinctive responses to danger. Some degree of social intelligence seems to be at work, too. The dreamer's mind is actively engaged in recognizing other characters, evaluating their intentions, and making quick tactical decisions about how to react to threats.

All of these features and qualities of aggressive nightmare have clear correlations with specific aspects of brain functioning during sleep, many of which we discussed in earlier chapters.

Vivid realism: Researchers have shown the overall level of electrical activity in the brain (as measured by the EEG) is basically the same in normal REM sleep as it is in the waking state. It seems likely that electrical output increases dramatically during intense nightmares of being chased or attacked, to levels far above the normal baseline output. The hyper-aroused condition of the brain supports people's visceral feelings that these dreams are no less real, and perhaps more real, than anything they experience in ordinary waking life. Researchers have also found the limbic system of the brain is particularly active in REM sleep, which is significant because the limbic system is involved in reality monitoring (i.e., being aware of the external world). In Mark Solms's neuropsychological research, patients with damage to the frontal-limbic region suffered severe impairments in their ability to monitor reality and distinguish dreaming from waking. Solms's findings suggest that if the electrical activity in this specific region of the brain were *stimulated* rather than *damaged*, it would further enhance the feelings of hyper-realism during an aggressive nightmare experience.

Sensory awareness: The normal course of REM sleep involves heightened activity in the occipital and temporal regions of the brain, which are associated with visual and auditory processing. In extremely frightening nightmares overflowing with complex images and sounds, it seems likely these particular neural systems are working at very high levels of activation. Another finding from Solms is that spatial cognition in dreaming (the ability to perceive one's surroundings and physically navigate through them) depends on the inferior parietal region of the brain, which is normally active in REM sleep. This implies that unusually kinetic nightmares with long sequences of vigorous chasing, hiding, and fighting may be neurologically correlated with extreme activation in the brain's inferior parietal region.

Fear response: Many researchers have found heightened activity during REM sleep in various parts of the limbic system, particularly the amygdala and hippocampus, both of which are related to emotion, memory, and instinctual responses. The amygdala is well known for its central role in the brain's response to frightening situations.[22] If any part of the brain is highly stimulated during aggressive nightmares, it would have to be the amygdala. Also very active in REM sleep is the anterior cingulate cortex, which connects the amygdala to the prefrontal parts of the brain. The anterior cingulate is vital to the brain's "executive cognitive system" of focused attention and decision-making. This neurological circuit between the limbic system and the prefrontal cortex enables an extremely fast connectivity between instincts and awareness. During the experience of a terrifying nightmare of being chased or attacked, the limbic-prefrontal circuit of the brain may be operating at its maximal capacity.

Social intelligence: The medial prefrontal cortex has been identified as an important neural substrate for social intelligence. It plays a necessary role in giving people the ability to perceive and empathize with other people's feelings and intentions ("theory of mind"). This part of the brain is known to be active in REM sleep, and it seems likely to have a strong influence on people's experiences in vivid nightmares in which they have extensive interactions with the monstrous aliens and other aggressive antagonists.

Let us pause for a moment and consider a larger fact that emerges from all of this research. The brain systems most likely to be centrally involved in aggressive nightmares are normal, natural parts of the human sleep cycle. We do not have to invoke anything radically new in how the brain works; we can account for the experiential qualities of aggressive nightmares by drawing on solid, evidence-based research that already exists. This means that big dreams like these can be best explained neurologically as *intensifications* of what the brain is already doing in sleep. Such dreams are unusually dynamic expressions of the neural power of the ordinary dreaming process, amplified to extreme but not necessarily pathological levels.

Threat Simulations

We have enough data now to discuss the possibility that aggressive nightmares may have an adaptive function. Recall the epigraph to this chapter, when Chanticleer awakened from a harrowing nightmare that left his "heart racing from fear." He went on to describe the dream to his wife, Pertelote:

> I dreamt that roaming up and down a while
> Within our yard I saw a kind of beast,
> A sort of hound that tried or seemed at least
> To try and seize me . . . would have killed me dead!
> His colour was a blend of yellow and red,
> His ears and tail were tipped with sable fur
> Unlike the rest; he was a russet cur.
> Small was his snout, his eyes were glowing bright.
> It was enough to make one die of fright.[23]

Chanticleer and Pertelote engaged in a long and quite scholarly debate about the proper way to classify the dream, with both of them making accurate and insightful references to ancient philosophers, famous writers, and medical authorities. (It should be noted that Chanticleer was a rooster, and Pertelote was a hen.) Pertelote took the position of a skeptic, using the best scientific information of her time (the fourteenth century) to argue that Chanticleer's dream was nothing but the meaningless side effect of an imbalance of bodily humors. She tried to shame him into agreement by questioning his masculinity: "Have you no manly heart to match your beard? And can a dream reduce you to such terror? Dreams are a vanity, God knows, pure error."[24] Chanticleer responded by describing several reports from history of people whose dreams accurately predicted events in their waking lives: "Dreams have quite often been significations as well of triumphs as of tribulations. . . . My dream undoubtedly foretells confusion, it bodes me ill, I say."[25]

Yet in the end Chanticleer ignored his own ominous interpretation, and with Pertelote's scornful, humiliating words ringing in his ears he went out into the barnyard like it was any other day. There he encountered "a coal-tipped fox of sly iniquity" who had sneaked into the yard during the night—a fox whose shape, fur, and coloring matched in all details the appearance of the beast in Chanticleer's dream. Suffice it to say that Chanticleer escaped with his life only because the fox was even more foolish and vain than the rooster.

This whimsical story from several hundred years ago illuminates the basic principle behind one of the better theories about the potentially adaptive function of aggressive nightmares. The *threat simulation theory*

(TST) developed by Antti Revonsuo and Katja Valli uses ideas from evolutionary psychology to analyze dream experiences in terms of the survival needs of our species. The TST claims that nightmares of being chased or attacked are rooted in a dreaming function that simulates likely threats and dangers in waking life so people will be better prepared to deal with such problems should they arise in waking life. By creating a virtual reality of what it would feel like to be violently attacked or chased, the nightmares provide people with an opportunity to practice possible responses to these kinds of survival-threatening situations. Revonsuo emphasized the heightened realism of physical actions in dreaming:

> Mental imagery of motor actions uses the same motor representations and central neural mechanisms that are used to generate actual actions; moreover, dreamed action is experientially far more realistic than mere imagined action. Therefore we have good reasons to believe that dreamed action is equivalent to real action as far as the underlying brain mechanisms are concerned. . . . [T]he dream-production system can be seen as an ancestral defense mechanism comparable to other biological defense mechanisms whose function is to automatically elicit efficient protective responses when appropriate cues are encountered.[26]

Presumably the early humans who had alarming dreams like these were better able to defend themselves against a variety of threats, increasing their chances of survival compared to those humans who did not have such dreams. Thus, a threat-simulating propensity of dreaming would eventually be incorporated by natural selection into the innate mental machinery of our species.

Similar ideas have been developed over the years by other researchers. Jung spoke of "the prospective function" of dreams; Montague Ullman said dreaming worked to maintain an optimal state of "vigilance"; Frederick Snyder viewed sleep and dreaming as a "sentinel" system to prepare for environmental danger; Rosalind Cartwright argued that dreams serve as "rehearsals" for future actions; and Jeremy Taylor has focused on recurrent nightmares as warnings of psycho-spiritual danger in the dreamer's waking life.[27] All of them agree with the TST that dreaming is oriented toward future challenges, with some kind of preparatory function that improves a person's ability to survive and adapt successfully in the waking world.

Revonsuo's original formulation of the TST in 2000 received a great deal of criticism for its shortcomings. It did not explain the large portion of dreams that do not involve threats, it did not fit well with research on PTSD nightmares, it made questionable assumptions about prehistoric human life, and it was hazy about the mechanisms that lead from threat-simulating dreams to improved waking behavior. If it were presented as a general theory of all dreams, the TST would clearly be unsupportable. But as a more focused explanation for the big dreaming prototype of aggressive nightmares, the TST works pretty well, and so do the parallel theories of Jung, Ullman, and the others. They all emphasize the practical benefits of frightening, worst-case-scenario dreams in terms of preparing the dreamer's mind and body for the possibility of similar situations arising in waking life. The carry-over effects guarantee the nightmare dangers will make an extremely vivid and alarming impression on waking awareness. "God turn my dream to good and guard all here" was Chanticleer's instinctively cautious, security-minded response to his nightmare.

The TST concentrates on literal threats, but the simulations can portray metaphorical dangers, too. For example, a frightening dream of being attacked by a wolf may not reflect an actual danger from wolves in waking life. Instead, the wolf may be a metaphor for some person or situation in the dreamer's life that feels "wolf-like." This metaphorical process helps to explain the high incidence of monsters, aliens, and other fantastic beings in people's nightmares. These are fantasy characters with no literal, physical connection to the waking world, which makes them especially appealing targets for a variety of metaphorical meanings having to do with amorphous fears and ambiguous dangers.

Concluding Response

Nightmares following a severe trauma may require professional help to diminish and if possible eliminate the pathologically intrusive dreams. But not all nightmares are caused by trauma. Indeed, one might say that threat-simulating nightmares of being chased or attacked are driven by an instinctive desire to avoid future traumas by increasing waking awareness of possible dangers in the environment. With its strong carry-over effects, cross-cultural motifs, and deep roots in the brain's activities in sleep, the aggressive prototype of big dreaming can be regarded as an adaptive psychological function with beneficial effects on our evolutionary chances for survival.

10

Sexual

Take a little nap where the roots all twist,
Squished a rotten peach in my fist,
And dreamed about you, woman

THE PRESIDENTS OF THE UNITED STATES OF AMERICA,
"PEACHES"

Opening Question

Do sexual dreams promote immoral behavior?

The most scandalizing thing about dreaming is the way it sets loose a perverse phantasmagoria of erotic feelings and desires that often deviate dramatically from waking life standards. With no apparent concern for traditional morality or common decency, dreams break every sexual taboo there is, doing so with vivid realism and in elaborate anatomical detail. In his autobiographical work *Confessions*, the early Christian theologian Augustine (354–430 C.E.) described his experiences of sexual dreams. Augustine had taken a vow of chastity after his conversion to Christianity, but he was surprised and dismayed to find he continued having sexual dreams with highly arousing content: "[I]n my memory . . . there still live images of acts which were fixed there by my sexual habit. . . . While I am awake they have no force, but in sleep they not only arouse pleasure but even elicit consent, and are very like the actual act."[1] Augustine admitted his dreams had so much "force upon my flesh" that they violated the moral boundaries of his new religious life, leading him to wonder if he needed to separate his waking identity from the shady source of those nocturnal temptations: "During this time of sleep surely it is not my true self? . . . [H]ow great a difference between myself at the time when I am asleep and myself when I return to the waking state."

Whether or not one shares Augustine's religious faith, a great many people do agree with his skeptical wariness toward sexual dreams that unleash inappropriate desires and crude animal passions best kept under strict moral control.

Initial Response

Vivid sexual dreams reflect an innate brain/mind capacity for imaginatively priming the human reproductive system.

At the other end of the relational axis from aggressive dreams (figure III.1), sexual dreams represent a second prototypical form of the dreaming imagination. Physically realistic dreams of sexual experience are widely distributed throughout the human population, and they can be extremely memorable when they occur. If we use the term "sexual" in the biologically broad sense of "procreative," including not just romantic activity but also pregnancy and childbirth, we find evidence showing that sexual dreams provide survival-enhancing stimulation to the human reproductive process. Big dreams of sexuality envision a wide variety of possibilities, opportunities, and obstacles in people's procreative lives. Whether or not they violate conventional standards of social morality, these dreams serve the valuable evolutionary function of sparking people's sexual desires and preparing them for reproductive behaviors.

Data and Discussion
Frequencies

The methodological challenges of dream research become most difficult with the study of sexual dreams. For understandable reasons of privacy and discretion, many people are reluctant to share the details of their dreams with sexual themes. Added to that, many religious traditions (e.g., Buddhism, Christianity, and Islam) warn their members to beware of the moral dangers of sexual dreams. For people influenced by these traditions, such warnings put negative pressure on their willingness to talk openly and honestly about their experiences. All of this means that research based on surveys and interviews will probably understate the frequency of sexual dreams to an unknown degree.

With those cautions in mind, let us consider some of the evidence about how many people have had such dreams. We can start by returning to the TDQ mentioned in the previous chapter, this time looking at people's answers to the question, "Have you ever had a dream of sexual experience?" This is perhaps the most general question that could be asked about the phenomenon. The results appear in table 10.1.

The "no answer" response for the Arab Israeli participants in Giora et al.'s 1972 study reflects the fact that their version of the TDQ had to exclude the question on sexual experiences: "[T]he school principals of the Arab girls did not allow it to appear in the questionnaire."[2] A similar cultural reluctance to answer this question may account for the relatively

Table 10.1 Typical Dreams: Sexual

Surveys	Number of total participants	Percent answering "yes"
Griffith et al. 1958		
American male	134	93
American female	116	36
Japanese male	132	85
Japanese female	91	43
Giora et al. 1972		
Kibbutz female	114	62
Kibbutz male	102	76
Arab female		no answer
Arab male		no answer
Nielsen et al. 2001		
Canadian female	840	73
Canadian male	341	85
Schredl et al. 2004		
German female	376	86
German male	68	93
Nasser and Bulkeley 2009		
Jordanian total	279 f, 47 m	25

Table 10.1 Continued

Surveys	Number of total participants	Percent answering "yes"
Demographic Surveys 2007 and 2010 combined		
American female	1,436	51
American male	2,239	67
Demographic Survey 2010 by gender and age		
American female 18–29	58	84
American female 30–49	233	73
American female 50–64	471	59
American female 65+	288	39
American male 18–29	144	82
American male 30–49	436	75
American male 50–64	809	70
American male 65+	517	60

low frequency (25%) of sexual dreams reported in the Jordanian survey of mostly female Arab college students in 2009.

All the other surveys showed high, and in some cases very high, frequencies of people having at least one memorable dream of sexual experience. As noted earlier, survey results like these probably understate the frequency of sexual dreams, so the findings here indicate this type of dream is a familiar experience for a significant majority of the general population. This supports the notion that such dreams emerge from hardwired brain/mind capacities shared by everyone in our species.

In each of the different cultures sampled by these studies, the males reported higher frequencies of sexual dreams than the females did. The Griffith et al. study in 1958 had the biggest gender gap, with the American and Japanese males (93% and 85%) answering yes at about double the rate of the American and Japanese females (36% and 43%). The Schredl et al. study in 2004 had the narrowest male/female gender gap (93% vs. 86%).

The 2010 Demographic Survey included an older group of participants, with a median age between 50 and 64. This makes it different from the other TDQ studies, all of which used college students in their late teens and early twenties. Looking at the 2010 survey results by age group, an interesting pattern appears. The frequency of "yes" answers was highest for the youngest group, with the females slightly higher than the males. Then the frequency diminished for the older age groups, especially for the females, and a significant gender gap appeared in the oldest age group, with males at 60% and females at 39%.

We do not know if this means the older people are less likely to have had sexual dream experiences, or if they are less likely to remember having had such experiences. The greater likelihood of memory impairments in older groups is undoubtedly a factor here, although it is also possible that cultural and social changes over the past several decades have made younger people (especially females?) more willing to report their sexual dreams.

Those are open questions to be explored in future research. For now, the TDQ evidence seems fairly clear that younger people are more likely than older people to report dreams of sexual experiences. Males are more likely than females to report such dreams, especially when they reach older age.

Further insights come from analyzing the 2010 Demographic Survey results in relation to other demographic variables. As seen in table 10.2, the "yes" frequencies vary only slightly among people who do or do not have a college degree. The same is true regarding annual income: there is no big difference in sexual dream frequencies between the poorest and wealthiest people.

However, large differences appear in relation to the factors of political ideology and religious worship service attendance.[3] As discussed earlier, these two demographic variables have considerable overlap in the current American social landscape, so it makes sense to see the same basic pattern in both cases. People on the political Left and/or people who rarely or never attend religious worship services are significantly more likely to report sexual dreams than are people on the political Right and/or people who attend religious worship services once a week or more. The difference is not absolute; people who are religiously active and politically conservative also report sexual dreams at high frequencies. But people who are on the political Left and are not religiously active report even higher frequencies of dreams with sexual experiences. This basic difference appears in all age groups. For example, younger conservatives report more sexual dreams than older conservatives do, but not as many as younger liberals and progressives.

Another way of measuring the frequency of sexual dreams is to analyze large collections of dreams from various groups and individuals, using the word search method to count how many reports have at least one

Table 10.2 2010 Demographic Survey Responses to Typical Dreams: Sexual

	Education, female	
	No college degree	College degree +
	Percent	Percent
Yes	54	61
No	38	31
Not sure	8	7

	Education, male	
	No college degree	College degree +
	Percent	Percent
Yes	68	70
No	24	23
Not sure	8	6

	Personal finances, female					
	<$25,000	$25,000–$35,000	$35,000–$50,000	$50,000–$75,000	$75,000–100,000	$100,000+
	Percent	Percent	Percent	Percent	Percent	Percent
Yes	63	50	53	63	64	66
No	29	45	36	27	29	30
Not sure	8	5	11	9	7	4

	Personal finances, male					
	<$25,000	$25,000–$35,000	$35,000–$50,000	$50,000–$75,000	$75,000–$100,000	$100,000+
	Percent	Percent	Percent	Percent	Percent	Percent
Yes	75	75	70	69	71	73
No	17	18	24	25	23	22
Not sure	8	7	6	5	6	5

(continued)

Table 10.2 Continued

Political ideology, female					
Progressive	Liberal	Moderate	Libertarian	Conservative	Very Conservative
Percent	Percent	Percent	Percent	Percent	Percent
Yes					
70	69	58	65	45	50
No					
23	22	36	29	48	40
Not sure					
6	9	7	6	8	10

Political ideology, male					
Progressive	Liberal	Moderate	Libertarian	Conservative	Very Conservative
Percent	Percent	Percent	Percent	Percent	Percent
Yes					
85	80	70	76	63	62
No					
11	16	22	21	29	31
Not sure					
4	4	9	3	8	7

reference to a sexually related word. Of course, this approach is vulnerable to the same problem of self-censorship as we found with the TDQ method. Some people are reluctant to share the sexual details of their dreams, even in anonymous settings with complete protection of their personal identities. As a consequence, the word search results probably represent the lower end of the actual frequencies in the general population.

Table 10.3 shows the results of searching for sexually related words in the sets of dreams I have been combining into the SDDb male and female baselines.

These results indicate sexual themes are not especially frequent in the ordinary course of dream recall. There is still a gender gap, but a slight one, with the males somewhat more likely than the females to have sexually related words in their dreams.

The picture becomes more complex when we apply the same word search process to a series of dreams from particular individuals. Table 10.4 presents the results of searching for sexually related words in 10 of the longest individual series in the SDDb, several of which have already been mentioned in earlier chapters.

Table 10.3 Frequencies of Sexually Related Words in the Baselines

	Surveys	
	Number of total dreams	Percent of dreams having at least one reference to sexuality
HVDC females	490	4
HVDC males	491	11
Miami Home	125	7
Miami Lab	187	6
International Survey females	790	7
International Survey males	645	5
Santa Clara Dreams	811	5
Demographic Surveys females	1004	3
Demographic Surveys males	665	4

Each of these individuals regularly recorded his or her dreams in a written journal over a lengthy period of time. The results in table 10.4 show great variability in their frequencies of sexual content, from 0% for the natural scientist and 1% for Will at the low end to 38% for Bea's second journal at the high end. Right away, this tells us that the gender gap is not absolute. Males can have very low frequencies of sexual references and females can have very high frequencies.

The differences in the frequencies displayed in table 10.4 seem to have less to do with gender per se, and more to do with the waking life circumstances of the dreamers. The natural scientist was a 39-year-old bachelor at the time he recorded his dreams, and he apparently had little or no romantic life. Will was a melancholy, emotionally troubled young man in his twenties who also had no romantic life to speak of. Bea, by contrast, was involved in her most serious romantic relationship and first sexual experiences of her life during the time of her second journal. The frequencies of sexual themes in these three people's dreams accurately reflected the importance of sexual concerns, interests, and experiences in their waking lives.

The wide variability among individuals suggests that the prototype of sexually themed dreaming is a latent potential in everyone, but it may not be activated in some people's lives, depending on their personal circumstances and cultural context.

Table 10.4 Frequencies of Sexually Related Words in Individual Dream Series

Series	Number of total dreams	Percent of dreams having at least one reference to sexuality
Natural scientist	234	0
Barb Sanders 250	250	20
Van	185	18
Bea journal 1	223	18
Bea journal 2	63	38
Lawrence	206	5
RB	51	18
Paul	136	8
Lola	102	14
Will	96	1
Jordan	50	11

Motifs

As with aggressive nightmares, sexual dreams can be qualitatively ana-lyzed and studied in terms of their recurrent motifs. Although people's reluctance to talk about sexuality makes it hard to gauge how often certain specific themes and narrative scenarios occur, we can still identify a few motifs that appear especially prominent.

The first would simply be the *ecstasy of sexual arousal*, often leading to physical orgasm. The nineteenth-century psychologist Julius Nelson referred to these experiences as "gonekboles," and researchers today use terms like "nocturnal emissions" and "wet dreams" to refer to a phenome-non that occurs in both males and females, especially during adolescence and early adulthood (more on this later). The carry-over effects of these cli-mactic dreams are unmistakable in terms of their highly arousing impact on the individual's body, exactly as would occur during a sexual encounter in waking life. This is what Augustine meant when he admitted his sexual dreams were so physically realistic they felt "very like the actual act."

A second motif has to do with *violations of taboos* in the individual's culture about inappropriate sexual behavior. This is the licentious streak in dreaming that prompted the ancient Greek philosopher Plato to warn people against the "bestial and savage" part of the soul that takes over the mind in sleep: "It does not shrink from attempting incestual inter-course, in its dream, with a mother or with any man or god or beast. . . .

[A] terrible, fierce, and lawless class of desires exists in every man, even in those of us who have every appearance of being decent people. Its existence is revealed in dreams."[4] Different societies draw the lines in different places between what is and is not allowed sexually, but every human community has some kind of moral code about people's sexual behavior. Dreams have a disturbing tendency to flout those codes and portray people engaging in a colorful variety of illicit situations that go far beyond their actual waking life experiences.

Pregnancy and childbirth is a third motif that should be included in a discussion of the sexual prototype of big dreaming. Of course, men's dreams rarely have this motif, but for women dreams of pregnancy and childbirth can be very powerful experiences, particularly in adolescence and early adulthood. Sometimes the dreams accompany an actual pregnancy, and other times they occur before the woman has ever been pregnant. An example of the latter came in the 2013 Demographic Surveys, with the following dream report from a 25-year-old woman who was single with no children: "I think I was *pregnant* in the dream. It felt so real! I could feel kicking. I remember walking in the dream. I just kept walking and ran in to people who were surprised to see me. That is all I can really remember, but it felt so real!" Many religious traditions such as Hinduism, Jainism, Buddhism, and Christianity have stories about women experiencing divine conception dreams heralding their pregnancy with a special child whose birth will bring new life, energy, and wisdom into the world.[5] This motif is widely distributed historically and culturally, and it seems to make a considerable impact on people's waking awareness when it occurs.

Reverse Engineering the Brain's Activities in Sexual Dreams

Highly memorable dreams about sexuality occur to so many people from so many different backgrounds that we can feel confident the experiences are generated at some level by cognitive and neurological functions shared all across our species. If we pursue that idea, it raises the question of what might be the most likely brain/mind systems involved in producing such experiences. To answer that question, we have to try reverse engineering these dreams.

Looking at the various motifs and themes of sexual dreaming, it seems that several experiential qualities have to be accounted for. One is the vivid realism and acute perceptual sensitivity of these dreams—just like aggressive nightmares, they feel completely real while they are happening, as real as anything that occurs in waking life. Another quality to explain is the complex social cognition that goes into the dreamer's intimate interactions with other characters. This includes all the thought processes, emotional evaluations, spoken conversations, and nonverbal communications that occur in these dreams. A third quality has to do with the physiological responses of sexual arousal, which in many cases produce feelings of extreme pleasure. Fourth, there is the tendency to portray incredibly strange and counterfactual scenarios that seem far removed from actual waking reality.

Here again, we do not have to look far to find plausible, scientifically grounded explanations for these recurrent features of sexual dreaming.

Vivid realism: The brain's capacity to generate an internal state of high arousal in sleep is well known, thanks to several decades of EEG studies measuring patterns of neuroelectrical activity through the sleep cycle. During sexual experiences in waking life, people's brains are clearly operating at very high levels of overall arousal. There is every reason to believe the same neural processes are at work in the sexual experiences of dreaming, helping to enhance their lifelike qualities and sharpening their sensory perceptions. These processes involve increased activation in the frontal-limbic, occipital, temporal, and inferior parietal regions of the brain, as discussed in the previous chapter. Neuroscientists have also found that visual stimuli have a more sexually arousing effect on men than on women, and this might account for some of the gender gap in sexual dreaming, since the brain regions responsible for visual imagination are highly active during REM sleep.[6]

Social intelligence: Despite their long reputation as "bestial" and "savage," sexual dreams frequently include rational thoughts and reflections that indicate the workings of high-order cognition devoted to interpersonal relations. This points to a probable role for the medial prefrontal cortex, which underlies our "theory of mind" ability to recognize other people's thoughts, feelings, and intentional behaviors. In sexual dreams with a great deal of conversation, flirting, and/or seduction, the prefrontal cortex is also likely to be very active. This part of the brain is associated with focused attention and goal-seeking strategies, and it is usually less active in PS than in waking. But the prefrontal cortex seems to come back online during certain kinds of lucid and metacognitive dreaming (to be discussed later in the book), and something similar may happen in sexual dreams when the dreamer's awareness becomes intensely focused on, and attentive to, his or her romantic partner.

Physiological responses: In chapter 3 we discussed what happens to the body during sleep, including a significant increase in blood flow to the genitals during REM sleep for both men and women. The neurological triggers for these bodily changes are located deep in the brainstem, indicating their long evolutionary history in our species. Not all dreams have overtly sexual content, so we cannot say that sexual dreams are caused by this automatic physiological system. Instead, we can say that sexual dreams intensify that system, building on the natural cycles of genital arousal to generate a thoroughly realistic sexual experience that sweeps the individual toward the ultimate conclusion of the process. The subjective feelings of pleasure that often accompany these dreams suggest an active role for the brain's "reward circuit" centered in the mesolimbic region, with the neurotransmitter dopamine surely involved. Oxytocin, a neurotransmitter associated with sexual pleasure, orgasm, and childbirth, also seems highly likely to factor into these dreams.

Extremely strange content: The hyper-associative capacities of the brain during sleep make it possible for sexual dreaming to range far beyond the ordinary boundaries of waking sexual behavior. The strangeness of these dreams seems to result from several things that typically happen in the brain during paradoxical sleep: (1) neuroelectrical activities in many parts of the brain rise to very high levels; (2) there is a big drop in production of the inhibitory neurotransmitter GABA; and (3) the brainstem starts pulsing with PGO spikes, which Hobson has described as lightning bolts in the brain. All of these factors combine to produce a lively imaginative environment in the dreaming mind with less inhibitory control and more neural energy than ordinary waking consciousness. The weirdness of some sexual dreams is not evidence that dreaming itself is inherently random or dysfunctional. As we have seen, dreams can and frequently do simulate ordinary waking reality with perfect fidelity. When a dream takes a sexually bizarre turn, it more likely reflects an unusually creative, playful, and perhaps metaphorical mode of cognition in sleep, working in concert with the other brain/mind processes most active in this prototype of big dreaming.

Procreative Simulations

When Revonsuo presented his threat simulation theory in a 2000 issue of *Behavioral and Brain Sciences*, the article was accompanied by several commentaries that questioned various aspects of the theory.[7] Much of the criticism was misguided, in my view, but one insightful theme came up in several of the responses that had to do with other kinds of simulations in dreams besides threats. Revonsuo took little interest in this possibility, but other researchers proposed that if dreams can simulate threats, they can surely simulate other aspects of life, too. Tore Nielsen and Anne Germain pushed this point to its logical conclusion: "In fact, it could be argued that *any* dream content with a high overall prevalence is a candidate for supporting a biological function analogous to that of threat simulation."[8] This is exactly the right way to frame the question, because it takes seriously the empirical data about what people do and do not typically dream about. One piece was missing from Nielsen and Germain's analysis, however. Researchers should be looking for any dream content with high overall prevalence and tangible carry-over effects into waking life. Those are the kinds of dreams most likely to influence and guide people's behavior in biologically adaptive ways. Threat-simulating nightmares have both of these qualities, and so do "gonekboles" and other highly memorable dreams of sexual experience.

One way of testing the idea that sexual dreams are adaptive simulations is to look at survey data asking people if they ever dreamed about sexual experience before becoming sexually active in waking life. The Demographic Survey 2010 included this question, and the results are presented in table 10.5, sorted by age and gender.

The gender gap is back, with males answering "yes" to this question much more often than the females in all age groups. The age gap is equally as prevalent, with all the younger groups having higher frequencies than the older groups. Unlike most other facets of dream content in which young females tend to have the highest frequencies and older men have the lowest, the situation is reversed for sexual dream content: young males tend to have the highest frequencies, and older women have the lowest.

The high proportion of "not sure" responses is very unusual; no other question in this or any other SDDb survey has elicited so many ambivalent, non-committal answers. I suspect these are covert "yes" answers, which the participants could not, for whatever reason, bring themselves to openly declare. Whether or not that is true, the numerous "not sure" responses show once again how difficult it can be to gain accurate and complete information about this topic.

Taking that caution into account, the findings in table 10.6 are still consistent with the idea that sexual dreams have the effect of priming the reproductive system. Dreams, in this view, serve an adaptive function by creating realistic simulations of sexual experiences as a way of preparing

Table 10.5 Sexual Dreams before Sexual Activity
in the 2010 Demographic Survey

	Female (N = 613)			
	18–29	30–49	50–64	65+
	Percent	Percent	Percent	Percent
Yes	55	31	17	11
No	22	37	39	48
Not sure	22	32	44	42

	Male (N = 1,326)			
	18–29	30–49	50–64	65+
	Percent	Percent	Percent	Percent
Yes	76	55	44	37
No	8	16	24	30
Not sure	15	29	33	33

the individual for what such activities will feel like, rehearsing possible responses to romantic partners, and imagining the conception of new life. Many people dream about sex before actually having sex: this simple fact has not been fully appreciated by psychologists, doctors, or evolutionary biologists, but it tells us something crucial about the normal place of dreaming in the healthy development of human sexuality.

Medical researchers have found several pieces of evidence indicating that sexual problems correlate with sleep problems. Men with sleep apnea often suffer from erectile dysfunction, and narcoleptics are more likely than non-narcoleptics to be impotent. People with insomnia usually report a simultaneous loss of sexual desire, as do people suffering from depression, a libido-sapping condition that includes disturbed sleep as a major symptom. It remains unclear how exactly the causal relations work between sleep and sexuality, but we do know that a disruption in one can easily lead to disruptions in the other.

An intriguing connection has appeared between REM sleep deprivation and waking sexual behavior. According to sleep researcher Max Hirshkowitz, some of the early REM-deprivation studies in animals measured many aspects of how the loss of sleep impacted the given animal:

Perhaps one of the most dramatic and unexpected findings was a substantial increase in sexual activity in many laboratory animals deprived of REM sleep. Increased sexual pursuit and mounting occurred in both normal and hyposexual animals. Cats and rats would sometimes have frenzied sexual activity and mount virtually anything, including blocks of wood.[9]

Hirshkowitz goes on to cite research in which REM-deprived humans were more likely to seek and gaze at sexual images than non-deprived participants.[10] Taken together, these findings suggest that when the normal processes of sleep and dreaming are blocked, the sexual energies usually expressed in dreaming leak out into the waking world. There seems to be some kind of homeostatic balance between regular sleep and normal sexual functioning, a balance that can easily be thrown off kilter. If further research could shed more light on this relationship, it could have enormous public policy implications (e.g., what if poor sleep conditions increase the risk of domestic abuse or sexual assault?)

Deprivation experiments have their limits, of course, so we should be cautious about putting too much weight on these studies. But the results are consistent with the idea that a healthy process of simulating sexual experience in dreaming is connected to healthy sexual behavior in waking.

What about shockingly immoral, taboo-violating dream content? What could be beneficial or adaptive about that?

We may consider at least three possible explanations for dreams with feelings, images, and behaviors that violate the individual's beliefs about sexual morality in waking life.

The first comes from Freud, who referred to the sexual character of humans as "polymorphously perverse," meaning that every one of us is born with a multiplicity of sexual desires and erotic attractions, not all of which focus directly on reproduction (hence their "perversity"). During the course of psychological development, and with the guidance/ constraint of cultural education, people learn to channel those various desires in a (more or less) unified direction. But the socially forbidden desires still exist within the psyche, and dreams are a natural place for them to express themselves. Freud made it clear that recognizing these polymorphous sexual feelings does not automatically mean one should act on them. To Augustine's concern about the threat that sexual dreams pose to his "true self," Freud would say the only threat comes from conceiving one's self too narrowly and ignoring powerful aspects of one's own human nature. The experience of bizarre, taboo-breaking sexual dreams reflects the deep psychological reality of our multifaceted sexual desires.

Another explanation for especially strange sexual dreams refers to conceptual metaphor theory. Freud was often accused of interpreting every dream image as a symbol of repressed sexuality. Now that we know more about the cognitive processes behind metaphorical thinking and creativity, it seems just as likely that sexual experiences in dreams can metaphorically express many other nonsexual meanings. Especially when the sexual activity is bizarre or unrealistic, the dream's significance is more likely to be metaphorical than literal. For example, several years ago a colleague told me she had a dream of an adulterous affair with a co-worker. The dream shocked her because she loved her husband and was not physically attracted to her co-worker. But then she realized that, seen as a metaphor, the dream accurately reflected her waking life concern that she was devoting all her creative energies to her work and not enough to her marriage. This dream certainly did not prompt her to act out the dream, as Augustine might fear. Rather, it gave her a new awareness of the emotional dynamics of her waking life, using the familiar and attention-grabbing experience of sexuality as a metaphorical target for the source meaning of serious but hard-to-articulate marital worries.

A third possible explanation has to do with the evolutionary advantages of sexual versus asexual reproduction.[11] In asexual reproduction, a parent passes its genome directly to its offspring, creating exact genetic replicas (clones) of itself. This means the creature is unalterably committed to its basic form and structure, which makes it more vulnerable to unanticipated changes in the environment. The advantage of sexual reproduction is that it mixes genetic materials from two parents, producing an endless stream of new combinations that enhance the adaptive flexibility of the species as a whole. The human species has definitely benefited from sexual diversity, and we can see in people's "bizarre" sexual dreams the strong evolutionary impulse to seek novel avenues of procreative pursuit. From this perspective, Augustine's concerns are probably justified. Whatever rules and boundaries cultures try to impose on human sexuality, there will always remain an instinctual pressure to explore sexual experiences beyond those limits.

Concluding Response

Sexual dreams do not promote immoral behavior, but they do make people more aware of the complexity and power of sexual desire in their lives. This prototype of big dreaming functions like a neurally hard-wired course in sex education—here is what you need to know about what it will feel like, what could go frighteningly wrong, and what could go pleasurably right.

If one is committed to the absolute, infallible truth of a strict moral code, then dreaming will probably always seem like a frightening source of evil temptation. If, however, one thinks in terms of the long-term adaptive needs of the human species, then sexual dreams appear as a valuable part of the mind–body system devoted to creating a healthy and prosperous future for our progeny.

II

Gravitational

Last night, Mother, I saw a dream.
There was a star in the heavens.
Like a shooting star of Anu it fell on me.
I tried to lift it; too much for me.
I tried to move it; I could not move it.

The Epic of Gilgamesh

Opening Question

Are falling dreams merely the revived memories of games from childhood?

The consensus among nineteenth-century European psychologists was that "typical" dreams like falling could be scientifically explained as the internal effects of external causes. For example, a sleeping person's arm might drop abruptly out of bed, leading to a dream of suddenly plunging off a cliff. In *The Interpretation of Dreams* Freud acknowledged that external causes like this could play a role, but he said a better explanation came from memories of childhood experiences. Falling dreams, he claimed, "reproduce impressions of childhood; they relate, that is, to games involving movement, which are extraordinarily attractive to children."[1] Starting with babies being affectionately tossed in the air and caught by relatives, these games extend to swings, see-saws, hopscotch, and dancing. The physical sensations generated by such games provide the raw material for dreams of falling later in life.

This kind of simple, physically grounded explanation removes the need for any further claims about the significance or functions of falling dreams.

Initial Response

Falling dreams express an innate awareness of gravity as a primordial force of life and a shaper of human existence.

This prototype of highly memorable dreaming has received relatively little attention from scientific researchers, but it occurs at least as often as the other prototypes, and probably more so. Gravitational dreams produce intense, vertiginous bodily sensations that dramatically carry over into waking awareness. In many cases people wake up with a violent start, as if they were actually falling and about to hit the ground. Other gravitational themes regularly appear in dreams (such as paralysis, a collapsing environment, or tidal waves), each with its own vivid carry-over effects. Freud may have a piece of the truth with his notion of childhood memories, but gravitational dreams do more than simply replicate games of movement from earlier in life. In their most extreme form, these dreams stimulate in people an uncanny awareness of the cosmic forces of physics and their pervasive influence on human existence.

Data and Discussion
Frequencies

The first two chapters of this part focused on the *relational* axis of the typology in figure III.1, with aggressive dreams at the left end of the spectrum and sexual dreams at the right. In this chapter and the one that follows we turn to the *elemental* axis, with gravitational dreams at the lower end and mystical dreams at the higher. These two prototypes share a central concern with entropy and the forces of physical reality. Gravitational dreams, as I conceive them, reflect an existential awareness of the dangers posed by these forces. The dreamer is threatened not by other characters, but by the laws of nature. This marks a difference from chasing dreams, with which falling dreams are often lumped in the general category of "nightmares." In a chasing dream the fear arises from a violent social interaction with another character; the frightening experience occurs within some kind of social context. Gravitational dreams often have little or no social context. They tend to have few characters or social interactions, and their negative emotions revolve around a stark, pitiless, and solitary encounter with the inanimate powers that hold sway over all of life.

Numerous researchers have noted the high frequency of falling dreams in various populations from cultures across the world. Table 11.1 shows the TDQ results for the question, "Have you ever had a dream of falling?"

Table 11.1 Typical Dreams: Falling

	Number of total participants	Percent answering "yes"
Griffith et al. 1958		
American male	134	62
American female	116	73
Japanese male	132	59
Japanese female	91	59
Giora et al. 1972		
Kibbutz female	114	73
Kibbutz male	102	69
Arab female	101	52
Arab male	308	46
Nielsen et al. 2001		
Canadian female	840	74
Canadian male	341	73
Schredl et al. 2004		
German female	376	74
German male	68	75
Nasser and Bulkeley 2009		
Jordanian total	279 f, 47 m	69
Demographic Surveys 2007 and 2010 combined		
American female	1,436	53
American male	2,239	44
Demographic Survey 2010 by gender and age		
American female 18–29	58	69
American female 30–49	233	61

(*continued*)

Table 11.1 Continued

	Number of total participants	Percent answering "yes"
Demographic Survey 2010 by gender and age		
American female 50–64	471	56
American female 65+	288	45
American male 18–29	144	62
American male 30–49	436	55
American male 50–64	809	43
American male 65+	517	33

In all the surveys, the question about falling dreams was at or near the top of the highest frequencies of "yes" answers.[2] Women were slightly higher in some of the surveys, but not in all. The SDDb demographic surveys have the same age pattern found in previous chapters, with younger people reporting more falling dreams than older people, for both men and women.

The additional variables in the demographic surveys revealed no differences in education, but a moderately higher proportion of falling dreams for people at the lower end of the income scale, especially for the men (table 11.2). People on the political Left (again, especially the men) reported more falling dreams than people on the political Right.

These differences are not huge and should be interpreted with caution. Statistical chance may be distorting the results, and/or they could be confounded with other variables.[3] Still, we should not rule out the possibility of a genuine signal in the noise here, a clue to the cultural symbolism of gravitational dreams and their relevance to people in different kinds of life situations. We will return to that prospect later in the chapter.

Like the other prototypes of big dreaming, gravitational dreams are highly memorable when they occur, but they do not occur frequently in the ordinary course of dreaming.[4] This is shown in tables 11.3 and 11.4, which present the word search findings for the "Falling" category in the SDDb baselines and in several series from individual dreamers.

The results indicate how many dreams include at least one reference to a word related to falling. No appreciable difference between men and women appears in the baselines. Several of the individual series have frequencies very similar to those of the baselines. Bea is the youngest individual in this group (ages 14–21 during the time of her journal) and Paul the oldest (ages 79–80 during the time of his journal), and the differences

Table 11.2 2010 Demographic Survey Responses to Typical Dreams: Falling

	Education, female	
	No college degree	College degree +
	Percent	Percent
Yes	53	56
No	42	38
Not sure	5	6

	Education, male	
	No college degree	College degree +
	Percent	Percent
Yes	46	44
No	47	51
Not sure	6	5

	Personal finances, female					
	<$25,000	$25,000–$35,000	$35,000–$50,000	$50,000–$75,000	$75,000–$100,000	$100,000+
	Percent	Percent	Percent	Percent	Percent	Percent
Yes	61	59	56	59	53	55
No	31	36	39	39	41	40
Not sure	8	4	5	2	6	5

	Personal finances, male					
	<$25,000	$25,000–$35,000	$35,000–$50,000	$50,000–75,000	$75,000–$100,000	$100,000+
	Percent	Percent	Percent	Percent	Percent	Percent
Yes	57	50	48	47	43	44
No	40	44	47	48	52	52
Not sure	3	6	6	5	5	5

(continued)

Table 11.2 Continued

| Political ideology, female | | | | | |
| Progressive | Liberal | Moderate | Libertarian | Conservative | Very Conservative |
Percent	Percent	Percent	Percent	Percent	Percent
Yes	62	54	54	51	51	56
No	33	38	43	45	42	42
Not sure	5	9	4	4	7	2

| Political ideology, male | | | | | |
| Progressive | Liberal | Moderate | Libertarian | Conservative | Very Conservative |
Percent	Percent	Percent	Percent	Percent	Percent
Yes	54	52	45	46	40	42
No	39	42	47	48	56	55
Not sure	6	7	8	6	4	4

in their falling dream frequencies (12% vs. 3%) are consistent with the age drop-off already noted.

Greater individual variability emerges in the dream series of Van and Will, both of whom were men in their early twenties. As noted in chapter 9, Van was an avid video game player, and themes from those games influenced the content of his dreams in many ways. What looked to me like frequent nightmares were, according to Van, exciting and enjoyable adventures that felt just like his best gaming experiences. The unusually high proportion of falling references in Van's dreams makes more sense in the personal context of his gaming experiences. For Will, some of his falling references were not about himself but about a local waterfall, or the autumnal season of "Fall"; many of the other references involved him "falling asleep" in his dreams, which is quite a rare phenomenon. In chapter 7 we discussed Will's melancholy temperament and struggles with mental illness. Although we would need more personal information to know for sure, the recurrence of falling themes in his dreams seems to accurately reflect the tenuous, fragile conditions of his psychological health in waking life during this period of time.

Table 11.3 Frequencies of Falling-Related Words in the Baselines

	Surveys	
	Number of total dreams	Percent of dreams having at least one reference to falling
HVDC females	490	7
HVDC males	491	10
Miami Home	125	6
Miami Lab	187	7
International Survey females	790	9
International Survey males	645	10
Santa Clara Dreams	811	9
Demographic Surveys females	1,004	5
Demographic Surveys males	665	5

Motifs

The classic version of this big dream prototype is the *downward plunge*: a helpless fall from some higher point toward a shattering impact with the ground. It can be a fall off a building, a ledge, a cliff, or a tall ladder. It can involve an airplane going down, a bridge collapsing, or a car swerving off the side of the road. In each case, the central motif is the feeling of being seized by gravity and pulled inescapably down, down, down. In many cases people awaken just before they hit the ground, suddenly bolting upright in bed, flooded with vivid carry-over sensations. Sometimes people become spontaneously lucid during falling dreams and consciously change the outcomes. More rarely, the dreamer actually hits the ground and either magically survives like a cartoon character, or "dies" in the dream, while still maintaining some degree of awareness after the dream body's demise.

The motif of *paralysis* in dreaming shares a similar feeling of vulnerability to impersonal, irresistible forces that deprive one's body of strength and volition. In dreams of paralysis people become impotent prisoners of gravity. The dreamer cannot move, run, speak, or sometimes even breathe. The epigraph quote from *Epic of Gilgamesh*, about the hero being helplessly pinned to the ground by a fallen star, is an example of this kind of experience from more than 4,000 years ago. Here is another more contemporary example from a male college student in his late teens:

Table 11.4 Frequencies of Falling-Related Words in Individual Series

Series	Number of total dreams	Percent of dreams having at least one reference to falling
Natural scientist	234	7
Barb Sanders 250	250	7
Van	185	21
Bea journal 1	223	13
Bea journal 2	63	5
Lawrence	206	7
RB	51	6
Paul	136	3
Lola	102	14
Will	96	28
Jordan	90	8

I lie in bed, and feel helpless and insignificant. I feel as if I am the size of an ant, and I can barely lift my arms and legs. Then fear sets in, and everything in my room moves. Then out of nowhere, a shadow enters at the center of my room. The black shadow, which I cannot describe exactly, slowly extends his hand toward me, and as the hand moves closer it grows larger. Out of panic and fear, I try to pull the sheets over myself, but I can't.[5]

Physical movements that require little effort in waking become agonizingly difficult in these dreams. In this young man's dream, the fear of his own physical immobility is magnified by the strange, unnatural movements of other entities in the dream that he does not understand and cannot control or defend against.

Another gravitational motif goes beyond the falling of the dreamer's body to envision *total entropy* (i.e., the falling, collapse, decay, and destruction of everything around the dreamer). There is a "Murphy's Law" quality to these dreams—whatever can go wrong, does go wrong. Sometimes this motif takes hold in a relatively mundane setting: the dreamer is late for an appointment, then can't find the car keys, gets lost on the streets, forgets the name of the other person, spills the coffee, on and on and on, one problem after another in a seemingly endless series of failures and misfortunes. In other dreams this motif expands to encompass the natural world, as in the following report from one of the female college students in the Hall and Van de Castle Norms:

> I dreamt I was walking across a bridge and just as I got across, the bridge fell in. I then kept walking along a road. Alongside were trees lining the road. I suddenly heard a tremendous thud, and when I turned around, a tree had fallen just behind me. I was walking along a road high above a ravine and just as I stepped around a curve, the road gave way behind me.

The dreamer barely stays ahead of the destructive forces of entropy and chaos. This motif turns the dynamics of the "classic" gravitational dream inside out. Rather than the dreamer falling through space, space is falling around the dreamer. Several scenes from the 2011 film *Inception*, directed by Christopher Nolan, draw upon similar kinds of high-entropy dream experiences to generate a terrifying sense of a crumbling world.

Dreams of *enormous waves* can also be considered a gravitational motif. The late Ernest Hartmann, a psychoanalytic psychiatrist and one of the great dream researchers of the past several decades, often talked about tidal wave dreams as the best examples of an intense "central image" in dreaming.[6] For Hartmann, these dreams reflected especially vivid expressions of human emotion as a natural force. In the waking world, ocean waves are the fluid embodiment of massive gravitational interactions between the earth, moon, and sun. The waves in dreams can grow to monstrous proportions, representing another source of danger that continually threatens to overwhelm human life.[7] As an example, a 44-year-old man from the 2011 Memorable Dreams survey reported this as the most vivid dream of his life: "I can remember being on a beach and hearing screaming as a huge tidal wave is coming, and trying to run as fast as I could to get into a building. But I woke up before it hit me or the building."[8]

A final motif to consider has to do with what I call *titanic* dreams. In Greek mythology the Titans were the Elder Gods, the primordial deities born of heaven and earth who ruled over the cosmos for untold ages. Classicist Edith Hamilton described the Titans in these terms:

> They had the shattering, overwhelming strength of earthquake and hurricane and volcano. In the tales about them they do not seem really alive, but rather to belong to a world where as yet there was

no life, only tremendous movements of irresistible forces lifting up the mountains and scooping out the seas. The Greeks evidently had some such feeling because in their stories, although they represent these creatures as living beings, they make them unlike any form of life known to man.[9]

A titanic dream tends to be unusually abstract and disembodied, yet filled with tremendous force and power. The dreamer is often the only character present, and the settings are mostly empty and devoid of life. Naturally people find such dreams difficult to put into words, which means their reports can sound vague or nonsensical. But that is misleading; the experiences are real and impactful, no matter how hard they are to verbalize. Titanic dreams can be understood as the most extreme form of the gravitational prototype. The human world falls away and the dreamer descends into a realm of pure physics: gravity, mass, energy, speed, momentum. The following example comes from a female college student:

> My most memorable dream contains no characters. It starts off looking like a crumpled sheet of paper, with areas of light and dark. The areas of light and dark move away, revealing many more points of light and areas of dark. It becomes almost like a television screen of static, only there isn't movement on an individual level, but the entire area begins to move and roll. A big ball appears and rolls over the area, and I start to fall back into the area until it feels as though I reach the atomic level. I wake up with an unpleasant feeling.[10]

The "unpleasant feeling" mentioned by this young woman seems less about fear than a deeper, more visceral kind of disorientation. In titanic dreams people leave ordinary reality far behind, becoming captive witnesses to the mysterious movements and interactions of elemental forces that have no apparent connection to human life. Ian R. MacLeod, a British science-fiction writer, shared this recurrent childhood dream in the 1996 collection *The Tiger Garden: A Book of Writers' Dreams*:

> I saw myself standing on a vast plain. The sky was grainy and dark. . . . The land was a flat grey expanse marked with lines like strips of floor boarding that narrowed toward the horizon. Far away from

me, at the center of this empty scene, a vertical disturbance of the air would soon begin. At first it was to be nothing more than a shimmer midway between the plain and the sky. But I knew as I watched it that the shimmer would soon become a long spindle-like thread, spinning madly, and slowly thickening in the middle. The spindle was blurred and whitish, already impossibly huge. I sensed as it grew that it was dragging in the whole world around it. . . . [I]t gave off a huge sense of energy. Unable to move, I always feared that the thing would soon engulf me."[11]

We have no research-based statistics about the frequency of titanic dreams, but my strong impression is they occur more often among children than older people. I have also found they can be triggered by fevers and other kinds of illnesses that disrupt sleep. People with mental illnesses may have more of them; many of Will's dreams had eerie titanic themes, far more than in any other individual series I have studied.

Reverse Engineering

Even though dreams like these envision worlds quite far removed from present reality, they are still grounded in the mental and physical processes of the individual's sleeping body. The recurrent qualities of gravitational dreams implicate several specific brain/mind systems that seem to be involved in producing such experiences. Following the reverse engineering method, we can use these recurrent qualities to identify the most likely connections between gravitational dreaming experiences and the neurophysiology of sleep.

To start, we can point to brain/mind systems that do not seem especially active in gravitational dreams. For instance, the neural networks that underlie social cognition have no apparent role in these dreams, given that they have very few characters, social interactions, or spoken communications. Most other dreams have a great deal of social thought and behavior, as we have seen, so this marks an unusual and distinctive feature of gravitational dreams. The difficulty in verbally describing such dreams may derive from the absence of precisely those mental faculties associated in waking life with ordinary language and social discourse.

What parts of the brain are active in these dreams, then? Humans and other mammals perceive gravity primarily through the *vestibular system*, a sophisticated and very fast sensory network that connects the inner ear, brainstem, eyes, and muscular activities throughout the body. Crucial for coordinated movement, balance, and clear vision, the vestibular system enables us to orient our bodies with respect to gravity. Portions of this network are highly active during PS, particularly the reticular formation in the brainstem and the eyes as they twitch under their lids. In gravitational dreams it seems the whole vestibular network becomes hyper-activated, generating extraordinary inner ear sensations and projecting intense signals that would lead, in waking, to immediate physical movement and muscular effort all over the body. There is some research showing a direct role for the vestibular system in REM sleep,[12] and also research showing that experimental stimulation of the vestibular system can impact people's dream content. According to Kenneth Leslie and Robert Ogilvie's 1996 study, "vestibular stimulation leads to a number of changes in dream mentation, including increased self-reflectiveness, lucid mentation, vestibular imagery, and bizarreness.... The exact mechanism by which vestibular stimulation influences lucid mentation is unclear; possibilities include increased subcortical arousal, changes in eye movements that then affect mentation, and increased vestibular imagery and bizarreness that in turn trigger more lucid mentation."[13] This connection between vestibular activity and lucidity makes good sense in relation to the quality of heightened sensory awareness in gravitational dreams.

In cases where these dreams involve feelings of physical paralysis, constricted movement, and arduous struggle, we can look to brain/mind systems that produce the atonia of sleep. As discussed in chapters 2 and 3, atonia is the automatic relaxation of the major muscle groups. The neurotransmitter glycine plays a key role in atonia by blocking the movement signals from the sleeping brain and preventing our bodies from physically acting out those movements. The thalamus in the limbic system also has a big influence on atonia. The thalamus serves as a kind of gatekeeper between the brain and the physical actions of the body, relaying neural signals in both directions. During sleep the thalamus is very active, suggesting it is involved in both generating realistic physical sensations in dreams and blocking those sensations from leading to actual somatic movements.

Knowing this about the brain's functioning in sleep, we can infer that gravitational dreams involve some kind of unusual activity with the thalamus and/or the neurotransmitter glycine. A hyperactive thalamus could overwhelm the dreaming mind with the neurological tension between the simultaneous imperatives to *move* and *not move*. Extremely elevated levels of glycine might prompt dreams of intense pressure and immobility. A precipitous decline in glycine levels might produce dreams of dangerously uncontrolled movements and falls.

There is clearly a reality basis to these dreams, given that the dreamer's body is effectively paralyzed and has no muscle tone during the ordinary process of sleep. But this cannot be the whole explanation. As shown in table 11.3, most people's dreams have references to falling fewer than 10% of the time. In other words, more than 90% of people's dreams do not include any references to falling. If the natural atonia of sleep were the cause of gravitational dreams, then we have to ask why all dreams are not falling dreams, since all dreams occur in neurophysiological conditions of atonia. Evidently the dreaming mind is more than capable of ignoring the body's immobilized condition and weaving elaborate imaginative experiences of vigorous physical movement.

Some gravitational dreams have a great deal of overlap with the parasomnia of sleep paralysis, as discussed in chapter 3. Episodes of sleep paralysis usually occur during the transition between waking and sleeping, and again between sleeping and waking. They involve a disorienting and often alarming combination of a motionless, atonic body and a vigilant, semi-conscious mind. Sleep paralysis is not pathological in itself, even though the experiences can be quite unsettling. But medical research has shown that greater vulnerability to sleep paralysis can be a common symptom of several kinds of psychopathology. This highlights the possible connection between gravitational dreams and mental and physical illness mentioned earlier. When people are sick, feverish, or mentally disturbed in some way, they seem to have a greater propensity toward entropic dreaming.

This suggests that gravitational dreams could, at one level, provide accurate reflections of the threatening disintegration of the individual's mind—the dream world is falling apart, just as the person's mind is in danger of breaking down.

These dreams may also reflect the heightened activation of the body's immune system as it fights the illness at a cellular level, seeking to restore health and balance. We already know the immune system is very active in sleep, so it requires no great leap to infer that in conditions of sickness these immunological processes will be even more intensely active than usual. Gravitational dreams could be the psychological expressions of this deep biological impulse to confront the inner dangers and strive against them.

Entropic Simulations

Since Freud, no psychologist has tried to make a serious case that these dreams have any particular function or significance. And yet, gravitational dreams are one of the most pervasive and memorable types of dreaming in human experience. They generate vividly realistic portrayals of a wide variety of physical movements and activities, all while the body remains motionless in bed. Indeed, despite their neglect from other research-ers, I find these dreams to be among the most remarkable creations of the sleeping mind. If I close my eyes in waking, I can easily imagine an aggressive or sexual scenario that generates some degree of emotional response. But I could never consciously imagine a falling scenario that would make me feel the same head-spinning, gut-wrenching sensations I experience in dreams of falling. The dreaming imagination seems to display its greatest powers of simulating physical reality when it throws us into the merciless clutches of gravity.

What purpose, then, might these vivid entropic simulations serve? If they are neither memories of childhood games nor responses to external physical stimuli, why do they occur so frequently and memorably through-out the human population?

Following the threat simulation theory of Revonsuo, we could propose a possible function that helped our distant primate ancestors, who origi-nally lived and slept in trees far above the ground (see chapter 2). Those primates presumably faced a real and constant danger of falling from the branches whenever their sleeping bodies became atonic. Periodically hav-ing very realistic and frightening dreams of falling might, in such circum-stances, have the adaptive benefit of making the individual more alert and vigilant about the security of his or her physical position in the trees. The primates whose waking awareness was most impacted by these dreams might gain a survival advantage in terms of a lower chance of injury or death from falling, compared to those less impacted by the dreams.

Like many theories in evolutionary psychology, this one is rather spec-ulative and difficult to prove experimentally. But it does help to frame the question in terms that connect the recurrent dream patterns with sci-entific knowledge about the evolution of our species. Based on the best of current evolutionary research, it is no exaggeration to say the human mind bears the deep neurological imprint of those tree-dwelling primates. Their brains have grown and developed into our brains. Their worst fears are still our worst fears, in waking and in dreaming.

Still, this is a partial explanation at best, highlighting just one of several potential levels of meaning in these dreams.

Not all of these meanings are literally about physical movements or behaviors. Some gravitational dreams have metaphorical dimensions in which falling provides the experiential source for many possible targets of meaning. George Lakoff's research has identified a number of conceptual metaphors with relevance to gravitational dreams and their many motifs: *up is good, down is bad, help is support, action is self-propelled motion*, and *freedom is lack of constraint*.[14] According to Lakoff, our minds naturally use experiences from physical space to create metaphorical maps for our conceptual thinking. (He calls this the "spatialization of form" hypothesis.) If this is true, then the reality-simulating powers of gravitational dreams may provide an especially unconstrained arena for metaphorical thought and expression.

In *Metaphors We Live By*, Lakoff and Johnson said, "the major metaphor in our culture is *happy is up*." Countless phrases in ordinary language embody the belief that *up* is good, right, strong, and controlled. To be *down*, then, is metaphorically to be unhappy, bad, wrong, weak, uncontrolled, and out of sync with the mainstream of society. This network of negative metaphorical meanings may help account for some of the TDQ results discussed earlier. For instance, people at the lower end of the income scale reported somewhat more falling dreams than did the people with the highest annual incomes (61% vs. 55% for the females, 57% vs. 44% for the males). It seems plausible that lower-income people are more likely to feel "down," unhappy, and powerless in their lives compared to high-income people, and these personal finance experiences are accurately reflected in their dreams.

In the 2008 book *American Dreamers* I studied the dream lives of several people who were experiencing severe financial difficulties and whose dreams metaphorically expressed their economic anxieties with gravitational themes. One of these people, "Richard," was a security guard at a hospital where the management had repeatedly cut staff positions to save money, putting extra burdens on the remaining employees. Richard desperately needed the job to support his wife and daughter—he knew he might be the next one fired—so he tried to control his frustration and perform his duties. But a flashpoint for him and many of his co-workers was the hospital cafeteria, whose quality and efficiency had declined drastically due to the budget cuts. Here is a dream Richard had early in the study:

I was standing in our cafeteria's cash register line at work. The next thing I knew, the line became an obstacle course to get your food. I was up on a roof of a tall building, trying to walk across a plank bridging two roofs. On the roof across on the other side were two halves of a tuna sub sandwich I ordered. As I was about to step onto the plank, an earthquake shook and my bridge fell. Roofs and buildings everywhere were in various states of ruin. People were scrambling about everywhere! Some were in fear, while others were angry that they couldn't get to their food. People were fighting over food that others had.[15]

Richard said the dream gave him a strange but honest portrayal of his feelings about the situation at work: the tenuous nature of his employ-ment, the danger of losing his financial balance, the physical decay of the hospital infrastructure, the deteriorating morale and civility of the other employees ... It all came through in this metaphorical image of the caf-eteria falling and collapsing around him.

Do people with very high incomes also have gravitational dreams like these? Yes, they certainly do, but perhaps not as frequently as people with fewer financial resources and less economic control over their lives. The metaphorical possibilities of falling dreams might be more experientially relevant for people at the lower end of the income scale.

A similar principle may be at work with the differences in falling dream frequencies between people on the Left and Right of the American political spectrum (58% vs. 53% for the females, 53% vs. 40% for the males). Broadly speaking, it is fair to say that conservatives value tradi-tional beliefs and practices, and they promote social policies that preserve order, authority, and Judeo-Christian morality. Perhaps they have slightly fewer falling dreams because they feel more solidly anchored in their principles. Liberals and progressives, meanwhile, are more inclined to value new ideas about improving society, particularly for underprivileged people, and they favor policies that embrace cultural and religious diver-sity. They may have somewhat more falling dreams because they are less attached to the social status quo.

Another angle on the cultural symbolism of gravitational dreams comes from the study Lana Nasser and I did in 2009 with a group of Jordanian college students. Nasser's research has focused on contemporary Arabic experiences with possession by the *jinn* (sometimes referred to in English as *genies*; more about them in chapter 13). The *jinn* are trickster-like spiritual beings from pre-Islamic mythology who afflict people with a variety of physical and psychological maladies. In addition to the standard questions on the TDQ, Nasser and I added a few questions specifically tailored to help illuminate this issue. One of these new questions was, have you ever dreamed of a *jinn* or *shaitan?* In Arabic cultures the *jinn* are widely believed to appear in dreams, and *shaitan* is a well-known demon related to the *jinn*, so this question gave us a way of gauging people's familiarity with *jinn* experiences. A total of 22% of the participants answered yes to this question. Nasser and I then looked at how the females who answered "yes" to the *jinn* question responded to the other TDQ questions, and an interesting pattern appeared: the biggest differences between the "yes-*jinn*" and "no-*jinn*" women all related to gravitational themes. The yes-*jinn* women had much higher frequencies of dreams about falling, being on the verge of falling, being half awake and paralyzed in bed, and being smothered and unable to breathe.[16] According to Nasser's research, the most likely victims of *jinn* possession are unmarried young women with low status in their communities.[17] Combined with the TDQ findings, this suggests their higher frequencies of various kinds of gravitational dreams can be interpreted as metaphorically accurate reflections of their waking life experiences of social weakness and vulnerability.

A further twist on these metaphorical meanings comes from a recent study by Mary Walsh, a psychotherapist with expertise in trauma treatment.[18] In her study Walsh worked at a school for troubled adolescents with harrowing personal backgrounds of physical abuse, sexual violence, drug and alcohol addiction, gang activities, and a host of other problems. For a period of several weeks Walsh taught several groups of teenagers some simple biofeedback methods for self-regulating their breathing and heart rates (trauma victims are often very erratic on these measures), and she talked with them about their dreams. Over the course of her study she was able to track the changes in their physiological coherence and compare them with changes in their dream content. Surprisingly, she found their dreams from later in the process had many *more* references to falling than the earlier dreams (15% later vs. 2% earlier).[19] Walsh expected the improved physiological coherence would have lowered the frequency of this theme, but in her conversations with the teenagers it emerged that some of the falling dreams actually reflected a degree of therapeutic progress. At least some kind of movement and narrative action occurred in these dreams, which was an improvement over the static, frozen images of their early dreams. One of the adolescents, "Jesse," told Walsh that his old recurrent dream of being in a fight on top of a skyscraper had changed during the training. In the new dream he fell off the skyscraper, going down and down until he finally hit the ground. Jesse interpreted the dreams "as a warning 'not to live on the edge,' and [he] associated hitting the ground with 'hitting the bottom' and facing his addiction."[20] In the context of his difficult life circumstances, this counted as an empowering metaphorical insight.

Gravitational dreams can express many possible meanings, both literal and metaphorical. The experiential power of these dreams is rooted in the sleeping brain and body, but it would be a mistake to conclude the dreams are caused by automatic neurophysiological processes. It seems instead that the dreaming imagination uses these processes when it sees fit, as raw materials to craft images, sensations, and narratives that are relevant to the circumstances of the individual's waking life.

Concluding Response

All forms of life on earth, and presumably elsewhere in the universe, struggle against entropy, against the tendency toward disarray, disorder, and death. Gravitational dreams reflect that fundamental concern of every living being. These chthonic expressions of the dreaming imagination stimulate a heightened awareness of the physical realities and limitations of our existence, yielding deep and unsettling insights into the elemental forces that reign over everyone and everything.

This is true not only for those toward the bottom of the social hierarchy but also for those at the top. The *Epic of Gilgamesh* told such a tale. No one was greater or more powerful than Gilgamesh—he was the mightiest of ancient kings. Unrivalled on the battlefield, his power knew no limits, and soon he began oppressing the people of his city of Uruk: "day and night he oppresses the weak . . . Gilgamesh does not let the young woman go to her mother, the girl to the warrior, the bride to the young groom." The suffering people prayed to the gods for deliverance from his tyranny. That was when Gilgamesh had the dream of a star falling upon him, and to his horror he found himself powerless against it. The titanic nightmare launched Gilgamesh on a long and dangerous journey that eventually led him down to the land of the dead, where he found that even the most powerful man in the world must ultimately yield to the finitude of human existence.

12
_____

Mystical

Toto, I have a feeling we're not in Kansas anymore.
DOROTHY GALE, *The Wizard of Oz*

Opening Question

Do dreams of magical powers weaken people's minds and encourage superstitious thinking?

Dreams that portray fantastic abilities and impossible events are incompatible with rational, fact-based explanations of the world. People who take such dreams seriously run the risk of diminishing their ability to perceive reality apart from the distorting effects of their own wishes and desires. One of the earliest thinkers to challenge irrational superstitions like these was Wang Ch'ung (27–97 C.E.), a Chinese philosopher from the Han Dynasty era who wrote about astronomy, meteorology, and other fields of natural science.[1] Ch'ung took a dim view of the popular belief that each human has an immortal soul apart from his or her material body. Why, he asked, do spirits always appear wearing clothes? Do clothes have spirits, too, that accompany their wearers to Heaven? Or do heavenly clothes-makers await us once we arrive? The logical absurdities of such beliefs should make us wary of unrealistic dreams that seem to validate those notions and give them further credibility.

Initial Response

Mystical dreams express a deep cognitive imperative to think beyond what is to imagine what might be.

Some dreams defy the downward pull of entropy. Instead, they rise above gravity, death, and disorder. I refer to them collectively as "mystical" because they envision powers that transcend the ordinary limitations of physical reality. Like the other prototypes of big dreaming, mystical dreams are relatively rare in frequency, but highly memorable and impactful when they do occur. They include hyper-realistic dreams of flying, haunting visitation dreams from people who have died, and aesthetically complex dreams of astonishing beauty. In all these cases the sleeping brain seems to be working at the highest levels of integrated creativity. The psychological impact of mystical dreams is not to encourage naïve superstition but to stimulate an adaptive and distinctly human sense of possibility and hope beyond the given realities of current waking life.

Data and Discussion
Frequencies

Moving now to the opposite end of the elemental axis, we shift from life-sapping gravitational dreams to uplifting, life-affirming mystical dreams in which people overcome the myriad threats, dangers, and vulnerabilities that plague them in other types of dreaming. In these dreams there is power, not weakness; freedom, not constraint; joy, not terror. Murphy's Law is suspended, at least for a time.

As with other prototypical dreams, these ones have a long history, with reports from many parts of the world going back thousands of years. Here, for example, is a classic flying dream from ancient Rome, as recorded by Artemidorus in his dream interpretation manual from the second century c.e.: "A man who was living in Rome dreamt that he flew around the city near the rooftops and that he was elated by his adept flying. And all those who looked at him were struck with admiration."[2]

Visitation dreams have an even more illustrious historical and cross-cultural background. Dreams of dead ancestors are a prominent and well-known experience found in virtually every indigenous culture studied by Western anthropologists and ethnographers. The Australian Aborigines developed elaborate myths and rituals around these kinds of dreams, and so did Native American cultures like the Iroquois and Ojibwa.[3] Many African communities likewise paid special attention when people who had died appeared as if alive again in their dreams.[4] Descriptions of visitation dreams appear in sacred texts from ancient India, China, and Mesopotamia.[5] There can be little doubt this kind of dreaming experience is pervasive throughout our species.

The TDQ asks participants about both flying and visitation dreams, and the results in table 12.1 show they occur somewhat less frequently than the other prototypes.

A few slight gender differences appear—males have some of the highest frequencies of flying dreams, and females have mostly higher frequencies of visitation dreams. There may be cultural factors at work

Table 12.1 Typical Dreams: Flying and Visitation

	Number of total participants	Flying dreams Percent answering "yes"	Visitation dreams Percent answering "yes"
Griffith et al. 1958			
American male	134	32	40
American female	116	35	53
Japanese male	132	46	52
Japanese female	91	46	66
Giora et al. 1972			
Kibbutz female	114	40	52
Kibbutz male	102	61	39
Arab female	101	43	70
Arab male	308	44	73
Nielsen et al. 2001			
Canadian female	840	44	39
Canadian male	341	58	38
Schredl et al. 2004			
German female	376	63	46
German male	68	66	38
Nasser and Bulkeley 2009			
Jordanian total	279 f, 47 m	26	46

(continued)

Table 12.1 Continued

	Number of total participants	Flying dreams Percent answering "yes"	Visitation dreams Percent answering "yes"
Demographic Surveys 2007 and 2010 combined			
American female	1,436	38	51
American male	2,239	41	38
Demographic Survey 2010 by gender and age			
American female 18–29	58	57	55
American female 30–49	233	58	53
American female 50–64	471	46	57
American female 65+	288	33	51
American male 18–29	144	48	35
American male 30–49	436	50	39
American male 50–64	809	47	42
American male 65+	517	33	34

in some of the variations, too. The Germans, for instance, reported many more flying than visitation dreams, while the Israeli Arabs and Jordanians reported the reverse (i.e., many more visitation than flying dreams). Do these differences reflect distinctive features of their respective cultures? Perhaps. We would need much more data before saying anything conclusive. But it is a reasonable question to ask, the kind of question that can be answered with empirical evidence.

The SDDb demographic surveys found a sharp drop-off for older people in the frequencies of flying dreams, but no such decline in the frequencies of visitation dreams. Both the men and women reported about the same proportions of visitation dreams at all ages, with the highest frequency among 50–64 year olds, and only a little less among people 65 and older. Perhaps this is another instance of the continuity principle at work. Compared to younger participants, people in the older age groups are presumably more likely to have concerns about death and dying and to know people who have died. Other kinds of dreaming may fade in significance over the course of the life cycle, but visitation dreams seem to become more important and memorable the older one gets.

Table 12.2 Frequencies of Flying-Related Words in the Baselines and Individual Series

Series	Number of total dreams	Percent of dreams having at least one reference to flying
Baseline females	3,095	4
Baseline males	2,113	6
Natural scientist	234	4
Barb Sanders 250	250	4
Van	185	11
Bea journal 1	223	4
Bea journal 2	63	5
Lawrence	206	4
RB	51	10
Paul	136	0
Lola	102	4
Will	96	8
Jordan	90	9

Dreams like these, although highly impactful and memorable, do not occur very often, as demonstrated by word search analyses of people's most recent dreams. Table 12.2 shows that a small percentage of dream reports from either demographic surveys or individual journals make any reference to flying, and some of the ones that do use flying-related words are about planes or birds, not the dreamer's own flight.

In most cases the males had slightly more flying references than the females. The individuals with the highest frequencies, Van and Will, were both young men. When added to the TDQ results, these findings suggest a modest but real tendency of males toward more frequent dreams of flying.

Motifs

The two major motifs of the mystical dreaming prototype have already been noted: *flying* and *visitations from the dead*. These motifs share the quality of defying the entropic limitations of ordinary physical existence. Flying dreams are liberations from gravity, and visitation dreams are liberations from death. Both of these motifs have multiple variations in terms of different settings, feelings, and outcomes. Some flying dreams involve soaring journeys into the sky, while others portray the dreamer hovering or floating closer to the ground. Sometimes people have total control over their direction and speed, while at other times their flight is more erratic and unpredictable. Exhilarating dreams of flying can abruptly turn into frightening nightmares of falling—recall Rose's dream from chapter 8, about flying up into the heavens but then being pulled back down into her bedroom by her husband.

Visitation dreams likewise have many variations, from joyful reunions to terrifying warnings, from wise words of advice to angry accusations of neglect. A literary reference to the latter kind of visitation dream came at the end of Homer's *Iliad*, when the ancient Greek warrior Achilles dreamed of his close friend Patroklos, who had just been slain in battle:

> The ghost came and stood over his head and spoke a word to him: "You sleep, Achilles, you have forgotten me; but you were not careless of me when I lived, but only in death. Bury me as quickly as may be, let me pass through the gates of Hades. . . . "

In the dream Achilles promised he would do so, and he asked Patroklos to stay:

> "But stand closer to me, and let us, if only for a little, embrace, and take full satisfaction from the dirge of sorrow." So he [Achilles] spoke, and with his own arms reached for him [Patroklos], but could not take him, but the spirit went underground, like vapour, with a thin cry, and Achilles started awake, staring, and drove his hands together, and spoke, and his words were sorrowful: "Oh, wonder! Even in the house of Hades there is left something, a soul and an image, but there is no real heart of life in it."[6]

The emotional poignancy of a dream visitation from the dead comes through clearly in this ancient story. Achilles's mournful vision does not lead him to deny death, but rather to try understanding it more fully, and more maturely.

Other mystical motifs, although less common than flying and visitation dreams, also share the quality of transcending basic physical limitations in waking life. Dreams of *breathing underwater* occur to some people, often generating the same kind of surprised delight and joyful freedom of movement found in flying dreams. Dreams of amazing *good fortune*, like making a miraculous shot in a game or winning the lottery, are experiences of beating the odds—in situations where an individual would ordinarily be doomed to failure, the dreamers enjoy incredible luck and surprising success. Dreams of extraordinary *beauty* can have mystical, otherworldly qualities in their complex combinations of aesthetically brilliant sights, sounds, and sensations, giving the dreamer a lasting impression of creative novelty beyond the drab constraints of ordinary life.

Now that all four big dream prototypes have been introduced, we can begin talking about hybrid cases with features of more than one prototype. The flying dreams that can suddenly shift into falling dreams are one such hybrid. Another one might be called "mystically aggressive" dreams in which the individual gains a magical advantage over the enemy in warfare. For instance, the Muslim prophet Muhammad reportedly dreamed of a sword that was broken and then magically restored to full strength, and he interpreted the dream as divine support for his army in their upcoming battles.[7] Likewise, there are "mystically sexual" dreams in which the individual has an ecstatically satisfying interaction, perhaps in magically enhanced surroundings or with an idealized partner. Many big dream experiences have elements of more than one prototype, which should not be surprising given the boundless creativity of the dreaming imagination.

Reverse Engineering

The widespread recurrence of these mystical dream motifs is strong evidence they have some basis in the general functioning of the human brain during sleep. Of course, no direct neuroscientific research has been done to explore this question. That is due in part to the rarity of mystical dreams, which makes them hard to observe and study. It is also partly due to the reluctance of modern investigators to devote valuable time and resources to the study of something that seems obscure, bizarre, and irrelevant for any practical purposes. With so little empirical research to prove otherwise, this attitude can become a self-fulfilling prophecy.

The reverse engineering approach is especially useful here in showing how the experiential qualities of mystical dreams can be correlated with activities in several well-known regions and systems in the sleeping brain. In other words, we can plausibly show that mystical dreams have naturalistic roots. There is no need to abandon a scientific perspective when studying this realm of human experience. By carefully examining the most prominent features of these dreams and considering them in relation to current research on brain/mind functioning, we can propose realistic hypotheses about how they connect to each other.

The vivid realism we have noted in the other big dream prototypes reaches an even greater level of intensity in mystical dreams. Dreams of being chased, or having sex, or falling off a cliff are representations of things that could actually happen to a person; they might be improbable or unlikely, but no laws of physics would be violated if they occurred in waking life. Mystical dreams, however, are twice removed from the waking world. They generate extremely realistic representations of things that could not happen in actual life, physically impossible things like flying and dead people coming back to life. These dreams make the unreal feel more real than waking reality.

How does the sleeping brain accomplish such remarkable feats? Several neural systems contribute to the process. The limbic system is very likely involved, especially the frontal-limbic circuits that Solms has found to be crucial for reality-monitoring and distinguishing waking from dreaming. The positive emotions that often accompany mystical dreams also have their neural foundations in the limbic system. Dreams in general tend to have more fear than happiness, and neuroscientists have done more research on negative than positive emotions, so the dreaming-limbic connection is especially clear in cases of frightening nightmares. But mystical dreams of ecstatic joy and exhilaration also have their neural roots in this part of the brain, and these roots reach far back into evolutionary history. In a 2006 review article on the neurobiology of positive emotions, Jeffrey Burgdorf and Jaak Panksepp found "there are probably several distinct forms of positive affect, but all are closely related to ancient sub-neocortical limbic brain regions we share with other mammals."[8] This research supports the basic idea that our brains have a deeply programmed ability to generate a variety of emotions, both negative and positive, in both waking and dreaming experience.

The vestibular system that connects the inner ear, eyes, and brainstem presumably plays a central role in mystical dreams of flying, just as it does in gravitational dreams of falling. Whereas in falling dreams the vestibular system generates a sense of weakness and loss of control, in flying dreams the opposite sensations arise of energy, freedom, and autonomous movement through space. The function of the vestibular system in waking life is to maintain a constant, finely tuned sense of one's body in relation to gravity. In ordinary dreams the feeling of one's body in gravitational space is usually preserved without any noticeable difference from waking, suggesting the vestibular system remains online during the dream state. If so, the rare but highly memorable experience of flying in a dream may depend on extraordinary activities in this vital neural network.

Visitation dreams are, by definition, socially interactive experiences, and this means the various brain/mind networks involved in social cognition are going to contribute to their formation. Foremost among these is the medial prefrontal cortex, which supports the human capacity to empathize with other people, appreciate the reality of their subjective experiences, and develop a "theory of mind" to help interpret their feelings, thoughts, and motivations. This part of the brain is quite active in REM sleep, and it seems to be a direct contributor to the abundance of characters and social interactions in most dreams—recall Mary Calkins's 1893 comment that "the dream world is well-peopled." Visitation dreams focus intensely on a person (sometimes an animal) who is no longer alive in the waking world. The dreamer feels a strong sense of the *realism* of that particular character, and as they interact the dreamer often tries to understand the other person's subjective desires and intentions. These are exactly the features of psychological experience most closely associated with the empathetic abilities generated by the medial prefrontal cortex.

A drawback to the reverse engineering approach is that it can easily slide into overly simplistic modular thinking about how the brain works. Modular thinking means looking at bits and pieces of the brain in isolation from each other. The problem is that in reality, brain processes never operate in complete isolation but are always parts of dynamic networks of widely distributed neural systems that constantly influence and shape each other's functioning. Cross-modal activities are pervasive in healthy neurological life. This is particularly true of sophisticated, high-order cognitive abilities like memory, language, reasoning, problem-solving, and dreaming.

Neuroscientists are still early in the process of learning how to analyze and model such massively complex interactions. The study of mystical dreams may actually be relevant to this effort by illuminating specific instances of cross-modal functioning. For example, dreams of otherworldly beauty and aesthetic wonder bring together many different cognitive elements and weave them into a greater, harmonious whole. The following case comes from Roger Knudson's 1999 article "Significant Dreams: Bizarre or Beautiful?" in which he explored a particularly memorable dream reported by a 48-year-old man who was a lifelong musician:

I was dreaming about trees. The trees were all blowing. The wind was blowing, and some were blowing that way and some were blowing this way. And it was a counterpoint of trees, and I was hearing it. There was music, too. They were all sort of going different ways. Then gradually they all started to line up toward this climax, and I realized then in that dream how to write a climax in music. It was part musical, but it was also very visual. I could hear music, although I don't remember if it was Beethoven [a big influence on him at the time]. I was watching the trees and the leaves in the trees. I could almost see the leaves in the trees. The leaves were notes if you will. The trees were made up of notes—almost like an LSD trip. I could see it and hear it. And there was counterpoint like the lines in a Bach fugue that will go different ways.[9]

The dream occurred when the man was 22 years old, and it remained a vivid presence in his mind for more than 25 years afterwards, inspiring him to pursue a lifelong career of teaching, composing, and playing music. What made the dream so striking and memorable was the dramatic *synesthesia* of sight, sound, thought, and movement. Synesthesia means a merging of perceptions from different senses, leading people to say things like they can *hear* colors or *see* ideas. In this dream, the leaves of the trees became musical notes, and the movement of the leaves became the aesthetically pleasing flow of a musical composition toward a creatively satisfying climax. Knudson emphasized that in the process of recounting his dream the man felt compelled to use hand motions, draw pictures, and lay out musical scores to convey what the dream was like. The cross-modal creativity of his dream extended beyond what merely written or spoken language could communicate.

Simulations of Transcendence

The findings considered so far make it clear that mystical dreams are neither random nonsense nor symptoms of mental illness. These kinds of dreams are highly structured, cognitively complex, and psychologically meaningful to the individuals. They have strong carry-over effects both mentally and physically, and they remain vivid memories for many years after the original experience. Far from pathological, mystical dreams seem to reflect a healthy brain/mind system working at extreme levels of intensity.

It is important at this stage to concentrate on the experiential qualities of the dreams themselves and bracket out the religious, spiritual,
and metaphysical meanings that people have historically associated with
them. Those meanings will be explored in greater detail in the next part.
Before we can get to that discussion, however, we need to understand as
much as possible about the neurocognitive roots of these dreams and their
impact on the dreamer.

The previous chapters in this part have discussed the various prototypes of big dreaming as simulations of various kinds of universal human
experience—threats of physical aggression, opportunities for sexual
reproduction, and dangerous encounters with gravity. What kind of experiences could mystical dreams be simulating, since they often portray
supernatural events and abilities completely outside the realm of actual
reality?

The answer, I believe, is that these dreams simulate *possibility*. Not
what is, but what might be. As we have discussed throughout the book,
human beings are distinguished by a uniquely powerful capacity to create, imagine, and innovate. The evolutionary history of our species has
given us unusually large and densely interconnected brains endowed
with tremendous cognitive flexibility. The survival benefits of having
such brains are significant and far-reaching. They gave our earliest ancestors a big advantage over other species in adapting to new habitats and
changing environmental circumstances. They enabled the development
of long-term memory, language, art, culture, and science. They gave rise
to consciousness.

If all this is true, it provides us with a better conceptual framework
for looking at mystical dreams. In this view they should be understood
as expressions of the innate creativity of the human brain/mind system
liberated from all waking constraints. Such dreams are like mental yoga,
enabling people to stretch their awareness beyond the limits of ordinary
existence to explore alternative realities and modes of being. The remarkable neuroplasticity of human sleep helps to establish ideal conditions for
dreaming experiences that transcend the here-and-now to imagine the
what-would-happen-if.

In flying dreams, the simulation has to do with physical power and
individual freedom. The elements of the sleep cycle come together to create a vividly realistic experience of liberation from gravity and from all that
gravity represents. What seems impossible is not necessarily so. Many flying dreams can be easily recognized as metaphorical expressions of some

kind of personally significant meaning, as Lakoff pointed out in his 1991 article on dreams and metaphors. The cultural significance of the "happy is up" metaphor can be directly mapped onto flying dreams, and so can a host of other positive meanings ("good is up," "strong is up"). In some flying dreams, especially those that shift into falling dreams, there may be negative metaphors at work suggesting detachment and lack of grounding ("his head is in the clouds," "she's a space cadet").

In visitation dreams, the simulation is interpersonal. Someone emotionally close to the dreamer is dead and gone, but the dream creates a space in which that person appears alive and able to interact once again, if only for a short time and in cryptic language. The extraordinary realism of the dead person's presence in the dream seems to rely on the coordinated activities of many high-order neural systems and psychological abilities, particularly those involving empathy, social intelligence, and theory of mind. Visitation dreams stretch the limits of ordinary social cognition and broaden the sphere of people's empathetic potential. They expand the range of what counts as a mind to theorize about.

Prototypical Patterns of Dreaming

The four-part mapping laid out in this part is certainly not the only typology ever devised to account for the many variations of highly memorable dreaming. On the contrary, such typologies go back to the beginning of recorded history. Some of the earliest texts ever written were manuals of dream interpretation that systematically categorized people's dreams in terms of the origins, contents, and meanings. Many of these texts are discussed in *Dreaming in the World's Religions*. Here, I want to compare my typology with those of other modern psychologists who have studied similar kinds of dreams.

As the book's title indicates, I take Jung's notion of "big dreams" as the starting point for modern psychological research on this topic. Jung's usage of the term derived primarily from his clinical work with mentally disturbed adults. He found that when he asked his patients about their most memorable dreams from childhood, they gave him dramatic reports of powerful, meaning-rich experiences that could still be clearly remembered many years later.[10] As he explored and interpreted these remarkable dreams, Jung realized they accurately foreshadowed the developmental course of the individual's life, revealing fundamental personality characteristics and long-term challenges.

Jung's approach to big dreams was both more focused and more expansive than mine. As a clinician, he concentrated on the dreams' therapeutic value for his suffering patients. As a psychological theorist, he regarded big dreams as one of many ways in which people tap into the *collective unconscious* of the human psyche and encounter universal *archetypes* like the shadow, persona, trickster, anima/animus, and Self. My approach is deeply indebted to Jung, and I can see many possible connections that could be pursued with his clinical work and theoretical ideas. In this book, however, my aim has been to develop a broad mapping of big dreams using empirical data from many fields of study. These data, and the arguments I build from them, should make sense to readers whether or not they have any clinical training, and whether or not they accept Jung's metapsychology.

Other psychologists have pursued Jung's notion of big dreams in greater depth, seeking a more nuanced understanding of the transformative role of these dreams in people's lives. For instance, psychologist Roger Knudson, whose work on beauty in dreaming was mentioned earlier, has written several excellent articles about highly significant and memorable dreams. These articles combine the ideas of Jung and depth psychologist James Hillman to argue for the importance of imagery and imagination in the study of big dreams. The key feature of big dreaming experience, according to Knudson, is the aesthetic power of especially vivid images: the "image, its life never pinned down, never literalized into a fixed concept or 'meaning,' remains an animating, enlivening presence in the psychic life of the dreamer."[11] The long-term memorability of a dream can be understood not by analyzing specific items of its content but by appreciating the aesthetic image itself, which serves over time as an inexhaustible source of psychological energy and personal insight.

These qualities of dream imagery cannot be easily studied using conventional scientific methods. As discussed earlier in the chapter, my approach does try to account for the aesthetic dimensions of dreaming. But digital technologies and statistical calculations cannot substitute for the kind of deeply probing, finely grained, empathetically sensitive methods of interpretation used by Knudson, Hillman, and others in the Jungian lineage.

Some psychologists have pushed beyond the binary categories of "big" and "little" in trying to account for the varieties of big dreaming experience. Harry Hunt's 1989 book *The Multiplicity of Dreams* has served as an indispensable touchstone in this effort for a generation of researchers (including Knudson and myself). Hunt argued that the essential starting point for dream psychology is the development of a full and detailed phenomenology of dreaming in all its varied forms, from the ordinary to the extraordinary. Once we have such a phenomenology, then we can determine which theoretical perspectives are most helpful in understanding the data. But we are not there yet:

> Dream psychology, in its haste for its own Darwin, has bypassed the necessary foundations of a Linnaeus. The various available systems of quantitative content analysis are complex and reliable, and they correlate to a degree with cognitive, physiological, and personality variables, but they are still reminiscent of attempting to classify the natural order of species by first, ever so precisely, measuring length of limb, size of tooth, body weight, and so on—disregarding whether the animal is a reptile, fish, bird, or mammal.[12]

Hunt's creative synthesis of evidence from cognitive psychology, anthropology, and history enables him to propose a "natural order of dream forms," with each type of dream involving a distinctive combination of visual-spatial and conceptual-verbal processes.[13] The complex multidimensionality of his "dream diamond" model makes it difficult to summarize, but among the various dream types Hunt describes are *personal-mnemonic* dreams, regarding common matters in the dreamer's waking life; *medical-somatic* dreams, relating to physiological processes in the dreamer's body; *prophetic* dreams, presenting omens or images of the future; and *archetypal-spiritual* dreams, with vivid, subjectively powerful encounters with numinous force, often also including extremely strong physical or "titanic" sensations.

Needless to say, my approach has been guided by Hunt's call for dream researchers to establish the "foundations of Linnaeus," meaning the eighteenth-century Swiss botanist Carl Linnaeus, whose naturalistic observations provided the raw material necessary for Darwin to develop the theory of evolution. I agree with Hunt that before we can try to explain the nature and significance of big dreams we need to gather high-quality evidence from many different sources, including laboratory and natural settings. Hunt's model, however, goes beyond mine in identifying several specific kinds of dreaming interaction between the visual-spatial and conceptual-verbal capacities of the mind. My approach is simpler than his, and perhaps more simplistic.

Since 1991 Don Kuiken and his colleagues have been studying recurrent patterns in "impactful dreams," meaning dreams with an ongoing influence on people's thoughts and feelings after waking. Like Hunt, Kuiken has advocated for greater attention to the *multiplicity* of dreams, and he argues against the idea that dreaming has a single, universal function. "Perhaps," Kuiken said, "dreaming *is* a sufficiently uniform phenomenon to consistently serve some function or integrated set of functions. On the other hand, perhaps dreaming is only *apparently* uniform because differences among kinds of dreaming—and among the functions of different kinds of dreaming—have not received sufficient research attention."[14]

Kuiken's research, involving highly detailed analyses of small sets of dreams from college student volunteers, initially identified four types of dreaming with distinct clusters of content: *existential dreams* (distressing, concerned with separation and personal integrity); *anxiety dreams* (frightening, concerned with threats to physical well-being); *transcendent dreams* (ecstatic, concerned with magical accomplishments); and *mundane dreams* (little emotion, unimpactful). His later study added a fifth class, *alienation dreams*, which are moderately impactful and express emotional agitation and concerns about relations with other people. Kuiken and his colleagues have developed elaborate coding systems to separate their sample dreams into typical clusters: "in general, these clusters were differentiable according to six categories of properties: 1) emotions and feelings, 2) goals and concerns, 3) movement style, 4) sensory phenomena, 5) dreamer perspective, and 6) dream endings. Each cluster exhibited distinct profiles of properties from these six categories."[15]

This typology has many points of contact with my approach, starting with its emphasis on the waking impact (or carry-over effects) of the dreams. Kuiken's existential dreams share some similarities with my gravitational dreams; his categories of anxiety and transcendent dreams are comparable to my aggressive and mystical prototypes, respectively. His system has no comparable category for sexual dreams, and mine has no direct parallel to alienation dreams.

Other researchers have proposed additional typologies of highly memorable dreaming, all of which have their merits and drawbacks.[16] I have tried to learn from each of them and contribute something new that hopefully advances our shared enterprise. To understand the multiplicity of dreams requires a multiplicity of sources of evidence, hence my emphasis on cross-cultural and historical reports, demographic surveys, psychological experiments, and brain imaging studies. In developing my set of prototypes I have given priority to the most transparent sources of data, so other researchers can access and study the same material. New digital technologies have created the scholarly opportunity, and the responsibility, of documenting one's sources of information in finely grained detail. Properly designed databases can protect the privacy and confidentiality of research participants while providing access to other investigators interested in further analysis of the data, either to verify its legitimacy, critique its shortcomings, or to extend it in new directions. The best way to promote future progress in the scientific study of dreams is to insist on the transparency and accessibility of primary research data.

Closing Response

There is no evidence that mystical dreams like flying and visitations from the dead are caused by cognitive deficiencies or brain pathologies. On the contrary, scientific evidence from many different sources indicates that these dreams emerge from healthy brain/mind systems operating with unusual degrees of cross-modal coordination and creativity. Experiences of the mystical prototype of dreaming can certainly play a role in people's religious lives, but not simply as literal proof of superstitious beliefs. The influence of these dreams is more a matter of stimulating people's capacities for hope and imagination, envisioning possibilities beyond the limits of present reality ("*Somewhere over the rainbow* ... "). According to the latest findings of evolutionary biology, those are precisely the qualities that best define our species and account for our adaptive success. Being able to dream the impossible is what makes humans *human*.

PART IV

Religious Experience

13
Demonic Seduction

Because from the very beginning of her creation
She was but in a dream.

Genesis Rabbah

Opening Question

Do religions exploit people's nightmares?

As the Roman satirist Petronius first observed almost 2,000 years ago, "It is fear that first brought gods into the world."[1] Throughout history, religions have taken advantage of the fears that naturally arise in nightmares, using those anxieties to manipulate people's feelings and instill ideas in their minds they might not accept in less frightened and vulnerable conditions. Religious teachings about demons, ghosts, and evil spirits exploit the human propensity to experience terrifying dreams, filling people's minds with irrational worries about supernatural beings intent on doing them harm. These beliefs lead people to rely even more strongly on the religious authorities to provide them with spiritual protection, thus leading to a self-sustaining cycle of cynical deception and emotional abuse.

Initial Response

Nightmares of demonic seduction stimulate greater awareness of real procreative dangers.

Religions have devised many different ways of using human fears as tools of oppression, and we can easily recognize the fictional aspects of many religious stories about supernatural beings. But that does not fully explain the mutual interaction of nightmares and religious teachings about demons. Scientific research on highly intensified nightmares can help us better understand the experiential origins of the primal fears that religions try to guide and influence. A closer investigation of a particular type of spirit possession—demonic seduction—reveals a host of unconscious cognitive processes at work, all revolving around dangers to sexuality and procreation. The empirical study of sleep and dreams will help to illuminate the various brain/mind activities involved in generating these vivid nocturnal experiences.

Data and Discussion
Case Study: Sana

This chapter begins the final part of the book, which moves from dreaming to religious experience. Having developed a large base of knowledge about sleep and dreams in the previous three parts, we may now apply that knowledge to the cognitive scientific study of religious experiences in various traditions around the world. In this way we can test and refine the classic hypothesis that dreaming plays an important role in the origins of religion.

To focus the process, I have selected four specific areas of religious experience found in many traditions around the world—demonic seduction, prophetic vision, healing rituals, and contemplative practice. Rather than trying to explain all aspects of all religions, our chances of success will be better if we concentrate on a few kinds of recurrent, widely distributed experiences and try to identify as precisely as we can the connections between big dreams, brain/mind functioning, and religious beliefs and practices.[2]

Each chapter in this part starts with a brief case study that illuminates some of the personal and cultural dimensions of that specific area of religious experience. Here, the case study is drawn from the ethnographic work of Lana Nasser and her conversations with "Sana," a 28-year-old single woman living in Jordan.[3] In the course of several interviews in 2004 Sana described her experiences of being possessed by the *jinn* (*genie* or *genies*), fiery, shape-shifting spirits with origins in the earliest mythology and folklore of the Arabian Peninsula. When Islam arose in the seventh century C.E., it rejected the worship of all other ancient Arabic gods and goddesses in favor of the one God, Allah. The jinn were an exception, however. They were accepted into the new Muslim cosmology and given their own chapter (72) in the Qur'an, in which they accepted their submission to Allah's monotheistic reign. In the centuries since then, the jinn have played a shadowy and spiritually ambivalent role in Muslim life. They are admired as the inspirations for great poetry and music, but more often they are blamed for maliciously causing illnesses, misfortunes, and problems of various kinds.[4]

Sana, who was training to work in a beauty shop, began suffering the signs of possession soon after her boyfriend broke off their relationship, a sudden emotional blow that followed several other jarring developments in her life, including family financial troubles and her father's marriage to a second wife. Sana found herself plagued by a host of physical and psychological symptoms: "moodiness and aggression, depression, appetite loss, insomnia, visual and auditory hallucinations, stomach bloating, and obsessive thoughts about her lover being with other women or about her father dying."[5] She also had bad dreams and nightmares of being attacked by the jinn: she said, "[Y]ou feel something choking you, you want to get up—you can't—you want to open your eyes—you can't."[6] Sana also had dreams in which the jinn would drown her in water and repeatedly carry her high in the air then drop her down to the ground. At one point she had a dream that gave her a clear vision of the jinn that was possessing her: he appeared "like in a TV screen ... tall, slender, good-looking ... not human ... with gold and red lines around his eyes ... his hair was long and he had it tied in a ponytail, and he was dressed normally, like humans, a black T-shirt, a pair of jeans, a belt."[7]

Sana said she felt the jinn was trying to prevent her from getting married, because the jinn loved her and wanted her to love only him. By making her less physically attractive and socially appealing to the outside world, the jinn was keeping Sana for himself so they could be eternal lovers in the spirit world. He gave Sana the magical power of anticipating the future, but she tried not to be tempted by that prophetic gift: "Sana prayed to God to stop this sixth sense of feeling things before they happened because it brought her much worry and was at times deceiving."[8]

Comparative Religions

Sana reported dreams of paralysis, impaired breathing, sensations of flying and then falling, and romantically tinged encounters with a deceptively attractive evil spirit, along with heightened sensitivity toward the future. Are these demonic dream themes unique to Sana, or do they also appear in the dreams of other people in other religious and cultural contexts?

Sana is certainly not alone in Muslim culture, where men as well as women can suffer from jinn possession. In a man's case, the jinn may take a female form, as noted by anthropologist Victor Crapanzano in his study of the jinn beliefs and experiences of religiously devout Muslim men in contemporary Morocco. Crapanzano found these men were especially wary of a certain jinn known as A'isha Qandisha, a she-demon "capable of appearing as a beauty or a hag, but always with the feet of a camel or some other hoofed animal. . . . She is always libidinous, quick-tempered, and ready to strangle, scratch, or whip anyone who insults her or does not obey her commands."[9] In dreams A'isha Qandisha comes to the men in an appealing disguise and seduces them into marrying her and becoming her exclusive lover: "She may require them [the men] to wear old and dirty clothes and never cut their hair or fingernails; she often restricts their sexual activities."[10]

Islam incorporated many aspects of older Jewish biblical teachings and traditions, and Muslim beliefs about A'isha Qandisha may have been influenced by Jewish myths about Lilith, Adam's first wife. These myths arose from the double creation stories in the Book of Genesis—the first one (1:26–27) portrayed the simultaneous creation of a male and a female human, while in the second one (2:7–25) Adam was created first, then Eve was created from one of his ribs. To explain what happened to the woman who came before Eve, stories arose of Lilith, a long-haired woman who lost her human identity and was transformed into a night-dwelling succubus forever haunting people in their sleep. In the *Babylonian Talmud*, a collection of Jewish teachings dating from 200 B.C.E. to 300 C.E., there are several passages that warned people about Lilith attacking them in their dreams. Men who slept alone were considered especially vulnerable to her sexual persuasions, leading to involuntary wet dreams; Lilith allegedly used their semen to spawn multitudes of demon babies. Pregnant women who dreamed of Lilith were at risk of having miscarriages or abnormal births.[11]

This constellation of demonic dream themes does not only appear in Abrahamic traditions but also in other cultures around the world. For example, among the Kuma people of New Guinea mentioned in chapter 8, the men worry about dreams of *masalai*, evil bush spirits who take the form of strange girls in order to tempt the men into dangerous sexual encounters that can lead to illness and death.[12] According to anthropologist Rosalind Shaw, the Temne people of West Africa often suspect that a man who has become ill or suffered a financial misfortune must have formed a sexual relationship in his dreams with a female water spirit called *an-yaron*. If the man stays obedient to *an-yaron*, she will give him good fortune, but if he defies her she may kill him or drive him insane. Temne women who suffer from menstrual irregularities, stomach pains, or miscarriages are often diagnosed as having succumbed in dreams to the sexual allures of bush spirits.[13]

Not all demonic attacks have a direct connection to sexuality and reproduction, but many of them do. Pregnant women are especially likely to be threatened by such assaults, as indicated by this incantation from the ancient Hindu text the *Rig Veda* (1200–900 B.C.E.) used to protect the embryo inside the womb: "Let *Agni* the killer of demons unite with this prayer and expel from here the one whose name is evil, who lies with disease upon your embryo, your womb. . . . The one who by changing into your brother, or your husband or your lover, lies with you, who wishes to kill your offspring—we will drive him away from here. The one who bewitches you with sleep or darkness and lies with you— we will drive him away from here."[14] This prayer reflects a widespread, cross-cultural belief that demons concentrate their malevolent energies on human procreation, threatening to disrupt and destroy people's ability to create new life. Aligned with this belief is an anxious awareness that dreams provide evil spirits with a convenient portal into people's minds and bodies.

Few religious traditions can top medieval and early modern Christianity for its ruthlessly aggressive efforts to battle against demons appearing in dreams. A twelfth-century compilation of Church law, the *Decretum Gratiani*, included a section known as the "Canon Episcopi," which described the grave dangers posed by people who engaged in heretical practices like divination and magic. This text, which governed official Church policies for the next several centuries, focused on the misbehavior of "certain wicked women" who claimed to fly on wild beasts during the night. These women were deluded by the shape-shifting wiles of Satan into believing in the reality of their sinful dream experiences. Christian authorities were instructed to eradicate such beliefs by all means necessary and to replace them with the explanation that ordinary people's dreams are merely the nonsensical productions of their individual minds.

This approach was expanded and intensified in the *Malleus Maleficarum* ("The Hammer of Witches"), a manual written in 1484 to guide Church officials in hunting down and punishing people who consorted with demons.

Dreams were presented in the *Malleus* as one of the ways that witches communicated with the Devil and gained favors from him. In a section detailing various heretical superstitions, special mention was made of:

> the unholy dreams of witches. For when they do not wish . . . to be bodily transferred to a place, but desire to see what their fellow-witches are doing, it is their practice to lie down on their left side in the name of their own and of all devils; and these things are revealed to their vision in images. And if they seek to know some secret, either for themselves or for others, they learn it in dreams from the devil, by reason of an open, not a tacit, pact entered into with him.[15]

The close association of witchcraft and dreaming in Christian demonology had devastating consequences during the seventeenth-century witch trials in the New England colonies. Some of these trials allowed the use of "spectral evidence" in considering the guilt or innocence of the people (mostly young women) accused of witchcraft. Spectral evidence involved testimony by one person that another person had appeared to him or her in a dream with the devilish intention of leading the dreamer astray. The validity of this source of information depended on the premise, well established in official Christian teachings for many centuries, that witches and demons can enter into people's dreams at night and tempt them with immoral desires. Everyone involved in the New England court proceedings believed this to be true, and thus it made a perverse kind of sense that a person on trial for witchcraft could be condemned as guilty based on the dreams other people experienced about the accused. The more intense and unusual (and erotic) their dreams, the stronger the evidence against the accused person.

Examples like these make it clear that people in many different religious traditions throughout history have regarded dreams as a potential source of interaction with evil spirits and seductive demons. This is truly a cross-cultural phenomenon, and possibly a universal feature of human communities. How can we account for such a distinctive constellation of dream-related religious beliefs and experiences, found in so many different places and times?

Psychology and Cognitive Science

At its best, the study of religion draws on the coordinated findings of many academic disciplines. One of those disciplines has traditionally been psychology, going back at least as far as William James and his Gifford Lectures at the University of Edinburgh in 1902–1903, soon thereafter published as *The Varieties of Religious Experience*. In those lectures James argued that psychology, as a science of the human mind, could play a valuable role in explaining why certain themes and patterns recur in religious experiences. He pointed to the already well-established concept of the *subconscious* as the most important bridge between psychology and the study of religion. The subconscious (or *unconscious* in today's terminology) means those parts of the mind outside of normal waking awareness. James used the best available scientific evidence to argue that religious experiences

> [F]requently connect themselves with the subconscious part of our existence. . . . [I]n religion we have a department of human nature with unusually close relations to the transmarginal or subliminal. . . . Our intuitions, hypotheses, fancies, superstitions, persuasions, convictions, and in general all our non-rational operations, come from it. It is the source of our dreams, and apparently they may return to it. . . . It is also the fountain-head of much that feeds our religion. In persons deep in the religious life, as we have now abundantly seen—and this is my conclusion—the door into this region seems unusually wide open; at any rate, experiences making their entrance through that door have had emphatic influence in shaping religious history. . . . Let me then propose, as an hypothesis, that whatever it may be on its farther side, the "more" with which in religious experience we feel ourselves connected is on its hither side the subconscious continuation of our conscious life.[16]

In the 100+ years since James gave his lectures, psychological research on the unconscious has expanded dramatically. Freud, Jung, and others in the broad tradition of depth psychology made enormous strides through the twentieth century, and in the early years of the twenty-first century cognitive scientists have continued to make progress with innovative experimental methods.[17] We today are in a better position than ever to make good on James's claim by illuminating in finer detail the specific connections between religious experiences and unconscious psychological processes.

To accept this claim, we also have to accept James's point about the limitations of a psychological analysis of religious experience. We do not know what else may be involved in these experiences on their "farther side," or even if there is a farther side. What psychology can do is explain some of the recurrent features of religious experience in relation to unconscious processes outside the sphere of ordinary consciousness. This approach allows us to recognize a naturalistic basis for strong, numinous feelings of being connected to something "more" than oneself in religious experiences, something "greater," "bigger," and "more powerful." From a psychological perspective, such feelings are accurate representations of what happens when one's consciousness is flooded with an unusual surge of thoughts, feelings, and energies from the unconscious—the mind suddenly expands its range of awareness and its access to previously unknown depths and dimensions of the self.

However, a psychological analysis says nothing one way or another about the separate existence of gods, angels, or any other supernatural beings. James proposed an evidence-based theory about natural, albeit extraordinary, phenomena in the human psyche.

New research in the cognitive science of religion (CSR) can be understood in the same terms. The findings of CSR investigators help to explain the "hither side" of religious experience, giving us a better understanding of many aspects of unconscious mental processing and their involvement in religious beliefs and practices. As with any psychological approach, CSR neither proves nor disproves any particular metaphysical claims; this limitation has not changed. But cognitive science has brought a fresh air of empirical curiosity to the psychology of religion, and its value should become clear in the coming chapters.

Returning to demonic seductions in dreams, the initial question from a psychological perspective is whether they can somehow be explained in relation to the workings of the unconscious. The answer would seem to be yes, according to a young, pre-psychoanalytic Sigmund Freud, writing a letter to his friend Wilhelm Fliess in January 1897:

> Do you remember that I always said that the medieval theory of possession held by the ecclesiastical courts was identical with our theory of a foreign body and the splitting of consciousness? But why did the devil who took possession of the poor things invariably abuse them sexually and in a loathsome manner? Why are their confessions under torture so like the communications made by my patients in psychiatric treatment?[18]

This letter reflected some of Freud's earliest insights and speculations about the unconscious, prior to writing *The Interpretation of Dreams* (1900) or any of his other major psychoanalytic works. Like James, Freud could see the explanatory potency of this concept, not only in clinical practice but also in the comparative study of religion. Religious reports of seductive demons could be explained as symbolic expressions of unconscious feelings, desires, and fantasies that had been repressed and denied by the conscious mind. Following this line of reasoning, the intensity of the feelings of fear and repulsion in the dreams could provide a way of measuring the degree of unconscious repression—the more "loathsome" the demon, the more deeply repressed the underlying wish.

The idea of a demons–unconscious connection remained in common currency among American and European psychologists through most of the twentieth century. Freud's first biographer, Ernest Jones, wrote an influential 1951 book *On the Nightmare* in which he attributed belief in the devil to the "exteriorization of ... repressed wishes."[19] However, psychoanalysts never launched any systematic efforts to gather more information that might help clarify the empirical contours of this hypothesis. Freud had the evidence of his psychiatric practice, plus his personal readings in history. The same was true of Jones and other psychoanalysts, all of whom recognized the intuitive appeal of this line of thought but did little to extend it with more objective sources of evidence from a wider range of scientific disciplines.

More recently, cognitive scientists have applied new findings about the unconscious to the study of religion, demons, and possession experiences. The best work so far using this approach is Emma Cohen's *The Mind Possessed* (2007), in which she combined ethnographic observations of an Afro-Brazilian healing cult with a cognitive scientific analysis of mental processes that operate "beneath the surface of conscious awareness."[20] Cohen argued that the study of religion and culture should focus less on clever but fruitless interpretations and more on new scientific discoveries about the general functioning of the human mind. Her cognitively informed approach was meant to challenge "the dominant agenda of anthropological scholarship, in which the sole mandate of epistemological relativism produces a situation in which anything goes, provided that it is suitably presented."[21] The best way to promote genuine progress in our understanding of possession is for researchers to ground themselves in the latest findings about "the architecture of the mind":

> [C]ultural phenomena are informed and constrained by tacit mental operations. The cognitive tools responsible for the generation and acquisition of ideas constitute a relatively fixed, generic mental

architecture, the product of human evolution. Insofar as these processes are generalizable across all humans, they provide instructive
insights into the causes of cross-cultural recurrence and spread of
spirit beliefs and related practices.[22]

Cohen's methodological approach is entirely consistent with the long
lineage of James, Freud, and other psychologists who first speculated about
applying the science of the unconscious to the study of religious experiences. Like those earlier psychologists, Cohen did not try to answer metaphysical questions about the reality of demonic possession: "Whether or not
spirits are real, perceptions and understandings of what they are, what they
do, and what they mean are only ever located in human minds."[23] Cognitive
science can help us better understand the "hither" side of possession experiences, but it can say nothing one way or another about their "farther" side.

Influenced by CSR investigators like Justin Barrett, Pascal Boyer,
Dan Sperber, and Harvey Whitehouse, Cohen concentrated her study
on the cognitive aspects of people's beliefs about possession, specifically
the unconscious mechanisms that support the "transmissive success"
of those beliefs: some religious ideas spread more easily and intuitively
than others through large populations. These ideas are more "successful" because they have a quicker, better fit with the innate cognitive systems of the human mind. Cohen argued that the religious beliefs of her
Afro-Brazilian informants were especially compelling to them and easy
to transmit to others because they fit so smoothly with the unconscious
cognitive processes involved in recognizing people, animals, and other
self-directed beings (what CSR calls "agency detection"). Through the
long course of evolution, humans have developed highly sophisticated
mental abilities to identify other "agents" in the environment and make
inferences about their behavior and intentions. Whatever the ontological
status of the Afro-Brazilian spirits (a "farther side" question), Cohen's participants found it cognitively convenient to perceive and think about the
spirits as independent, self-directed beings.

The Afro-Brazilian spirits were not just agents, however. They were
supernatural agents because they had no physical bodies and were privy
to secret sources of information. This made them categorically different
from all other natural agents. Other than these differences, though, the
spirits behaved almost entirely like ordinary humans. This "minimally
counterintuitive" quality made them even easier to remember, discuss,
and share with other people—the spirits were unusual enough to be

noticeable and interesting, yet not so unusual that it was difficult to recall their main characteristics.

Cohen's analysis has considerable merit, and the notion of minimally counterintuitive supernatural agents will be used frequently in this and later chapters. But like many other researchers in CSR, Cohen focused more on how ideas are *transmitted*, and less on the *experiential origins* of those ideas. The cognitive functions of greatest interest to CSR researchers tend to be memory and social intelligence, not imagination and creativity. This takes nothing away from the CSR findings, but it helps explain why so little discussion of dreaming, sexual dynamics, or altered states of consciousness can be found in Cohen's work or in the works of her main CSR influences.[24]

Sleep and Dreaming

Freud and his followers had a good insight about the unconscious roots of demonic seductions in dreams, but limited data to support it. Cohen and her CSR colleagues have a great deal of new information about unconscious mental operations, but they have not (yet) applied it to this specific area of religious experience. Here is the first opportunity for dream research to contribute to CSR and the psychological analysis of religion.

Recall the *jinn* possession of Sana, discussed at the beginning of the chapter. If we consider her physical and mental symptoms in light of current knowledge about sleep and dreaming, we can immediately highlight several points of significance.

First, a general observation: Sana perfectly matches the research-based profile of someone who is likely to be an unusually troubled sleeper and vivid dreamer. As discussed in previous chapters, the most prolific and wide-ranging dreamers tend to be women more often than men, and younger people more often than older people. Furthermore, people who are socially or economically marginalized face much greater risks of sleep disorders and insomnia. Sana, as an unmarried, working-class young woman with tenuous family support, had all the demographic characteristics of a person we would expect to experience a relatively high frequency of unsettled sleep and intensified dreaming. Demographics are not destiny, of course, but the sociological reality is that older, prosperous men are less likely to be big dreamers or victims of spirit possession than younger, poorer women.

Second (and supporting the first point), Sana's dreams have many qualities of sleep paralysis, with her sensations of constricted breathing, physical immobility, and external pressure.[25] This does not mean, however, that her experiences were pathological in ultimate causation. It simply means that Sana's possession very likely involved, among other things, the activation of the brain/mind systems that underlie sleep paralysis.

In many cultures around the world people have come to believe that specific demons are responsible for causing sleep paralysis—the *incubus* and *succubus* of early European folklore, for instance. The "Old Hag" belief of the early settlers of Newfoundland is another example.[26] Contemporary Newfoundlanders still report being "hagged" in their sleep by a menacing presence. A 20-year-old college student told anthropologist David J. Hufford, "You are dreaming and you feel as if someone is holding you down. You can do nothing only cry out. People believe that you will die if you are not awakened."[27] Sana's dreams were pervaded by similar feelings of an evil entity seizing control of her body and trying to do her harm. The cross-cultural recurrence of this theme strongly suggests that the "sleeping body/waking mind" dynamics of sleep paralysis play a generative role in cases of demonic seduction in dreaming.

As a third point, it should be emphasized that Sana's possession dreams included more than just the sensations often associated with sleep paralysis. In fact, her experiences involved elements of all four prototypes of big dreaming: the gravitational sensation of falling, the aggressive motif of an invasion of personal space, the mystical motifs of flying and magical powers, and the subtly sexual image of the jinn as a stylish young man who wanted to marry her. These prototypical features indicate that Sana's experience of possession was driven, at least in part, by intensified activity in the various brain/mind systems involved in big dreaming. This means we cannot reduce her case to the effects of just one kind of dream and its corresponding neural substrate. Sana's possession stimulated the whole of her dreaming imagination.

The sexual dimensions of Sana's experiences may be muted in her reports, given the evidence we have seen of lower frequencies of sexual dreams reported by Arab populations. But this too is a recurrent theme in many reports of demonic possession around the world, and research on big dreams can help in explaining its unconscious roots. As discussed in chapter 10, the ordinary rhythms of the sleep cycle include periods of increased blood flow to the genitals, providing a natural, internally generated source of sexual stimulation in everyone's dream life. Added to this, the lower levels in REM sleep of the inhibitory neurotransmitter GABA enable these libidinal energies to seek expression in ways the waking mind might not ordinarily allow. These innate features of our sleeping brains set the stage for dreams of seductive demons leading us astray, especially in cultural contexts of constricted or forbidden sexual expression. Members of ascetic traditions in both Christianity and Buddhism have struggled through the centuries with the difficulty of controlling these kinds of dreams, in which celibate monks battle against the procreative impulses of their own bodies.

A fourth point combines dream research with CSR: the jinn pursuing Sana in her dreams can be regarded as a minimally counterintuitive supernatural agent. We have seen in previous chapters how realistically the dreaming imagination can portray our social relations and the people with whom we interact in daily life. In Sana's case the innate social intelligence of her sleeping mind extended beyond the sphere of ordinary, familiar characters to engage with a mythic being of legendary religious significance. The jinn is a spiritual being made of fire, and thus decidedly nonhuman and supernatural, but he can also appear as an ordinary, indeed very attractive human male. Like any other person he has intentions and goals, and like any other person he can communicate with others and try to align his interests with theirs. As Cohen and other CSR researchers have shown, beliefs in supernatural agents can have the effect of stimulating a great deal of inferential thinking about those agents—what they are like, what they can and cannot do, why they are attacking, how to defend against them, and so forth. For Sana, the belief that she was possessed by a jinn seemed to have this same cognitive effect of stimulating her to think more intently about her problems and the difficult circumstances of her life. The jinn became the central figure in Sana's mental and physical dis-ease, the spiritual personification of all her symptoms. The jinn gave her a religious and psychological framework in which she could try to make better sense of what was happening to her and how she might get better. The cognitive benefits of thinking of her situation in terms of jinn possession may actually have had a therapeutic effect.

This kind of exploration could continue in much more detail, of course. Indeed, I can easily imagine a deeper, book-length exploration of a particular case study of demonic possession, using larger collections of dream data and expanded access to personal, familial, and cultural information. But for now, the goal has been to identify some specific ways that dream research can help in the psychological analysis of demonic possession. The discussion so far has suggested that:

- Dreams of seductive demons can happen to anyone, but they are more likely to occur to socially and economically marginalized people, especially young women, and to sexually constrained people like ascetic monks;
- Sleep paralysis plays a role in generating many of the experiential qualities;
- All four big dream prototypes can be involved, especially the procreative motifs of sexual dreaming;
- The dreamers interact with the demons as social characters, often as minimally counterintuitive supernatural agents.

These characteristics apply not only to Sana's case but also to the other cross-cultural examples mentioned earlier. If we take all this evidence into account, we can offer some possible explanations and testable hypotheses that apply to this area of religious experience. Dreams of demonic seduction reflect a natural combination of innate brain/mind capacities in sleep. They have unconscious psychological roots that are independent of culture, which means these kinds of dream experiences probably occur to some portion of the population in every human community, whether people openly report them or not, whether the religious authorities welcome them or not. The brain/mind capacities involved in demonic dreams are not pathological in themselves, although they may become more highly activated at times of illness, stress, and poor health. The dreams seem to occur most often in situations revolving around threats to sexuality, pregnancy, and childbirth. They have the effect of stimulating a great deal of social cognition, inferential reasoning, metacognitive awareness, and bodily arousal with physical carry-over sensations. They provoke greater consciousness of the dangers, and the pleasures, of trying to fulfill the deep biological imperative to create new life.

The evidence from sleep and dream research is potentially compatible with other kinds of explanations of demonic possession. Sana had a family life filled with Oedipal drama, so a more detailed psychoanalytic study of her dreams would certainly find much to consider. Historians and social scientists could further illuminate the cultural influences that gave shape and substance to her interactions with the jinn. As we know from previous chapters, such influences can have a big impact on the dreaming imagination. But the key point is that the social and historical factors are not working with a blank slate—there is a pre-cultural substrate of dreaming that makes use of cultural material but remains independent from it, emerging from deeper unconscious processes in the evolved architecture of the human mind. These unconscious processes are necessary, though not sufficient, conditions for experiences of demonic seduction in dreaming to occur.[28]

Concluding Response

Beliefs about demonic seduction in dreams have a basis in real psychological experience and real biological concerns about potential threats to procreation. These dreams are not simply the products of irrational ignorance, misplaced fear, or religious conditioning, but are instead expressions of innately creative powers of the imagination in sleep, powers shared by all members of our species.

Prophetic Vision

What the dreams I've had from mid-March to now,
which is to say scores and scores of them,
mean is that: This is prophetic knowledge.
The Exegesis of Philip K. Dick

Opening Question

Do allegedly prophetic dreams delude people into accepting the irrational claims of diviners, astrologers, and soothsayers?

In his 2008 book *The God Delusion*, Richard Dawkins proposed a "general theory of religion as an accidental by-product—*a misfiring of something useful*."[1] Putting his theory in psychological terms, Dawkins said that religious beliefs and practices may be explained as the results of malfunctioning "modules" of cognitive processing in the brain. These modules are normally directed toward useful activities, but when something goes wrong they can spin off in strange and pointless directions, with little or no connection to their originally valuable functions.[2] This seems to be the case when people have hallucinatory visions and hyper-realistic dreams that allegedly predict things to come. Religions take advantage of these cognitive misfirings to persuade people that prophetic dreams and other divinatory practices can provide accurate information about the future, particularly if the dreams come from authoritative experts like priests or shamans.

Initial Response

Big dreams can prompt intense activation of the brain/mind processes devoted to visual imagination and creative forethought.

Some forms of illness may prompt strange dreams and nightmares, but that does not mean all dreaming is pathological. As we have seen, dreaming reflects a natural, healthy, and adaptive mode of brain/mind functioning, a mode that sometimes reaches extraordinarily high degrees of cognitive sophistication. Dreams cannot be explained (away) as the results of psychological "misfirings." Religious reports of prophetic dreaming can be better understood as experiences involving the neural processes of visual imagination responsible for generating the intense imagery and prospective insights characteristic of many big dreams. I collectively refer to these processes as the "autonomous visionary capacity," meaning an innate neurocognitive network that orients the sleeping mind toward the visual apprehension of future possibilities.

Data and Discussion
Case Study: Perpetua

People in religions all over the world have looked to dreams for glimpses of the future, seeking information beyond what is given by the ordinary senses. Whether the prophetic power is attributed to the gods, the travels of the dreamer's soul, or some other spiritual force, there is a nearly universal belief that dreams offer a means of expanding the individual's range of temporal perception and gaining knowledge about potentially harmful or beneficial events in the future. Although often compared to other divinatory practices like astrology, crystal gazing, reading entrails, and so forth, prophetic dreaming is different in having a well-understood naturalistic foundation in the workings of the sleeping mind. This foundation has a long evolutionary history in our species that predates the appearance of religious teachings, authorities, and traditions. Religions may indeed manipulate and abuse people's beliefs about their prophetic dream experiences, but the experiences themselves emerge from deeply rooted capacities in the human psyche.

To begin exploring these capacities in more detail, let us consider another case study, this one drawn from earlier in history. It involves a young Roman woman named Perpetua, who lived in the prosperous Mediterranean city of Carthage in the late second century c.e., during the reign of Septimius Severus. Perpetua was an educated member of a well-to-do family, but when she converted to the new religion of Christianity she came into conflict with the Roman imperial government and its requirement that everybody participate in rituals of fidelity to the emperor and the gods. Perpetua refused, and so she was imprisoned and sentenced to death.

During her time in prison Perpetua recorded a diary. She had given birth a few months previously (her diary does not mention a husband), and she wrote about her worries for the infant child, whom she was secretly breast-feeding in her jail cell. She wrote about terrible arguments with her distraught father, who begged his daughter to change her mind. And, she wrote about her dreams.

The first dream came in response to a question prompted by her brother, also a Christian convert, who said to her, "My lady, my sister, you are now greatly blessed; so much so that you can ask for a vision, and you will be shown if it [the imprisonment] is to be suffering unto death or a passing thing." In other words, would she receive a pardon, as many other Christian prisoners had, or would her sentence be carried out? Perpetua did as her brother suggested, praying for such a vision as she fell asleep. She then reported having a dream blending Christian imagery with surrealistic details from her own personal situation:

> I saw a bronze ladder, marvelously long, reaching as far as heaven, and narrow too: people could climb it only one at a time. And on the sides of the ladder every kind of iron implement was fixed: there were swords, lances, hooks, cutlasses, javelins, so that if anyone went up carelessly or not looking upwards, she would be torn and her flesh caught on the sharp iron. And beneath the ladder lurked a serpent of wondrous size, who laid ambushes for those mounting, making them terrified of the ascent . . . [With the encouragement of another convert in the dream, Perpetua stepped on the head of the serpent and rose up the ladder, praying for safety. Once she reached the top of the ladder she found herself in a mystical scene of pastoral bliss:] I saw an immense space of garden, and in the middle of it a white-haired man sitting in shepherd's garb, vast, milking sheep, with many thousands of people dressed in shining white standing all around. And he raised his head, looked at me, and said, "You are welcome, child." And he called me, and gave me, it seemed, a mouthful of the *caseo* he was milking; and I accepted it in both my hands together, and ate it, and all those standing around said: "Amen." And at the sound of that word I awoke, still chewing something indefinable and sweet. And at once I told my brother, and we understood that it would be mortal suffering; and we began to have no more hope in the world.

Perpetua's dream directly incorporated a great deal of imagery from classic Christian belief and iconography—the malevolent serpent, the ladder to heaven, the benevolent shepherd, the shining white garments. But the climactic moment of the dream came in the experience of eating the *caseo*, variously translated as cheese, milk, or sweet curds. This was the moment when Perpetua awoke, with that vividly pleasant taste sensation carrying over into waking awareness.[3]

Comparative Religions

Perpetua recorded three more dreams of prophetic import in her diary, which we will discuss later in the chapter. Focusing for the moment on her first dream, we can identify the key recurrent themes also found in reports of prophetic dreams from other religious traditions around the world.

Most important, Perpetua's dream came during a time of acute personal crisis. This is true of many other prophetic dreams occurring in relation to some kind of major change, transition, or difficulty in the dreamer's waking life. Death and dying represent one such moment of crisis, and many prophetic dreams are believed to herald the dreamer's imminent demise. The great Chinese sage Confucius (551–479 B.C.E.) reportedly had a dream foretelling his death a few days later. In the dream Confucius was sitting between two pillars in a royal hallway where funeral rituals were held, and "the sacrificial offerings [were] in full view."[4] No other people were in attendance, however, and Confucius understood this as a portent that the funeral would soon be his own.

Another ancient philosopher, Socrates (470–399 B.C.E.), also told of a strange dream that predicted his impending death. The Platonic dialogue known as the *Crito* opened with Socrates asleep in his prison cell while the Athenian authorities awaited the arrival of a ceremonial boat that would signal the time for his execution for crimes against the state religion. His friend Crito was sitting in the cell when Socrates awoke just before dawn, and Socrates immediately declared the boat in question would not arrive that day:

Crito: What makes you think that?
Socrates: I will try to explain. I think I am right in saying that I have to die on the day after the boat arrives?
Crito: That's what the authorities say, at any rate.

Socrates: Then I don't think it will arrive on this day that is just begin-
    ning, but on the day after. I am going by a dream that I had in the
    night, only a little while ago. It looks as though you were right not
    to wake me up.
Crito: What was the dream about?
Socrates: I thought I saw a gloriously beautiful woman dressed in white
    robes, who came up to me and addressed me in these words: "Socrates,
    'To the pleasant land of Phthia on the third day thou shalt come.'"
Crito: Your dream makes no sense, Socrates.
Socrates: To my mind, Crito, it is perfectly clear.

As Socrates foresaw, the boat did not arrive that day. Soon afterwards
he took his own life by drinking a cup of hemlock.[5]

At the other end of the life cycle, auspicious dreams are often believed
to attend the births of special children. The Jain Dharma and Buddhist
traditions of India both tell stories of beneficial prophetic dreaming
in pregnancy,[6] and so does Christianity in the first two chapters of the
Gospel of Matthew, including this dream of Joseph: "But while he thought
on these things, behold, the angel of the Lord appeared unto him in a
dream, saying, Joseph, thou son of David, fear not to take unto thee Mary
thy wife: for that which is conceived in her is of the Holy Ghost."[7]

Prophetic dreaming is not just about the future, but about *important
things* that will happen in the future. Along with death and birth, frequent topics include religious initiations, military battles, family conflicts, health problems, hunting prospects, threatening weather, and
cultural crises. Future-gazing dreams seem to be stimulated by any situation that is emotionally charged, extremely important, and yet unclear
in its outcome. An intense desire to know is frustrated by the difficulty
of predicting or influencing the coming results. Reaching the limits of
ordinary conscious thought and reasoning, people look for ways to extend
their perceptual abilities farther ahead in time. Dreaming has served in
cultures all over the world as a widely accessible resource in these mantic
pursuits.

A second notable quality in Perpetua's dream was its striking visual
imagery, with a host of aesthetically complex and vividly rendered elements. Many other prophetic dreams also include highly memorable
images of people, places, and activities that, in the dreamer's mind at
least, are directly and meaningfully connected to the future. The images
do not always take bizarre or supernatural forms; what matters most is

the intensity of the visual sensations. The power of the image provides an experiential confirmation of the dream's premonitory meaning.

Several Native American traditions have made a special practice of attending to the visual imagery in their dreams and using it to guide future behavior, both individually and collectively. According to Lee Irwin in his 1993 book *The Dream Seekers*, the native cultures of the Great Plains are especially attuned to their visionary dreams: "[T]he vision is recognized as a form of encounter with mythically defined sources of personal empowerment and as a manifestation of the mysterious contents of a visionary world."[8] Along the same lines, an early twentieth-century anthropologist made the following observation about the Blackfoot Indians, one of the nomadic groups who ranged across the prairies of what is now Canada and the United States: "[A] dream, especially if it is a strong one—that is, if the dream is very clear and vivid—is almost always obeyed. As dreams start them [the Blackfoot] on the war path, so, if a dream threatening bad luck comes to a member of a war party even if in the enemy's country and just about to make an attack on a camp, the party is likely to turn about and go home without making any hostile demonstrations."[9]

These Native American beliefs about the power of visionary dreaming cannot be dismissed as the foolish superstitions of tribal peoples. Similar ideas have been developed in the highly literate teachings of Sufi Islam, Tibetan Buddhism, and Eastern Orthodox Christianity, among others. Reports of visually powerful, future-oriented dreams appear in religious traditions all over the world, indicating this is another specific type of cross-cultural religious experience centering on intensified dreaming.

Psychology and Cognitive Science

Here, then, is a second opportunity to apply dream-focused research from psychology and cognitive science to the study of religion. Before going further, however, we should acknowledge the many uncertainties that arise in trying to explain the psychological dynamics of prophetic dream visions. To start, how do we know a supposedly prophetic dream really came true? Perhaps it was just a coincidence with no real predictive meaning. Why should we believe someone who claims to have such dreams? People in crisis situations are obviously desperate for any source of help, and this makes them more likely to fantasize about what might happen in the future. How can we ever know the dreamers are not simply fabricating their reports, either consciously or unconsciously?

These questions show how difficult it is to study this aspect of religiously significant dreaming. We can never know with certainty whether or not people are telling the truth about their experiences, and coincidental results are always a possibility. In light of such concerns, it would be tempting to dismiss the whole subject as unworthy of serious investigation.

However, even taking these skeptical questions into account, there remains a psychological core to these dreams, a core that can be plausibly explained as the outgrowth of naturalistic processes in the mind during sleep. Cognitive scientists have begun to map these processes and show in greater detail than ever before how they impact religious beliefs and practices. We may never be able to prove the veracity of any one particular dream report, but we can definitely shed light on the psychological dynamics that make it possible for people to experience real, visually intensified dreams that strike them as prophetic.

As noted in the previous chapter, CSR researchers have not spent much time exploring the unconscious mental activities that generate dreams. But one of the early models of CSR, the "modes of religiosity" theory of anthropologist Harvey Whitehouse, has taken seriously the religious impact of intense visual experiences and tried to explain their effects in terms of unconscious mental processes.[10] Whitehouse's approach can provide some initial ideas about how cognitive science may be relevant to a better understanding of prophetic dreaming.

Whitehouse himself emphasized that his theory was not meant to neatly divide the world's religions into two separate camps.[11] What he called the *doctrinal* and *imagistic* modes of religiosity referred to two different tendencies that have shaped the various ways people express and practice their religions. In the doctrinal mode, religious activities become larger and more standardized, with less emotional arousal and weaker social bonds. In the imagistic mode, religious activities develop in smaller and more idiosyncratic groups, with greater emotional arousal and closer social bonds. Using cognitive scientific research, Whitehouse argued that these two modes of religiosity have an intuitive appeal to humans everywhere because of their close fit with two different kinds of memory. The doctrinal mode depends a great deal on *procedural memory*, the system devoted to specific actions (such as tying your shoe, or performing a church ritual). The imagistic mode, however, relies primarily on *episodic memory*, the system that stores unique experiences of great meaning and emotional arousal (such as your first kiss, or a divine revelation).

Our interest lies with the imagistic mode, which Whitehouse regarded as the evolutionarily older of the two: "[T]he presence of the imagistic mode almost certainly predates the emergence of the doctrinal mode by a very substantial margin."[12] Whitehouse never focused any particular attention on dreaming, but his account of imagistic religiosity has many points of connection with our previous discussions of big dreams. The preeminent features of religious experiences in the imagistic mode, according to Whitehouse, are *low frequency* and *high arousal*: they do not occur often, but when they do occur they carry an extraordinary emotional impact. Exactly the same can be said of big dreams, of course. As an anthropologist, Whitehouse was more inclined to study the behavior of groups, but what he said about religious rituals could also apply to intensified visionary dreaming: "[R]arely performed and highly arousing rituals invariably trigger vivid and enduring episodic memories among the people who participate in them."[13]

If big dreams may be fairly considered a generative source of imagistic religiosity, then what else can Whitehouse's CSR analysis tell us? At least two things. First, even though the imagistic mode appeared earlier in human history, Whitehouse noted that in modern society it usually occupies a marginal position compared to doctrinal religion: "[I]t is precisely within those populations that lack access to the authoritative corpus of religious teachings . . . that we find the greatest profusion of imagistic practices."[14] This seems consistent with the role dreams have often played through history of providing an unorthodox religious resource for people with relatively little power and low social status.

A second point from Whitehouse's analysis has to do with the immediate cognitive after-effects of an imagistic religious experience. Whitehouse said these experiences often prompt people to engage in "spontaneous exegetical reflection," that is, an urgent mental need to ponder what just happened and what it might mean.[15] Following such an experience people often feel their minds overflowing with a sudden torrent of thoughts, feelings, and possible interpretations, stimulating further lines of thought that feed into wider cognitive networks. All of this works to encode the experience into long-term memory and facilitate its compelling effects on the mind. As Whitehouse observed, "rare and climactic rituals evoke abundant inferences, producing a sense of multivalence and multivocality of religious imagery, experienced as personal and unmediated inspiration."[16] I suggest this sudden profusion of thought is the cognitive equivalent of the carry-over effects of big dreams discussed in Part III. The CSR notion of spontaneous exegetical reflection can help to clarify these carry-over effects and their long-lasting psychological impact on the individual.

Dream Research

Left unaddressed in Whitehouse's work is the question of how the imagistic experiences arise in the first place. Something or other apparently just happens, and then the cognitive functions of memory, exegetical reflection, and cultural transmission take over. Whitehouse and other CSR researchers have many excellent things to say about those secondary functions, but not so much about the primary experiences that set the whole process in motion (other than hint about their possibly pathological nature).

We can do better with the help of scientific knowledge about big dreaming. Start with the etymological fact that in many languages all across the world, the word for "dream" relates to words for seeing, sight, and the eyes (discussed in chapter 5). This is strong cross-cultural evidence of a predisposition in the human mind toward visual sensations in dreaming. The other senses may become active, too, but for the majority of people sight is by far the most prevalent. As noted in chapter 8, the only cases where I have found fewer references to sight than sound are in the dreams of blind people.[17] This makes perfect sense in light of the continuity hypothesis: people who lack visual perception in waking life are less likely to have visual perceptions in their dreams.[18]

The predominance of visual experience is not merely an artifact of language or description. It has a solid basis in the brain's functioning during sleep. Our knowledge about this comes from two different sources of neuroscientific research, which converge on the same central point of agreement with etymological history. First, brain imaging studies have shown that REM sleep brings a lowering of activity in the neural regions devoted to sensory input from the eyes (V1, the primary visual cortex).[19] At the same time, REM sleep stimulates higher activity in the brain regions associated with visual imagination and internal imagery (the medial temporal lobe and fusiform gyrus). This pattern of neural activation in REM sleep is exactly what we would expect to find if people through history have been accurately describing their dreams as "visions in sleep."

Further confirmation comes from Mark Solms and his neuropsychological study of more than 300 hospital patients suffering from a variety of injuries and diseases affecting the brain.[20] Solms found a key neurological distinction—a "double dissociation"—between waking eyesight and the experience of visual dreaming. People with damage to the primary visual processing area of the brain continue to have dreams with normal visual imagery, while people with damage to parts of the brain responsible for inner imagination lose all visual dreaming, even though their primary visual processes remain intact and healthy. Thus, people whose external eyesight is fine may have no visual experience in their dreams, while people who have gone blind can still in many cases have visual dreams.

Seeing in dreaming is a *different kind of seeing* than seeing in waking.

Considering these findings in the broader cross-cultural context, we begin to understand that humans are born, not only with tremendous powers of external visual perception but also with an *autonomous visionary capacity* that can create a seemingly limitless variety of vividly realistic scenarios in our minds during sleep. This capacity for the spontaneous emergence of intense imagistic experience appears to be a natural and healthy feature of the human psyche.

It certainly arises often enough in big dreams. Each of the four prototypes discussed in Part III has many instances of intensified visual sensations that enhance the emotional impact and memorability of the experiences. The images can vary widely in their content—from horrible monsters to beautiful lovers, from everyday reality to otherworldly realms—but they all share a tremendous perceptual power and vividness that sets them apart from other dreams. Reports of extreme visual imagery such as overwhelming brilliance and shining white light also pervade these dreams.

So, there is strong scientific evidence supporting the notion that the brain/mind system has innate capacities in dreaming for intensified visual experience.

There is also abundant evidence showing that dreaming functions in part as a psychological means of simulating the future and anticipating possibilities that might arise in waking life. The big dreaming prototypes all revolve around future possibilities and scenarios with relevance for survival, reproduction, and healthy adaptation. There is nothing magical or supernatural about this; it simply reflects the way our minds have evolved to think about the temporal environment. The brain that spends the day engaged in future-oriented thought (planning, preparing, anticipating, scheduling) is also the brain that sleeps at night and remains engaged in many of those same cognitive processes, preoccupied by the same concerns and challenges of waking life. The difference is that in sleep the brain has greater powers of neuroplasticity, an extended range of cognitive creativity, wider associative networks, less executive control, and looser constraints on what can and cannot be thought.

Put these sleep-based capacities for spontaneous visionary experience and unconstrained creative forethought together, and you get a perpetual neurocognitive source of imagistically rich prophetic dreaming. Religions may take advantage of this source of premonitory insight, but they did not create it. The capacities are built into the evolved architecture of our brains, primed by unconscious processes that almost inevitably stimulate a flow of conscious waking thought (akin to what Whitehouse calls spontaneous exegetical reflection). In situations of acute crisis and mortal danger, it would make sense for these capacities to intensify their adaptive functioning, prompting stronger visions with greater impact and memorability.

There is a naturalistic basis for prophetic visionary dreaming in the workings of the mind in sleep. These kinds of dreams cannot be simply dismissed as cognitive misfirings. Other aspects of religion may be explained in that way, but Dawkins's theory does not fit well with empirical research showing that dreaming arises from the normal functioning of neurocognitive processes devoted to adaptive forethought.

Dawkins himself has questioned the limitations of a maximally skeptical view of dreaming, in a tweet he posted on December 26, 2013:

Are dreams epiphenomenal or have they Darwinian survival value? I find "tidying the hard disk" (Evans, Crick) to be not a big enough theory.[21]

"Evans" is Christopher Evans, a British psychologist and computer scientist, who wrote *Landscapes of the Night: How and Why We Dream* (1983, posthumously edited by his son Peter Evans). "Crick" is Francis Crick, Nobel Prize winner in 1962 with James Watson for their discovery of DNA. In 1983 Crick co-wrote a paper in the prestigious journal *Nature*, titled "The Function of Dream Sleep." Both Evans and Crick compared the human brain to a kind of biological computer, and this analogy led to their dismissive analysis of dreams as neurologically equivalent to parasitic computer codes that must periodically be wiped clean from the hard drive. Dawkins, however, found this viewpoint not "big enough." He seemed to regard the brain-computer analogy as too narrow in accounting for the role of dreaming in human life, thus opening the door to new research that treats dreaming not as a random by-product of sleep but as a potentially adaptive mode of brain/mind functioning that contributes to human survival and reproduction.

Dawkins would probably never consider taking the further step of connecting dreams to religion. After all, he has made plain his resolutely atheistic outlook: "Religious beliefs are irrational. Religious beliefs are dumb and dumber: super dumb."[22] At the same time, Dawkins also expresses his admiration for the tremendous creative power of the human brain, the emergence of which he believes marked a unique transitional moment in the history of life on earth:

> It seems likely that, after the *Homo Sapiens* singularity, evolution may never be the same again. The Singularity . . . resulted from the natural evolution of the human brain, which, under the blind forces of natural selection, expanded to the point where, all unforeseen, it overreached itself and started to behave insanely from the selfish gene's point of view. . . . The big brain achieved the evolutionarily unprecedented feat of genuine foresight: became capable of calculating long-term consequences beyond short term selfish gain.[23]

What Dawkins referred to as the brain "overreaching itself" is very much what I am trying to describe as an aspect of human dreaming, particularly in big dreams where the sleeping mind is overreaching in many different ways. Dawkins says this new cognitive freedom enabled humans to channel their genetic instincts in alternative, self-chosen directions, guided by a greater ability to anticipate future possibilities and imagine better life prospects. I completely agree with this, and would simply add that the brain's newfound powers extended to dreaming as well as waking mentation, as part of an overall boost in neurocognitive functioning in our species.

None of this would likely persuade Dawkins to think of religion as less than "super dumb." But the chief goal of a CSR analysis is to identify the brain/mind functions that most likely give rise to specific types of religious phenomena. This kind of analysis cannot say whether those phenomena are dumb or smart, good or bad, ontologically real or illusory. All we can do is highlight the "hither side" psychological processes that correspond most closely to their recurrent features. Here, we have found evidence suggesting the human brain has evolved with innate tendencies to have visually intense, future-oriented dreams, and these dreams are frequently woven into people's religious systems of meaning and belief.[24]

Such was the case with Perpetua. We will never know if she really dreamed the dreams she reported in her diary. But we do know, based on cognitive scientific knowledge, that a normal person in her circumstances would be highly primed to experience intense dreams with strong visual images and anticipatory themes.

All four of the dreams she recorded had these qualities. Her first one followed a practice of *dream incubation* (to be discussed more in the next chapter), prompted by her brother's suggestion to pray for a prophetic vision. The dream's dramatic imagery was surely influenced by one of the great night visions in the Bible, Jacob's dream of the heavenly ladder in the Book of Genesis: "And he dreamed, and behold a ladder set up on the earth, and the top of it reached to heaven: and behold the angels of God ascending and descending on it."[25]

The memorability of Perpetua's dream was further enhanced by the unusual carry-over effect of the sweet taste of *caseo*, a detail that turned out to have enormous metaphorical significance for her. A few days after this dream, Perpetua's child no longer needed to nurse, having grown old enough to start eating solid food. Perpetua welcomed this development as a minor miracle: "And somehow, through God's will, [the baby] no longer needed the breast, nor did my breasts become inflamed—so I was not tormented with worry for the child, or with soreness."[26] Her dream anticipated the transition from milk to solid food in her child, which metaphorically mirrored her impending transition from nursing mother to religious martyr.[27] Just as she no longer needed to worry about the child's survival, she no longer had to worry about her own survival.

Perpetua's second and third dreams related to another brother who had died many years before, and her anxieties about the fate of his soul—an especially urgent concern for members of her religious group. These two dreams also had striking visual images (her brother's face, a pool of water) involving a pressing question about the immediate future: What would her own death bring?

After these three dreams, after the baby had stopped nursing, and after her father had raged at her one last time ("wasted and worn . . . he began to tear out the hair of his beard and fling it on the ground"[28]), Perpetua had a fourth and final dream. In this dream she was taken from the prison to the amphitheater, where a huge crowd had gathered to watch the spectacle. At this point Perpetua suddenly changed her gender: "And I was stripped naked, and became a man."[29] From the other side of the arena "a man of amazing size came out—he towered even over the vault of the amphitheater."[30] The two warriors prepared for a wrestling match to the death:

> And we joined combat, and fists began to fly. He tried to grab my feet, but I struck him in the face with my heels. And I felt airborne, and began to strike him as if I were not touching ground. But when I saw there was a lull, I locked my hands, clenching my fingers together, and so caught hold of his head; and he fell on his face, and I trod upon his head. The populace began to shout, and my supporters to sing jubilantly. . . . And triumphantly I began to walk towards the Gate of the Living. And I awoke. And I knew I should have to fight not against wild beasts but against the Fiend; but I knew the victory would be mine.[31]

Her diary ended there. The next day Perpetua was brought from the prison to the amphitheater where a large crowd, gathered to celebrate the birthday of the Emperor's son, cheered as she was mauled to death by lions.

Concluding Response

To grant a degree of small-p prophetic power to dreaming is not to believe in magical powers, divine interventions, or happy endings. Our brains have evolved to continually think about the future in waking and dreaming, and this ability has given us enormous cognitive freedom to anticipate, adapt, and respond intentionally to life's varying circumstances, both positive and negative. In dreaming, our powers of forethought are boosted by an innate neural capacity to generate spontaneous visionary experiences during sleep. These visionary dreams can make strong and lasting impressions on waking awareness, stimulating extensive conscious reflection about their potential meanings and anticipatory significance. Such dreams naturally lend themselves to religious interpretations. These interpretations may have some merit if they remain focused on the specific content of the dreams and the circumstances of the dreamer's life.

15

Ritual Healing

One, two, Freddy's coming for you
Three, four, better lock your door
Five, six, grab a crucifix
Seven, eight, gonna stay up late
Nine, ten, never sleep again
A Nightmare on Elm Street

Opening Question

Are claims about the healing power of dreams just another form of desperate, irrational religious thinking?

Illness, suffering, and death can strike anyone, at any time. The human condition involves an anxious awareness of our inescapable mortality, our perpetual vulnerability to a sudden blow to physical health. Many people become frantic for magical relief when they fall sick, thus creating a lucrative market for priests, shamans, and other alleged "healing experts" who claim to work miracles. In the final pages of his highly influential 1996 book *How the Mind Works*, cognitive psychologist Steven Pinker argued that this kind of deceptive "hocus pocus" lies at the heart of religion: "Religion is a desperate measure that people resort to when the stakes are high and they have exhausted the usual techniques for the causation of success. . . . In culture after culture, people believe that the soul lives on after death, that rituals can change the physical world and divine the truth, and that illness and misfortune are caused and alleviated by spirits, ghosts, saints, fairies, angels, demons, cherubim, djinns [*sic*], devils, and gods. . . . Shamans and priests are Wizards of Oz who use special effects, from sleight-of-hand and ventriloquism to sumptuous temples and cathedrals, to convince others that they are privy to forces of power and wonder."[1] Religions, in Pinker's view, are merely organized bands of spiritual hucksters preying on scared, sick people who have exhausted their options with conventional medical treatments, making them all too eager to accept the dubious methods and illogical beliefs of faith healers.

Initial Response

Dream-based rituals and practices can stimulate a natural placebo effect that aids the body's innate capacities for healing, recovery, and self-repair.

During the normal course of human sleep the immune system becomes highly active, performing a variety of essential tasks for bodily health. Religiously inspired dream rituals can have the medically useful function of enhancing those endogenous healing processes. What Western researchers call the "placebo effect" can be activated in certain kinds of dreams, particularly in big dreams with highly memorable images, characters, and emotions. These dreams can boost the physiological impact of the placebo effect and mobilize the body's own illness-fighting defenses.

Data and Discussion
Case Study: Aristides

As Pinker correctly noted, people in cultural traditions all over the world have drawn on religious beliefs and practices to help alleviate their physical suffering and protect them against illness. In many of these traditions dreaming has served as a therapeutic resource providing insight into the causes of sickness, guidance in treating the symptoms, and hope for the ultimate restoration of good health. The dreams often have an explicitly religious dimension to them, but they also have direct connections to the physiological state of the dreamer's body. Rather than assuming a categorical opposition between religious and secular methods of healing, we should take seriously the mounting evidence of a dynamic interplay of physical, psychological, and cultural forces in the healing process, an interplay we can see with special clarity in dreaming experience.

The historical background to this aspect of human religiosity has deep roots in the ancient teachings of many traditions. One of the best illustrations of dream-based religious healing practices comes from the same cultural world as Perpetua's, just a few years before her birth, in much more favorable conditions. The Roman orator Aelius Aristides was born in

117 C.E., to a wealthy family in what is now Turkey.[2] At a young age he was sent to study in the nearby city of Smyrna, a major center of Roman education specializing in classical Greek culture. The Romans had recently expanded their territorial control across the eastern Mediterranean into Asia Minor, and this prompted a burst of interest in the literature, philosophy, and science of ancient Greece. A new group of scholars emerged—the *sophists*—whose deep knowledge of the Greek intellectual heritage made them highly valued in Roman society as speakers, writers, and governmental advisors. Smyrna had a lively community of sophists, and from them Aristides received an extensive education in the theory and practice of classical oratory. Showing great talent from an early age, he traveled to Athens and Egypt to give public lectures and participate in philosophical debates, taking the first steps in what looked to be a promising career as a professional sophist.

The next challenge for Aristides would be making a trip to Rome itself, the capital city of the empire, so he could demonstrate his skills to the leading orators of the day. But unfortunately Aristides became ill and had to cut the trip short before engaging in any of his planned activities. He returned to Smyrna, where his condition grew worse. He suffered severe headaches, nausea, diarrhea and muscular aches that made it impossible to work or appear in public. At some point he decided to leave Smyrna in search of a more favorable place to rest and recuperate.

He traveled to the city of Pergamon, a prosperous imperial outpost along the eastern Mediterranean coastline. Pergamon had benefited in recent years from major Roman investment in its public works, and one of the biggest projects was the expansion and upgrade of an ancient spa on the outskirts of the city. The spa was dedicated to the Greek healing god Asclepius, and his worship was not only allowed but actively encouraged by the Roman authorities. The Pergamon spa eventually became one of the largest Asclepian temples in the world. People like Aristides journeyed across great distances, from many different parts of the empire, to visit the temple and seek help for their physical and mental ailments. The Asclepian shrine served, in effect, as a state-of-the-art hospital and therapy center for these visitors and for the growing citizenry of Pergamon itself, which reached a population of 200,000 by the time of Aristides's arrival.

One of the primary tools used by the priests at all Asclepian temples was *dream incubation*. We know a great deal about this practice at Pergamon from Aristides's dream diary, which he titled *The Sacred Tales*.[3]

People reached the temple by walking along a beautiful half-mile colonnade, paved in smooth stone and lined with sculptures, leading down into a wooded valley with a natural spring at the base. Large statues of Asclepius welcomed the visitors into the temple grounds, where the walls were inscribed with testimonials from people whose ills had been cured by the god. Visitors spent their days resting, praying, and bathing in the spring waters. At night the priests brought them into the *abaton*, the inner sanctum of the temple, to lie down on a *kline* or ritual bed. While non-poisonous serpents slithered freely on the floors (snakes were the god's favored animal), the ailing supplicants slept in hopes of receiving a dream from Asclepius that would heal them immediately, or at least offer guidance about methods to relieve their suffering. In the morning they awoke and shared their dreams with the temple priests, who helped interpret the dreams and discussed possible remedies and treatments based on the incubated visions of the god.

The acute symptoms of Aristides's illness lasted two years, during which time various parts of his body were afflicted with pain and dysfunction, including earaches, toothaches, asthma, fevers, and a host of intestinal problems. While at the temple he practiced dream incubation regularly, and over time he developed a very intimate relationship with Asclepius, a relationship whose intensity corresponded with an eventual return to better health (although other illnesses plagued him throughout his life). Reflecting on the ups and downs of his experiences at the temple, Aristides said:

I almost got rid of all my disease, save that when the god gave me signs and changed my [medical] regimen, I myself was ready to act in this way, but the evil counsel of my comrades prevailed, who pretending to wisdom and seeming to have a certain cleverness in these matters, explained my dreams rather unnaturally and said that the god expressly indicated that it was necessary to keep to the same things. . . . By experience I learned well that I was right. . . . For whenever the god prescribed and clearly stated them, the same regimen and the same things brought to my body and to my spirit salvation and strength and comfort and ease and high spirits, and every good thing. But when some other person advised me and missed the intention of the god, they brought everything opposite to this. How is this not the greatest sign of the god's power?[4]

Comparative Religions

In a 2004 article on cross-cultural practices of dream incubation, Kimberley Patton outlined three elements that typically characterize the efforts people in various traditions have made to stimulate special kinds of dreaming experience.[5] First is *intentionality* (i.e., the purpose or reason for seeking a dream). The intentionality manifests itself in prayers, rites of purification, fasting, and a host of pre-sleep activities that focus the mind on a particular question or concern. Second is *locality*, the setting where the dream-seeking individual will sleep. Rituals of dream incubation usually emphasize localities far removed from the normal, mundane, and ordinary sphere of life and closer to whatever the individual considers sacred, beautiful, and mysterious. Classic settings include mountains, caves, graveyards, and shrines. The third element Patton identifies is *epiphany*, meaning the dream experience itself, interpreted as a response to the focus of pre-sleep intentionality. As with all dreams, the epiphanies can be more or less direct in their relevance to the individual's waking concerns, requiring both literal and metaphorical methods of analysis.

Patton's model certainly applies to Aristides. His intentionality centered on his physical ailments; his locality was the aesthetically pleasing Asclepian temple at Pergamon; and his epiphany was a series of vivid dreams that tracked the course of his illness and recovery. Patton's model also applies to the Muslim practice of *istikhara*, which goes back to the sayings (*hadiths*) of the Prophet Muhammad, when he encouraged his followers to perform certain prayers and ritual actions to elicit good dreams and protect against bad ones.[6] Other forms of divination are forbidden in Islam, but istikhara has become an acceptable method of petitioning for divine counsel and guidance in times of great uncertainty and anxiety, such as during a life-threatening illness. Istikhara may be practiced anywhere, so the locality criterion is not strictly observed, although the most ardent seekers usually favor spiritually charged settings like mosques, the tombs of saints, and caves (where Muhammad received his original revelations). Before sleep the individual engages in ritual cleansings, prays for guidance, and then lies down on the right side, with the right hand to the right ear, and repeats the name of Allah until falling asleep. The resulting dreams are interpreted as meaningful indications of divine favor or disfavor regarding the individual's concerns in waking life.

A medieval Jewish text described a "dream question" ritual (*she-elat chalom*) that has many of the same features as the Asclepian and Muslim incubation practices.[7] Like them, it starts with changes in diet, purifications, immersions in water, and extensive prayers and scriptural recitations. But the Jewish ritual prescribes the opposite body posture from the one in Islamic istikhara. According to this text, the individual should:

> Sleep on the left side. Sleep alone in your bed and alone in the house, and be careful to have clean underwear, bed, and sheets. . . . The customary practice is to compose this request [the dream question] in writing and read from it. After completing everything that has been mentioned, you should then place the request and the prayer under your pillow and concentrate your thoughts upon the request, so that you will fall asleep while contemplating the formulation.[8]

Other religious and spiritual traditions around the world have also looked to dreams for insights about illness and health. For instance, researchers have found that dreams play a role in the healing practices of Australian and South Pacific island cultures, Amazonian tribal groups, Tibetan medicine, and African indigenous traditions.[9] In his book about dreams in Native American history, Lee Irwin said, "[T]he visionary origins of cultural technologies are essential to the healing and medicinal practices of all Plains peoples. It would be no exaggeration to say that the majority of healing techniques are received in visions and dreams."[10]

To highlight these similarities does not mean we should ignore the many significant differences in such religiously and culturally diverse practices. But it must be admitted the basic parallels are quite striking, and they do encourage further psychological analysis. In a wide variety of cultures and periods of history, people perform rituals to elicit special dreams that provide insights into the state of their health, treatments and remedies for illness, and curative blessings from divine beings. These cross-cultural behaviors suggest the activation of deeply rooted, species-wide brain/mind processes that should be comprehensible, at least to some degree, in cognitive scientific terms.

Psychology and Cognitive Science

Here is our third opportunity to use psychological and cognitive scientific research on dreams to investigate a specific area of religious experience. As in previous chapters, we should start by acknowledging the limits to this approach, stating what it can and cannot explain.

Of course, we are unable to prove whether or not the divine beings appearing in these dreams actually exist, and we cannot verify all the personal details that people include in their reports. Sick people are naturally prone to wishful thinking about regaining their health, and unscrupulous charlatans will always be ready to offer them magical cures, for a price. These factors of human greed and gullibility make it difficult to distinguish fantasy from reality in dream incubation practices. Furthermore, many illnesses last for a certain period of time and then go away of their own accord. This means that when a sick person practices dream incubation and then gets better, we cannot know for sure if the dream incubation actually caused the improvement in health, or if the illness simply reached its natural conclusion by coincidence at the same time as the incubation practice. These issues must be taken into account in any attempt to explain the psychological and religious dynamics of dream incubation.

For some people, the biggest limitation here might be the way dream incubation seems to violate the basic premise of modern medicine, by ignoring the actual physiological workings of the body and naively accepting the allegedly healing effects of thoughts, prayers, and dreams. In this view, the only way to explain a practice like dream incubation is to debunk it with real scientific evidence.

Unfortunately, researchers are finding it harder than ever to separate the mind from the body, or to reduce mental activities to inconsequential by-products of physical processes. Real scientific evidence is increasingly pointing to a dynamic interplay between mind and body, with causal forces working in both directions.

An important voice in this area is James W. Jones, a psychologist of religion and author of *Contemporary Psychoanalysis and Religion* (1993) and *Can Science Explain Religion?* (2015). Jones has a professional practice as a clinical psychotherapist, giving him a deep familiarity with people's experiences of illness and health. He also has a background in the philosophy of science, providing him a sophisticated framework for understanding the interaction of mind and body in the healing process. Jones's methods and approach place him squarely within the intellectual domain of the cognitive science of religion. But few other CSR scholars know as much as Jones does about the practical dimensions of healing and their relevance for the study of religion and brain/mind science.

In a 2005 book chapter titled "Brain, Mind, and Spirit—A Clinician's Perspective, or Why I Am Not Afraid of Dualism," Jones challenged the philosophical premise of *physicalism*, which is widely accepted among cognitive scientists. Physicalism asserts that all mental phenomena can ultimately be explained as the secondary psychological effects of primary physical causes. Jones argued that physicalism "is not adequate to the data of psychoneuroimmunology."[11] In other words, current scientific findings about the enormously complex interactions of the brain, the mind, and the immune system cannot be explained in purely physical terms. Jones pointed to several therapeutic practices (e.g., hypnosis, mental imagery, biofeedback, and meditation) whose effectiveness refutes a simplistic, bottom-up model of causation that goes in one direction only, from brain to mind. Research has shown that therapeutic approaches like these can have measurable effects on various neural functions and bodily systems, particularly the immune system. These well-documented experiences of top-down causation—the mind influencing the brain—are incompatible with a strictly physicalist outlook. Jones encouraged CSR researchers to develop explanatory models based on current evidence rather than outmoded assumptions: "The kind of self-regulation currently being demonstrated in psychophysiological laboratories and clinical practice, involving hypnosis, biofeedback, and meditation, demands a robust account of mental causation."[12]

Jones's work helps clear the way for a better CSR approach to religious healing practices.[13] This approach recognizes a mutual relationship between mind and body, with causative influences moving in both directions. In philosophical terms we might call it "interactive dualism."

Perhaps the strongest evidence in support of this approach comes from research on the *placebo effect*. In medical experiments, a "placebo" is an empty, inert substance (like a sugar pill) given to people in a control group, for comparison with the effects of a real substance given to a different group of people. If those in the latter group improve their condition at a higher rate than the people who took the placebo, the difference is counted as evidence in favor of the medical effectiveness of the real substance.

What is often overlooked, but plainly there for all to see, is the tremendous medical effectiveness of the placebos themselves. Even though people in control groups are given a substance specifically designed to have no medical impact, they often experience a measurable improvement in their health and well-being. For instance, researchers have found that between 25% and 60% of people with depression report a lessening of their symptoms after treatment with a placebo pill.[14] A 2002 study by Andrew Leuchter and colleagues showed that placebo treatments actually change the neural functioning in people's brains (particularly in the pre-frontal cortex), in ways that are different from other medical treatments but real and significant nevertheless.

Other maladies that respond well to placebo treatments include anxiety disorders, gastro-intestinal problems, sexual dysfunction, asthma, swelling, fever, and pain of various kinds. In many of these cases, the beneficial effects seem to emerge from increased activity in the immune system, including the release of endorphins and other endogenous opioids, along with hormones like dopamine.[15] These internally produced substances help to lessen pain, recover from stress and trauma, and stimulate cell and tissue regeneration.

Much remains unknown about the neurophysiological changes associated with the placebo effect. But we do know that what launches these changes is *belief*, belief of a special kind. People who benefit from a placebo treatment believe they are receiving it from a sympathetic and skilled authority: someone they trust, someone they feel confident is trying to care for them. The physical changes depend on a positive, reassuring relational context in which the patients believe that specific efforts are being made to relieve their suffering. If a placebo is given within that kind of intimate interpersonal setting, the healing effects are most likely to occur.[16] According to Dylan Evans in his 2004 book *Placebo: Mind over Matter in Modern Medicine*, "only if you believe that a medical intervention is taking place, and that it works for the condition you are suffering from, will the placebo response be activated."[17]

The placebo effect has its limits, of course. It cannot cure cancer, stitch a wound, or mend a broken bone. But an abundance of evidence has shown that it can diminish suffering and speed healing in a variety of ways, for a variety of serious ailments. A certain kind of mental activity—belief in the skills and good intentions of one's caregiver—can produce measurably beneficial effects in psychophysiological functioning.[18]

The power of the placebo effect poses an ethical challenge for doctors and clinicians who might consider incorporating it more consciously into their practice. When does the goal of healing conflict with the obligation to be honest? The placebo effect definitely works, but only by misleading people into accepting treatments that are intended to be medically ineffective. Should doctors and clinicians actively deceive their patients to stimulate a placebo response? How could that be done without violating the patients' right to know all their options and make informed choices about their treatment?

These are not easy questions to answer. It does seem, however, that medical science should put more energy into responsibly cultivating the therapeutic potentials of the placebo effect, considering its low cost and high impact for various maladies.

More attention should also be given to the placebo's lesser known shadow twin, the *nocebo* effect. A nocebo is a medically empty substance that produces a negative physical impact on people because they believe the substance will harm them. For obvious ethical reasons, little experimental research has been done on this phenomenon. But anthropologists have found nocebo-like effects reported in various cultures where people hold strong spiritual beliefs about witchcraft, sorcery, and black magic.[19] In many cultures people can become genuinely ill and even die when they believe they have been afflicted by an evil curse. American film director Wes Craven got the idea for his *Nightmare on Elm Street* movies from newspaper reports of sudden nocturnal deaths among Cambodian immigrants in the Los Angeles area. Doctors at the local hospitals could not explain why these people had suddenly died, but other Cambodian immigrants from the Hmong cultural tradition said the people had been killed by evil spirits known to strike in nightmares, leaving no outside trace of their attacks.[20]

Placebo and nocebo responses are further evidence that mental beliefs, intentions, and images can influence various aspects of bodily functioning, for good and for ill. As Jones has pointed out, there are many other therapeutic practices that also demonstrate the tangible effects of "downward causation," from the mind to the body. In light of all this research data, it should no longer seem strange or unscientific to consider the potential medical value of rituals of dream incubation.

Dream Research

What, then, are the specific mechanisms that might facilitate the beneficial effects of dream incubation? The answer comes from several different studies and research findings, many of which we have already discussed, all pointing in the same general direction.

Start with the vital activities of the immune system during sleep, when a host of regenerative substances (e.g., human growth hormone, interleukin-1, tumor necrosis factor, and prolactin) are released throughout the body. Anything people do to enhance their capacity for deep, long, restful sleep is likely to enhance the functioning of their immune system.

Virtually all dream incubation rituals emphasize the creation of a quiet, undisturbed setting for sleep—precisely what one would do if the medical goal were to promote immunological health.

Research on neuroplasticity during sleep and dreaming also bears directly on this question. The early studies of neuroplasticity focused on people who had suffered strokes and other forms of brain damage, causing them major losses of mental and physical functioning.[21] In many cases these deficits proved temporary, as their brains found innovative ways to rewire themselves to regain the lost abilities. The remarkable flexibility of the human brain provides a valuable healing resource in times of illness and injury.[22] Recall now the claim by Maquet and his colleagues that "sleep is a favorable condition for brain plasticity." Their research suggested that sleep provides an optimum neurological setting for all the important repairing, rewiring, and regenerating work that supports healthy brain functioning. Once again, we can see that anything that helps people sleep better will also help the internal healing processes of their own brains and bodies.

In terms of dream content, we can point to the continuity hypothesis and the abundant evidence showing that people's dreams accurately reflect the most meaningful and emotionally salient concerns of their waking lives. This means that sick people are already primed to dream a great deal about their illnesses and their efforts to get better. Incubation rituals amplify this natural oneiric tendency. The rituals have the effect of enhancing the individual's awareness of dreaming–waking continuities and drawing more conscious attention to their literal and metaphorical dimensions of meaning.

As we saw in chapter 5, people's dream recall frequencies are quite flexible and can be increased by fairly simple methods. Dream incubation rituals push those recall efforts to a maximal degree, doing everything possible (using special prayers, diet, clothing, location, timing, and posture) to elicit powerful dreams that can be clearly preserved in mind. No deception, magic, or hocus-pocus is involved here. The incubation rituals work because they skillfully build on the basic psychological predispositions of the dreaming imagination.

Let us set aside religious history for a moment, and think about the issue strictly in terms of current scientific research. If a person with an urgent concern in waking life, like a health crisis, makes a deliberate and sustained effort to remember more dreams about that specific concern, what is the likelihood of the person's success? Based on the best available evidence about dream recall and content frequencies, we would have to say the person has a very good chance of dreaming about the crisis. Even if the person were not making any extra effort to increase recall, we would predict his or her regular dream content would have an elevated frequency of references to illness and healing. But add in the factors of conscious intentionality, special locations, pre-sleep preparations, and so on, and the likelihood rises to near certainty that the person will succeed in experiencing and remembering at least some health-related dreams.

At one level, then, we can say with confidence that for people suffering an illness, incubation rituals are likely to be quite effective in stimulating greater recall of dreams with a high proportion of content relating to their health concerns.

The question now becomes one of impact. Do these incubated dreams have any real effect on the illness, or do they simply mirror what is happening in the body?

The evidence here is less direct, but it still leads in a compelling direction. A good source of information about dreams and healing comes from clinical work with PTSD. As we noted earlier, clinicians have found that people with PTSD often experience a change in their dreaming over the course of their healing. Immediately after the trauma people tend to have graphic, repetitive nightmares of the incident, accompanied by extreme fear and distress. Then over time, and with the help of therapy and other forms of caregiving, the nightmares gradually turn into "dreamier" dreams, with more varied settings, characters, and feelings. The trauma may still appear in these later dreams, but it no longer dominates the whole oneiric world. An increased playfulness and imaginative freedom in dreaming corresponds with a diminished severity of PTSD symptoms.

It makes sense, based on the continuity principle, that a lessening of trauma symptoms would cause a change in dreaming. It also makes sense, based on the mind–body research we just discussed, that changes in dreaming might cause a lessening of trauma symptoms. If it is true, as a great deal of scientific evidence has shown, that mental activities can influence physical processes, then we should at least entertain the possibility that certain dreams may have genuinely curative effects. With PTSD victims, who are often psychologically frozen by their traumatizing experience, the healing process may begin with the simple recovery of some degree of creative vitality in their dream world, reminding them what it feels like to pursue free, open-ended possibilities beyond the grip of the painful, panic-stricken memories.

With other illnesses and ailments, it seems the curative effects of dreaming derive from a triggering of the placebo response. When sick people believe that a trusted caregiver is actively trying to help them get better, their symptoms tend to diminish in severity. The key element in this process—belief—can be stimulated not only in waking life but in dreaming, too. If we go back to the dream incubation rituals performed by Aristides and others at the ancient Asclepian temples, we can see that their practices worked to cultivate a powerful belief in the benevolent presence and intentions of the healing god. As Aristides himself declared, the more he trusted in the divine care of Asclepius, the more his health improved. From a CSR perspective, we might say his devout faith in the god created the ideal conditions for a strong dream-mediated placebo response. The details of his treatments, some of which seem quite bizarre to modern eyes (e.g., bathing in frigid waters, bloodletting, and enemas), matter less than his implicit belief in the healing power of Asclepius. This belief depended almost entirely on his revelatory dreams, dreams that were shaped by incubation rituals specifically designed to elicit highly impactful visionary experiences.

The strong likelihood that certain dreams can prompt a placebo response gives us a way of psychologically accounting for the prevalence of incubation rituals and dream healing practices throughout the world. For Aristides, the powerful and trusted authority trying to help him was Asclepius. For a Christian it might be Jesus, a saint, or an angel. For a Muslim it might be a special teacher or Imam. For an Australian Aborigine it might be a mythic ancestor. The rituals may involve sleeping on the right side or the left side, high on a mountain top or deep within a cave—these are all means to the same basic end of stimulating a mystically charged dream that gives experiential power to the individual's belief in the active presence of a benevolent caregiver.

These divine healers, it is important to note, meet two principal CSR criteria for minimally counterintuitive supernatural agents. Asclepius and the other deities possess magical powers and secret knowledge, but otherwise they talk and behave like ordinary human beings. The combination of these qualities seems perfectly suited for stimulating a placebo response. Asclepius and other divine healers have (1) supernatural healing abilities that people believe can help them in a time of crisis, plus (2) human characteristics that make it easier for people to form caring relationships with them. From a CSR perspective, rituals that seek to incubate dreams of healing gods can be seen as reasonable techniques for helping people activate their own inner powers of psychophysiological recovery.

Concluding Response

Religious rituals of dream incubation have a considerable degree of therapeutic effectiveness because they promote deep, sound sleep and because they stimulate dreams of particular relevance to the individual's illness, potentially leading to a placebo response that relieves some of his or her symptoms. To be clear, placebo treatments do not have infinite powers, but experimental evidence has shown they do benefit ailing people in a variety of ways, such as reducing inflammation, diminishing pain, lowering stress, and boosting the immune system. Religiously oriented rituals of dream incubation have all the characteristics necessary to trigger strong placebo effects. It may be the case, as Pinker has said, that spiritual hucksters take advantage of people's willingness to believe in healing miracles. But we should not for that reason overlook the empirical evidence that certain kinds of belief can have a genuinely curative impact. The ancient practitioners of dream incubation seemed to understand this when they developed rituals aimed at eliciting powerful, highly memorable dreams with precisely those qualities of intensified belief that modern scientists have found are key to activating the placebo effect.

FIGURE 15.1 Rod of Asclepius © JPL Designs / Shutterstock

Anyone today who goes to a doctor's office probably walks past several signs and emblems featuring the symbol shown in figure 15.1. Few people, however, know that the symbol represents the rod of Asclepius, as a visual reminder of where the healing sciences of our civilization began. The two greatest and most influential physicians of classical antiquity, Hippocrates (460–370 B.C.E.) and Galen (129–200 C.E.), were both originally trained as Asclepian priests. Hippocrates was born into a family of doctors at the Asclepian temple of Cos, and Galen served as a dream interpreter at the Pergamon sanctuary, overlapping in time with Aristides.[23] The roots of modern Western medicine may truly be said to lie among the slithering snakes of the temples of Asclepius.

Contemplative Practice

"So I wasn't dreaming, after all," she said to herself,
"Unless—unless we're all part of the same dream.
Only I do hope it's *my* dream, and not the Red King's!
I don't like belonging to another person's dream."
LEWIS CARROLL, *Alice's Adventures in Wonderland and
through the Looking-Glass*

Opening Question

*Why should anyone pay attention to aberrant, esoteric states of consciousness
like lucid dreaming?*

Cognitive scientists have made enormous progress in recent years in their
efforts to explain the neurocognitive processes involved in normal daily
activities like speech, perception, inferential reasoning, and short-term
memory. This record of success has prompted skepticism toward the
study of experiences that lie outside the regular sphere of ordinary mental
life. Pascal Boyer's 2001 book *Religion Explained: The Evolutionary Origins
of Religious Thought* adopted this skepticism as his cardinal methodological principle. He dismissed the approach of William James and others
who explored unusual and anomalous religious experiences, and instead
he advocated for a tight focus on the mind in its normal, ordinary mode
of functioning. "We can understand religion much better," Boyer said, "if
we take into account that the processes that create 'belief' are the same in
religion and in everyday matters."[1] There is no need, in this view, for any
special study of the varieties of religious experience or altered states of
consciousness. All we need to know is how the mind operates in normal
circumstances, and then we can show how religion hijacks those ordinary
psychological processes. As Boyer succinctly put it, "religious concepts are
parasitic upon other mental capacities."[2]

Initial Response

Contemplative practices of lucid dreaming can generate intensified modes of consciousness that stretch the mind far beyond its ordinary range of awareness.

In addition to Boyer's "White Swan" method of focusing on the psychology of ordinary mental life, much can be learned from a "Black Swan" approach toward exceptional religious experiences and their corresponding effects on brain/mind functioning. Many religious traditions have rituals, teachings, and meditative techniques aimed at helping people cultivate heightened awareness within their dreams. As neuroscientific research has recently confirmed, these practices can be very effective at stimulating extremely memorable and thought-provoking experiences of lucidity and metacognition.

Data and Discussion
Case Study: Myoe

The close connection between dreaming and meditation will be a prominent theme in this chapter, so it makes sense to start with a case study of someone who deeply explored the spiritual potentials of both pursuits.

Few people have ever done more in that regard than Myoe Shonin, a Buddhist monk and teacher who lived in medieval Japan. Born in 1173, Myoe was trained in traditional contemplative practices going back several centuries to the original arrival of Buddhism in Japan in the sixth and seventh centuries c.e. These practices included an emphasis on images, visions, and dreams, along with a variety of other mind-altering rituals and activities. We know a great deal about Myoe's life and teachings thanks to the historical research of George J. Tanabe, Jr. and his 1992 book *Myoe the Dreamkeeper: Fantasy and Knowledge in Early Kamakura Buddhism.* "His story," Tanabe said of Myoe, "is of a sustained quest for dream-visions."[3] Myoe belonged to an early strand of Buddhism in which people devoted themselves to the practice of multiple techniques for generating visionary images, which were then shared, interpreted, and used as templates for future image-seeking pursuits. Commenting on the historical context of Myoe's life, Tanabe said that "Buddhism in Asia is a treasure trove of images, particularly of visions produced by fantasy, the primary faculty involved in that most important of Buddhist practices, meditation."[4]

In his analysis Tanabe made a subtle distinction between fantasy and imagination, but both his terms are consistent with our broader use in this book of "imagination" in the waking and dreaming states. Myoe and his monastic colleagues were lifelong practitioners of time-honored spiritual disciplines aimed at eliciting vivid experiences of the imagination, and the foremost of these disciplines was meditation. According to Tanabe, "meditation is a technique for stimulating or even controlling the mental faculty of fantasy to produce visions, which are either spontaneous or prescribed by instructions sometimes passed down for generations and across cultures."[5] Myoe's visionary experiences had aspects of both, the spontaneously created and the culturally structured. He and other monks tried so hard to activate the image-creating faculty of their minds because they found the resulting dream-visions to be valuable guides in their ongoing quest for enlightenment.

Myoe's experiences in waking, sleeping, dreaming, and meditating often blurred into each other. He made a point of recording his night dreams when they seemed particularly significant, and he kept a journal of these dreams for more than 30 years, from the age of 23 up until a few years before his death in 1232 at the age of 59. The journal had 185 dream reports, which were originally written and illustrated in Myoe's own hand (not by a disciple or later hagiographer). The dreams included plenty of strange, fragmentary, and trivial content, along with several instances of Myoe behaving in embarrassing and inappropriate ways—all of which suggests the journal is a reasonably direct and accurate rendering of his dream life.

A blind analysis of his dreams would have little trouble identifying Myoe as a practicing Buddhist monk. The dreams are filled with references to Buddhist teachers, temples, beliefs, rituals, practices, and postures. This is just as we would expect, given that these religious matters were Myoe's primary concerns in waking life. His dreams are populated by many different characters, including religious colleagues, nuns, people from town, members of the imperial government, several different animals, and a variety of supernatural beings. Not all of the dreams have emotional references, but many of them express vivid feelings of joy, wonder, and delight related to his religious activities in the waking world. At the same time, some of the dreams portray strongly negative emotions (fear, anger) and aggressive social interactions, along with sexual encounters that clearly surprised the chaste monk. Myoe's experiences of dreaming, as recorded in his journal, covered the full range of what we know today to be the ordinary patterns of human dream content. Even though he led a very unusual life in terms of the ascetic intensity of his meditative practices, Myoe's dreams were still grounded in the hard-wired processes of the human mind during sleep.

There was never a eureka moment in his recorded dreams when Myoe suddenly exclaimed, "I am dreaming!" Rather, his dreams were permeated by an alert, expansive, and highly metacognitive awareness of himself and the world. He seems to have experienced not just lucid *dreams*, but lucid *dreaming* as a stable mode of oneiric consciousness. Here is one of the more complex dreams in the journal:

> On the night of the 20th day of the 9th month of the same [1220], I had a dream about a large object which resembled a sheep in the sky. It went through unending transformations. Sometimes it was like a light, sometimes it resembled a human figure. When it was like an aristocrat wearing a cap, it suddenly changed into a commoner who descended to the ground. The priest Girin [a disciple of Myoe's] was there. He looked at it, was disgusted, and detested it. It turned to me and seemed to want to say something. I thought to myself that this was a constellation that had transformed and manifested itself. I thought highly of it. I wanted to resolve my uncertainty [about what it was]. Then it turned to me and said, "Many [priests] should not accept the faith and offerings of other people." Then I understood it. I asked it, "Where will I be reborn next?" It replied, "In the Trayastrimsas Heaven." I asked, "When I am reborn there, will I already be unattached to the five desires and be practicing the Buddha's way?" It replied, "Yes." The heavenly being said, "Shouldn't you keep from burning your head?" I replied, "Yes." I thought, My next life will be good. Why do I try to anticipate it? I think it was telling me that I need only do what I must before people in this world. Again I said, "Will you always protect me like this?" It said, "Yes." Then I awoke.[6]

Several elements in this dream require specific knowledge of Myoe's waking life context to understand. For example, the "priest Girin" was one of Myoe's disciples who later wrote a biography about him. The "Trayastrimsas Heaven" was the second of six heavens in Buddhist cosmology. The comment about "burning your head" was, Tanabe suggested, "an admonition against any radical procedures such as self-immolation described in the *Lotus Sutra*."[7] In other words, do not commit suicide as a shortcut from this existence to a higher spiritual level.

Beyond those particular details, though, there is a remarkable degree of mental calm and cognitive clarity in this dream. Despite the bizarre metamorphoses of the object/entity/person, Myoe approached it with a serene and open-minded curiosity about what it could teach him. In the ensuing dialogue he asked his deepest religious questions, and the responses from the entity were surprising, illuminating, and reassuring. In effect, Myoe's dream served him as a spiritual classroom where he could learn how to improve his contemplative techniques and further develop his visionary capacities.

Comparative Religions

Instances of lucid dreaming can be found in many cultures and periods of history, and so can efforts to cultivate such dreams via incubation rituals, meditation, and other contemplative methods. This probably goes back to the Paleolithic people who created and worshipped in the fantastically painted caves of southern Europe. The caves were used by various groups over thousands of years, and as we discussed in chapters 2 and 5, it is very likely that descending into these subterranean sanctuaries had a consciousness-altering effect. Whether or not people actually slept in the caves and tried to incubate dreams (they probably did, but we do not know for sure), their dream lives were surely impacted in dramatic fashion by the experience of going down into these mysterious, shadowy, spectacularly illustrated caverns.

Most traditions have a special class or group of people who engage in dream-stimulating practices as a lifelong discipline, striving to expand the range of their imaginative awareness and deepen their understanding of life and reality. For Paleolithic groups these were the shamans, people who, in anthropologist Barbara Tedlock's words, "listen to and amplify an inner expression of the psyche."[8] Ancient Hindu and Buddhist traditions had numerous sages, mystics, and meditators who cultivated heightened states of consciousness in sleep and dreaming. The passage from the *Brihadaranyaka Upanishad* quoted as the epigraph in chapter 2 goes on to mention the metacognitive verses of an earlier Hindu teaching: "*Subduing by sleep the bodily realm, / Remaining awake, he contemplates the sleeping senses.*"[9] Other Hindu texts gave instructions about how to develop greater awareness in dreaming as a step toward greater awareness in waking, ultimately leading to an understanding of the self-created nature of all realities.[10] The Indian Buddhist sage Naropa (1016–1100) sought this goal, and he made dreaming a central feature of his system of Tantric Yoga.[11] Naropa taught his disciples to incubate lucid dreams by performing special prayers, chants, visualizations, breathing exercises, and bodily postures. Once the disciples gained a higher degree of awareness within the dream state, they were deemed ready to pursue additional practices aimed at developing greater powers of consciousness across all states of being, from waking to dreaming, from living to dying to being reborn.

Influenced to some degree by Indian traditions, the mystical strand of Islam known as Sufism has also emphasized the importance of gaining more conscious clarity in the dream state. Over many centuries the Sufis have looked to their dreams for guidance, instruction, and inspiring imagery. Using highly refined methods of istikhara, they have studiously prepared their minds for unusually intense dream experiences with heightened metacognition.[12] Henri Corbin, one of the great Western scholars of Sufism, explained that these consciousness-altering practices led the Sufis to develop a theory of a third world, *alam al-mithal*, between the two worlds of internal thought and external perception. According to Corbin's study of the early Sufi masters, the visionary realm of alam al-mithal can be understood as:

> a world of autonomous forms and images. . . . It is a perfectly real world preserving all the richness and diversity of the sensible world but in a spiritual state. . . . Neither the physical senses nor the pure intellect are the organs apprehending this world; it is grasped by "suprasensible senses," essentially an *imaginative consciousness*. As we have said, we must be careful not to confuse this imaginative power with "fantasy," or imaginal reality with the imaginary.[13]

Corbin's notion of an "imaginative consciousness" in Sufi practice fits well with many of the themes discussed in this chapter, and the book as a whole. Unfortunately, the Sufis have suffered a great deal of persecution through history for their unorthodox religious beliefs and psychospiritual investigations.

Native American traditions have preserved similar visionary practices over the course of many centuries, right into the modern era. Lee Irwin's work has already been mentioned as an excellent guide to these traditions, along with the studies of Barbara Tedlock and Dorothy Eggan. A good recent example of Native American dream incubation comes from Ruby Modesto, a member of the Cahuilla people of Southern California. Born in 1913, Modesto learned the traditional shamanic methods preserved by the Cahuilla since ancient times, and she served her community as an herbalist and healer until her death in 1980. In her autobiography she described a dream incubation method for "real Dreaming," taught to her by her uncle, also a traditional Cahuilla healer:

> The way you do that is by remembering to tell yourself to go to sleep in your first-level ordinary dream. You consciously tell yourself to lay down and go to sleep. Then you dream a second dream. This is the second level and the prerequisite for real Dreaming. Uncle Charlie called this process "setting up dreaming." You can tell yourself ahead of time where you want to go, or what you want to see, or what you want to learn. On the third level you learn and see unusual things, not of this world. The hills and terrain are different. On both the second and third dream levels you can talk to people and ask questions about what you want to know.[14]

Modesto was not describing lucid dreams in the sense of explicitly thinking within the dream that one is dreaming. Like the Sufis and Tantric Buddhists, she focused her heightened awareness not on herself but on the imaginal world and its endless possibilities for exploration, discovery, and insight.

These kinds of intensive dream practices may seem utterly alien to contemporary Westerners. But, in fact, the same basic idea can be found at the very roots of our civilization, in one of the greatest works of classical philosophy, Plato's *Republic* (fifth century B.C.E.). At several points in the *Republic* Plato made it clear that dreams should be avoided because they can cloud people's rational thinking with dangerous animal passions. Nevertheless, he allowed for the possibility that a person with philosophical training might actually benefit from what is essentially a practice of dream incubation:

> But I fancy that a man who is of healthy body and sound mind, before he goes to sleep, stirs up the reasoning part within him and feasts it on noble arguments and problems, and so comes to peace and understanding with himself. The desiring element he neither

starves nor surfeits in order that it may go to sleep and not trouble the best part with its joy or with its sorrow, but may leave it [his reason] undisturbed, alone by itself, to inquire into and stretch out the apprehension of what it does not know, whether of things past or present or future. . . . In such case you know that he comes nearer to grasping the truth than at any other time, and the visions of his dreams are never unlawful.[15]

Unfortunately we have no evidence that Plato or his followers ever actually tried such a dream incubation practice. He granted it as a logical possibility within his philosophical system, but apparently pursued it no further than that.

Psychology and Cognitive Science

Modern researchers have found it difficult to scientifically study altered states of consciousness, particularly in dreams.[16] The experiences are so rare, unpredictable, and context-specific that it can be hard to observe and measure them in controlled experimental settings. Furthermore, many religious traditions and schools of practice consider these experiences to be precious personal secrets that should be hidden and not shared with others. This, of course, adds to the difficulty of analyzing them psychologically and evaluating their impact on people's thinking and behavior.

The biggest exception to this problem has been research on meditation, which neuroscientists have been actively examining for several years now. As an object of scientific study, meditation has considerable advantages. People who are meditating sit still and motionless for long stretches of time, allowing investigators to apply any number of measuring devices that can track the neurophysiological correlates of their mental experiences. The best current technologies for brain imaging (e.g., fMRI, PET, and SPECT) are perfectly suited for these conditions, making it possible to observe what happens in people's brains when they meditate. As we shall see, the discoveries of this line of research bear directly on our understanding of dreams.

James Austin's 1998 work *Zen and the Brain* explored the effects of Zen meditation on people's neural functioning. He found that enlightenment experiences correlated with several specific changes in the brain: diminished activity in the limbic system, particularly the fear-detection circuits of the amygdala; diminished activity in the prefrontal systems involved in the executive functions of ordinary consciousness; and diminished activity in the parietal lobe areas responsible for orientation in space.[17] We would expect these changes to correspond to a psychological experience of low emotion, low intentionality, and feelings of merger between self and world. Sure enough, Zen meditation aims at producing a mode of altered consciousness with exactly those qualities. According to Austin's neuroscientific research, it does so by generating a major reconfiguration of brain functioning.

A somewhat different picture emerged from the research of Andrew Newberg and Eugene D'Aquili, who used the SPECT brain imaging technique to study Buddhist meditators and Franciscan nuns in prayer. In both groups they found more activation in the prefrontal cortex and less activation in the brain regions responsible for sensory perception and bodily orientation. In contrast to the low-prefrontal activity of Austin's Zen meditators, the contemplatives studied by Newberg and D'Aquili showed higher activity in the prefrontal executive regions involved in self-awareness and focused attention. Newberg and D'Aquili attributed this to their participants' strenuous mental efforts to concentrate on the object of their meditation/prayer, which, when combined with the dramatically lower sensory input, produced a major alteration in their consciousness. In such a neurological condition, lacking any of the information normally used to define self and world and yet highly aroused and attentive, the brain would interpret its experience as suddenly devoid of boundaries. According to Newberg and D'Aquili, "the brain would have no choice but to perceive that the self is endless and intimately interwoven with everyone and everything the mind senses."[18]

Yet another brain pattern associated with meditation was identified by Hans Lou and colleagues in 1999, when they used PET scans to study Hindu yoga teachers while performing the imagery-centered, multi-step relaxation technique known as *yoga nidra*.[19] Lou et al. found the participants had increased neural activation in precisely those brain regions one would predict would be stimulated during this kind of meditation: the visual cortex in the posterior part of their brains was activated during a phase of intense visualization; the brain regions devoted to bodily awareness and control were more active during a reflection on the weight of the limbs; and the prefrontal cortex showed markedly less activation throughout as the executive control of the mind yielded to the flow of visual images and bodily sensations.[20]

More studies like these could be mentioned, but several important points emerge from the ones just discussed. First, meditation works. It has tangible, measurable effects on neurological functioning. Second, the resulting brain alterations are not pathological or harmful. Normal, healthy people can engage in these practices, with no damage to their ordinary cognitive abilities. Third, different contemplative practices produce different patterns of brain activation. This means there is no single, all-encompassing model for explaining the effects of meditation on the brain. It depends on the specific type of meditation a person is practicing, which is going to generate distinctive patterns of brain/mind functioning.[21] These patterns may or may not overlap with the neural correlates of other types of meditation. And fourth, there seems to be a "practice effect": the neurological impact gets stronger over time as people become more skilled and experienced with their contemplative methods.

These are all significant findings, and they highlight several neurocognitive processes in meditation that directly relate to the religious practices of lucid dreaming.

Dream Research

Although slumbering people move around somewhat more than sitting meditators, the state of sleep is sufficiently calm and quiet to be studied using current brain imaging technologies. This line of research has led to the realization that lucid dreaming may be closer, in neurological terms, to meditation than it is to either ordinary REM sleep or waking consciousness.

For millennia, people have known about the possibilities of heightened awareness in dreaming. Only in recent decades, however, have Western scientists recognized that lucid dreams actually occur to a fairly large portion of the population.[22] Neither Freud nor Jung took any special interest in them, and as late as 1960 a prominent philosopher, Norman Malcolm, wrote a well-regarded book that rejected the very concept of lucid dreaming. Malcolm argued that self-awareness in dreaming was a logical impossibility, since sleep is, by definition, a state that lacks consciousness.[23] It was not until the late 1970s, with the parallel laboratory studies of Keith Hearne and Stephen LaBerge, that convincing scientific evidence emerged to support the reality of self-awareness in sleep.[24] Hearne and LaBerge used EEG technology to perform experiments in which the participants (themselves included) already had the ability to induce lucidity in their dreams. When they slept in the laboratory, EEG monitors recorded their brain waves as they passed through the various stages of sleep. As soon as the participants reached a point of lucidity in their dreams, they performed a predetermined series of eye movements that were designed to show up on the EEG readings. These eye movements would be signals that the participants were indeed conscious at a time when, according to the EEG, their brains were asleep.

Since the early work of Hearne and LaBerge, numerous studies of lucid dreaming have been conducted that fill out the picture of what seems to be happening in the mind and brain during these unusual states of consciousness. These studies have revealed a broad array of metacognitive abilities that can appear in dreaming. Lucidity, in the sense of self-awareness, is just one of the high-order cognitive functions that researchers have found in dreaming. Other functions include volition, selective attention, self-monitoring, self–regulation, memory, planning, decision-making, and inferential reasoning. Virtually any mental ability that people have in waking can also appear in dreaming.

In a 1993 study Sheila Purcell and colleagues developed a nine-point scale for measuring different levels of self-reflectiveness in dreaming, from 1 ("dreamer not in dream; objects unfamiliar; no people") to 9 ("dreamer can consciously reflect on the fact that he or she is dreaming").[25] Purcell et al. found that their participants were more likely to experience intermediate levels (3–7) of self-reflectiveness in their dreams, rather than total lucidity (9) or a total lack of reflectiveness (1). These intermediate levels included extended processes of thought while dreaming, detailed conversations with other characters, noticing oddities and incongruities in the environment, and simultaneously participating in the dream while observing it from a third-person perspective. All of these phenomena indicate the presence of highly sophisticated mental abilities during sleep. Purcell and her colleagues concluded that the metacognitive potentials of dreaming have no innate limitations:

> The present results indicate that the inhibitory constraints on this process are implicit in the organization of the dreamer rather than the dreaming. The lifting of these constraints, their reorganization, can be effected through the mechanisms of attention and intention on what is to be reorganized. The constraints on this response are therefore not implicit in dreaming itself, although this view of dreaming has been widely held.[26]

This is a truly dramatic claim that might get lost in the scholarly prose. Putting it differently, the upper limits of metacognitive dreaming are set by the individual's mental framework, not by the capacities of dreaming itself. These limits can be changed if the mental framework is changed. People can have more metacognition in their dreams if they strive to do so (by using "the mechanisms of attention and intention").[27]

A similar point was made by psychologist Tracey Kahan, who has performed several studies on the specific mental processes that appear in dreaming and how they relate to waking thought. Commenting on Purcell et al.'s work, Kahan said it was consistent with other research showing that "metacognition can be increased simply by increasing one's attention to the reporting of dreams and reinforcing the intention to notice the process or content characteristics of one's dreams."[28] In her own research Kahan has found that the differences between waking and dreaming thought are quantitative, not qualitative. The same mind is at work in both states. Waking and dreaming have more similarities than differences, and the differences are not absolute but relative: varying patterns and frequencies of the same basic mental capacities.

Other psychologists, including Jayne Gackenbach, Harry Hunt, Alan Moffitt, and Miloslava Kozmova, have added to our understanding of the many possible states of consciousness in dreaming.[29] Gackenbach and Hunt, in particular, have argued in favor of the idea that, in terms of brain/mind functioning, lucid dreaming is very closely related to meditation. Gackenbach's studies have shown that experienced transcendental meditators have much more metacognitive dreaming than do people who have never meditated, and Hunt's work has shown that lucid dreaming experiences include many of the same mental attributes reported in the contemplative practices of various religious traditions.

In his 2014 article "Lucid Dreaming as Sleep Meditation," James Pagel observed that when people meditate they often enter states that qualify as sleep according to their EEG measurements. Particularly when monks and nuns curtail their normal amounts of sleep and practice intensive meditation for long periods of time, a merging of waking, sleeping, and dreaming consciousness becomes almost inevitable. As Pagel noted, this merging is reflected in their brain functioning: "Electrophysiologically, both focused meditation and lucid dreaming are associated with high levels of alpha and beta/gamma frequencies."[30] Both states look very much alike in terms of their distinctive patterns of brain wave activity. Pagel cautioned that lucid dreaming as observed in a laboratory does not necessarily reflect the metacognitive dream experiences of people during the natural course of their lives, or during their contemplative practices. However, he still argued that the best neuroscientific evidence to date is remarkably consistent with the teachings of many religious traditions and schools of meditation. "Lucidity may be best viewed," Pagel said, "as a trainable meditative-like state that, unlike most other forms of meditation, is developed and elaborated while in the state of sleep."[31]

With the help of these researchers, we can draw the following conclusions. Lucidity and various forms of metacognition are innate potentials of the dreaming imagination. They may emerge spontaneously, and they may be taught and cultivated. The experiences often have the carry-over effect of destabilizing people's perceptions of ordinary reality, leading them to wonder if the "real" world is just one kind of reality among many others. Religious traditions have developed incubation rituals and meditative practices to stimulate these natural potentials for heightened awareness and channel them in particular directions. Although religions do not create these dreams, they do help to frame the oneiric realizations in a meaningful context. This is no small service, because the destabilizing experience of an intense lucid dream can be quite frightening. Like the fretful Alice in her perilous journey through Wonderland, people tend not to like the idea of shifting in and out of different realities and modes of perception, with different configurations of brain/mind functioning. And yet, this is precisely the goal of many forms of meditation, such as that of the Buddhist monk Myoe: to reach a state of awareness where the distinctions of waking, sleeping, and dreaming no longer matter, where consciousness can freely explore the farthest reaches of its own latent abilities.

Closing Response

The value of studying altered states of consciousness like meditation and lucid dreaming is that they reveal powerful brain/mind capacities that are innate in our species, yet lie dormant in the ordinary course of most people's lives. If we focused only on the mental activities of normal life, we would never know about these other neurocognitive possibilities. Research on lucid dreaming has revealed that (1) people can truly experience heightened self-awareness during sleep, (2) this ability can be trained and improved by various methods, and (3) it overlaps in many ways with the altered states of consciousness people experience in meditation. At least in the case of lucid dreaming, religious teachings and practices are not "parasitic" on the mind, but rather provide useful guides for people interested in exploring the metacognitive potentials of human consciousness.

Conclusion

When, after infinities of chaos, the first men came,
The Great Old Ones spoke to the sensitive among them
by molding their dreams; for only thus could
Their language reach the fleshy minds of mammals.

H. P. LOVECRAFT, *The Call of Cthulhu*

TYLOR, NIETZSCHE, AND the others quoted in the introduction were correct. Dreaming is indeed a primal wellspring of religious experience and belief. Scientific research on dreaming has shown that the naturalistic workings of the sleeping brain can generate hyper-realistic visions, deeply creative insights, and extraordinary states of awareness. These innate qualities of dreaming have interacted with people's religious lives in a variety of ways. In the four areas we examined in detail—demonic seduction, prophetic vision, ritual healing, and contemplative practice—the evidence is strong that the neurocognitive architecture of sleep sets the stage for vivid and highly memorable dream experiences that many people find religiously meaningful.

Alas, we cannot prove or disprove the reality of the gods, demons, ghosts, and other supernatural beings that populate people's religious dreams. As William James said more than a century ago, a psychological approach to religion can help us understand the "hither side" activities of the unconscious mind, but it cannot tell us anything about the ontological status of what lies on the "farther side." Still, we can at least dispel the outdated notion that unusually intense and memorable dreams are caused by some kind of malfunctioning in the brain. Current scientific research indicates that big dreams are products of the brain working at peak levels of imaginative power and integration. Religions have always been drawn to such dreams because they open people's minds to new possibilities beyond the limits of ordinary existence.

Of course, religions differ in terms of how many possibilities they want people thinking about. Some traditions welcome the unpredictable revelations of dreaming, while other traditions emphatically do not. This suggests some testable hypotheses. Any religious group that opposes imagery or visual representations of the divine is likely to have trouble with dreaming, because dreaming is an inexhaustible source of vivid, spiritually charged visionary experiences. The same goes for any religious group that tries to impose strict controls on sexual expression—dreams are going to be a problem for them because of the irrepressible sexual energies that naturally course through the dreaming process. And it seems probable that any religious group with a fundamentalist outlook (meaning a fixed and unyielding attachment to a set of theological doctrines) will avoid contact with dreams because of their tendency toward heretical, boundary-crossing, taboo-violating content.

One more hypothesis arises from this study. I suspect that dreaming is a primal wellspring not only of religious experience, but of skeptical philosophy, too.[1] Dreaming is not opposed to skepticism. On the contrary, dreaming gives birth to skeptical consciousness. When people awaken from a dream (particularly a big dream), they immediately face a profound metaphysical question, one that has puzzled philosophers for ages: How does the reality of the dream relate to the reality the waking world? This question echoes throughout human life as a conceptual template for critical thought and reflection.

This last hypothesis reflects back on the overall structure of the book. Even though I have written each chapter as an argument against someone whose ideas I reject, I could not have formulated my own ideas without the help of the skeptical questions raised by that person. Ultimately, dreaming and skepticism feed and nourish each other. Skepticism about dreaming is an outgrowth of dreaming itself. To study dreaming, then, requires a full and unrestrained embrace of skeptical consciousness and all that it implies.

Darwin's Dream of a Double Execution

Throughout the book I have taken evolutionary theory as the basic framework for discussing human mental life. This is standard practice in the cognitive science of religion, where Darwinian ideas remain highly influential. To close, then, I would like to consider a little-known dream that

Charles Darwin himself experienced during a tumultuous period in his personal and professional life. He recorded the dream in one of his private notebooks when he was 29 years old, and it seems to be an accurate, contemporaneous report of his subjective experience at that time.

Two years after his life-altering voyage aboard the *HMS Beagle*, Darwin was working feverishly to develop the early ideas that turned into his theory of evolution. In his notebooks he called this a process of "mental rioting."[2] The full force and radical implications of evolutionary theory had begun to dawn on him. Darwin realized how much resistance his ideas would generate from religious authorities, who would accuse him of threatening the moral order of society by equating humans with animals. He worried that telling other people about his theory would brand him as a criminal, as if he were "confessing a murder."[3] At the same time, he knew that he was on the brink of a momentous scientific discovery, and he wanted to devote all his energy to the pursuit of that lofty and exciting goal. Complicating matters further was the pressure he felt to end his bachelor status. The rest of his family was less interested in his research than in seeing him properly settled, and the selection of a matrimonial partner was reaching a critical moment of decision. On top of everything, his health was terrible. For months he had been suffering a variety of physical ailments, including stomach problems, headaches, and heart palpitations. During this turbulent time, when Darwin was in "his deepest radical phase"[4] and pondering the best way to lead a happy and scientifically fruitful life, he had this dream:

> Sept. 21st [1838]. I was witty in a dream in a confused manner. I thought that a person was hung and came to life, and then made many jokes about not having run away and having faced death like a hero. Then I had some confused idea of showing a scar behind (instead of front) (having changed hanging into his head cut off) as a kind of wit, showing he had honourable wounds. . . . There was the feeling of banter and joking.[5]

When Darwin spoke of this dream as "witty," he seems to have meant it had unusual elements of whimsy, spontaneity, and intellectual creativity. Although it contained ghoulish imagery and references to violence, the tone of the dream was light-hearted and playful. Darwin was struck upon awakening by the impression that the man's execution had suddenly changed from hanging to decapitation because he remembered *in the dream* the details of medical research showing the fatal damage caused by hanging. Somehow his recall of the anatomical knowledge had prompted the dreaming process to shift the method of execution so the wounds would seem more plausibly survivable. This mid-dream switch clearly impressed Darwin as an instance of clever innovation on the part of his sleeping mind.

Three elements remained the same in both executions: a fatal blow to the neck, a miraculous recovery, and an attitude of triumphant heroism. The disruption caused by the recall of medical information did not change the dream's fundamental trajectory, which led in what we would have to call a mystical direction. The experience transpired in a strangely liminal and detached space where Darwin said "all these ideas came one after another, without ever comparing them, I neither doubted them or *believed* them."[6] Throughout the dream he was a disembodied observer witnessing the cheerfully noble behavior of someone who sacrificed himself for a greater cause and then magically defied the finality of physical death.

A motif of Christian resurrection can certainly be discerned here, despite Darwin's atheistic beliefs and tepid feelings about organized religion. But the dream was not calling him to the clergy. It was rather an inspiring vision of playful heroism, showing him the virtues of someone who freely accepted a death sentence for the sake of honor and then emerged undefeated and unbowed, with spirits still high and head still attached to body. For a person like Darwin, about to take the momentous step of pledging the rest of his life to the twin causes of evolutionary science and domestic tranquility, this would likely appeal to him as quite a good dream, indeed.

Acknowledgments

THIS BOOK HAS been many years in the making. Several people, groups, and institutions have helped along the way.

For nearly 30 years I have benefitted from the friendship of many brilliant and talented members of the International Association for the Study of Dreams, with special input on this project from Tracey Kahan, Ryan Hurd, Ernest Hartmann, Lana Nasser, Stanley Krippner, Roger Knudson, Jeremy Taylor, Michael Schredl, Katja Valli, James Pagel, Don Kuiken, Jayne Gackenbach, Fariba Bogzaran, Daniel Delauriers, Tore Nielsen, Antonio Zadra, and Harry Hunt.

The faculty, staff, and students at the Graduate Theological Union in Berkeley, California, have been wonderful companions and intellectual partners over the years, especially Lewis Rambo, Mark Graves, Steven Bauman, Patricia M. Davis, Mary Walsh, Archie Smith, Arthur Holder, and Eleanor Rosch (from U.C. Berkeley).

Several members of the American Academy of Religion have offered invaluable guidance and support in pursuing these psychological and cognitive scientific approaches to the study of religion and dreams, including James W. Jones, Kirk Bingaman, David Hogue, John McDargh, Kimberley Patton, Bonnie Miller-McLemore, Pamela Cooper-White, Ann Taves, Jeffrey Kripal, and Robert Sears.

In addition to building their enormously useful Dreambank.net database, G. William Domhoff and Adam Schneider have generously assisted with gathering dream data, developing analytic methods, and statistically modeling the results.

Kurt Bollacker did the original design and engineering work that laid the groundwork for the highly flexible functionality of the SDDb. The web design team at Graybox in Portland has done a great job of enhancing the accessibility of the user interface.

I am grateful for the expert advice on several specific passages in the book provided in the final stages by Patrick McNamara, Hank Glassman, and Sara Arber. The anonymous readers of the original proposal and the final manuscript gave many useful ideas for improving the final text. The Oxford University Press editor for this project, Cynthia Read, has been helpful and encouraging every step of the way.

The members of my immediate family—Hilary, Dylan, Maya, and Conor—have cheered me on through the marathon journey of the writing process. Their love and support make all dreams possible.

Notes

INTRODUCTION

1. David Hume, *A Treatise of Human Nature* (New York: Oxford University Press, 2000).

2. Nicholas Nassim Taleb, *The Black Swan: The Impact of the Highly Improbable* (New York: Random House, 2007).

3. "Not all dreams are of equal importance. Even primitives distinguish between 'little' and 'big' dreams, or, as we might say, 'insignificant' and 'significant' dreams. Looked at more closely, 'little' dreams are the nightly fragments of fantasy coming from the subjective and personal sphere, and their meaning is limited to the affairs of everyday. That is why such dreams are easily forgotten, just because their validity is restricted to the day-to-day fluctuations of the psychic balance. Significant dreams, on the other hand, are often remembered for a lifetime, and not infrequently prove to be the richest jewel in the treasure-house of psychic experience." C. G. Jung, "On the Nature of Dreams," in *Dreams*, translated by R. F. C. Hull (Princeton, NJ: Princeton University Press, 1974), 76.

4. For example, Mark Graves, *Mind, Brain, and the Elusive Soul: Human Systems of Cognitive Science and Religion* (Burlington, VT: Ashgate, 2008); Ilkka Pyysiainen, *How Religion Works: Towards a New Cognitive Science of Religion* (Leiden: Brill Academic, 2003); Istvan Czachesz and Tamas Biro, eds., *Changing Minds: Religion and Cognition through the Ages* (Leuven: Peeters, 2011); Dimitris Xygalatas, *The Burning Saints: Cognition and Culture in the Fire-Walking Rituals of the Anastenaria* (New York: Routledge, 2014); and T. M. Luhrmann, *When God Talks Back: Understanding the American Evangelical Relationship with God* (New York: Knopf, 2012).

5. For exceptions see Lohmann, *Dream Travelers: Sleep Experiences and Culture in the Western Pacific* (New York: Palgrave Macmillan, 2003) and Patrick McNamara, *An Evolutionary Psychology of Sleep and Dreams* (Westport, CT: Praeger, 2004).

6. In many ways this approach follows the one advocated by Ann Taves in *Religious Experience Reconsidered: A Building-Block Approach to the Study of Religion and Other Special Things* (Princeton, NJ: Princeton University Press, 2011).

7. http://sleepanddreamdatabase.org.

8. http://sleepanddreamdatabase.org/dream/person?personid=zogby_052110:41575.

9. http://sleepanddreamdatabase.org/dream/person?personid=harris_2011:034914.

10. http://sleepanddreamdatabase.org/dream/person?personid=harris_2011:001227.

11. http://sleepanddreamdatabase.org/dream/person?personid=harris_2011:056308.

CHAPTER 1

1. *New York Times*, May 31, 1908, SM1.

2. According to Steven Pinker in *How The Mind Works* (New York: W.W. Norton, 1997), "The mind is a system of organs of computation, designed by natural selection to solve the kinds of problems our ancestors faced in their foraging way of life, in particular, understanding and outmaneuvering objects, animals, plants, and other people... Their operation [the organs or modules of the mind] was shaped by natural selection to solve the problems of the hunting and gathering life led by our ancestors in most of our evolutionary history" (21).

3. See the section on "Chronobiology," in Meir H. Kryger, Thomas Roth, and William C. Dement, *Principles and Practice of Sleep Medicine*, 4th ed. (Philadelphia: Elsevier Saunders, 2005).

4. See C. A. Czeisler, "The Human Circadian Timing System and Sleep-Wake Regulation," in *Principles and Practice of Sleep Medicine*, ed. Meir H. Kryger, Thomas Roght, and William C. Dement, 4th ed. (Philadelphia: Elsevier Saunders, 2005), 375–394.

5. See the several articles about the effects of sleep deprivation in Mary A. Carskadon, ed., *Encyclopedia of Sleep and Dreaming* (Farmington Hills, MI: Gale Cengage, 1993).

6. I. V. Zhdanova, "Fishing for Sleep," in *Evolution of Sleep: Phylogenetic and Functional Perspectives*, ed. Patrick McNamara, Robert Barton, and Charles Nunn (New York: Cambridge University Press, 2010), 243: "Larvae either float with their heads down or stay in a horizontal position close to the bottom of the tank. Adult fish typically float either in horizontal position or with the head slightly upward, showing occasional small pectoral fin movements."

7. Jerome Siegel, "Sleep Viewed as a State of Adaptive Inactivity," *Nature Reviews Neuroscience* 10 (2009): 747–753.

8. Oleg Lyamin, Julia Pryaslova, Peter Kosenko, and Jerome Siegel, "Behavioral Aspects of Sleep in Bottlenose Dolphin Mothers and Their Calves," *Physiology and Behavior* 92 (2007): 725–733.

9. Ibid.

10. Oleg Lyamin, Peter Kosenko, Jennifer Lapierre, Lev Mukhametov, and Jerome Siegel, "Fur Seals Display a Strong Drive for Bilateral Slow-Wave Sleep While on Land," *Journal of Neuroscience* 28 (2008): 12614–12621.

11. Bijal Trivedi, "Need Sleep? Birds May Have Shortcut to Second Wind," *National Geographic News*, October 28, 2010. http://news.nationalgeographic.com/news/2003/11/1112_031112_tvbirdnaps.html.

12. See Eugene Aserinsky and Nathaniel Kleitman, "Regularly Occurring Periods of Eye Motility, and Concomitant Phenomena, during Sleep," *Science* 118 (1953): 273–274; William Dement and Christopher Vaughan, *The Promise of Sleep* (New York: Dell, 1999); Michel Jouvet, *The Paradox of Sleep: The Story of Dreaming*, trans. Laurence Garey (Cambridge, MA: MIT Press, 1999).

13. See Ruben Rial, Mourad Akaarir, Antoni Gamundi, M. Cristina Nicolau, and Susana Esteban, "The Evolution of Wakefulness: From Reptiles to Mammals," in *Evolution of Sleep: Phylogenetic and Functional Perspectives*, ed. Patrick McNamara, Robert Barton, and Charles Nunn (New York: Cambridge University Press, 2010), 183.

14. Niels Rattenborg and Charles Amlaner, "A Bird's-Eye View of the Function of Sleep," in *Evolution of Sleep: Phylogenetic and Functional Perspectives*, ed. Patrick McNamara, Robert Barton, and Charles Nunn (New York: Cambridge University Press, 2010), 155.

15. Philip Steven Low, Sylvan Shank, Terrence Sejnowski, and Daniel Margoliash, "Mammalian-Like Features of Sleep Structure in Zebra Finches," *Proceedings of the National Academy of Sciences* 105 (2008): 9081–9086.

16. Rattenborg and Amlaner, "A Bird's-Eye View of the Function of Sleep," 157.

17. Charles Nunn, Patrick McNamara, Isabella Capellini, Brian Preston, and Robert Barton, "Primate Sleep in Phylogenetic Perspective," in *Evolution of Sleep: Phylogenetic and Functional Perspectives*, ed. Patrick McNamara, Robert Barton, and Charles Nunn (New York: Cambridge University Press, 2010), 131–133.

18. Ibid., 126–127.

19. Quoted in Rial et al., "The Evolution of Wakefulness," 174.

20. The *Guinness Book of World Records* no longer accepts attempts to break this record, out of concern for the aspirants' health.

21. For more on thermoregulation in sleep, see Kryger et al., *Principles and Practices of Sleep Medicine.*

22. Siegel, "Sleep Viewed as a State of Adaptive Inactivity."

CHAPTER 2

1. Antonio Damasio, *The Feeling of What Happens: Body and Emotion in the Making of Consciousness* (San Diego, CA: Harcourt, 1999), 315.

2. The material in the following paragraphs draws primarily upon the archeological histories of Steven Mithen in *The Prehistory of the Mind: The Cognitive*

Origins of Art, Religion, and Science (London: Thames and Hudson, 1996) and David Lewis-Williams in *The Mind in the Cave: Consciousness and the Origins of Art* (London: Thames and Hudson, 2004).

3. Mithen, *The Prehistory of the Mind*, 11.

4. The material in the following paragraphs draws upon several general sources on sleep, including Jim Horne, *Sleepfaring: A Journey through the Science of Sleep* (New York: Oxford University Press, 2007); Rosalind Cartwright, *The 24-Hour Mind: The Role of Sleep and Dreaming in Our Emotional Lives* (New York: Oxford University Press, 2010); James Pagel, *The Limits of Dream: A Scientific Exploration of the Mind/Brain Interface* (Waltham: Academic Press, 2010); William Dement and Christopher Vaughan, *The Promise of Sleep* (New York: Dell, 1999); and Edward Pace-Schott et al., *Sleep and Dreaming: Scientific Advances and Reconsiderations* (Cambridge: Cambridge University Press, 2003). It also relies on Mary A. Carskadon, ed. *Encyclopedia of Sleep and Dreaming* (Farmington Hills, MI: Gale Cengage, 1993) and Meir H. Kryger, Thomas Roth, and William C. Dement, *Principles and Practice of Sleep Medicine*, 4th ed. (Philadelphia: Elsevier Saunders, 2005).

5. See Kryger et al., *Principles and Practice of Sleep Medicine*, 112, 552.

6. Ibid., 102.

7. Howard Roffwarg, Joseph Muzio, and William Dement, "Ontogenetic Development of the Human Sleep-Dream Cycle," *Science* 152 (1966): 604–619.

8. Kryger et al., *Principles and Practice of Sleep Medicine*, 92. It would be more accurate to say this is true for terrestrial mammals. As we have seen, ocean-dwelling mammals like dolphins and whales have no apparent PS. We should be careful not to equate PS with intelligence, since dolphins and whales clearly have remarkable cognitive abilities.

9. Kafui Dzirasa et al., "Dopaminergic Control of Sleep-Wake States," *Journal of Neuroscience* 26 (2006): 10577–10589.

10. Carskadon, *Encyclopedia of Sleep and Dreaming*, 383.

11. Ibid.

12. Pierre Maquet, Carlyle Smith, and Robert Stickgold, eds., *Sleep and Brain Plasticity* (New York: Oxford University Press, 2003), 80.

13. For more on the anatomy of the brain, see Eric Kandel et al., *Principles of Neural Science*, 5th ed. (New York: McGraw Hill, 2012) and Richard Thompson, *The Brain: A Neuroscience Primer* (New York: Worth Publishers, 2000).

14. Thien Thanh Dan-Vu et al., "Spontaneous Neural Activity during Human Slow Wave Sleep," *Proceedings of the National Academy of Sciences* 105 (2008): 15160–15165.

15. Ibid.

16. Roar Fosse and G. William Domhoff, "Dreaming as Non-Executive Orienting," in *The New Science of Dreaming*, ed. Patrick McNamara and Deirdre Barrett (Westport, CT: Praeger, 2007), 2: 49–78. See also John Herman, "Reflexive and

Orienting Properties of REM Sleep Dreaming and Eye Movements," in *Sleep and Dreaming: Scientific Advances and Reconsiderations*, ed. Edward Pace-Schott, Mark Solms, Mark Blagrove, and Steven Harnad (Cambridge: Cambridge University Press, 2003), 161.

17. Christof Koch, *The Quest for Consciousness: A Neurobiological Approach* (Englewood, CO: Roberts and Company, 2004), 108–109.

18. Kieran Fox et al., "Dreaming as Mind Wandering: Evidence from Functional Neuroimaging and First-Person Content Reports," *Frontiers in Human Neuroscience* 7 (2013): 412. See also G. William Domhoff, "The Neural Substrate for Dreaming: Is It a Subsystem of the Default Network?" *Consciousness and Cognition* 20 (2011): 1163–1174. For an overview of this area of research, see Marcus Raichle and Abraham Snyder, "A Default Mode of Brain Function: A Brief History of an Evolving Idea," *NeuroImage* 37 (2007): 1083–1090.

CHAPTER 3

1. King James translation.

2. For example, 6:9 ("How long wilt thou sleep, O sluggard? When wilt thou arise out of thy sleep?") and 19:15 ("Slothfulness casteth into a deep sleep; and an idle soul shall suffer hunger.")

3. I. V. Zhdanova, "Fishing for Sleep," in *Evolution of Sleep: Phylogenetic and Functional Perspectives*, ed. Patrick McNamara, Robert Barton, and Charles Nunn (New York: Cambridge University Press, 2010), 242.

4. Mary A. Carskadon, ed., *Encyclopedia of Sleep and Dreaming* (Farmington Hills, MI: Gale Cenage, 1993), 360.

5. William Dement and Christopher Vaughan, *The Promise of Sleep* (New York: Dell, 1999), 270.

6. Carskadon, *Encyclopedia of Sleep and Dreaming*, 618.

7. Ibid., 537.

8. This is why people in freezing conditions should not sleep.

9. Carskadon, *Encyclopedia of Sleep and Dreaming*, 175 and following.

10. Ibid., 183.

11. Jim Horne, *Sleepfaring: A Journey through the Science of Sleep* (New York: Oxford University Press, 2007), 39. See also William Killgore et al., "The Effects of 53 Hours of Sleep Deprivation on Moral Judgment," *Sleep* 30 (2007): 345: "These findings suggest that sleep deprivation impairs the ability to integrate emotion and cognition to guide moral judgments, although susceptibility to the effects of sleep loss on this ability is moderated by the level of emotional intelligence"; Y. Harrison and Jim Horne, "One Night of Sleep Loss Impairs Innovative Thinking and Flexible Decision Making," *Organizational Behavior and Human Decision Processes* 78 (1999): 128: "Recent findings with

clinically oriented neuropsychological tests suggest that one night without sleep causes particular impairment to tasks requiring flexible thinking and the updating of plans in the light of new information. . . . [S]leep deprivation led to more rigid thinking, increased perseverative errors, and marked difficulty in appreciating an updated situation"; Carskadon, *Encyclopedia of Sleep and Dreaming*, 179–180: "RSD [REM sleep deprivation] in animals also increased certain behaviors, including aggressive, sexual, locomotor, pleasure-seeking, and feeding behaviors. One theory about these findings is that RSD increases the excitability of the brain substrate responsible for drive-related behaviors."

12. Carskadon, *Encyclopedia of Sleep and Dreaming*, 183: "The interaction of situational and test characteristics predicts that it should be relatively easy to remain awake playing a stimulating game but difficult to memorize a large number of Latin words under time pressure or to write an original play."

13. Dement and Vaughan, *The Promise of Sleep*, 244 and following. See also Carskadon, *Encyclopedia of Sleep and Dreaming*, 181.

14. This is truer of NREM than REM sleep, as the former is more closely regulated than the second. See Irwin Feinberg, "Hobson on the Neuroscience of Sleep: A Case of Persistent REM Tunnel Vision," *American Journal of Psychology* 117 (2004): 621–627.

15. See Pierre Maquet, Carlyle Smith, and Robert Stickgold, eds., *Sleep and Brain Plasticity* (New York: Oxford University Press, 2003).

16. See, for example, Robert Vertes and Kathleen Eastman, "The Case against Memory Consolidation in REM Sleep," in *Sleep and Dreaming: Scientific Advances and Reconsiderations*, ed. Edward Pace-Schott, Mark Solms, Mark Blagrove, and Stevan Harnad (Cambridge: Cambridge University Press, 2003), 75–84; and Bjorn Rasch and Jan Born, "About Sleep's Role in Memory," *Physiological Reviews* 93 (2013): 681–766.

17. Some researchers do not include learning and memory as instances of neuroplasticity; they want to preserve the main denotation of the word for larger scale changes. I prefer a broader definition that helps us understand the processes of change at varying scales.

18. Maquet et al., *Sleep and Brain Plasticity*, 1, italics in the original.

19. See Erica Goode, "Rats May Dream, It Seems, of Their Days at the Mazes," *New York Times*, January 25, 2001, for an account of Matthew Walker's research.

20. Maquet et al., *Sleep and Brain Plasticity*, 79–80.

21. Quoted in Sharon Begley, *Train Your Mind, Change Your Brain: How a New Science Reveals Our Extraordinary Potential to Transform Ourselves* (New York: Ballantine Books, 2007), 5.

22. Ibid.

23. Ibid., 29.

24. Daniel Kripke et al., "Mortality Associated with Sleep Duration and Insomnia," *Archives of General Psychiatry* 59 (2002): 131–136. See also Horne, *Sleepfaring*, 189–192.

25. Carskadon, *Encyclopedia of Sleep and Dreaming*, 397.

26. Ibid., 499.

27. Ibid., 577.

28. See Ryan Hurd, *Sleep Paralysis: A Guide to Hypnogotic Visions and Visitors of the Night* (Los Altos, CA: Hyena Press, 2010); David Hufford, *The Terror That Comes in the Night: An Experience-Centered Study of Supernatural Assault Traditions* (Philadelphia: University of Pennsylvania Press, 1982); Shelley Adler, *Sleep Paralysis: Night-Mares, Nocebos, and the Mind–Body Connection* (New Brunswick, NJ: Rutgers University Press, 2011).

CHAPTER 4

1. Heraclitus, *Fragments*, trans. T. M. Robinson (Toronto: University of Toronto Press, 1987), Fragment 89.

2. The following discussion has been influenced by the research of Katie Glaskin and Richard Chenhall, eds., *Sleep around the World: Anthropological Perspectives* (New York: Palgrave Macmillan, 2013); Roger Ekirch, *At Day's Close: Night in Times Past* (New York: W. W. Norton, 2005); and Roger Lohmann, ed., *Dream Travelers: Sleep Experiences and Culture in the Western Pacific* (New York: Palgrave Macmillan, 2003).

3. See Richard Shweder et al., "Who Sleeps by Whom Revisited: A Method for Extracting the Moral Goods Implicit in Practice," *New Directions for Child and Adolescent Development* 67 (1995): 21–29: "The practice of determining who sleeps by whom in a family household is a symbolic action that simultaneously expresses and realizes some of the deepest moral ideals of a cultural community" (21).

4. Roger Lohmann, "Sleeping among the Asabano: Surprises in Intimacy and Sociality at the Margins of Consciousness," in *Sleep around the World*, ed. Glaskin and Chenhall, 39–40.

5. See Glaskin and Chenhall, *Sleep around the World*, xi.

6. Diana Adis Tahhan, "Sensuous Connections in Sleep: Feelings of Security and Interdependency in Japanese Sleep Rituals," in *Sleep around the World*, ed. Glaskin and Chenhall, 59.

7. Much could also be said about Spanish and Latin American traditions of an afternoon *siesta*.

8. Ekirch, *At Day's Close*, 279–280.

9. Ibid., 276.

10. Genesis 28:11.

11. Mary A. Carskadon, ed., *Encyclopedia of Sleep and Dreaming* (Farmington Hills, MI: Gale Cengage, 1993), 454–455.

12. The 2013 International Bedroom Poll. The survey was conducted by telephone. Gender data were not included in the analysis. http://www.prnewswire.com/ news-releases/national-sleep-foundation-2013-international-bedroom-poll-first-to-explore-sleep-differences-among-six-countries-222192101.html.

13. See, for example, the National Sleep Foundation's 2007 study on "Women and Sleep," http://sleepfoundation.org/sleep-polls-data/sleep-in-america-poll/ 2007-women-and-sleep.

14. Sara Arber et al., "Sleep and Society," in *The Oxford Handbook of Sleep and Sleep Disorders*, ed. Charles Morin and Colin Espie (New York: Oxford University Press, 2012), 223–247. The Surrey Sleep Research Centre offers many resources for researchers on its website: http://www.surrey.ac.uk/fhms/research/centres/ ssrc/.

15. Sara Arber et al., "Gender and Socio-Economic Patterning of Self-Reported Sleep Problems in Britain," *Social Science & Medicine* 68 (2009): 288.

16. The survey was conducted by Greenberg Quinlan Rosner in 2007, using random-digit-dialing methods of recruiting a representative sample of participants. The percentages from this study represent weighted results, not raw results. They have been weighted by Greenberg Quinlan and Rosner to better approximate the demographic profile of the US population. The raw, unweighted data in the SDDb yield slightly different results.

17. This survey was conducted by Zogby Interactive in 2010, using online methods with a random subset from a demographically diverse group of participants. The percentages from this study represent raw results drawn from the SDDb, with no weighting.

18. These results reflect weighted calculations intended by the polling company, YouGov, to represent the demographics of the US population as a whole. The raw, unweighted data in the SDDb yield slightly different results.

19. As a contemporary example, see Charles Graeber's article for *Wired Magazine*, "Inside the Mansion—and Mind—of Kim Dotcom, the Most Wanted Man on the Net": "Kim Dotcom is rich enough to work however and wherever he wants. And what he wants is to work from bed. His bed of choice is a remarkable piece of custom Swedish craftsmanship.... Each one takes some 160 hours to produce and is signed by a master bed-maker who lays out the most perfect matrix of horsehair, cotton, flax, and wool.... Kim has surrounded himself with luxury, but what he prizes above all other indulgences is pure, deep sleep.... For sleep of the finest quality, for epicurean, luxury slumber, total silence is required and enforced. The gardeners do not mow, the cleaners do not clean. The cooks chop quietly in other wings, the nannies tend the children in

another house. When he sleeps the mansion holds its breath. Kim can't provide a schedule. He doesn't have to. It's his house."

20. A recent study by Yetish et al. suggests that the effects of modernization may be less negative than my portrait indicates for normal sleep length. Yetish and colleagues studied the sleep patterns of contemporary people living in three pre-industrial societies (the Hadza from Tanzania, the Tsimane from Bolivia, and the San from Namibia) and found that they tended to sleep no longer than do people in modern industrialized societies, with averages of 6 to 7 hours a night. This is a small sample, of course (3 groups, 94 total adults), but the results should temper any extreme claims that modern sleep is vastly worse than premodern sleep. See Gandhi Yetish, Hillard Kaplan, Michael Gurven, Brian Wood, Herman Pontzer, Paul R. Manger, Charles Wilson, Ronald McGregor, and Jerome M. Siegel, "Natural Sleep and Its Seasonal Variations in Three Pre-industrial Societies," *Current Biology* 25 (2015): 1–7.

CHAPTER 5

1. Antonio Damasio, *The Feeling of What Happens: Body and Emotion in the Making of Consciousness* (San Diego, CA: Harcourt, 1999), 83, emphasis in the original.

2. The Old Norse language uses a similar word, *draugry*, to mean ghost or apparition.

3. Lexicographer Robert K. Barnhart, quoted in Sarah White, "Dreamwork as Etymology," *Dreaming* 9 (1999): 17. White also highlighted the etymology of the French word for dream, *rêve*, which goes back to the Old French *rev-erie*, for "revelry, raving, delirium," with connections to *esver*, "to wander." This term appears in Modern English as *reverie*, "musing, daydreaming, lost in pleasant thoughts." And, White pointed out that although they seem similar, the German word *traum* is not etymologically related to the word *trauma*, which comes from the root word *ter*, which means twist, turn, or wound.

4. Kasia Szpakowska, "Through the Looking Glass: Dreams in Ancient Egypt," in *Dreams: A Reader on the Religious, Cultural, and Psychological Dimensions of Dreaming*, ed. Kelly Bulkeley (New York: Palgrave, 2001), 31.

5. E. R. Dodds, *The Greeks and the Irrational* (Berkeley: University of California Press, 1951), 104.

6. Serinity Young, "Buddhist Dream Experience: The Role of Interpretation, Ritual, and Gender," in *Dreams*, ed. Bulkeley, 11.

7. Robert Knox Dentan and Laura McClusky, "'Pity the Bones by Wandering River Which Still in Lovers' Dreams Appear as Men,'" in *The Functions of Dreaming*, ed. Alan Moffitt, Milton Kramer, and Robert Hoffmann (Albany: State University of New York Press, 1993), 489–548.

8. Pamela Stewart and Andrew Strathern, "Dreaming and Ghosts among the Hagen and Duna of the Southern Highlands, Papua New Guinea," in *Dream Travelers: Sleep Experiences and Culture in the Western Pacific*, ed. Roger Lohmann (New York: Palgrave Macmillan, 2003), 43–60.

9. Aristotle, "On Dreams," in *The Collected Works of Aristotle*, ed. R. McKeon (New York: Random House, 1941), 619; see also, "From all this, then, the conclusion to be drawn is, that the dream is a sort of presentation, and, more particularly, one which occurs in sleep" (625).

10. For more on the definitions of dreaming, see James Pagel, *The Limits of Dream: A Scientific Exploration of the Mind/Brain Interface* (New York: Academic Press, 2010), 22 and following.

11. Aristotle, "On Dreams," 619.

12. Michel Jouvet, *The Paradox of Sleep: The Story of Dreaming*, trans. Laurence Garey (Cambridge, MA: MIT Press, 1999), 82.

13. Kelly Bulkeley, *Dreaming in the World's Religions: A Comparative History* (New York: New York University Press, 2008), 269.

14. David Lewis-Williams, *The Mind in the Cave: Consciousness and the Origins of Art* (London: Thames and Hudson, 2004), 252.

15. Kelly Bulkeley, *The Wondering Brain: Thinking About Religion With and Beyond Cognitive Neuroscience* (New York: Routledge 2005), 112–113.

16. Chris Scarre, "Painting by Resonance," *Nature* 338 (1989): 382.

17. See, for example, Michael Winkelman, *Shamanism: A Biopsychosocial Paradigm of Consciousness and Healing* (Santa Barbara, CA: ABC-Clio, 2010); David Whitley, *Cave Paintings and the Human Spirit: The Origin of Creativity and Belief* (Amherst, NY: Prometheus Books, 2009); Brian Hayden, *Shamans, Sorcerers, and Saints: A Prehistory of Religion* (Washington, DC: Smithsonian Books, 2003); and Barbara Tedlock, *The Woman in the Shaman's Body: Reclaiming the Feminine in Religion and Medicine* (New York: Bantam, 2005).

18. These results reflect weighted calculations intended by the polling company, YouGov, to represent the demographics of the US population as a whole. The raw, unweighted data in the SDDb yield slightly different results.

19. R. Stepansky et al., "Austrian Dream Behavior: Results of a Representative Population Survey," *Dreaming* 8 (1998): 25.

20. Kathryne Belicki, "Recalling Dreams: An Examination of Daily Variation and Individual Differences," in *Sleep and Dreams: A Sourcebook*, ed. Jayne Gackenbach (New York: Garland Publishing, 1986), 192.

21. Calvin Yu, "Dream Intensity Scale: Factors in the Phenomenological Analysis of Dreams," *Dreaming* 20 (2010): 113; "Testing the Factorial Structure of the Dream Intensity Scale," *Dreaming* 22 (2012): 289.

22. Michael Schredl, "Gender Differences in Dreaming," in *The New Science of Dreaming*, ed. Patrick McNamara and Deirdre Barrett (Westport, CT: Praeger, 2007), 2:32.

23. Michael Schredl, "Dream Recall: Models and Empirical Data," in *The New Science of Dreaming*, ed. McNamara and Barrett, 2: 79–114.
24. Pagel, *The Limits of Dream*, 152.
25. Ibid., 153.
26. Ibid.
27. Ibid.
28. Schredl, "Dream Recall: Models and Empirical Data," 89.
29. In his short treatise "On Dreams," Aristotle suggested that non-dreamers might eventually gain the ability to dream as they grew older. "There are cases of persons who in their whole live have never had a dream, while others dream when considerably advanced in years, having never dreamed before.... But it is not surprising that, as age advances, a dream should at length appear to them. Indeed, it is inevitable that, as a change is wrought in them in proportion to age or emotional experience, this reversal [from non-dreaming to dreaming] should occur also" (625).
30. Dominic Beaulieu-Prevost and Antonio Zadra, "Dream Recall Frequency and Attitude towards Dreams: A Reinterpretation of the Relation," *Personality and Individual Differences* 38 (2005): 919–927; "Absorption, Psychological Boundaries and Attitude towards Dreams as Correlates of Dream Recall: Two Decades of Research Seen through a Meta-Analysis," *Journal of Sleep Research* 16 (2007): 51–59.
31. Prevost and Zadra, "Dream Recall Frequency," 924–925.

CHAPTER 6

1. Thomas Nashe, "Terrors of the Night, or, A Discourse of Apparitions," in *Thomas Nashe: Selected Writings*, ed. Stanley Wells (Cambridge, MA: Harvard University Press, 1965), 153–155.
2. Quoted in Jim Horne, *Sleepfaring: A Journey through the Science of Sleep* (New York: Oxford University Press, 2007), 168–169.
3. Francis Crick and Graeme Mitchison, "The Function of Dream Sleep," *Nature* 304 (1983): 114.
4. J. Allan Hobson, *The Dreaming Brain* (New York: Basic Books, 1988).
5. Owen Flanagan, "Dreaming Is Not an Adaptation," in *Sleep and Dreaming: Scientific Advances and Reconsiderations*, ed. Edward Pace-Schott, Mark Solms, Mark Blagrove, and Stevan Harnad (Cambridge: Cambridge University Press, 2003), 147–150.
6. Hobson, *The Dreaming Brain*; G. William Domhoff, *The Scientific Study of Dreams: Neural Networks, Cognitive Development, and Content Analysis* (Washington, DC: American Psychological Association, 2003). Antti Revonsuo's "The Reinterpretation of Dreams: An Evolutionary Hypothesis of

the Function of Dreaming," in *Sleep and Dreaming*, ed. Pace-Schott et al., 85–109, referred to those who follow Hobson's approach as "reticular activation theorists," leading to an unflattering acronym.

7. Eugene Aserinsky and Nathaniel Kleitman, "Regularly Occurring Periods of Eye Motility, and Concomitant Phenomena, during Sleep," *Science* 118 (1953): 273–274.

8. David Foulkes, "Dream Reports from Different Stages of Sleep," *Journal of Abnormal and Social Psychology* 65 (1962): 14–25.

9. Tore Nielsen, "A Review of Mentation in REM and NREM Sleep: 'Covert' REM Sleep as a Possible Reconciliation of Two Opposing Models," in *Sleep and Dreaming*, ed. Pace-Schott et al., 59–74. Recently, Calvin Yu and colleagues have found that a precisely calibrated awakening schedule can yield nearly 100% dream recall from REM sleep. See Calvin Yu, "Toward 100% Dream Retrieval by Rapid-Eye-Movement Sleep Awakening: A High-Density Electroencephalographic Study," *Dreaming* 24 (2014): 1–17.

10. Domhoff, *The Scientific Study of Dreams*, 148.

11. See, for example, Erin Wamsley et al., "Circadian and Ultradian Influences on Dreaming: A Dual Rhythm Model," *Brain Research Bulletin* 71 (2007): 347–354.

12. Tracey Kahan, "The 'Problem' of Dreaming in NREM Sleep Continues to Challenge Reductionist (Two Generator) Models of Dream Generation)," in *Sleep and Dreaming*, ed. Pace-Schott et al., 957, emphasis in the original.

13. Ibid.

14. In a review of Hobson's 2002 book *Dreaming: An Introduction to the Science of Sleep*, Irwin Feinberg had this to say about Hobson's "persistent REM Tunnel Vision": "The subtitle . . . is misleading because Hobson discusses only REM sleep, which makes up only 25% of human sleep time. . . . Most investigators soon realized that the REM-dreaming relationship is seriously flawed. But this book demonstrates that Hobson's theories remain fixated at the early developmental stage of modern sleep research."

15. Mark Solms, *The Neuropsychology of Dreams: A Clinico-Anatomical Study* (Mahwah, NJ: Lawrence Erlbaum, 1997).

16. This list draws on Kelly Bulkeley, *The Wondering Brain: Thinking About Religion With and Beyond Cognitive Neuroscience* (New York: Routledge, 2005), 33.

17. Solms, *The Neuropsychology of Dreams*, 153, 241–242, emphasis in the original. The final phrase is a quote from Hobson and McCarley. The quote continues: "If psychological forces are equated with higher cortical functions, it is difficult to reconcile the notion that dreams are random physiological events generated by primitive brainstem mechanisms, with our observation that global anoneira is associated not with brainstem lesions resulting in basic arousal disorders, but rather with parietal and frontal lesions resulting in spatial-symbolic and motivational-inhibitory disorders. These observations suggest that dreams are both generated and represented by some of the highest mental mechanisms."

18. Calvin Hall and Robert Van de Castle, *The Content Analysis of Dreams* (New York: Appleton-Century-Crofts, 1966).

19. Carolyn Winget and Milton Kramer, *Dimensions of Dreams* (Gainesville: University of Florida Press, 1978), vii.

20. G. William Domhoff and Adam Schneider, "Studying Dream Content Using the Archive and Search Engine on DreamBank.net," *Consciousness and Cognition* 17 (2008): 1238–1247.

21. Brent Berlin and Paul Kay, *Basic Color Terms: Their Universality and Evolution* (Berkeley: University of California Press, 1969).

22. The next most common basic colors in the Berlin and Kay schema are green, yellow, blue, and brown.

CHAPTER 7

1. See Justin Barrett, *Why Would Anyone Believe in God?* (Walnut Creek, CA: AltaMira Press, 2004).

2. See Stewart Guthrie, *Faces in the Clouds: A New Theory of Religion* (New York: Oxford University Press, 1992).

3. Julius Nelson, "A Study of Dreams," *American Journal of Psychology* 1 (1888): 367.

4. Ibid., 391.

5. Ibid., 398.

6. Mary Calkins, "Statistics of Dreams," *American Journal of Psychology* 5 (1893): 311.

7. Ibid., 321.

8. Ibid., 325.

9. Ibid., 329.

10. Ibid., 315.

11. Ibid., 329.

12. James Ralph Jewell, "The Psychology of Dreams," *American Journal of Psychology* 16 (1905): 34, numbers 3, 5, 9, 10, 11, 14, and 16. The other conclusions he draws are (1) more difficult to assess in relation to the findings of contemporary research, or (2) valid but less directly relevant to the current discussion.

13. Madison Bentley, "The Study of Dreams: A Method Adapted to the Seminary," *American Journal of Psychology* 26 (1915): 208.

14. Ibid.

15. Jeremy Carrette, "Post-Structuralism and the Psychology of Religion: The Challenge of Critical Psychology," in *Religion and Psychology: Mapping the Terrain*, ed. Diane Jonte-Pace and William Parsons (London: Routledge, 2001).

16. Freud's most substantial reference to Calkins came in chapter 5 of *The Interpretation of Dreams*, trans. James Strachey (New York: Avon Books, 1965), on the topic of "Material and Sources of Dreams." Freud was arguing that not

all aspects of dreaming derive from physical causes, and he cited Calkins's research as empirical support for his view: "[I]t is impossible to attribute the wealth of ideational material in dreams to external nervous stimuli alone. Miss Mary Whiton Calkins examined her own and another person's dreams for six weeks with this question in mind. She found that in only 13.2 percent and 6.7 percent of them respectively was it possible to trace the element of external sense-perception; while only two cases in the collection were derivable from organic sensations. Here we have statistical confirmation of what I had been led to suspect from a hasty survey of my own experiences" (254–255). Calkins's quantitative research helped Freud show that physiological dream theories are inadequate. This set the stage for his effort to develop a psychological approach to the study of dreams.

17. Dorothy Eggan, "The Manifest Content of Dreams: A Challenge to Social Science," *American Anthropologist* 54 (1952): 481.

18. Ibid., 479.

19. Dorothy Eggan, "Dream Analysis," in *Studying Personality Cross-Culturally*, ed. Bert Kaplan (Evanston, IL: Row, Peterson, 1961), 570, emphasis in original.

20. Quoted in G. William Domhoff, "Dreams Are Embodied Simulations That Dramatize Conception and Concerns: The Continuity Hypothesis in Empirical, Theoretical, and Historical Context," *International Journal of Dream Research* 4 (2011): 52.

21. Calvin S. Hall and Vernon J. Nordby, *The Individual and His Dreams* (New York: Signet, 1972), 122–123.

22. Ibid., 54. For more on the Barb Sanders analysis, see G. William Domhoff, *The Scientific Study of Dreams: Neural Networks, Cognitive Development, and Content Analysis* (Washington, DC: American Psychological Association, 2003).

23. Richard Wolman and Miloslava Kozmova, "'Last Night I Had the Strangest Dream': Varieties of Rational Thought Processes in Dream Reports," *Consciousness and Cognition* 16 (2007): 838–849.

24. Ibid., 10.

25. Tracey Kahan and Stephan LaBerge, "Dreaming and Waking: Similarities and Differences Revisited," *Consciousness and Cognition* 20 (2011): 494–515.

26. Ibid., 509.

27. See Michael Schredl and Friedrich Hofmann, "Continuity Between Waking Activities and Dream Activities," *Consciousness and Cognition* 12 (2003): 306: "The findings support the notion of continuity between waking and dreaming but the study also clearly demonstrated that an unspecific, global formulation of this hypothesis is not valid."

28. Kelly Bulkeley and G. William Domhoff, "Detecting Meaning in Dream Reports: An Extension of a Word Search Approach," *Dreaming* 20 (2010): 77–95.

29. Kelly Bulkeley, "Dreaming in Adolescence: A 'Blind' Word Search of a Teenage Girl's Dream Series," *Dreaming* 22 (2012): 240–252.

CHAPTER 8

1. Sigmund Freud, *The Interpretation of Dreams*, trans. James Strachey (New York: Avon Books, 1965), 376–377, 313. See also: "[D]reams, like all other psychopathological structures, regularly have more than one meaning" (182); "Not only are the elements of a dream determined by the dream-thoughts many times over, but the individual dream-thoughts are represented in the dream by several elements" (318); and further discussions on 213 and 253.

2. Frederick Crews and Kelly Bulkeley, "Dialogue with a Skeptic," in *Dreams: A Reader on the Religious, Cultural, and Psychological Dimensions of Dreaming*, ed. Kelly Bulkeley (New York: Palgrave, 2001), 368.

3. Frederick Snyder et al., "Phenomenology of REM Sleep Dreaming," *Psychophysiology* 4 (1968): 375.

4. J. Allan Hobson et al., "Dream Bizarreness and the Activation-Synthesis Hypothesis," *Human Neurobiology* 6 (1987): 157–164.

5. Richard Bonato et al., "Bizarreness in Dreams and Nightmares," *Dreaming* 1 (1991): 56.

6. Antti Revonsuo and Christina Salmivalli, "A Content Analysis of Bizarre Elements in Dreams," *Dreaming* 5 (1995): 169–188.

7. George Lakoff and Mark Johnson, *Metaphors We Live By* (Chicago: University of Chicago Press, 1980), 5.

8. Ibid., 221.

9. George Lakoff, "How Metaphor Structures Dreams: The Theory of Conceptual Metaphor Applied to Dream Analysis," in *Dreams*, ed. Bulkeley, 273.

10. Mark Landau et al., eds., *The Power of Metaphor: Examining Its Influence on Social Life* (Washington, DC: American Psychological Association, 2013).

11. Ibid.

12. Kelly Bulkeley, "Dream Interpretation: Practical Methods for Pastoral Care and Counseling," *Pastoral Psychology* 49 (2000): 101 and following.

13. Sandu M. Iordache, *Palliative People's Dreams and Dream-Related Perceptions and Interpretations: A Mixed-Method Investigation*. Unpublished dissertation. (Auckland: University of Auckland, 2012).

14. For example, Anthony Pellegrini, *The Role of Play in Human Development* (New York: Oxford University Press, 2009). I write about this in more detail in "Dreaming Is Play: A Response to Freud," in *Visions of the Night: Dreams, Religion, and Psychology*, ed. Kelly Bulkeley (Albany: State University of New York Press, 1999), 59–66.

15. See J. Bruner et al., eds., *Play: Its Role in Development and Evolution* (New York: Basic Books, 1976); J. Huizinga, *Homo Ludens: A Study of the Play Element in Culture* (Boston: Beacon Press, 1955); Gordon Burghardt, *The Genesis of Animal Play: Testing the Limits* (Cambridge, MA: MIT Press, 2005); and Suzanne Held and Marek Spinka, "Animal Play and Animal Welfare," *Animal Behavior* 81 (2011): 891–899.

16. The only adjustments would be "REM dreaming" in the first paragraph, and "dream-sharing" as a process that builds interpersonal trust. And there is no evidence (yet) that turtles dream.

17. Peretz Lavie and Hanna Kaminer, "Dreams That Poison Sleep: Dreams in Holocaust Survivors," *Dreaming* 1 (1991): 11–22.

18. Ibid., 19.

19. Deirdre Barrett, ed., *Trauma and Dreams* (Cambridge, MA: Harvard University Press, 1996); Ernest Hartmann, *Dreams and Nightmares: The Origin and Meaning of Dreams* (New York: Basic Books, 2000).

20. D. W. Winnicott, *Playing and Reality* (London: Tavistock Publications, 1971), 38, 50. Winnicott goes on to connect all the dots: "In playing, the child manipulates external phenomena in the service of the dream and invests chosen external phenomena with dream meaning and feeling. There is a direct development from transitional phenomena to playing, and from playing to shared playing, and from this to cultural experiences" (51).

21. G. William Domhoff, "The Neural Substrate for Dreaming: Is It a Subsystem of the Default Network?" *Consciousness and Cognition* 20 (2011): 1163–1174.

22. Marcus Raichle and Abraham Snyder, "A Default Mode of Brain Function: A Brief History of an Evolving Idea," *NeuroImage* 37 (2007): 1083–1090. See also Randy L. Buckner et al., "The Brain's Default Network: Anatomy, Function, and Relevance to Disease," *Annals of the New York Academy of Sciences* 1124 (2008): 1–38.

23. Ibid., 1.

24. See Domhoff, "The Neural Substrate for Dreaming"; and Silvina Horovitz et al., "Decoupling of the Brain's Default Mode Network during Deep Sleep," *Proceedings of the National Academy of Sciences* 106 (2009): 11376–11381.

25. Domhoff, "The Neural Substrate for Dreaming," 1173.

CHAPTER 9

1. Thomas Reid, quoted in Chris Olsen, "Forgotten Perspectives on Lucid Dreaming from the Enlightenment through the Early Twentieth Century," in *Lucid Dreaming: New Perspectives on Consciousness in Sleep*, ed. Ryan Hurd and Kelly Bulkeley (Westport, CT: ABC-Clio, 2014), 2: 94–95.

2. See Eleanor Rosch, "Principles of Categorization," in *Concepts: Core Readings*, ed. Eric Margois and Stephen Laurence (Cambridge, MA: MIT Press, 1999),

196, 197: "By prototypes of categories we have generally meant the clearest cases of category membership defined operationally by people's judgments of goodness of membership in the category.... In short, prototypes appear to be just those members of a category that most reflect the redundancy structure of the category as a whole."

3. This paragraph draws much of its language from Kelly Bulkeley, *Dreaming in the World's Religions: A Comparative History* (New York: New York University Press, 2008), 271–274.

4. A night terror is a disorder of sleep sometimes accompanied by brief images; it usually occurs in the first half of the night. A nightmare is an extremely frightening dream that often awakens a person; it usually occurs in the second half of the night. See chapter 3.

5. Tore Nielsen and Ross Levin, "Nightmares: A New Neurocognitive Model," *Sleep Medicine Reviews* 11 (2007): 296.

6. C. G. Seligman, "Type Dreams: A Request," *Folklore* 34 (1923): 376–378; and "Presidential Address: Anthropology and Psychology: A Study of Some Points of Contact," *Journal of the Royal Anthropological Institute of Great Britain and Ireland* 54 (1924): 13–46.

7. Richard Griffith et al., "The Universality of Typical Dreams: Japanese vs. Americans," *American Anthropologist* 60 (1958): 1173–1179; Z. Giora et al., "Dreams in Cross-Cultural Research," *Comprehensive Psychiatry* 13 (1972): 105–114; Tore Nielsen et al., "The Typical Dreams of Canadian University Students," *Dreaming* 13 (2003): 211–235; Lana Nasser and Kelly Bulkeley, "The Typical Dreams of Jordanian College Students," in *Dreaming in Christianity and Islam: Culture, Conflict, and Creativity*, ed. Kelly Bulkeley, Kate Adams, and Patricia Davis (New Brunswick, NJ: Rutgers University Press, 2009), 200–216; Michael Schredl et al., "Typical Dreams: Stability and Gender Differences," *Journal of Psychology* 138 (2004): 485–494.

8. We might speculate about the cultural significance of the variations reported in these studies. For example, the relatively low frequencies of chasing/attacked dreams among the Israeli Arab women (51%) and the mostly female Jordanians (48%) is intriguing and may reflect something distinctive about gender relations in Arab cultures. Until more TDQ studies are done with a wider variety of populations, we cannot be sure what to make of statistical variations like this.

9. Jorge Luis Borges, "Nightmares," in *Seven Nights*, trans. Eliot Weinberger (New York: New Directions, 1984), 32.

10. Ibid.

11. In terms of conceptual metaphor theory, a dream motif can be the target of many different source concepts.

12. In some cases there may be some intermingling of externally focused awareness with the dreaming experience. For example, the king appeared in Borges's

bedroom at dawn, which Borges thought was probably the time when the dream was in fact occurring.

13. The comparisons involved searching reports of 25 words of more for the terms "bed," "beds," and "bedroom." The reports came from 205 women and 208 men in the most recent dream sets, and from 231 women and 183 men in the worst nightmares set.

14. Participant ID: zogby_052110:32661.

15. Homer, *The Iliad*, trans. Richard Lattimore (Chicago: University of Chicago Press, 1951), Book 22, lines 199–201.

16. Charlotte Beradt, *The Third Reich of Dreams*, trans. A. Gottwald (Chicago: Quadrangle Books, 1966), 40.

17. Marie Reay, "The Sweet Witchcraft of Kuma Dream Experience," *Mankind* 5 (1962): 460–461.

18. In Griffith et al.'s study, 25.6% of the Americans and 27.8% of the Japanese answered "yes" to the question about a dream of killing someone. In Nielsen et al.'s study, 24.3% of the Canadians answered "yes." In Giora et al.'s study, 34.3% of the Israeli Kibbutz residents and 25.4% of the Israeli Arabs answered "yes." In Nasser and Bulkeley's study, 12% of the mostly female Jordanians answered "yes." In all but one group (the Japanese), the males answered "yes" at a considerably higher frequency than did the females.

19. Participant ID harris_2011:010210.

20. Herodotus, *Histories*, 2.139, discussed in Stephanie West, "And It Came to Pass That Pharaoh Dreamed: Notes on Herodotus 2:139," *Classical Quarterly* 37 (1987): 262–271.

21. See Steven Pinker, *How the Mind Works* (New York: W. W. Norton, 1997), 21, 22: "[P]sychology is engineering in reverse. In forward engineering, one designs a machine to do something; in reverse engineering, one figures out what a machine was designed to do. . . . The rationale for reverse engineering living things comes, of course, from Charles Darwin."

22. See Nielsen and Levin, "Nightmares: A New Neurocognitive Model." See also Joseph Ledoux, *The Emotional Brain: The Mysterious Underpinnings of Emotional Life* (New York: Simon and Schuster, 1998); and Jaak Panksepp, *Affective Neuroscience: The Foundations of Human and Animal Emotions* (New York: Oxford University Press, 2004).

23. Geoffrey Chaucer, "The Nun's Priest's Tale," in *The Canterbury Tales* (trans. Nevill Coghill), in *Great Books of the Western World*, ed. Mortimer J. Adler (Chicago: Encyclopaedia Britannica, 1952), 362.

24. Ibid.

25. Ibid., 363, 365.

26. Antti Revonsuo, "The Reinterpretation of Dreams: An Evolutionary Hypothesis of the Function of Dreaming," in *Sleep and Dreaming: Scientific Advances and Reconsiderations*, ed. Edward Pace-Schott, Mark Solms, Mark Blagrove, and Stevan Harnad (Cambridge: Cambridge University Press, 2003), 97, 104.

27. For further discussion, see Kelly Bulkeley, "Dreaming Is Play II: Revonsuo's Threat Simulation Theory in Ludic Context," *Sleep and Hypnosis* 6 (2004): 125 and following.

CHAPTER 10

1. Augustine, *Confessions*, trans. Henry Chadwick (Oxford: Oxford University Press, 1991), 10:30.
2. Z. Giora et al., "Dreams in Cross-Cultural Research," *Comprehensive Psychiatry* 13 (1972): 109.
3. The data for the religious worship service attendance are not included in table 10.2, but can be found at the SDDb website under "Sample Data."
4. Plato, *The Republic*, trans. A. D. Lindsay (New York: E. P. Dutton, 1957), 336.
5. See Kelly Bulkeley, *Dreaming in the World's Religions: A Comparative History* (New York: New York University Press, 2008).
6. Stephan Hamann et al., "Men and Women Differ in Amygdala Response to Visual Sexual Stimuli," *Nature Neuroscience* 7 (2004): 411–416.
7. The entire issue was later republished as Edward Pace-Schott et al., eds., *Sleep and Dreaming: Scientific Advances and Reconsiderations* (Cambridge: Cambridge University Press, 2003).
8. Tore Nielsen and Anne Germain, "Post-Traumatic Nightmares as a Dysfunctional State," in *Sleep and Dreaming: Scientific Advances and Reconsiderations*, ed. Edward Pace-Schott, Mark Solms, Mark Blagrove, and Stevan Harnad (Cambridge: Cambridge University Press, 2003), 191, emphasis added. Two additional responses are also worth quoting. From James Bednar, "Internally-Generated Activity, Non-Episodic Memory, and Emotional Salience in Sleep," in *Sleep and Dreaming*, ed. Pace-Schott et al., 120: "Given that threats are not the only situations biologically important to humans, ancestral or otherwise, a much more intuitive hypothesis would be that dreams simulate biologically-significant situations in general." From Anne Germain et al., "The Prevalence of Typical Dream Themes Challenges the Specificity of the Threat Simulation Theory," in *Sleep and Dreaming*, ed. Pace-Schott et al., 152: "[C]onsistencies in the prevalence of typical dream themes in multiple study samples offer only limited support for the idea that dreaming is threat simulation. These findings would be more consistent with a less specific version of the theory that postulates simulations of positive, as well as negative, and of current, as well as ancestral, dream themes."
9. Mary A. Carskadon, *Encyclopedia of Sleep and Dreaming* (Farmington Hills, MI: Gale Cengage, 1993), 536.
10. De La Pena Zarcone and William Dement, "Heightened Sexual Interest and Sleep Disturbance," *Perceptual and Motor Skills* 39 (1974): 1135–1141.
11. E. O. Wilson, *Sociobiology: The New Synthesis*, 25th Anniversary ed. (Cambridge, MA: Belknap Press, 2000), 315: "[T]he advantage of sexual reproduction lies in

the much greater speed with which new genotypes are assembled.... To diversify is to adapt; sexually reproducing populations are more likely than asexual ones to create new genetic combinations better adjusted to changed conditions in the environment."

CHAPTER 11

1. Sigmund Freud, *The Interpretation of Dreams*, trans. James Strachey (New York: Avon Books, 1965), 305. The same passage is also found in a later section of the book, on page 428.
2. Richard Griffith et al., "The Universality of Typical Dreams: Japanese vs. Americans," *American Anthropologist* 60 (1958): 1173–1179, used other questions about falling; the frequencies here come from the "falling, with fear" question from their survey.
3. For instance, wealthy, politically conservative people are more likely to be older than younger, so the findings about income and political ideology may reflect the more important difference among age groups.
4. Freud made a similar observation in *The Interpretation of Dreams*, when he admitted it was difficult to gather enough material on falling dreams to analyze and explain them properly (306).
5. Originally quoted in Kelly Bulkeley, *Transforming Dreams* (New York: John Wiley & Sons, 2000), 79, from a college student participant in research I conducted during the 1990s.
6. Ernest Hartmann, *Dreams and Nightmares: The Origin and Meaning of Dreams* (New York: Basic Books, 2000).
7. Additionally, dreams of earthquakes, tornados, and storms can have the same qualities of massive, overwhelming power in different elemental guises.
8. Slightly edited for clarity. Participant harris_2011:043446.
9. Edith Hamilton, *Mythology* (New York: Mentor, 1969), 64–65.
10. Originally quoted in Bulkeley, *Transforming Dreams*, 84, from a college student participant in research I conducted during the 1990s.
11. Nicholas Royle, *The Tiger Garden: A Book of Writer's Dreams* (London: Serpent's Tail, 1996), 154.
12. O. Ponpeiano, "Vestibular Influences during Sleep," in *Handbook of Sensory Physiology: Vestibular System*, Part I: *Basic Mechanisms*, ed. H. H. Kornhuker (New York: Springer-Verlag, 1974). See also John Herman, "Reflexive and Orienting Properties of REM Sleep Dreaming and Eye Movements," in *Sleep and Dreaming: Scientific Advances and Reconsiderations*, ed. Edward Pace-Schott, Mark Solms, Mark Blagrove, and Stevan Harnad (Cambridge: Cambridge University Press, 2003), 161, emphasis in the original: "It is proposed that a constant property of vivid REM dreaming is the sensation of orientation in the dreamt space, or the hallucinated impression that the dreamer is physically present in the dreamt scene, in three-dimensional space. The dreamer

is directionally oriented and aware of a spatial relationship to the persons or objects present in the dream. The sensation of orientation is made possible by cortical-subcortical mechanisms, including the vestibular system. The associated eye movements are related to reflexive and orienting responses to the dreamt surround via feedback loop connecting cortex to vestibular nuclei. *It is postulated that the sense of orientation is the phenomenological equivalent in dreaming to the continuous vestibular activation during REM sleep.*"

13. Kenneth Leslie and Robert Ogilvie, "Vestibular Dreams: The Effect of Rocking on Dream Mentation," *Dreaming* 6 (1996): 1–16.

14. George Lakoff, "How Metaphor Structures Dreams: The Theory of Conceptual Metaphor Applied to Dream Analysis," in *Dreams: A Reader on the Religious, Cultural, and Psychological Dimensions of Dreaming*, ed. Kelly Bulkeley (New York: Palgrave, 2001), 280.

15. Kelly Bulkeley, *American Dreamers* (Boston: Beacon Press, 2008), 121–122.

16. Lana Nasser and Kelly Bulkeley, "The Typical Dreams of Jordanian College Students," in *Dreaming in Christianity and Islam: Culture, Conflict, and Creativity*, ed. Kelly Bulkeley, Kate Adams, and Patricia Davis (New Brunswick, NJ: Rutgers University Press, 2009), 209.

17. Lana Nasser, "The Jinn: Companion in the Realm of Dreams and Imagination," in *Dreaming in Christianity and Islam*, ed. Bulkeley et al.

18. Mary C. Walsh, *Prophetic Imagination and the Neurophysiology of Trauma in Traumatized Adolescents*. Unpublished doctoral dissertation (San Anselmo: San Francisco Theological Seminary, 2014).

19. Ibid., 231.

20. Ibid., 255.

CHAPTER 12

1. Wang Ch'ung, quoted in Roberto Ong, *The Interpretation of Dreams in Ancient China* (Bochum: Studienverlag Brockmeyer, 1985), 67, 69–70.

2. Artemidorus, *The Interpretation of Dreams*, trans. Robert White (Park Ridge, NJ: Noyes Press, 1975), 238.

3. See Roger Lohmann, ed., *Dream Travelers: Sleep Experiences and Culture in the Western Pacific* (New York: Palgrave Macmillan, 2003); and Lee Irwin, *The Dream Seekers: Native American Visionary Traditions of the Great Plains* (Norman: University of Oklahoma Press, 1994).

4. M. C. Jedrej and Rosalind Shaw, eds., *Dreaming, Religion, and Society in Africa* (Leiden: E. J. Brill, 1992).

5. Wendy Doniger O'Flaherty, *Dreaming, Illusion, and Other Realities* (Chicago: University of Chicago Press, 1984).

6. Homer, *The Iliad*, trans. Richard Lattimore (Chicago: University of Chicago Press, 1951), Book 23, lines 54–107.

7. Marcia Hermansen, "Dreams and Dreaming in Islam," in *Dreams: A Reader on the Religious, Cultural, and Psychological Dimensions of Dreaming*, ed. Kelly Bulkeley (New York: Palgrave, 2001), 75.

8. Jeffrey Burgdorf and Jaak Panksepp, "The Neurobiology of Positive Emotions," *Neuroscience and Biobehavioral Reviews* 30 (2006): 173. See also Eric Kandel et al., eds., *Principles of Neural Science*, 5th ed. (New York: McGraw Hill, 2012), 982 and following.

9. Roger Knudson, "Significant Dreams: Bizarre or Beautiful?" *Dreaming* 11 (2001): 170.

10. Carl Jung, *Children's Dreams: Notes from the Seminar Given in 1936–1940*, trans. Ernst Falzeder and Tony Woolfson (Princeton, NJ: Princeton University Press, 2008), 2.

11. Roger Knudson and Samuel Minier, "The On-Going Significance of Significant Dreams: The Case of the Bodiless Head," *Dreaming* 9 (1999): 244.

12. Harry Hunt, *The Multiplicity of Dreams: Memory, Imagination, and Consciousness* (New Haven, CT: Yale University Press, 1989), 97.

13. Ibid., 90.

14. Don Kuiken and Shelley Sikora, "The Impact of Dreams on Waking Thoughts and Feelings," in *The Functions of Dreaming*, ed. Alan Moffitt, Milton Kramer, and Robert Hoffmann (Albany: State University of New York Press, 1993), 424.

15. Ibid., 429.

16. For example, Stanley Krippner, Fariba Bogzaran, and Andre Percia de Carvalho's 2002 book *Extraordinary Dreams and How to Work with Them* (Albany: State University of New York Press, 2002) presented 13 categories of dreaming: creative, lucid, out of body, pregnancy, healing, dreams within dreams, collective dreams, telepathic, clairvoyant, precognitive, past life, initiation, spiritual, and visitation. Ranier Schonhammer's article "Typical Dreams: Reflections of Arousal," *Journal of Consciousness Studies* 12 (2005): 18–37, discusses research on various kinds of typical dreaming, although he does not offer an overarching model of his own. Jaak Panksepp suggested the remarkable notion that cats, too, have a multiplicity of dreams ("The Dream of Reason Creates Monsters: Especially When We Neglect the Role of Emotions in REM-States," in *Sleep and Dreaming: Scientific Advances and Reconsiderations*, ed. Edward Pace-Schott, Mark Solms, Mark Blagrove, and Stevan Harnad (Cambridge: Cambridge University Press, 2003), 201: "following destruction of their atonia mechanisms, cats exhibit at least four 'archetypal' REM-dreams—predatory intent, fearful withdrawal, angry assertiveness, and licking/grooming. These categories reflect primal emotional concerns of all mammals, elaborated by subcortical systems which may have had a more important role in the emergence of consciousness than is commonly recognized. In unpublished work, I have repeatedly found these four primal themes to prevail in human dream reports." From his earliest writings, Tore Nielsen has been investigating highly impactful dreams,

and in his neuroscientific work on the relationship between REM and NREM he coined the term "apex dreaming," which he describes as follows: "The term 'apex' dreaming is adopted to refer to a subcategory of dreaming that is distinguished by exceptional vividness, intensity, or complexity.... Apex dreaming [is] the most vivid, intense, and complex forms of dreaming: e.g., nightmare, sexual, archetypal, transcendental, titanic, existential, lucid" ("A Review of Mentation in REM and NREM Sleep: 'Covert' REM Sleep as a Possible Reconciliation of Two Opposing Models," in *Sleep and Dreaming: Scientific Advances and Reconsiderations*, ed. Edward Pace-Schott, Mark Solms, Mark Blagrove, and Stevan Harnad [Cambridge: Cambridge University Press, 2003], 61.)

CHAPTER 13

1. Petronius, *The Satyricon*, P. G. Walsh, trans. (New York: Oxford University Press, 2009).
2. For discussion of a similar approach, see Ann Taves, *Religious Experience Reconsidered: A Building-Block Approach to the Study of Religion and Other Special Things* (Princeton, NJ: Princeton University Press, 2011).
3. Lana Nasser, "The Jinn: Companion in the Realm of Dreams and Imagination," in *Dreaming in Christianity and Islam: Culture, Conflict, and Creativity*, ed. Kelly Bulkeley, Kate Adams, and Patricia Davis (New Brunswick, NJ: Rutgers University Press, 2009), 143–154.
4. See Amira El-Zein, *Islam, Arabs, and the Intelligent World of the Jinn* (Syracuse, NY: Syracuse University Press, 2009).
5. Nasser, "The Jinn," 148.
6. Ibid.
7. Ibid., 149.
8. Ibid., 148.
9. Victor Crapanzano, "Saints, Jnun, and Demons: An Essay in Moroccan Ethnopsychology," *Psychiatry* 38 (1975): 147.
10. Ibid.
11. Babylonian Talmud: *Niddah* 24b, threats to pregnancy; *Shabbat* 151b, threats to solitary sleeping men; *Erubin* 100b, her long hair.
12. Marie Reay, "The Sweet Witchcraft of Kuma Dream Experience," *Mankind* 5 (1962): 459–463.
13. Rosalind Shaw, "Dreaming as Accomplishment: Power, the Individual, and Temne Divination," in *Dreaming, Religion, and Society in Africa*, ed. M. C. Jedrej and Rosalind Shaw (Leiden: E. J. Brill, 1992), 46–47.
14. Wendy Doniger O'Flaherty, trans., *The Rig Veda* (London: Penguin Books, 1981), 292.
15. Heinrich Kramer and James Sprenger, eds., *The Malleus Maleficarum*, trans. Montague Summers (New York: Dover, 1971), 81.

16. William James, *The Varieties of Religious Experience* (New York: Mentor Books, 1958), 362, 366, 386.
17. See Henri Ellenberger, *The Discovery of the Unconscious: The History and Evolution of Dynamic Psychiatry* (New York: Basic Books, 1970); Peter Homans, *The Ability to Mourn: Disillusionment and the Social Origins of Psychoanalysis* (Chicago: University of Chicago Press, 1989); Edward Kelly et al., *Irreducible Mind: Toward a Psychology for the 21st Century* (Lanham, MD: Rowman & Littlefield, 2007); Ran R. Hassin, James S. Uleman, and John A. Bargh, eds. *The New Unconscious* (New York: Oxford University Press, 2005).
18. From January 17, 1897. Jeffrey Moussaieff Masson, *The Complete Letters of Sigmund Freud to Wilhelm Fliess, 1887–1904* (Cambridge, MA: Belknap Press, 1985), 224.
19. Earnest Jones, *On the Nightmare* (New York: Liveright, 1951), 155.
20. Emma Cohen, *The Mind Possessed: The Cognition of Spirit Possession in an Afro-Brazilian Religious Tradition* (New York: Oxford University Press, 2007), 86.
21. Ibid., 73. The passage continues: "Satisfactory ethnographic presentation may now privilege ambiguity over precision, erudition over substance, overdramatic vivification over faithful narration, and obscurity over clarity."
22. Ibid., 14.
23. Ibid., 63. See also 56.
24. Whitehouse's theory of imaginal versus doctrinal religiosity does address issues of altered states of consciousness. His work will be discussed in the next chapter.
25. For more on sleep paralysis, see Ryan Hurd, *Sleep Paralysis: A Guide to Hypnogogic Visions and Visitors of the Night* (Los Altos, CA: Hyena Press, 2010); Shelley Adler, *Sleep Paralysis: Night-Mares, Nocebos, and the Mind–Body Connection* (New Brunswick, NJ: Rutgers University Press, 2011); and David Hufford, *The Terror That Comes in the Night: An Experience-Centered Study of Supernatural Assault Traditions* (Philadelphia: University of Pennsylvania Press, 1982).
26. Hufford, *The Terror That Comes in the Night*. Hufford found that people often spoke of their experiences using the phrase, "I was hagged last night" (3).
27. Ibid., 2.
28. As Cohen said in *The Mind Possessed*, "Even if one demonstrates that regular mental architecture is something one must have to conceptualize spirit possession—a *necessary* condition—it does not follow that having this architecture is enough—a *sufficient* condition" (183, emphasis in the original).

CHAPTER 14

1. Richard Dawkins, *The God Delusion* (Boston: Houghton Mifflin, 2006), 188, emphasis added.

2. Ibid., 179.

3. This passage is drawn in part from a similar discussion in Kelly Bulkeley, *Dreaming in the World's Religions: A Comparative History* (New York: New York University Press, 2008).

4. Quoted in Roberto Ong, *The Interpretation of Dreams in Ancient China* (Bochum: Studienverlag Brockmeyer, 1985), 15–16.

5. For additional discussion of this passage, see *Dreaming in the World's Religions*, 147–148.

6. Ibid., 28–30, 80–83.

7. Matthew 1:20, Standard King James Version.

8. Lee Irwin, *The Dream Seekers: Native American Visionary Traditions of the Great Plains* (Norman: University of Oklahoma Press, 1994), 18.

9. Quoted in J. S. Lincoln, *The Dream in Primitive Cultures* (London: University of London Press, 1935), 86.

10. Harvey Whitehouse, *Modes of Religiosity: A Cognitive Theory of Religious Transmission* (Walnut Creek, CA: Altamira Press, 2004).

11. See Harvey Whitehouse and James Laidlaw, *Ritual and Memory: Toward a Comparative Anthropology of Religion* (Walnut Creek, CA: Altamira Press, 2004).

12. Whitehouse, *Modes of Religiosity*, 77.

13. Ibid., 70.

14. Ibid., 76.

15. Ibid., 72.

16. Ibid.

17. Collections of lucid dreams are the only other possible exception to the pre-eminence of visual perception. See Kelly Bulkeley, "Lucid Dreaming by the Numbers," in *Lucid Dreaming: New Perspectives on Consciousness in Sleep*, ed. Ryan Hurd and Kelly Bulkeley (Westport, CT: ABC-Clio, 2014), 1–22.

18. This seems to have been the case with Mary Calkins, author of the 1893 article "Statistics of Dreams," *American Journal of Psychology* 5 (1893): 311–343. She observed in her own dreams a 3:2 ratio of visual to auditory perception, but she interpreted that finding as discontinuous with her waking life because she felt much less visually oriented than most people. However, with the larger collections of dreams now at our disposal, we can say that Calkins's finding might be better interpreted as a continuity with her waking life, since a 3:2 visual to auditory perception ratio is somewhat on the low end compared to other series, which can be closer to 3:1 or 4:1. In other words, visual perception is not as predominant in her dreams as it is for other people, and this is continuous with her self-description as a relatively low-visual person.

19. A. R. Braun et al., "Dissociated Pattern of Activity in Visual Cortices and Their Projections during Human Rapid Eye-Movement Sleep," *Science* 279 (1998): 91–95; Pierre Maquet et al., "Functional Neuroanatomy of Human Rapid-Eye-Movement Sleep and Dreaming," *Nature* 383 (1996): 163; and E. A. Nofziger et al.,

"Forebrain Activation in REM Sleep: An FDG PET Study," *Brain Research* 770 (1997): 192–201.

20. Mark Solms, *The Neuropsychology of Dreaming: A Clinico-Anatomical Study* (Mahwah, NJ: Lawrence Erlbaum, 1997).

21. Dawkins tweet: https://twitter.com/richarddawkins/status/416140759247495168.

22. Richard Dawkins, "Atheists for Jesus," in *The Portable Atheist: Essential Readings for the Nonbeliever*, ed. Christopher Hitchens (New York: Da Capo, 2007), 308.

23. Ibid., 309.

24. In his *Exegesis* Philip K. Dick, one of the great science-fiction writers of the twentieth century, struggled with these same issues in relation to his own experiences of mystical visions and prophetic dreams, which started on February 3, 1972, and continued for several months after that. The depth and complexity of Dick's exploration of these dreams cannot be easily summarized; I hope to write a more detailed response to the *Exegesis* at some point in the future. See also his novel *Radio Free Albemuth* and the other stories in the "VALIS" series.

25. Genesis 28:12, Standard King James Version.

26. Quoted in Peter Dronke, *Women Writers of the Middle Ages: A Critical Study of Texts from Perpetua to Margeurite Porete* (Cambridge: Cambridge University Press, 1984), 3.

27. See Patricia Davis, "The Weaning of Perpetua: Female Embodiment and Spiritual Growth Metaphor in the Dream of an Early Christian Martyr," *Dreaming* 15 (2005): 261–270.

28. Dronke, *Women Writers of the Middle Ages*, 3.

29. Ibid., 4.

30. Ibid.

31. Ibid.

CHAPTER 15

1. Steven Pinker, *How the Mind Works* (New York: W. W. Norton, 1997), 554, 555.

2. A good source of information about Aristides is John Stephens, *The Dreams and Visions of Aelius Aristides: A Case-Study in the History of Religions* (Piscataway, NJ: Gorgias Press, 2013). For general information about the worship of Asclepius and the practice of dream incubation at his temples, see Emma Edelstein and Ludwig Edelstein, *Asclepius: Collection and Interpretation of the Testimonies* (Baltimore, MD: Johns Hopkins University Press, 1945).

3. See Aelius Aristides, *The Complete Works*, trans. Charles Behr (Leiden: E. J. Brill, 1981).

4. Ibid., 305 and following.

5. Kimberly Patton, "'A Great and Strange Correction': Intentionality, Locality, and Epiphany in the Category of Dream Incubation," *History of Religions* 43 (2004): 194–223.

6. See Hidayet Aydar, "*Istikhara* and Dreams: Learning about the Future through Dreaming," in *Dreaming in Christianity and Islam: Culture, Conflict, and Creativity*, ed. Kelly Bulkeley, Kate Adams, and Patricia Davis (New Brunswick, NJ: Rutgers University Press, 2009), 123–136.

7. Joel Covitz, *Visions of the Night: A Study of Jewish Dream Interpretation* (Boston: Shambhala, 1990).

8. Ibid., 135, 139.

9. Roger Lohmann, ed., *Dream Travelers: Sleep Experiences and Culture in the Western Pacific* (New York: Palgrave Macmillan, 2003); Waud Kracke, "Kagwahiv Mourning: Dreams of a Bereaved Father," in *Dreams: A Reader on the Religious, Cultural, and Psychological Dimensions of Dreaming*, ed. Kelly Bulkeley (New York: Palgrave, 2001), 175–188; Angela Sumegi, *Dreamworlds of Shamanism and Tibetan Buddhism: The Third Place* (Albany: State University of New York Press, 2008); M. C. Jedrej and Rosalind Shaw, *Dreaming, Religion, and Society in Africa* (Leiden: E. J. Brill, 1992).

10. Lee Irwin, *The Dream Seekers: Native American Visionary Traditions of the Great Plains* (Norman: University of Oklahoma Press, 1994), 193.

11. James W. Jones, "Brain, Mind, and Spirit—A Clinician's Perspective, or Why I Am Not Afraid of Dualism," in *Soul, Psyche, Brain: New Directions in the Study of Religion and Brain-Mind Science*, ed. Kelly Bulkeley (New York: Palgrave, 2005), 36.

12. Ibid., 39.

13. Jones's most recent book, *Can Science Explain Religion?*, is a more detailed assessment of the limits of current CSR research and the prospects for better studies in the future.

14. Andrew Leuchter et al., "Changes in Brain Function of Depressed Subjects during Treatment with Placebo," *Psychiatry Online* 159 (2002): 122.

15. The etymology of *endorphin* is relevant to our theme: from the Greek words *endon*, meaning "proceeding from within," and *morphine*, from Morpheus, the god of sleep. An endorphin is an internally generated possession by sleep.

16. Dylan Evans, *Placebo: Mind over Matter in Modern Medicine* (New York: Oxford University Press, 2004), 111–113.

17. Ibid., 80.

18. See also Fabrizio Benedetti, *Placebo Effects*, 2nd ed. (New York: Oxford University Press, 2014); and Arthur Shapiro and Elaine Shapiro, *The Powerful Placebo: From Ancient Priest to Modern Physician* (Baltimore, MD: Johns Hopkins University Press, 1997).

19. See Anne Harrington, ed., *The Placebo Effect: An Interdisciplinary Exploration* (Cambridge, MA: Harvard University Press, 1997); Robert Hahn and Arthur Kleinman, "Belief as Pathogen, Belief as Medicine: 'Voodoo Death' and the 'Placebo Phenomenon' in Anthropological Perspective," *Medical Anthropology Quarterly* 14 (1983): 3–19; Shelley Adler, *Sleep Paralysis: Night-Mares, Nocebos,*

and the Mind–Body Connection (New Brunswick, NJ: Rutgers University Press, 2011); Cecil G. Helman, "Placebos and Nocebos: The Cultural Construction of Belief," *Understanding the Placebo Effect in Complementary Medicine: Theory, Practice and Research,* ed. David Peters (London: Churchill Livingstone, 2001).

20. See Adler, *Sleep Paralysis.*
21. Jeffrey Schwartz and Sharon Begley, *The Mind and the Brain: Neuroplasticity and the Power of Mental Force* (New York: Regan Books, 2002).
22. Good resources are Kirk Bingaman, *The Power of Neuroplasticity for Pastoral and Spiritual Care* (Lanham, MD: Lexington Books, 2014); and David Hogue, *Remembering the Future, Imagining the Past: Story, Ritual, and the Human Brain* (Cleveland, OH: Pilgrim Press, 2003).
23. See Steven Oberhelman, "Galen, *On Diagnosis from Dreams,*" *Journal of the History of Medicine and Allied Sciences* 38 (1983): 36–47.

CHAPTER 16

1. Pascal Boyer, *Religion Explained: The Evolutionary Origins of Religious Thought* (New York: Basic Books, 2001), 311.
2. Ibid., 311, emphasis added.
3. George Tanabe, Jr., *Myoe the Dreamkeeper: Fantasy and Knowledge in Early Kamakura Buddhism* (Cambridge, MA: Harvard University Press, 1992), 12.
4. Ibid., 9.
5. Ibid., 10.
6. Ibid., 174.
7. Ibid., 249, n. 95.
8. Barbara Tedlock, *The Woman in the Shaman's Body: Reclaiming the Feminine in Religion and Medicine* (New York: Bantam, 2005), 103.
9. *Upanishads,* trans. P. Olivelle (Oxford: Oxford University Press, 1996), 59 and following.
10. See chapter 1 of Kelly Bulkeley, *Dreaming in the World's Religions: A Comparative History* (New York: New York University Press, 2008).
11. Glenn Mullin, ed. and trans., *The Six Yogas of Naropa* (Ithaca, NY: Snow Lion, 2006).
12. See A. Muhammad Ma'ruf, "Lucid Dreaming and the Sufis: Conflicts and Opportunities in the Modern West," in *Lucid Dreaming: New Perspectives on Consciousness in Sleep,* ed. Ryan Hurd and Kelly Bulkeley (Westport, CT: ABC-Clio, 2014), vol. 2, 265–290; Mehrdad Fakour, "A Devil's Sojourn in the Realm of Lucid Dreams," in *Lucid Dreaming,* ed. Hurd and Bulkeley, vol. 2, 161–178; and Marcia Hermansen, "Dreams and Dreaming in Islam," in *Dreams: A Reader on the Religious, Cultural, and Psychological Dimensions of Dreaming,* ed. Kelly Bulkeley (New York: Palgrave, 2001), 73–92.

13. Henri Corbin, "Visionary Dream in Islamic Spirituality," in *The Dream and Human Society*, ed. G. E. Von Grunebaum and Roger Callois (Berkeley: University of California Press, 1966), 407, emphasis in original. See also Fazlur Rahman, "Dream, Imagination, and *Alam al-Mithal*" in *The Dream and Human Society*, ed. Von Grunebaum and Callois, 409–420.

14. Ruby Modesto and Guy Mount, *Not For Innocent Ears: Spiritual Traditions of a Desert Cahuilla Medicine Woman* (Cottonwood, CA: Sweetlight Books, 1980), 26.

15. Plato, *The Republic*, trans. A. D. Lindsay (New York: E. P. Dutton, 1957), 336.

16. Notable exceptions are Etzel Cardena et al., *Varieties of Anomalous Experience: Examining the Scientific Evidence* (Washington, DC: American Psychological Association, 2000); Edward Kelly et al., *Irreducible Mind: Toward a Psychology for the 21st Century* (Lanham, MD: Rowman & Littlefield, 2007); and Jeffrey Kripal, *The Serpent's Gift: Gnostic Reflections on the Study of Religion* (Chicago: University of Chicago Press, 2008).

17. James Austin, *Zen and the Brain* (Cambridge, MA: MIT Press, 1998).

18. Andrew Newberg et al., *Why God Won't Go Away: Brain Science and the Biology of Belief* (New York: Ballantine, 2001), 6.

19. Hans Lou et al., "A 15O-H2O PET Study of Meditation and the Resting State of Normal Consciousness," *Human Brain Mapping* 7 (1999): 98–105.

20. This text follows pages 249–250 of Kelly Bulkeley, "Religious Conversion and Cognitive Neuroscience," in *The Oxford Handbook of Religious Conversion*, ed. Lewis Rambo and Charles Farhadian (New York: Oxford University Press, 2014), 240–255.

21. See James Pagel, "Lucid Dreaming as Sleep Meditation," in *Lucid Dreaming*, ed. Hurd and Bulkeley, 69: "[T]he typical electrophysiological effects associated with meditative practice vary based on the specific technique. A jumble of data from different techniques and traditions indicates that meditation clearly alters CNS electrophysiology; these changes in electrophysiology occur, however, in a variety of patterns based on meditative technique."

22. See Kelly Bulkeley, "Lucid Dreaming by the Numbers," in *Lucid Dreaming*, ed. Hurd and Bulkeley.

23. Norman Malcolm, *Dreaming* (London: Routledge & Kegan Paul, 1959).

24. See Bulkeley and Hurd, "Introduction," in *Lucid Dreaming*.

25. Sheila Purcell et al., "Waking, Dreaming, and Self-Regulation," in *The Functions of Dreaming*, ed. Alan Moffitt, Milton Kramer, and Robert Hoffmann (Albany: State University of New York Press, 1993), 212.

26. Ibid., 247.

27. Excellent studies of the various methods used to stimulate lucid dreaming include Tadas Stumbrys and Daniel Erlacher, "The Science of Lucid Dream Induction," in *Lucid Dreaming*, ed. Hurd and Bulkeley; and Tim Post,

"Educational Frontiers of Training Lucid Dreamers," in *Lucid Dreaming*, ed. Hurd and Bulkeley.

28. Tracey Kahan, "Consciousness in Dreaming: A Metacognitive Approach," in *Dreams*, ed. Bulkeley, 344.

29. See Jayne Gackenbach and Stephen LaBerge, eds., *Conscious Mind, Sleeping Brain: Perspectives on Lucid Dreaming* (New York: Plenum, 1988); Harry Hunt, *The Multiplicity of Dreams: Memory, Imagination, and Consciousness* (New Haven, CT: Yale University Press, 1989); Alan Moffitt, et al., *The Functions of Dreaming* (Albany: State University of New York Press, 1993); Richard Wolman and Miloslava Kozmova, "'Last Night I Had the Strangest Dream': Varieties of Rational Thought Processes in Dream Reports," *Consciousness and Cognition* 16 (2007): 838–849.

30. Pagel, "Lucid Dreaming as Sleep Meditation," 72.

31. Ibid.

CONCLUSION

1. See Thomas Nagel, *What Does It All Mean? A Very Short Introduction to Philosophy* (New York: Oxford University Press, 1987); John Cole, *The Olympian Dreams and Youthful Rebellion of Rene Descartes* (Urbana: University of Illinois Press, 1992).

2. Adrian Desmond and James Moore, *Darwin: The Life of a Tormented Evolutionist* (New York: W. W. Norton, 1991), 240.

3. Ralph Colp, "Charles Darwin's Dream of His Double Execution," *Journal of Psychohistory* 13 (1986): 277.

4. Desmond and Moore, *Darwin*, 249.

5. Charles Darwin, *Charles Darwin's Notebooks 1836–1844*, ed. Paul Barrett, Peter Gautrey, Sandra Herbert, David Kohn, and Sydney Smith (Ithaca, NY: Cornell University Press, 1987), 555. Notebook M, 143–144.

6. Ibid., 556, emphasis in the original.

Bibliography

Adler, Shelley. *Sleep Paralysis: Night-Mares, Nocebos, and the Mind–Body Connection.* New Brunswick, NJ: Rutgers University Press, 2011.

Aizenstat, Stephen, and Robert Bosnak, eds. *Imagination and Medicine.* New Orleans, LA: Spring, 2009.

Arber, Sara, Marcos Bote, and Robert Meadows. "Gender and Socio-Economic Patterning of Self-Reported Sleep Problems in Britain." *Social Science & Medicine* 68 (2009): 281–289.

Arber, Sara, Robert Meadows, and S. Venn. "Sleep and Society." In *The Oxford Handbook of Sleep and Sleep Disorders,* edited by Charles Morin and Colin Espie, 223–247. New York: Oxford University Press, 2012.

Aristides, Aelius. *The Complete Works.* Translated by Charles Behr. Leiden: E. J. Brill, 1981.

Aristotle. "On Dreams." In *The Collected Works of Aristotle.* Edited by R. McKeon. New York: Random House, 1941.

Artemidorus. *The Interpretation of Dreams.* Translated by Robert White. Park Ridge, NJ: Noyes Press, 1975.

Aserinsky, Eugene, and Nathaniel Kleitman. "Regularly Occurring Periods of Eye Motility, and Concomitant Phenomena, during Sleep." *Science* 118 (1953): 273–274.

Augustine. *Confessions.* Translated by Henry Chadwick. Oxford: Oxford University Press, 1991.

Austin, James. *Zen and the Brain.* Cambridge, MA: MIT Press, 1998.

Aydar, Hidayet. "*Istikhara* and Dreams: Learning about the Future through Dreaming." In *Dreaming in Christianity and Islam: Culture, Conflict, and Creativity,* edited by Kelly Bulkeley, Kate Adams, and Patricia Davis, 123–136. New Brunswick, NJ: Rutgers University Press, 2009.

Barrett, Deirdre, ed. *Trauma and Dreams.* Cambridge, MA: Harvard University Press, 1996.

Barrett, Justin. *Why Would Anyone Believe in God?* Walnut Creek, CA: AltaMira Press, 2004.

Beaulieu-Prevost, Dominic, and Antonio Zadra. "Absorption, Psychological Boundaries and Attitude Towards Dreams as Correlates of Dream Recall: Two Decades of Research Seen through a Meta-Analysis." *Journal of Sleep Research* 16 (2007): 51–59.

Beaulieu-Prevost, Dominic, and Antonio Zadra. "Dream Recall Frequency and Attitude Towards Dreams: A Reinterpretation of the Relation." *Personality and Individual Differences* 38 (2005): 919–927.

Bednar, James. "Internally-Generated Activity, Non-Episodic Memory, and Emotional Salience in Sleep." In *Sleep and Dreaming: Scientific Advances and Reconsiderations*, edited by Edward Pace-Schott, Mark Solms, Mark Blagrove, and Stevan Harnad, 119–120. Cambridge: Cambridge University Press, 2003.

Begley, Sharon. *Train Your Mind, Change Your Brain: How a New Science Reveals Our Extraordinary Potential to Transform Ourselves*. New York: Ballantine Books, 2007.

Belicki, Kathryne. "Recalling Dreams: An Examination of Daily Variation and Individual Differences." In *Sleep and Dreams: A Sourcebook*, edited by Jayne Gackenbach, 187–206. New York: Garland Publishing, 1986.

Benedetti, Fabrizio. *Placebo Effects*. 2nd ed. New York: Oxford University Press, 2014.

Bentley, Madison. "The Study of Dreams: A Method Adapted to the Seminary." *American Journal of Psychology* 26 (1915): 196–210.

Beradt, Charlotte. *The Third Reich of Dreams*. Translated by A. Gottwald. Chicago: Quadrangle Books, 1966.

Bingaman, Kirk. *The Power of Neuroplasticity for Pastoral and Spiritual Care*. Lanham, MD: Lexington Books, 2014.

Bonato, Richard, Alan Moffitt, Robert Hoffmann, and Marion Cuddy. "Bizarreness in Dreams and Nightmares." *Dreaming* 1 (1991): 53–61.

Borges, Jorge Luis. "Nightmares." In *Seven Nights*, translated by Eliot Weinberger. New York: New Directions, 1984.

Boyer, Pascal. *Religion Explained: The Evolutionary Origins of Religious Thought*. New York: Basic Books, 2001.

Braun, A. R., T. J. Balkin, N. J. Wesensten, F. Gwadry, R. E. Carson, M. Varga, P. Baldwin, G. Belenky, and P. Herscovitch. "Dissociated Pattern of Activity in Visual Cortices and Their Projections during Human Rapid Eye-Movement Sleep." *Science* 279 (1998): 91–95.

Bruner, J., A. Jolly, and K. Sylva, eds. *Play: Its Role in Development and Evolution*. New York: Basic Books, 1976.

Buckner, Randy L., Jessica R. Andrews-Hanna, and Daniel L. Schachter. "The Brain's Default Network: Anatomy, Function, and Relevance to Disease." *Annals of the New York Academy of Sciences* 1124 (2008): 1–38.

Bulkeley, Kelly. *American Dreamers*. Boston: Beacon Press, 2008.

Bulkeley, Kelly. "Dreaming in Adolescence: A 'Blind' Word Search of a Teenage Girl's Dream Series." *Dreaming* 22 (2012): 240–252.

Bulkeley, Kelly. *Dreaming in the World's Religions: A Comparative History.* New York: New York University Press, 2008.

Bulkeley, Kelly. "Dreaming Is Play: A Response to Freud." In *Visions of the Night: Dreams, Religion, and Psychology,* edited by Kelly Bulkeley, 59–66. Albany: State University of New York Press, 1999.

Bulkeley, Kelly. "Dreaming is Play II: Revonsuo's Threat Simulation Theory in Ludic Context." *Sleep and Hypnosis* 6 (2004): 119–129.

Bulkeley, Kelly. "Dream Interpretation: Practical Methods for Pastoral Care and Counseling." *Pastoral Psychology* 49 (2000): 95–104.

Bulkeley, Kelly. "Dream Recall and Political Ideology: Results of a Demographic Survey." *Dreaming* 22 (2012): 1–9.

Bulkeley, Kelly. "Lucid Dreaming by the Numbers." In *Lucid Dreaming: New Perspectives on Consciousness in Sleep,* edited by Ryan Hurd and Kelly Bulkeley, I: 1–22. Westport, CT: ABC-Clio, 2014.

Bulkeley, Kelly. "Religious Conversion and Cognitive Neuroscience." In *The Oxford Handbook of Religious Conversion,* edited by Lewis Rambo and Charles Farhadian, 240–255. New York: Oxford University Press, 2014.

Bulkeley, Kelly. *Transforming Dreams.* New York: John Wiley & Sons, 2000.

Bulkeley, Kelly. *The Wondering Brain: Thinking About Religion With and Beyond Cognitive Neuroscience.* New York: Routledge, 2005.

Bulkeley, Kelly, and G. William Domhoff. "Detecting Meaning in Dream Reports: An Extension of a Word Search Approach." *Dreaming* 20 (2010): 77–95.

Bulkeley, Kelly, and Ryan Hurd. "Introduction." In *Lucid Dreaming: New Perspectives on Consciousness in Sleep,* edited by Ryan Hurd and Kelly Bulkeley, vol. 1, xiii–xxxii. Westport, CT: ABC-Clio, 2014.

Burgdorf, Jeffrey, and Jaak Panksepp. "The Neurobiology of Positive Emotions." *Neuroscience and Biobehavioral Reviews* 30 (2006): 173–187.

Burghardt, Gordon. *The Genesis of Animal Play: Testing the Limits.* Cambridge, MA: MIT Press, 2005.

Calkins, Mary. "Statistics of Dreams." *American Journal of Psychology* 5 (1893): 311–343.

Cardena, Etzel, Steven Jay Lynn, and Stanley Krippner. *Varieties of Anomalous Experience: Examining the Scientific Evidence.* Washington, DC: American Psychological Association, 2000.

Carrette, Jeremy. "Post-Structuralism and the Psychology of Religion: The Challenge of Critical Psychology." In *Religion and Psychology: Mapping the Terrain,* edited by Diane Jonte-Pace and William Parsons, 110–126. London: Routledge, 2001.

Carskadon, Mary A., ed. *Encyclopedia of Sleep and Dreaming.* Farmington Hills, MI: Gale Cengage, 1993.

Cartwright, Rosalind. *The 24-Hour Mind: The Role of Sleep and Dreaming in Our Emotional Lives.* New York: Oxford University Press, 2010.

Chaucer, Geoffrey. "The Nun's Priest's Tale," in *The Canterbury Tales* (trans. Nevill Coghill), in *Great Books of the Western World*, edited by Mortimer J. Adler. Chicago: Encyclopaedia Britannica, 1952.

Cohen, Emma. *The Mind Possessed: The Cognition of Spirit Possession in an Afro-Brazilian Religious Tradition*. New York: Oxford University Press, 2007.

Cole, John. *The Olympian Dreams and Youthful Rebellion of Rene Descartes*. Urbana: University of Illinois Press, 1992.

Colp, Ralph. "Charles Darwin's Dream of His Double Execution." *Journal of Psychohistory* 13 (1986): 277–292.

Corbin, Henri. "The Visionary Dream in Islamic Spirituality." In *The Dream and Human Society*, edited by G. E. Von Grunebaum and Roger Callois, 381–408. Berkeley: University of California Press, 1966.

Covitz, Joel. *Visions of the Night: A Study of Jewish Dream Interpretation*. Boston: Shambhala, 1990.

Crapanzano, Victor. "Saints, Jnun, and Demons: An Essay in Moroccan Ethnopsychology." *Psychiatry* 38 (1975): 145–159.

Crews, Frederick, and Kelly Bulkeley. "Dialogue with a Skeptic." In *Dreams: A Reader on the Religious, Cultural, and Psychological Dimensions of Dreaming*, edited by Kelly Bulkeley, 361–377. New York: Palgrave, 2001.

Crick, Francis, and Graeme Mitchison. "The Function of Dream Sleep." *Nature* 304 (1983): 111–114.

Czachesz, Istvan, and Tamas Biro, eds. *Changing Minds: Religion and Cognition through the Ages*. Leuven: Peeters, 2011.

Czeisler, C. A. "The Human Circadian Timing System and Sleep-Wake Regulation," in *Principles and Practice of Sleep Medicine*, edited by Meir H. Kryger, Thomas Roth, and William C. Dement. 4th ed., 375–394. Philadelphia: Elsevier Saunders, 2005.

Damasio, Antonio. *The Feeling of What Happens: Body and Emotion in the Making of Consciousness*. San Diego, CA: Harcourt, 2000.

Dan-Vu, Thien Thanh, et al. "Spontaneous Neural Activity during Human Slow Wave Sleep." *Proceedings of the National Academy of Sciences* 105 (2008): 15160–15165.

Darwin, Charles. *Charles Darwin's Notebooks 1836–1844*. Edited by Paul Barrett, Peter Gautrey, Sandra Herbert, David Kohn, and Sydney Smith. Ithaca, NY: Cornell University Press, 1987.

Davis, Patricia. "The Weaning of Perpetua: Female Embodiment and Spiritual Growth Metaphor in the Dream of an Early Christian Martyr." *Dreaming* 15 (2005): 261–270.

Dawkins, Richard. "Atheists for Jesus." In *The Portable Atheist: Essential Readings for the Nonbeliever*, edited by Christopher Hitchens, 307–310. New York: Da Capo, 2007.

Dawkins, Richard. *The God Delusion*. Boston: Houghton Mifflin, 2006.

Dement, William, and Christopher Vaughan. *The Promise of Sleep.* New York: Dell, 1999.

Dentan, Robert Knox, and Laura McClusky. "'Pity the Bones by Wandering River Which Still in Lovers' Dreams Appear as Men.'" In *The Functions of Dreaming,* edited by Alan Moffitt, Milton Kramer, and Robert Hoffmann, 489–548. Albany: State University of New York Press, 1993.

Desmond, Adrian, and James Moore. *Darwin: The Life of a Tormented Evolutionist.* New York: W. W. Norton, 1991.

De Wall, Frans. *Chimpanzee Politics: Power and Sex among Apes.* Baltimore, MD: Johns Hopkins University Press, 2007.

Dick, Philip K. *The Exegesis of Philip K. Dick.* Edited by Pamela Jackson and Jonathan Lethem. Boston: Houghton Mifflin Harcourt, 2011.

Dodds, E. R. *The Greeks and the Irrational.* Berkeley: University of California Press, 1951.

Domhoff, G. William. "Dreams Are Embodied Simulations That Dramatize Conception and Concerns: The Continuity Hypothesis in Empirical, Theoretical, and Historical Context." *International Journal of Dream Research* 4 (2011): 50–62.

Domhoff, G. William. *Finding Meaning in Dreams: A Quantitative Approach.* New York: Plenum, 1996.

Domhoff, G. William. "The Neural Substrate for Dreaming: Is It a Subsystem of the Default Network?" *Consciousness and Cognition* 20 (2011): 1163–1174.

Domhoff, G. William. *The Scientific Study of Dreams: Neural Networks, Cognitive Development, and Content Analysis.* Washington, DC: American Psychological Association, 2003.

Domhoff, G. William, and Adam Schneider. "Studying Dream Content Using the Archive and Search Engine on DreamBank.net." *Consciousness and Cognition* 17 (2008): 1238–1247.

Dronke, Peter. *Women Writers of the Middle Ages: A Critical Study of Texts from Perpetua to Margeurite Porete.* Cambridge: Cambridge University Press, 1984.

Dzirasa, Kafui, Sidarta Ribeiro, Rui Costa, Lucas Santos, Shih-Chieh Lin, Andres Grosmark, Tatyana Sotnikova, Raul Gainetdinov, Marc Caron, and Miguel Nicolelis. "Dopaminergic Control of Sleep-Wake States." *Journal of Neuroscience* 26 (2006): 10577–10589.

Edelstein, Emma, and Ludwig Edelstein. *Asclepius: Collection and Interpretation of the Testimonies.* Baltimore, MD: Johns Hopkins University Press, 1945.

Eggan, Dorothy. "Dream Analysis." In *Studying Personality Cross-Culturally,* edited by Bert Kaplan, 551–557. Evanston, IL: Row, Peterson and Co., 1961.

Eggan, Dorothy. "The Manifest Content of Dreams: A Challenge to Social Science." *American Anthropologist* 54 (1952): 469–485.

Ekirch, Roger. *At Day's Close: Night in Times Past.* New York: W. W. Norton, 2005.

Ellenberger, Henri. *The Discovery of the Unconscious: The History and Evolution of Dynamic Psychiatry.* New York: Basic Books, 1970.

El-Zein, Amira. *Islam, Arabs, and the Intelligent World of the Jinn.* Syracuse, NY: Syracuse University Press, 2009.

Evans, Christopher. *Landscapes of the Night: How and Why We Dream.* Edited by Peter Evans. London: V. Gollancz, 1983.

Evans, Dylan. *Placebo: Mind over Matter in Modern Medicine.* New York: Oxford University Press, 2004.

Fakour, Mehrdad. "A Devil's Sojourn in the Realm of Lucid Dreams." In *Lucid Dreaming: New Perspectives on Consciousness in Sleep,* edited by Ryan Hurd and Kelly Bulkeley, vol. 2, 161–178. Westport, CT: ABC-Clio, 2014.

Feinberg, Irwin. "Hobson on the Neuroscience of Sleep: A Case of Persistent REM Tunnel Vision." *American Journal of Psychology* 117 (2004): 621–627.

Flanagan, Owen. "Dreaming Is Not an Adaptation." In *Sleep and Dreaming: Scientific Advances and Reconsiderations,* edited by Edward Pace-Schott, Mark Solms, Mark Blagrove, and Stevan Harnad, 147–150. Cambridge: Cambridge University Press, 2003.

Fosse, Roar, and G. William Domhoff. "Dreaming as Non-Executive Orienting." In *The New Science of Dreaming,* edited by Patrick McNamara and Deirdre Barrett, 2:49–78. Westport, CT: Praeger, 2007.

Foulkes, David. "Dream Reports from Different Stages of Sleep." *Journal of Abnormal and Social Psychology* 65 (1962): 14–25.

Fox, Kieran, Savannah Nijeboer, Elizaveta Solomonova, G. William Domhoff, and Kalina Christoff. "Dreaming as Mind Wandering: Evidence from Functional Neuroimaging and First-Person Content Reports." *Frontiers in Human Neuroscience* 7 (2013): 412.

Freud, Sigmund. *The Interpretation of Dreams.* Translated by James Strachey. New York: Avon Books, 1965.

Gackenbach, Jayne, and Stephen LaBerge, eds. *Conscious Mind, Sleeping Brain: Perspectives on Lucid Dreaming.* New York: Plenum, 1988.

Germain, Anne, Tore Nielsen, Antonio Zadra, and Jacques Montplaisir. "The Prevalence of Typical Dream Themes Challenges the Specificity of the Threat Simulation Theory." In *Sleep and Dreaming: Scientific Advances and Reconsiderations,* edited by Edward Pace-Schott, Mark Solms, Mark Blagrove, and Stevan Harnad, 151–152. Cambridge: Cambridge University Press, 2003.

Giora, Z., Y. Esformes, and A. Barak. "Dreams in Cross-Cultural Research." *Comprehensive Psychiatry* 13 (1972): 105–114.

Glaskin, Katie, and Richard Chenhall, eds. *Sleep around the World: Anthropological Perspectives.* New York: Palgrave Macmillan, 2013.

Goode, Erica. "Rats May Dream, It Seems, of Their Days at the Mazes." *New York Times,* January 25, 2001.

Graeber, Charles. "Inside the Mansion—and Mind—of Kim Dotcom, the Most Wanted Man on the Net." *Wired Magazine,* October 18, 2012. http://www.wired.com/2012/10/ff-kim-dotcom/all/.

Graves, Mark. *Mind, Brain, and the Elusive Soul: Human Systems of Cognitive Science and Religion.* Burlington, VT: Ashgate, 2008.

Griffith, Richard, Otoya Miyagi, and Akira Tago. "The Universality of Typical Dreams: Japanese vs. Americans." *American Anthropologist* 60 (1958): 1173–1179.

Guthrie, Stewart. *Faces in the Clouds: A New Theory of Religion.* New York: Oxford University Press, 1992.

Hahn, Robert, and Arthur Kleinman. "Belief as Pathogen, Belief as Medicine: 'Voodoo Death' and the 'Placebo Phenomenon' in Anthropological Perspective." *Medical Anthropology Quarterly* 14 (1983): 3–19.

Hall, Calvin, and Robert Van de Castle. *The Content Analysis of Dreams.* New York: Appleton-Century-Crofts, 1966.

Hall, Calvin S., and Vernon J. Nordby. *The Individual and His Dreams.* New York: Signet, 1972.

Hamann, Stephan, Rebecca Herman, Carla Nolan, and Kim Wallen. "Men and Women Differ in Amygdala Response to Visual Sexual Stimuli." *Nature Neuroscience* 7 (2004): 411–416.

Hamilton, Edith. *Mythology.* New York: Mentor, 1969.

Harrington, Anne, ed. *The Placebo Effect: An Interdisciplinary Exploration.* Cambridge, MA: Harvard University Press, 1997.

Harrison, Y., and Jim Horne. "One Night of Sleep Loss Impairs Innovative Thinking and Flexible Decision Making." *Organizational Behavior and Human Decision Processes* 78 (1999): 128–145.

Hartmann, Ernest. *Dreams and Nightmares: The Origin and Meaning of Dreams.* New York: Basic Books, 2000.

Hassin, Ran, James Uleman, and John Bargh, eds. *The New Unconscious.* New York: Oxford University Press, 2006.

Hayden, Brian. *Shamans, Sorcerers, and Saints: A Prehistory of Religion.* Washington, DC: Smithsonian Books, 2003.

Held, Suzanne, and Marek Spinka. "Animal Play and Animal Welfare." *Animal Behavior* 81 (2011): 891–899.

Helman, Cecil G. "Placebos and Nocebos: The Cultural Construction of Belief." In *Understanding the Placebo Effect in Complementary Medicine: Theory, Practice and Research,* edited by David Peters, 3–16. London: Churchill Livingstone, 2001.

Heraclitus. *Fragments.* Translated by T. M. Robinson. Toronto: University of Toronto Press, 1987.

Herman, John. "Reflexive and Orienting Properties of REM Sleep Dreaming and Eye Movements." In *Sleep and Dreaming: Scientific Advances and Reconsiderations,* edited by Edward Pace-Schott, Mark Solms, Mark Blagrove, and Stevan Harnad, 161. Cambridge: Cambridge University Press, 2003.

Hermansen, Marcia. "Dreams and Dreaming in Islam." In *Dreams: A Reader on the Religious, Cultural, and Psychological Dimensions of Dreaming,* edited by Kelly Bulkeley, 73–92. New York: Palgrave, 2001.

Hesiod. *Theogony*. Translated by D. Wender. New York: Penguin Books, 1973.

Hobson, J. Allan. *Dreaming: An Introduction to the Science of Sleep*. New York: Oxford University Press, 2003.

Hobson, J. Allan. *The Dreaming Brain*. New York: Basic Books, 1988.

Hobson, J. Allan, S. A. Hoffman, R. Helfand, and D. Kostner. "Dream Bizarreness and the Activation-Synthesis Hypothesis." *Human Neurobiology* 6 (1987): 157–164.

Hogue, David. *Remembering the Future, Imagining the Past: Story, Ritual, and the Human Brain*. Cleveland, OH: Pilgrim Press, 2003.

Homans, Peter. *The Ability to Mourn: Disillusionment and the Social Origins of Psychoanalysis*. Chicago: University of Chicago Press, 1989.

Homer. *The Iliad*. Translated by Richard Lattimore. Chicago: University of Chicago Press, 1951.

Homer. *The Odyssey*. Translated by Robert Fagles. New York: Penguin Classics, 1997.

Horne, Jim. *Sleepfaring: A Journey through the Science of Sleep*. New York: Oxford University Press, 2007.

Horovitz, Silvina, Allen Braun, Walter Carr, Dante Picchioni, Thomas Balkin, Masaki Fukunaga, and Jeff Duyn. "Decoupling of the Brain's Default Mode Network during Deep Sleep." *Proceedings of the National Academy of Sciences* 106 (2009): 11376–11381.

Horton, Lydiard. *The Dream Problem and the Mechanism of Thought*. Philadelphia: The Cartesian Research Society of Philadelphia, 1925.

Hufford, David. *The Terror That Comes in the Night: An Experience-Centered Study of Supernatural Assault Traditions*. Philadelphia: University of Pennsylvania Press, 1982.

Huizinga, J. *Homo Ludens: A Study of the Play Element in Culture*. Boston: Beacon Press, 1955.

Hume, David. *A Treatise of Human Nature*. New York: Oxford University Press, 2000.

Hunt, Harry. *The Multiplicity of Dreams: Memory, Imagination, and Consciousness*. New Haven, CT: Yale University Press, 1989.

Hunt, Harry. "New Multiplicities of Dreaming and REMing." In *Sleep and Dreaming: Scientific Advances and Reconsiderations*, edited by Edward Pace-Schott, Mark Solms, Mark Blagrove, and Stevan Harnad, 164–166. Cambridge: Cambridge University Press, 2003.

Hurd, Ryan. *Sleep Paralysis: A Guide to Hypnogogic Visions and Visitors of the Night*. Los Altos, CA: Hyena Press, 2010.

Iordache, Sandu. *Palliative People's Dreams and Dream-Related Perceptions and Interpretations: A Mixed-Method Investigation*. Unpublished dissertation. Auckland: University of Auckland, 2012.

Irwin, Lee. *The Dream Seekers: Native American Visionary Traditions of the Great Plains*. Norman: University of Oklahoma Press, 1994.

James, William. *The Varieties of Religious Experience*. New York: Mentor Books, 1958.

Jedrej, M. C., and Rosalind Shaw, eds. *Dreaming, Religion, and Society in Africa*. Leiden: E. J. Brill, 1992.

Jewel, James Ralph. "The Psychology of Dreams." *American Journal of Psychology* 16 (1905): 1–34.

Jones, Ernest. *On the Nightmare*. New York: Liveright, 1951.

Jones, James W. "Brain, Mind, and Spirit—A Clinician's Perspective, or Why I Am Not Afraid of Dualism." In *Soul, Psyche, Brain: New Directions in the Study of Religion and Brain-Mind Science*, edited by Kelly Bulkeley, 36–60. New York: Palgrave, 2005.

Jouvet, Michel. *The Paradox of Sleep: The Story of Dreaming*. Translated by Laurence Garey. Cambridge, MA: MIT Press, 1999.

Jung, Carl. *Children's Dreams: Notes from the Seminar Given in 1936–1940*. Translated by Ernst Falzeder and Tony Woolfson. Princeton, NJ: Princeton University Press, 2008.

Kahan, Tracey. "Consciousness in Dreaming: A Metacognitive Approach." In *Dreams: A Reader on the Religious, Cultural, and Psychological Dimensions of Dreaming*, edited by Kelly Bulkeley, 333–360. New York: Palgrave, 2001.

Kahan, Tracey. "The 'Problem' of Dreaming in NREM Sleep Continues to Challenge Reductionist (Two Generator) Models of Dream Generation." In *Sleep and Dreaming: Scientific Advances and Reconsiderations*, edited by Edward Pace-Schott, Mark Solms, Mark Blagrove, and Stevan Harnad, 167–169. Cambridge: Cambridge University Press, 2003.

Kahan, Tracey, and Stephen LaBerge. "Dreaming and Waking: Similarities and Differences Revisited." *Consciousness and Cognition* 20 (2011): 494–515.

Kandel, Eric, James Schwartz, Thomas Jessell, Steven Siegelbaum, and A. J. Hudspeth, eds. *Principles of Neural Science*. 5th ed. New York: McGraw Hill, 2012.

Kelly, Edward, Emily Williams Kelly, Adam Crabtree, Alan Gauld, Michael Grosso, and Bruce Greyson. *Irreducible Mind: Toward a Psychology for the 21st Century*. Lanham, MD: Rowman & Littlefield, 2007.

Killgore, William, Desiree Killgore, Lisa Day, Christopher Li, Gary Kamimori, and Thomas Balkin. "The Effects of 53 Hours of Sleep Deprivation on Moral Judgment." *Sleep* 30 (2007): 345–352.

Knudson, Roger. "Significant Dreams: Bizarre or Beautiful?" *Dreaming* 11 (2001): 166–177.

Knudson, Roger, and Samuel Minier. "The On-Going Significance of Significant Dreams: The Case of the Bodiless Head." *Dreaming* 9 (1999): 235–245.

Koch, Christof. *The Quest for Consciousness: A Neurobiological Approach*. San Diego, CA: Roberts and Company, 2004.

Kracke, Waud. "Kagwahiv Mourning: Dreams of a Bereaved Father." In *Dreams: A Reader on the Religious, Cultural, and Psychological Dimensions of Dreaming*, edited by Kelly Bulkeley, 175–188. New York: Palgrave, 2001.

Kramer, Heinrich, and James Sprenger, eds. *The Malleus Maleficarum*. Translated by Montague Summers. New York: Dover, 1971.

Kripal, Jeffrey. *The Serpent's Gift: Gnostic Reflections on the Study of Religion*. Chicago: University of Chicago Press, 2008.

Kripke, Daniel, Lawrence Garfinkel, Deborah Wingard, Melville Klauber, and Matthew Marler. "Mortality Associated with Sleep Duration and Insomnia." *Archives of General Psychiatry* 59 (2002): 131–136.

Krippner, Stanley, Fariba Bogzaran, and Andre Percia de Carvalho. *Extraordinary Dreams and How to Work with Them*. Albany: State University of New York Press, 2002.

Kryger, Meir H., Thomas Roth, and William C. Dement. *Principles and Practice of Sleep Medicine*. 4th ed. Philadelphia: Elsevier Saunders, 2005.

Kuiken, Don, and Shelley Sikora. "The Impact of Dreams on Waking Thoughts and Feelings." In *The Functions of Dreaming*, edited by Alan Moffitt, Milton Kramer, and Robert Hoffmann, 419–476. Albany: State University of New York Press, 1993.

Lakoff, George. "How Metaphor Structures Dreams: The Theory of Conceptual Metaphor Applied to Dream Analysis." In *Dreams: A Reader on the Religious, Cultural, and Psychological Dimensions of Dreaming*, edited by Kelly Bulkeley, 265–284. New York: Palgrave, 2001.

Lakoff, George, and Mark Johnson. *Metaphors We Live By*. Chicago: University of Chicago Press, 1980.

Landau, Mark, Michael Robinson, and Brian Meier, eds. *The Power of Metaphor: Examining Its Influence on Social Life*. Washington, DC: American Psychological Association, 2013.

Lavie, Peretz, and Hanna Kaminer. "Dreams That Poison Sleep: Dreams in Holocaust Survivors." *Dreaming* 1 (1991): 11–22.

Ledoux, Joseph. *The Emotional Brain: The Mysterious Underpinnings of Emotional Life*. New York: Simon and Schuster, 1998.

Leslie, Kenneth, and Robert Ogilvie. "Vestibular Dreams: The Effect of Rocking on Dream Mentation." *Dreaming* 6 (1996): 1–16.

Leuchter, Andrew, Ian Cook, Elise Witte, Melinda Morgan, and Michelle Abrams. "Changes in Brain Function of Depressed Subjects during Treatment with Placebo." *Psychiatry Online* 159 (2002): 122–129.

Lewis-Williams, David. *The Mind in the Cave: Consciousness and the Origins of Art*. London: Thames and Hudson, 2004.

Lincoln, J. S. *The Dream in Primitive Cultures*. London: University of London Press, 1935.

Lohmann, Roger, ed. *Dream Travelers: Sleep Experiences and Culture in the Western Pacific*. New York: Palgrave Macmillan, 2003.

Lohmann, Roger. "Sleeping among the Asabano: Surprises in Intimacy and Sociality at the Margins of Consciousness." In *Sleep around the World: Anthropological Perspectives*, edited by Katie Glaskin and Richard Chenhall, 21–45. New York: Palgrave Macmillan, 2013.

Lou, Hans, Troels Kjaer, Lars Friberg, Gordon Wildschiodtz, Soren Holm, and Markus Nowak. "A 15O-H2o PET Study of Meditation and the Resting State of Normal Consciousness." *Human Brain Mapping* 7 (1999): 98–105.

Low, Philip Steven, Sylvan Shank, Terrence Sejnowski, and Daniel Margoliash. "Mammalian-Like Features of Sleep Structure in Zebra Finches." *Proceedings of the National Academy of Sciences* 105 (2008): 9081–9086.

Lovecraft, H. P. "The Call of Cthulhu." In *The Colour Out of Space*, 45–75. New York: Jove/HBC Books, 1963.

Luhrmann, T. M. *When God Talks Back: Understanding the American Evangelical Relationship with God.* New York: Knopf, 2012.

Lyamin, Oleg, Peter Kosenko, Jennifer Lapierre, Lev Mukhametov, and Jerome Siegel. "Fur Seals Display a Strong Drive for Bilateral Slow-Wave Sleep While on Land." *Journal of Neuroscience* 28 (2008): 12614–12621.

Lyamin, Oleg, Julia Pryaslova, Peter Kosenko, and Jerome Siegel. "Behavioral Aspects of Sleep in Bottlenose Dolphin Mothers and Their Calves." *Physiology and Behavior* 92 (2007), 725–733.

Malcolm, Norman. *Dreaming.* London: Routledge & Kegan Paul, 1959.

Maquet, Pierre, J. M. Peters, J. Aerts, G. Delfiore, C. Degueldre, A. Luxen, and G. Franck. "Functional Neuroanatomy of Human Rapid-Eye-Movement Sleep and Dreaming." *Nature* 383 (1996): 163–166.

Maquet, Pierre, Carlyle Smith, and Robert Stickgold, eds. *Sleep and Brain Plasticity.* New York: Oxford University Press, 2003.

Ma'ruf, A. Muhammad. "Lucid Dreaming and the Sufis: Conflicts and Opportunities in the Modern West." In *Lucid Dreaming: New Perspectives on Consciousness in Sleep*, edited by Ryan Hurd and Kelly Bulkeley, 265–290. Westport, CT: ABC-Clio, 2014.

Masson, Jeffrey Moussaieff, trans. *The Complete Letters of Sigmund Freud to Wilhelm Fliess, 1887–1904.* Cambridge, MA: Belknap Press, 1985.

McNamara, Patrick. *An Evolutionary Psychology of Sleep and Dreams.* Westport, CT: Praeger, 2004.

McNamara, Patrick, Robert Barton, and Charles Nunn, eds. *Evolution of Sleep: Phylogenetic and Functional Perspectives.* New York: Cambridge University Press, 2010.

Mithen, Steven. *The Prehistory of the Mind: The Cognitive Origins of Art, Religion, and Science.* London: Thames and Hudson, 1996.

Modesto, Ruby, and Guy Mount. *Not for Innocent Ears: Spiritual Traditions of a Desert Cahuilla Medicine Woman.* Cottonwood, CA: Sweetlight Books, 1980.

Moffitt, Alan, Milton Kramer, and Robert Hoffmann, eds. *The Functions of Dreaming.* Albany: State University of New York Press, 1993.

Mullin, Glenn, ed. and trans. *The Practice of the Six Yogas of Naropa.* Ithaca, NY: Snow Lion, 2006.

Nagel, Thomas. *What Does It All Mean? A Very Short Introduction to Philosophy.* New York: Oxford University Press, 1987.

Nashe, Thomas. "Terrors of the Night, or, A Discourse of Apparitions." In *Thomas Nashe: Selected Writings*, edited by Stanley Wells, 143–175. Cambridge, MA: Harvard University Press, 1965.

Nasser, Lana. "The Jinn: Companion in the Realm of Dreams and Imagination." In *Dreaming in Christianity and Islam: Culture, Conflict, and Creativity*, edited by Kelly Bulkeley, Kate Adams, and Patricia Davis, 143–154. New Brunswick, NJ: Rutgers University Press, 2009.

Nasser, Lana, and Kelly Bulkeley. "The Typical Dreams of Jordanian College Students." In *Dreaming in Christianity and Islam: Culture, Conflict, and Creativity*, edited by Kelly Bulkeley, Kate Adams, and Patricia Davis, 200–216. New Brunswick, NJ: Rutgers University Press, 2009.

Nelson, Julius. "A Study of Dreams." *American Journal of Psychology* 1 (1888): 367–401.

Newberg, Andrew, Eugene D'Aquili, and Vince Rause. *Why God Won't Go Away: Brain Science and the Biology of Belief.* New York: Ballantine, 2001.

Nielsen, Tore. "A Review of Mentation in REM and NREM Sleep: 'Covert' REM Sleep as a Possible Reconciliation of Two Opposing Models." In *Sleep and Dreaming: Scientific Advances and Reconsiderations*, edited by Edward Pace-Schott, Mark Solms, Mark Blagrove, and Stevan Harnad, 59–74. Cambridge: Cambridge University Press, 2003.

Nielsen, Tore, and Anne Germain. "Post-Traumatic Nightmares as a Dysfunctional State." In *Sleep and Dreaming: Scientific Advances and Reconsiderations*, edited by Edward Pace-Schott, Mark Solms, Mark Blagrove, and Stevan Harnad, 190–191. Cambridge: Cambridge University Press, 2003.

Nielsen, Tore, and Ross Levin. "Nightmares: A New Neurocognitive Model." *Sleep Medicine Reviews* 11 (2007): 295–310.

Nielsen, Tore, Antonio Zadra, Valerie Simard, Sebastien Saucier, Philippe Stenstrom, Carlyle Smith, and Don Kuiken. "The Typical Dreams of Canadian University Students." *Dreaming* 13 (2003): 211–235.

Nofzinger, E. A., M. A. Mintun, M. B. Wiseman, D. J. Kupfer, and R. Y. Moore. "Forebrain Activation in REM Sleep: An FDG PET Study." *Brain Research* 770 (1997): 192–201.

Nunn, Charles, Patrick McNamara, Isabella Capellini, Brian Preston, and Robert Barton. "Primate Sleep in Phylogenetic Perspective." In *Evolution of Sleep: Phylogenetic and Functional Perspectives*, edited by Patrick McNamara, Robert Barton, and Charles Nunn, 123–144. New York: Cambridge University Press, 2010.

Oberhelman, Steven. "Galen, *On Diagnosis from Dreams.*" *Journal of the History of Medicine and Allied Sciences* 38 (1983): 36–47.

O'Flaherty, Wendy Doniger. *Dreams, Illusion, and Other Realities.* Chicago: University of Chicago Press, 1984.

O'Flaherty, Wendy Doniger, trans. *The Rig Veda.* London: Penguin Books, 1981.

Olsen, Chris. "Forgotten Perspectives on Lucid Dreaming from the Enlightenment through the Early Twentieth Century." In *Lucid Dreaming: New Perspectives on Consciousness in Sleep*, edited by Ryan Hurd and Kelly Bulkeley, 2: 93–125. Westport, CT: ABC-Clio, 2014.

Ong, Roberto. *The Interpretation of Dreams in Ancient China*. Bochum: Studienverlag Brockmeyer, 1985.

Pace-Schott, Edward, Mark Solms, Mark Blagrove, and Stevan Harnad, eds. *Sleep and Dreaming: Scientific Advances and Reconsiderations*. Cambridge: Cambridge University Press, 2003.

Pagel, James. *The Limits of Dream: A Scientific Exploration of the Mind/Brain Interface*. New York: Academic Press, 2010.

Pagel, James. "Lucid Dreaming as Sleep Meditation." In *Lucid Dreaming: New Perspectives on Consciousness in Sleep*, edited by Ryan Hurd and Kelly Bulkeley, 1: 63–76. Westport, CT: ABC-Clio, 2014.

Panksepp, Jaak. *Affective Neuroscience: The Foundations of Human and Animal Emotions*. New York: Oxford University Press, 2004.

Panksepp, Jaak. "'The Dream of Reason Creates Monsters' . . . Especially When We Neglect the Role of Emotions in REM-States." In *Sleep and Dreaming: Scientific Advances and Reconsiderations*, edited by Edward Pace-Schott, Mark Solms, Mark Blagrove, and Stevan Harnad, 200–202. Cambridge: Cambridge University Press, 2003.

Patton, Kimberley. "'A Great and Strange Correction': Intentionality, Locality, and Epiphany in the Category of Dream Incubation." *History of Religions* 43 (2004): 194–223.

Pellegrini, Anthony. *The Role of Play in Human Development*. New York: Oxford University Press, 2009.

Petronius. *The Satyricon*. Translated by P. G. Walsh. New York: Oxford University Press, 2009.

Pinker, Steven. *How the Mind Works*. New York: W. W. Norton, 1997.

Plato. *The Republic*. Translated by A. D. Lindsay. New York: E. P. Dutton, 1957.

Ponpeiano, O. "Vestibular Influences during Sleep." In *Handbook of Sensory Physiology: Vestibular System*. Part I: *Basic Mechanisms*, edited by H. H. Kornhuker, 1–16. New York: Springer-Verlag, 1974.

Post, Tim. "Educational Frontiers of Training Lucid Dreamers." *Lucid Dreaming: New Perspectives on Consciousness in Sleep*, edited by Ryan Hurd and Kelly Bulkeley, 1: 127–144. Westport, CT: ABC-Clio, 2014.

Purcell, Sheila, Alan Moffitt, and Robert Hoffmann. "Waking, Dreaming, and Self-Regulation." In *The Functions of Dreaming*, edited by Alan Moffitt, Milton Kramer, and Robert Hoffmann, 197–260. Albany: State University of New York Press, 1993.

Pyysiainen, Ilkka. *How Religion Works: Towards a New Cognitive Science of Religion*. Leiden: Brill Academic, 2003.

Rahman, Fazlur. "Dream, Imagination, and *Alam al-mithal*." In *The Dream and Human Society*, edited by G. E. Von Grunebaum and Roger Callois, 409–420. Berkeley: University of California Press, 1966.

Raichle, Marcus, and Abraham Snyder. "A Default Mode of Brain Function: A Brief History of an Evolving Idea." *NeuroImage* 37 (2007): 1083–1090.

Rasch, Bjorn, and Jan Born. "About Sleep's Role in Memory." *Physiological Reviews* 93 (2013): 681–766.

Rattenborg, Niels, and Charles Amlaner, "A Bird's-Eye View of the Function of Sleep." In *Evolution of Sleep: Phylogenetic and Functional Perspectives*, edited by Patrick McNamara, Robert Barton, and Charles Nunn, 145–171. New York: Cambridge University Press, 2010.

Reay, Marie. "The Sweet Witchcraft of Kuma Dream Experience." *Mankind* 5 (1962): 459–463.

Revonsuo, Antti. "The Reinterpretation of Dreams: An Evolutionary Hypothesis of the Function of Dreaming." In *Sleep and Dreaming: Scientific Advances and Reconsiderations*, edited by Edward Pace-Schott, Mark Solms, Mark Blagrove, and Stevan Harnad, 85–109. Cambridge: Cambridge University Press, 2003.

Revonsuo, Antti, and Christina Salmivalli. "A Content Analysis of Bizarre Elements in Dreams." *Dreaming* 5 (1995): 169–188.

Rial, Ruben, Mourad Akaarir, Antoni Gamundi, M. Cristina Nicolau, and Susana Esteban. "The Evolution of Wakefulness: From Reptiles to Mammals." In *Evolution of Sleep: Phylogenetic and Functional Perspectives*, edited by Patrick McNamara, Robert Barton, and Charles Nunn, 172–196. New York: Cambridge University Press, 2010.

Roffwarg, Howard, Joseph Muzio, and William Dement. "Ontogenetic Development of the Human Sleep-Dream Cycle." *Science* 152 (1966): 604–619.

Rosch, Eleanor. "Principles of Categorization." In *Concepts: Core Readings*, edited by Eric Margois and Stephen Laurence, 189–206. Cambridge, MA: MIT Press, 1999.

Royle, Nicholas, ed. *The Tiger Garden: A Book of Writer's Dreams*. London: Serpent's Tail, 1996.

Scarre, Chris. "Painting by Resonance." *Nature* 338 (1989): 382.

Schonhammer, Ranier. "Typical Dreams: Reflections of Arousal." *Journal of Consciousness Studies* 12 (2005): 18–37.

Schredl, Michael. "Dream Recall: Models and Empirical Data." In *The New Science of Dreaming*, edited by Patrick McNamara and Deirdre Barrett, 2: 79–114. Westport, CT: Praeger, 2007.

Schredl, Michael. "Gender Differences in Dreaming." In *The New Science of Dreaming*, edited by Patrick McNamara and Deirdre Barrett, 2: 29–47. Westport, CT: Praeger, 2007.

Schredl, Michael, and Friedrich Hofmann. "Continuity between Waking Activities and Dream Activities." *Consciousness and Cognition* 12 (2003): 298–308.

Schredl, Michael, Petra Ciric, Simon Gotz, and Lutz Wittmann. "Typical Dreams: Stability and Gender Differences." *Journal of Psychology* 138 (2004): 485–494.

Schwartz, Jeffrey, and Sharon Begley. *The Mind and the Brain: Neuroplasticity and the Power of Mental Force*. New York: Regan Books, 2002.

Seligman, C. G. "Presidential Address: Anthropology and Psychology: A Study of Some Points of Contact." *Journal of the Royal Anthropological Institute of Great Britain and Ireland* 54 (1924): 13–46.

Seligman, C. G. "Type Dreams: A Request." *Folklore* 34 (1923): 376–378.

Shapiro, Arthur, and Elaine Shapiro. *The Powerful Placebo: From Ancient Priest to Modern Physician*. Baltimore, MD: Johns Hopkins University Press, 1997.

Shaw, Rosalind. "Dreaming as Accomplishment: Power, the Individual, and Temne Divination." In *Dreaming, Religion, and Society in Africa*, edited by M. C. Jedrej and Rosalind Shaw, 36–54. Leiden: E. J. Brill, 1992.

Shweder, Richard, Lene Arnett Jensen, and William Goldstein. "Who Sleeps by Whom Revisited: A Method for Extracting the Moral Goods Implicit in Practice." *New Directions for Child and Adolescent Development* 67 (1995): 21–29.

Siegel, Jerome. "Sleep Viewed as a State of Adaptive Inactivity." *Nature Reviews Neuroscience* 10 (2009): 747–753.

Slone, Jason. *Theological Correctness: Why Religious People Believe What They Shouldn't*. New York: Oxford University Press, 2007.

Snyder, Frederick, Ismet Karacan, K. Van Tharp, Jr., and Jimmy Scott. "Phenomenology of REM Sleep Dreaming." *Psychophysiology* 4 (1968): 375.

Solms, Mark. *The Neuropsychology of Dreams: A Clinico-Anatomical Study*. Mahwah, NJ: Lawrence Erlbaum, 1997.

Stepansky, R., B. Holzinger, A. Schmeiser-Rieder, B. Saletu, M. Kunze, and J. Zeitlhofer. "Austrian Dream Behavior: Results of a Representative Population Survey." *Dreaming* 8 (1998): 23–30.

Stephens, John. *The Dreams and Visions of Aelius Aristides: A Case-Study in the History of Religions*. Piscataway, NJ: Gorgias Press, 2013.

Stewart, Pamela, and Andrew Strathern. "Dreaming and Ghosts among the Hagen and Duna of the Southern Highlands, Papua New Guinea." In *Dream Travelers: Sleep Experiences and Culture in the Western Pacific*, edited by Roger Lohmann, 43–60. New York: Palgrave Macmillan, 2003.

Stumbrys, Tadas, and Daniel Erlacher. "The Science of Lucid Dream Induction." In *Lucid Dreaming: New Perspectives on Consciousness in Sleep*, edited by Ryan Hurd and Kelly Bulkeley, 1: 77–102. Westport, CT: ABC-Clio, 2014.

Sumegi, Angela. *Dreamworlds of Shamanism and Tibetan Buddhism: The Third Place*. Albany: State University of New York Press, 2008.

Szpakowska, Kasia. "Through the Looking Glass: Dreams in Ancient Egypt." In *Dreams: A Reader on the Religious, Cultural, and Psychological Dimensions of Dreaming*, edited by Kelly Bulkeley, 29–44. New York: Palgrave, 2001.

Tahhan, Diana Adis. "Sensuous Connections in Sleep: Feelings of Security and Interdependency in Japanese Sleep Rituals." In *Sleep around the World: Anthropological Perspectives*, edited by Katie Glaskin and Richard Chenhall, 61–78. New York: Palgrave Macmillan, 2013.

Taleb, Nicholas Nassim. *The Black Swan: The Impact of the Highly Improbable*. New York: Random House, 2007.

Tanabe, George, Jr. *Myoe the Dreamkeeper: Fantasy and Knowledge in Early Kamakura Buddhism*. Cambridge, MA: Harvard University Press, 1992.

Taves, Ann. *Religious Experience Reconsidered: A Building-Block Approach to the Study of Religion and Other Special Things*. Princeton, NJ: Princeton University Press, 2011.

Tedlock, Barbara. *The Woman in the Shaman's Body: Reclaiming the Feminine in Religion and Medicine*. New York: Bantam, 2005.

Thompson, Richard. *The Brain: A Neuroscience Primer*. New York: Worth Publishers, 2000.

Trivedi, Bijal. "Need Sleep? Birds May Have Shortcut to Second Wind." *National Geographic News*, October 28, 2010. http://news.nationalgeographic.com/news/2003/11/1112_031112_tvbirdnaps.html.

Upanishads. Translated by P. Olivelle. Oxford: Oxford University Press, 1996.

Vertes, Robert, and Kathleen Eastman. "The Case against Memory Consolidation in REM Sleep." In *Sleep and Dreaming: Scientific Advances and Reconsiderations*, edited by Edward Pace-Schott, Mark Solms, Mark Blagrove, and Stevan Harnad, 75–84. Cambridge: Cambridge University Press, 2003.

Wamsley, Erin, Yasutaka Hirota, Matthew Tucker, Mark Smith, and John Antrobus. "Circadian and Ultradian Influences on Dreaming: A Dual Rhythm Model." *Brain Research Bulletin* 71 (2007): 347–354.

West, Stephanie. "And It Came to Pass That Pharaoh Dreamed: Notes on Herodotus 2:139." *Classical Quarterly* 37 (1987): 262–271.

White, Sarah. "Dreamwork as Etymology." *Dreaming* 9 (1999): 11–22.

Whitehouse, Harvey. *Modes of Religiosity: A Cognitive Theory of Religious Transmission*. Walnut Creek, CA: Altamira Press, 2004.

Whitehouse, Harvey, and James Laidlaw. *Ritual and Memory: Toward a Comparative Anthropology of Religion*. Walnut Creek, CA: Altamira Press, 2004.

Whitley, David. *Cave Paintings and the Human Spirit: The Origin of Creativity and Belief*. Amherst, NY: Prometheus Books, 2009.

Wilson, E. O. *Sociobiology: The New Synthesis*. 25th Anniversary edition. Cambridge, MA: Belknap Press, 2000.

Winget, Carolyn, and Milton Kramer. *Dimensions of Dreams*. Gainesville: University of Florida Press, 1978.

Winkelman, Michael. *Shamanism: A Biopsychosocial Paradigm of Consciousness and Healing*. Santa Barbara, CA: ABC-Clio, 2010.

Winnicott, D. W. *Playing and Reality*. London: Tavistock Publications, 1971.

Wolman, Richard, and Miloslava Kozmova. "'Last Night I Had the Strangest Dream': Varieties of Rational Thought Processes in Dream Reports." *Consciousness and Cognition* 16 (2007): 838–849.

Xygalatas, Dimitris. *The Burning Saints: Cognition and Culture in the Fire-Walking Rituals of the Anastenaria.* New York: Routledge, 2014.

Yetish, Gandhi, Hillard Kaplan, Michael Gurven, Brian Wood, Herman Pontzer, Paul R. Manger, Charles Wilson, Ronald McGregor, and Jerome M. Siegel. "Natural Sleep and Its Seasonal Variations in Three Pre-industrial Societies." *Current Biology* 25 (2015): 1–7.

Young, Serinity. "Buddhist Dream Experience: The Role of Interpretation, Ritual, and Gender." In *Dreams: A Reader on the Religious, Cultural, and Psychological Dimensions of Dreaming,* edited by Kelly Bulkeley, 9–28. New York: Palgrave, 2001.

Yu, Calvin. "Dream Intensity Scale: Factors in the Phenomenological Analysis of Dreams." *Dreaming* 20 (2010): 107–129.

Yu, Calvin. "Testing the Factorial Structure of the Dream Intensity Scale." *Dreaming* 22 (2012): 284–309.

Yu, Calvin. "Toward 100% Dream Retrieval by Rapid-Eye-Movement Sleep Awakening: A High-Density Electroencephalographic Study." *Dreaming* 24 (2014): 1–17.

Zarcone, De La Pena, and William Dement. "Heightened Sexual Interest and Sleep Disturbance." *Perceptual and Motor Skills* 39 (1974): 1135–1141.

Zhdanova, I. V. "Fishing for Sleep." In *Evolution of Sleep: Phylogenetic and Functional Perspectives,* edited by Patrick McNamara, Robert Barton, and Charles Nunn, 238–266. New York: Cambridge University Press, 2010.

Index

Numbers in *italics* indicate tables.

acetylcholine, 37, 38, 41
Activation-Synthesis model, 96
adaptive inactivity, 25–26
adenosine, 37
African bush elephants, sleep of, 19
agency detection, 222
aggressive dreams, 9, 146, 147, 209. *See also* nightmares
A'isha Qandisha, 216
alam al-mithal, 262
alarm clocks, 73, 91–92
alienation dreams, 209
American Dreamers (Bulkeley), 191–92
American golden plover, sleep of, 20
American Journal of Psychology, 114
Amlaner, Charles, 22
amygdala, 40, 41, 156, 265
animals
    aggressive, 153
    dreaming in, 81
anoneira, 98, 99
anoneirognosis, 98
anterior cingulated cortex, 41, 156
anthropology, as cognitive science, 82
anxiety dreams, 138, 209
an-yaron, 217
apex dreaming, 299n

apnea, 53, 173
Aquinas, Thomas, 10
Arber, Sara, 65
archaic *Homo sapiens*, 31, 33
archetypal-spiritual dreams, 208
archetypes, 207
architecture, sleep and, 61
Arctic tern, sleep of, 20
Aristides, Aelius, 243–45, 246, 254
Aristotle, 80, 112, 287n29
Artemidorus, 196
Asabano people, 59, 60
Asclepian temples, 244–45, 254
Asclepius, 254, 255–56
Aserinsky, Eugene, 96
asexual reproduction, 175
atonia, 38, 47, 53, 54, 188, 189
Augustine, 160, 168, 174
Austin, James, 264–65
Australopithecus afarensis, 30–31
autonomous visionary capacity, 229, 237

Babylonian Talmud, 216
Barrett, Justin, 222
basal forebrain, 41, 98
Basic Color Terms: Their Universality and Evolution (Berlin and Kay), 111

Beaulieu-Prevost, Dominic, 93
beauty, dreams of, 201
bedding, 61–63
bedrooms, as settings for nightmares, 152
behaviorism, 6
Bekoff, Marc, 136
Belicki, Kathryne, 90
belief, placebo effect and, 250, 254
Bentley, Madison, 116–17
Beradt, Charlotte, 152
Berlin, Brent, 109–11
Big Bang, 16–17
big brown bat, sleep of, 19
big dreams, 2. *See also* aggressive
    dreams; gravitational dreams;
    mystical dreams; sexual dreams
  active imagination and creativity, 228
  attentiveness to, 147
  carry-over effects of, 178, 204,
      235–36, 272
  cognitive science of religion and, 6–7
  cross-cultural occurrence of, 85
  gender and, 223
  hybrids of, 201, 224
  imagery in, 237
  imagistic religiosity and, 235
  as intensifications of the brain's sleep
      activity, 156
  metaphorical nature of, 273–74
  nightmares as, 146
  overreaching nature of, 239
  placebo effect of, 243
  prototypes of, 9, 147
  psychologists' studies of, 206–10
  source of, 236
birds, sleep of, 20–22
bizarreness, in dream content, 130–31
Blackfoot Indians, 233
black magic, 251
Black Swan approach, 2, 258
blind analysis, 123–27, 134–36
Bonato, Richard, 130–31

Bonnet, Michael H., 48
Borges, Jorge Luis, 151–52
bottlenose dolphins, sleep of, 19–20
Boyer, Pascal, 222, 257
brain
  activity of, during sleep, 21, 27,
      28, 34–38
  anatomy of, 38–42
  as computer, 238–39
  cross-modal functioning in, 203–4
  damage to, and dreams, 38–40,
      98–99, 236–37
  default mode network of, 139–40
  energy use by, 32
  enlightenment experiences
      and, 264–65
  evolutionary changes in, 28–32, 40
  imaging technology and, 39–40
  meditation and, 264–66
  neural connectivity in, 40
  neuroplasticity of, 39, 49–50,
      238, 252
  operating changes in, 33
  placebo treatments and, 249–50
  power of, during sleep, 238
  prayer and, 265
  regions of, involved in
      dreaming, 98–99
  size of, and effects on childbirth, 32
  survival functions of, for
      hominids, 32–33
  two hemispheres of, 39–40
  underdeveloped, in human
      newborns, 32
brainstem, 40–41, 45, 171, 171, 188
brainstem reductionism, 96, 97,
    99, 100
breathing underwater, dreams of, 200
Brihadaranyaka Upanishad, 261
Buckner, Randy, 139
Bulkeley, Kelly, 149
Bulkeley, Patricia M., 135

Burgdorf, Jeffrey, 202
Burghardt, Gordon M., 136
bush spirits, 216–17
Byers, John A., 136

Calkins, Mary, 100, 102, 115, 116, 117,
   203, 290–91n16, 301n18
Can Science Explain Religion (Jones), 248
Carleton University Scale of Impossibility
   and Improbability, 130
Carrette, Jeremy, 117
Cartwright, Rosalind, 158
cataplexy, 53
cats, dreaming by, 81
caves
   paintings in, 33, 83–85, 261
   used for sleeping and dreaming, 85
Center for the Sociology of Sleep, 65
cerebellum, 40
cerebral cortex, 40, 41
Chase, Michael H., 38
chasing dreams, 9, 152, 178
childbirth, as motif in sexual dreams, 169
childhood experiences, dreams and,
   177, 178
chimpanzee, common
   capacity of, for theory of mind, 29
   lives of, 29
   sleep of, 23
   social structures of, 29
Chimpanzee Politics (de Waal), 29
Christianity, response of, to demonic
   dreams, 217–18
circadian rhythms, 17–19, 45
climate, sudden changes in, 31–32
cognitive science, 6
   core disciplines of, 82
   prophetic dreaming and, 234–35
cognitive science of religion, 6–7, 220,
   222, 223, 248
   approach of, to religious healing
     practices, 249

big dreams and, 6
   dream research and, 225
   prophetic dreams and, 235
Cohen, Emma, 221–23, 225
cold-blooded creatures, sleep
   types in, 21
Coleridge, Samuel Taylor, 91
collective unconscious, 207
colors, in dreams, 109–11
communalism, 61
conceptual metaphor theory, 133, 175
Confessions (Augustine), 160
conflict, entrapped in, 152
Confucius, 231
consciousness
   alteration of, 265
   explanations for, 99–100
   imaginative, 262
   intensified modes of, 258
   merging of, 268–69
contemplative practice, 10, 214
   brain activity and, 265–66
   impact of, 266
*Contemporary Psychoanalysis and
   Religion* (Jones), 248
Content Analysis of Dreams, The (Hall
   and Van de Castle), 120
continuity, 113–27, 252
continuity hypothesis, 120, 122–25,
   198, 252
Corbin, Henri, 262
cortisol, 47
co-sleeping, 57, 59
Crapanzano, Victor, 216
Craven, Wes, 251
creation stories, 216
Crews, Frederick, 129, 132
Crick, Francis, 95–96, 238
Crito (Plato), 231–32
cross-modal functioning, 203–4
CSR. *See* cognitive science of religion
cultural texts, 8

Damasio, Antonio, 27–28, 78
Dan-Vu, Thien Thanh, 40
D'Aquili, Eugene, 265
Darwin, Charles, 273–74
Dawkins, Richard, 228, 238–39
daydreaming, 139
declarative memory, 50
Decretum Gratiani, 217
deep sleep, 35, 36
demand effects, 93
Dement, William, 46, 49
demographics
    dreaming and, 223
    sleeping and, 63–72
demographic surveys, 7
Demographic Surveys, 102, 106, 108,
        148, 149, 152, 153, 163, 164, 169,
        172, 180, 198
demonic seduction (possession)
        dreams, 10, 213–17, 220
    gender and, 223
    explanations for, 226–27
    unconscious and, 220–21, 223, 224–26
depression, 173
Descartes, René, 45, 100
Descartes' Error (Damasio), 27
De Somniis (Aristotle), 80–81
devil, belief in, 221
De Waal, Frans, 29
Dick, Philip K., 302n24
Dimensions of Dreaming, The
        (Winget and Kramer), 101
disciplinary amnesia, 117
discontinuities, 127, 129–40
disorders of arousal, 53–54
divine conception, dreams of, 169
doctrinal mode of religiosity, 234, 235
Dodds, E. R., 80
dolphins, sleep of, 19–20
Domhoff, G. William, 41–42, 96, 97,
        101–2, 120–21, 123–26, 134–35, 139, 140
dopamine, 37, 38, 171

Dotcom, Kim, 284–85n19
double dissociation, 99
downward plunge, 183
"dream," etymology of, 79–80, 236
Dreambank.net, 102, 123
"dream diamond" model, 208
dreamer, as aggressor, 153–54
dream incubation, 240, 244–48,
        251–55, 261–64
dreaming. *See also* dreams; lucid
        dreaming
    brain damage and, 38–40,
        98–99, 236–37
    brain regions involved in, 98–99
    categories of, 298n16
    consciousness in, 268
    curative effects of, 253–54
    demographics and, 223
    diversity in, 146–47
    evolutionary context of, 8
    flexibility of, 138
    human sexuality and, 173
    as imaginative play, 129–30,
        136–40, 171
    as intensified version of waking
        mind wandering, 42
    intentionality and, 246
    locality and, 246
    meditation and, 258, 259
    mental activities occurring during,
        121–22, 267–68
    metaphors and, 171. *See also* metaphors
    necessity of, 92
    neural triggers for, 97
    NREM sleep and, 96–97, 99. *See
        also* NREM sleep
    oriented toward future challenges, 158
    phenomenology of, 208
    religions and, 56, 272
    REM sleep and, 96–98, 99. *See also*
        REM sleep
    role of, 238–39

self-awareness in, 266–68
skeptical philosophy and, 272
spatial cognition in, 155–56
survival needs and, 158
as therapeutic resource, 243
unconscious processes during, 226–27
waking life and, 237–38
dreaming–waking continuities, 113–27, 131, 252
Dreaming in the World's Religions (Bulkeley), 3, 82–83, 206
Dream Problem and the Mechanism of Thought, The (Horton), 100
dreams. *See also* big dreams; dreaming; lucid dreams
aesthetics of, 207
in animals, 81
attacks in, 149–51
authenticity of, 8
bizarreness of, 130–31
black-swan approach to, 2
blind analysis of, 123–27, 134–36
of blind people, 127, 236, 237
brain damage and, 38–40, 98–99, 236–37
in brain's default mode network, 139–40
breaking sexual taboos, 160, 168–69
carry-over effects of, 151, 169, 168, 172, 209
cell biology and, 114
certainty regarding, 233–34
chases in, 149–51
coding systems for, 209
cognitive science of religion and, 6–7. *See also* cognitive science of religion
consistency in, 96, 107–8
defining, 80–81
double dissociation in, 99, 237
dreaming–waking continuities and, 80–81, 113–27, 131, 252
dreaming–waking discontinuities in, 127, 129–40
elements in, 108, *109*
emotional content of, 85, 107–8
forgotten, 1
form of, 121
as gauge of dreamer's religiosity, 124
hand-coding methods for, 101
highly memorable, 1, 3
influencing waking behavior, 172
low interest in, and dream recall, 93
manifest vs. latent content of, 117–18
meanings of, 2, 112, 128–29
metacognition in, 266–68
metaphorical nature of, 131–36. *See also* metaphors
mind wandering and, 139
mundaneness of, 129–30
obstacles to study of, 77–78
ordinary, 9
over-interpretation of, 112
passionate feelings in, 85
patterns of, 102–11, 113–27, 131
personal connection to, 113
physical reality in, experience with, 147
as presentations, 80–81
primal themes in, 298–99n16
psychoanalytic theory and, 118
psychological information in, 101
realistic, 130. *See also* lucid dreaming
reason for, 2
recall of, 86–94, 138, 252
reliable research on, 78
and religion, 3–5, 10, 82–83, 235, 239
reports of, 8, 77–78, 85–86
scientific study of, 100–106
seeing, 80
sensory references in, 127
as side effects of sleeping activity, 95
significance of, 1–2
as simulations, 172

dreams (*Cont.*)
skepticism regarding, as subject of scientific study, 77–78, 95–96
social interactions in, with other characters, 147
stimulation of, 246
surveys of, 1–2
trivial, 1–2
universality of, in humans, 82–83
visual imagery in, 85, 99, 236
word search analysis and, 101–5, 107–11, 123–25, 135–36, 164–68, 199
Dream Seekers, The (Irwin), 233
Dreams and Nightmares (Hartmann), 101
"Dream Struggle, The," 153
D-Sleep, 97
dualism, interactive, 249
Durkheim, Émile, 56

Edison, Thomas, 15, 16
EEG. *See* electroencephalograph
Eggan, Dorothy, 100, 102, 118–20, 124, 263
ekbole, 114
Ekirch, Roger, 60, 61
electroencephalograph, 34, 35
Elementary Forms of Religious Life, The (Durkheim), 56
elements, appearing in dreams, 108
Eliade, Mircea, 5
emotional expression, 108
encephalization, 32–33, 40
end-of-life dreams, 135
enlightenment, experiences of, and the brain, 264–65
entropy, 178, 184–85, 190
Epic of Gilgamesh, 183, 194
epiphany, 246
episodic memory, 234
Erikson, Erik, 136
Evans, Christopher, 238

Evans, Dylan, 250
Evans, Peter, 238
evolution, 8, 19, 45
brain changes and, 28–32, 40
dynamic nature of, 24
sexual dreams and, 161, 175
shaping the human mind, 16
evolutionary psychology, 112, 190
Exegesis (Dick), 302n24
existential dreams, 209
experimental studies, 8
explicit memory, 50

faith, 254
falling dreams, 9, 202, 206
age and, 180
becoming lucid during, 183
carry-over from, 183
feelings during, 183
frequency of, 178
gender and, 180
income and, 180, *181*
meaning of, 177
motifs in, 183–87
political ideology and, 180, *182*, 192
waking life and, 182
family, threats to, 153
fear, religion and, 213
Feeling of What Happens, The (Damasio), 27
Finding Meaning in Dreams (Domhoff), 101
fish, sleep of, 21–22
Flanagan, Owen, 95
flying dreams, 9, 196–97, 199–200, 202–3
age and, 198
gender and, 197
metaphorical aspect of, 205–6
nationality and, 198
word search analysis of, 199
Foulkes, David, 97, 101

Fox, Kieran, 42
Freud, Sigmund, 2, 5, 6, 113–14, 117–18,
    128–29, 174–75, 177, 178, 219–21,
    222, 223, 266, 290–91n16
frontal-limbic region, 98, 170, 202
fur seal, sleep of, 21
fusiform gyrus, 41
futons, 62

GABA, 37–38, 171, 224–25
Gackenbach, Jayne, 268
Galen, 256
Gardner, Randy, 49
genies. *See* jinn possession
Germain, Anne, 172
Giora, Z., 149, 162
global anoneira, 98, 99
Global Realism Scale, 130
glutamate, 37
glycine, 38, 188–89
God Delusion, The (Dawkins), 228
gonekboles, 114, 168
good fortune, dreams of, 200–201
Grammar of Dreams, A (Foulkes), 101
gravitational dreams, 9, 147, 149, 209
    brain activity during, 187–89
    carry-over effects of, 178
    cultural symbolism of, 180, 192–93
    evolutionary psychology and, 190
    frequency of, 178–83
    illness and, 187, 189
    income and, 191–92
    jinn possession and, 193
    lacking social context, 178
    meaning of, 177, 178, 191
    metaphorical dimensions of, 191–94
    physical sensations of, 178
    purpose of, 190
    sleep paralysis and, 189
    themes of, 178, 183–87
    therapeutic progress and, 193–94
gravity, awareness of, 177

Griffith, Richard, 149, 163
group sleeping, 57–60

Hall, Calvin, 100–101, 102, 120–21
Hall, G. Stanley, 114
Hamilton, Edith, 185–86
Hartmann, Ernest, 101, 185
healing, dreaming and
    effectiveness of, 253
    cognitive science and, 247–51
    dream incubation and, 244–48, 251–55
    placebo effect of, 243
    psychology and, 247–51
    religion and, 242, 243–48
health, sleep and, 45–49, 52–55
Hearne, Keith, 266–67
Heraclitus, 56, 74
Herodotus, 153–54
Hillman, James, 207
hippocampus, 40, 41, 156
Hippocrates, 256
Hirshkowitz, Max, 173–74
histamine, 37
Hobbes, Thomas, 4
Hobson, J. Allan, 95–96, 130, 171
Holocaust, survivors of,
    dreams and, 138
Homer, 74
hominids
    adaptability of, 31
    brain capacity of, 30–31
    migrating into Europe, 31
    sleeping patterns of, 57
    splitting from other primates, 29
Homo erectus, 30–31
Homo habilis, 30–31
Homo heidelbergensis, 31
Homo neanderthalis, 31
Homo sapiens sapiens, 32, 33. *See also*
    human beings
    paradoxical sleep in, levels of, 36
    sleeping brain of, 34–42

Hopi Native Americans, dream studies of, 100, 118–20
horizon of uncertainty, 17
Horne, Jim, 48
Horton, Lydiard, 100
How the Mind Works (Pinker), 242
Hufford, David J., 224
human beings. See also *Homo sapiens sapiens*
  cognitive freedom of, 239
  creative explosion for, 33
  dreaming in, universality of, 82–83
  migration of, 33
  mind of, evolution's shaping of, 16
  neurological capacities of, 33–34
  primed to notice other living beings, 112
  sexual character of, 174
  sleep efficiency of, 23–24
human growth hormone, 45–46
Hume, David, 2
Hunt, Harry, 207–9, 268
HVDC (Hall and Van de Castle) system, 101, 120–21
HVDC Male and Female Norm, 102, 106, 108, 124–25
hyperactive agency detector module, 112
hypnogogic hallucinations, 53

Iliad (Homer), 152, 200
illness, gravitational dreams and, 187, 189
imaging technology, 39–40
imagistic mode of religiosity, 234–35
immune system, 189
  placebo treatments and, 250
  sleep and, 46, 243, 251–52
impactful dreams, 209
implicit memory, 50
Inception (dir. Nolan), 185
incubus, 224
indigenous traditions, healing dreams and, 247

individualism, 60–61
inemuri, 59
inferior parietal region, 98, 155–56, 170
In Search of Dreams (Strauch and Meier), 101
insomnia, 64, 65–72, 173
intentionality, 246
interleukin-1, 45–46
International Survey, 102, 106
Interpretation of Dreams, The (Freud), 2, 117, 128–29, 177
Iordache, Sandu, 134–35
Irwin, Lee, 233, 262–63
Islam, dream incubation in, 246
isomorphism, 96
istikhara, 246

James, William, 6, 51, 218, 219–21, 222, 257, 271
Jewell, James Ralph, 116, 117
jinn possession, dreams of, 192–93, 214–16, 223–25
Johnson, Mark, 131, 132, 191
Jones, Ernest, 221
Jones, James W., 248–49, 251
Jouvet, Michel, 81
Judaism, dream incubation in, 246–47
Jung, Carl, 2, 6, 158, 159, 206–7, 219, 266, 277n3

Kahan, Tracey, 97–98, 102, 121–22, 268
Kamakura Buddhism, 258–59
Kaminer, Hanna, 138
Kay, Paul, 111
K-complexes, 34
Kleitman, Nathaniel, 95–96
Knudson, Roger, 203–4, 207
Kozmova, Miloslava, 121, 268
Kramer, Milton, 101
Kripke, Daniel, 51–52
Krippner, Stanley, 102

Kuiken, Don, 209
Kuma people, 153, 216

LaBerge, Stephen, 121–22, 266–67
Lakoff, George, 131–34, 191, 206
Landscapes of the Night (Evans), 238
latent content, 117–18
Lavie, Peretz, 138
learning, sleep and, 50
lesions, 39–41. *See also* brain,
    damage to
Leslie, Kenneth, 188
Leuchter, Andrew, 249–50
Levin, Ross, 148
Lewis-Williams, David, 83
Lilith, 216
limbic system, 40, 41, 155, 156,
    202, 265–66
Linnaeus, Carl, 208
little dreams, 147, 277n3
locality, 246
locus coeruleus, 40
Lohmann, Roger, 59
Lou, Hans, 265
lucid dreaming
    attentiveness to, 257
    awareness increased during, 258
    carry-over effect of, 269
    cultivation of, 261–64
    dream research and, 266–69
    inducing, 266–67
    meditation and, 266, 268–69
    metaphorical nature of, 260–61
    as mode of consciousness, 260
    cross-cultural occurrence of, 261–62
    prevalence of, 266
    psychology and, 264
    rejection of, 266
    religion and, 269
lucidity, vestibular activity and, 188
Lucretius, 4
Lucy, 29–30

MacLeod, Ian R., 186–87
Mahowald, Mark W., 54
Malcolm, Norman, 266
Malleus Maleficarum [The Hammer of
    Witches], 217–18
mammals
    cognitive abilities of, 22
    sleep of, 21–22
    water-dwelling, sleep of, 19–21
manifest content, 117–18
Maquet, Pierre, 50, 252
masalai, 216
materialism, 99–100
mattresses, 61–62
McCarley, Robert, 96
medial occipito-temporal structures, 98
medial prefrontal cortex, 156, 170, 203
medial temporal lobe, 41
medical-somatic dreams, 208
medication, effect of, on
    neurotransmitters, 37
meditation, 139
    dreaming and, 258, 259
    impact of, 266
    lucid dreaming and, 266, 268–60
    neural functioning and, 264–66
Meier, Barbara, 101
melatonin, 45, 47
Memorable Dreams, 185
memory
    REM sleep and, 50
    sleep and, 49
mental phenomena, source of, 249
mesolimbic region, 171
metacognition, 121–22, 267–68
metacognitive dreaming, 170
metaphors, 175
    big dreams and, 273–74
    dream content and, 131–36
    dreaming and, 171
    flying dreams and, 205–6
    gravitational dreams and, 191–94

metaphors (Cont.)
limits of, 132
lucid dreaming and, 260–61
prophetic dreams and, 240
sexual dreams and, 175
targets and sources of, 132
and the waking mind, 131–32
Metaphors We Live By (Lakoff
and Johnson), 131, 191
Miami Home/Lab Dreams, 102, 106, 108
micro-awakenings, 58
mind, as system of organs, 278n2
mind-body connection, 248–49
mind-body dualism, 100
Mind Possessed, The (Cohen), 221–22
mind wandering, 42, 139
Mitchison, Graeme, 95
modes of religiosity theory, 234–35
Modesto, Ruby, 263
modular thinking, 203
Moffitt, Alan, 268
monophasic sleep, 23
monstrous aliens, in nightmares, 153
Morales, Francisco R., 38
motifs, 151–52
mouse lemur, sleep of, 23
Muhammad, 201, 246
Multiplicity of Dreams, The (Hunt), 207–8
mundane dreams, 209
*Myoe the Dreamkeeper: Fantasy and
Knowledge in Early Kamakura
Buddhism* (Tanabe), 258–61
Myoe Shonin, 258–61
mystical dreams, 9–10, 147, 209, 210
brain activity during, 201–4
carry-over effects of, 204
frequency of, 196–99
function of, 205
hybrids with, 201
motifs of, 199–201
removed from the waking world, 202
simulating possibility, 205–6

superstitious thinking and, 195
types of, 196
mythical dreams, 225
myths, 5

naps, 59
narcolepsy, 53, 173
Naropa, 262
Nashe, Thomas, 95
Nasser, Lana, 149, 192–93, 214
National Sleep Foundation (NSF), 63
Native Americans
prophetic dreams and, 233
visionary practices of, 262–63
Neanderthals, culture of, 33
Nelson, Julius, 114, 116, 117, 168
neural circuitry, formation of, 51
neuroplasticity, 39, 49–51, 238, 252
neurotransmitters, 37
Newberg, Andrew, 265
newborns
altricial, 36
precocial, 36
Nielsen, Tore, 97, 148, 149, 172,
298–99n16
Nietzsche, Friedrich, 4–5, 271
nightmares, 126. *See also*
aggressive dreams
age and, 148–49
blocking of, 145–46
brain activity during, 146, 154–56
fear and, 213–14
frequency of, 147–51
gender and, 148–49
motifs in, 151–54
patterns in, 146
PTSD and, 138–39, 154
purpose of, 146, 156–59
realism of, 155, 158
recurring, 98
religion and, 213
sensory awareness and, 155–56

settings for, 152
social intelligence and, 155, 156
as threat simulations, 156–59
night terrors, 53–55, 293n4
nocebo effect, 251
nocturnal emissions. *See* wet dreams
Nolan, Christopher, 185
non-dreamers, 92–93
non-rapid eye movement sleep. *See*
NREM sleep
noradrenaline, 37, 40
northern fur seal, sleep of, 20
NREM sleep, 21
chemical activity during, 37
deprivation of, 47
dreaming and, 96–97, 99
memories and, 50
night terrors and, 53–54
sleepwalking and, 53
stages of, 34–35
NSF (National Sleep Foundation), 63

occipital region, 41, 155, 170
Odyssey (Homer), 74
O'Flaherty, Wendy Doniger, 5
Ogilvie, Robert, 188
Old Hag, 224
On the Nightmare (Jones), 221
orbital periodicity, 17
orexin, 37, 53
owl monkeys, sleep of, 23
oxytocin, 171

Pagel, James, 92–93, 268–69
Paleolithic art, 83–85, 261
Panksepp, Jaak, 202
paradoxical sleep, 21, 22, 42–43, 170
in cats, 81
energy use and, 25
function of, 36
and the human brain's early
development, 36

intense forms of, 25
neural firings during, 50
physical changes during, 171
proportion of, 36
vestibular system and, 188
parahippocampal gyrus, 40
paralysis, dreams of, 183–84, 188. *See
also* sleep paralysis
parasomnias, 55
parietal lobe, 265
Patton, Kimberley, 246
Pergamon spa, 244–45
Perpetua, 229–33, 240–41
personal-mnemonic dreams, 208
personal privacy, 60
personal space, invasion of, 152
Petronius, 213
PGO spikes, 35, 171
PGO waves, 41
physicalism, 248–49
physics, influence of, awareness of, 178
Piaget, Jean, 136
picture-gazing dreams, 232
pillows, 62
pineal gland, 45, 47
Pinker, Steven, 242, 243
*Placebo: Mind over Matter in Modern
Medicine* (Evans), 250
placebo effect, 249–51, 254
plasticity, 51
Plato, 168–69, 263
play
animal development and, 136–37
and the brain's default mode
network, 140
dreaming as, 129–30, 136–40, 171
features of, 137
therapeutic nature of, 139
polyphasic sleep, 23
pontine tegmentum, 41
Popper, Karl, 100
positive emotions, neurobiology of, 202

possession. *See* demonic possession
post-traumatic stress disorder, 138–39
   dreaming and, 253
   nightmares and, 154
Power of Metaphor, The
      (ed. Landau et al.), 132
prayer, brain activity and, 265
predation, sleep and, 19–20, 25
prefrontal cortex, 40, 156, 170, 265
prefrontal systems, 265
pregnancy, as motif in sexual
      dreams, 169
primary visual cortex, 41
primates
   cognitive innovations of, 23
   shifting to nighttime sleep, 23
   sleep consolidation in, 22–23
   sleep efficiency of, 23
   sleeping patterns of, 57
Principles of Psychology (James), 51
problem of inductive reasoning, 2
procedural memory, 50, 234
prolactin, 47
prophetic dreams, 208, 240
   carry-over effects of, 235–36, 240
   certainty regarding, 233–34
   of children, 232
   cognitive science and, 234–35
   cross-cultural religious experience
      of, 233
   delusional nature of, 228
   forecasting death, 231
   imagistic experience of, 234–37
   life change and, 231
   as metaphor, 240
   naturalistic basis for, 238
   psychology of, 233–36
   REM sleep and, 236
   sources of, 229, 236–39
   themes in, 231–32
   visual imagery in, 232–33
prophetic vision, 10, 214
Proverbs, book of, 44

PS. *See* paradoxical sleep
psychoanalysis, 6
psychology, used to study religion, 219–20
PTSD. *See* post-traumatic stress disorder
Purcell, Sheila, 267, 268

Raichle, Marcus, 139
Ramon y Cayal, Santiago, 51
rapid eye movement sleep. *See*
      REM sleep
rare events, importance of, 2
Rattenborg, Niels, 22
reality, bizarreness gauged against, 131
Reay, Marie, 153
rebound effect, 18, 24, 49, 63
Rechtschaffen, Allan, 24, 25
Reid, Thomas, 145–46
Religion Explained: The Evolutionary
      Origins of Religious Thought
      (Boyer), 257
religions. *See also* cognitive science of
      religion
   brain/mind functions and religious
      phenomena, 239
   comparative study of, 221
   describing big dreams, 3
   dreaming and, 239, 272
   experiential origins of, 3
   explanations of, evolution and, 8
   expression of, 234–35
   fear and, 213
   healing dreams and, 242, 243–48
   as hucksterism, 242–43
   lucid dreaming and, 269
   nightmares and, 213
   parasitic nature of, 257
   practices of, and social realities, 56
   prophetic dreams and, 228, 229, 238
   psychological approach to, 219–20, 271
   social and personal dimensions of, 56
   understanding of, 257
   worship in, and insomnia, 70–71
religiosity, modes of, 234–35

REM Behavior Disorder (REMBD), 53
REM latency, 54
REM sleep, 2, 21, 34
  anatomical shifts during, 41–42
  blood flow during, 171
  brain activation during, 85
  chemical activity during, 37–38
  compared to default network, 41–42
  deprivation of, 47, 173–74
  dreaming and, 96–98, 99
  efficiency of, 23–24
  GABA and, 224–25
  limbic system and, 41, 155, 156
  medial prefrontal cortex and, 203
  memories and, 50
  motionlessness during, 46–47
  muscle paralysis during, 38
  neural activity during, 41, 236
  onset of, 35, 46
  sensation in, of orientation in dreamt space, 296–97n12
  similarities of, with waking state, 35, 38
  vestibular system and, 188
  visual imagination and, 170
  visual processing during, 41
reptiles, sleep of, 21–22
Republic (Plato), 263
restless limb syndrome, 53
reticular activating system, 41
reverse engineering, 154
Revonsuo, Antti, 130, 158–59, 171–72, 190
Ricoeur, Paul, 5
Rig Veda, 217
ritual healing, 10
Roffwarg, Howard, 36

Sacred Tales, The (Aristides), 244–45
safety, group sleeping and, 58
Salmivalli, Christina, 130
Santa Clara Dreams, 102, 106
Scarre, Chris, 84
Schneider, Adam, 102, 123
Schredl, Michael, 90, 93, 149, 163

Scientific Study of Dreams, The (Domhoff), 101
SDDb. *See* Sleep and Dream Database
SDDb Baseline Dreams (baselines), 102–11
Seligman, C. G., 149
sensory awareness, nightmares and, 155–56
serotonin, 37
Seven Nights (Borges), 151
sexual dreams, 9, 114, 147, 224–25
  adaptive function of, 172–75
  age and, 163–64, 172
  brain/mind systems involved in, 169–71
  counterfactual scenarios in, 170, 171, 174–75
  cultural reluctance to discuss, 161–62, 166, 168, 172
  education and, *165*
  evolution and, 161, 175
  frequency of, 161–67
  gender and, 163–64, 167, 172
  immoral behavior and, 160–61, 168–69, 174–75
  as metaphorical expressions, 175
  moral dangers and, 161
  motifs in, 168–69
  neuroelectrical activity during, 171
  personal finances and, *165*
  physiological responses during, 170, 171
  political ideology and, 164, *166*
  priming the reproductive system, 161, 172–73
  religious worship service attendance and, 164
  social cognition and, 170
  survival and, 161
  understating of, 161, 163
  vividness of, 169–70
  waking life circumstances and, 167
  word search analysis of, 164–68
sexual problems, sleep problems and, 173

sexual reproduction, evolutionary
    advantage of, 175
Shabaka, King, 153–54
shaitan, 193
shamans, 84–85, 261
Shaw, Rosalind, 216–17
Sherrington, Charles S., 51
Siegel, Jerome, 25
singularity, 239
skepticism, dreaming and, 272
sleep
    activity during, 8, 21, 26, 27, 28,
        38–43, 46–47
    amount of, 52, 64
    ancestral environment for, 17
    animals living without, 18
    body temperature and, 46
    chemicals released during, 45–46
    circadian rhythms and, 18–19, 25
    cognitive functioning and, 22
    community beliefs about, 58
    conditions for, 64
    consolidation of, 22–23
    cultural influences on, 57
    cycles of, 34–35, 47, 48
    definition of, 18
    demographics and, 63–72
    education and, 65–71
    energy management and, 25
    ethnicity and, 64
    evolution and, 8, 16, 19, 45
    excessive, 44–45
    excessively short, 52
    flexibility of, 20–21, 25, 48, 55
    fluidity of, 59
    functions of, 24–26, 50
    gender and, 64–71
    healing during, 252
    health and, 45–49, 52–55
    homeostatic qualities of, 18
    imaging technology and, 39–40
    immune system and, 243, 251–52

income and, 65–71
as individual experience, 56
indispensability of, 48
learning and, 50
lifespan and, 52
material conditions of, 61–63
medication for, 37
memory and, 49
modern conditions for,
    73–74, 285n20
modifying cycles of, 48
monophasic, 23
mortality rates and 52
national differences in, 64
need for, 15–16
negative pressures on, 73–74
neural correlates of, 42–43
neuroscience of, 34
onset of, 46
of parents and children, 58
personal privacy in, 60
political ideology and, 65, 71
polyphasic, 23
problems with, and sexual
    problems, 173
in public, 59
quality of, 65
race and, 64
rebound effect with, 18, 24, 49, 63
with sexual mates, 58
sexual stimulation during, 171, 224
in single-gender groups, 58–59
skepticism about, 44
social dimension of, 57, 74
socioeconomic status and, 65, 72
solipsistic aspects of, 56, 57, 74
survival and, 25, 52
syndromes associated with, 52–53
thermoregulatory function of, 25
variability of, 24
weekends vs. work days, 63–64
sleep deprivation, 63

effects of, 48, 281–82n11
narcolepsy and, 53
socioeconomic status and, 65
studies of, 47–49
toleration of, 48–49
waking sexual behavior and, 173–74
Sleep and Dream Database, 7–8, 65,
  90, 102
sleep efficiency, 23
sleep factors, 37
sleep laboratories, 1
sleep paralysis, 53, 54–55, 147, 189,
  223–24. *See also* paralysis,
  dreams of
sleepwalking, 53, 54–55
slow wave sleep, 21, 22, 35
  human growth hormone and, 46
  neural activity during, 40
Snyder, Frederick, 101, 130, 158
Socrates, 231–32
Solms, Mark, 98–99, 155–56,
  202, 236–37
sophists, 244
sorcery, 251
spatialization of form hypothesis, 191
spectral evidence, 218
Sperber, Dan, 222
Spiegel, Jerome, 19
spindles, 34
spirits, counterintuitive quality
  of, 222–23
spontaneous exegetical reflection, 235
Stepansky, R., 86–90
Strauch, Inge, 101
subconscious, 219
subjective data, problems with, 86
succubus, 224
Sufism, 262
Summa Theologica (Aquinas), 10
supernatural agents, 222–23, 225
Sutton-Smith, Brian, 136
Swainson's thrush, sleep of, 20–21

swefn, 79
SWS. *See* slow wave sleep
synesthesia, 204
Szpakowska, Kasia, 80

Taleb, Nicholas Nassim, 2
Tanabe, George J., Jr., 258–61
Tantric Yoga, 262
Taylor, Jeremy, 158
TDQ. *See* Typical Dreams Questionnaire
Tedlock, Barbara, 261, 263
Temne people, 216–17
temporal limbic structures, 98
temporal region, 41, 155, 170
terrestrial life, rhythm of, 16–17
Terrors of the Night, The (Nashe), 95
thalamus, 41, 188
thematic sets, 8
theory of mind, 22, 29, 156, 170, 203
Third Reich of Dreams, The (Beradt), 152
threat simulation theory, 157–59,
  171–72, 190
Tiger Garden, The: A Book of Writers'
  Dreams (MacLeod), 186–87
titanic dreams, 185–87
transcendent dreams, 209
transportation words, metaphorical
  nature of, 135
TST. *See* threat simulation theory
tumor necrosis factor, 45–46
Tylor, Edward B., 4, 271
Typical Dreams Questionnaire, 149–51,
  153, 161–62, 178, 191, 193, 197

Ullman, Montague, 158, 159
unconscious, 219

Valli, Katja, 158
Van de Castle, Robert, 100–101, 102, 120
Varieties of Religious Experience, The
  (James), 218
vestibular system, 187–88, 202–3

video games, dreams and, 126
violence, ideological form of, 152
visions, 4
visitation dreams, 196–97, 199–200, 206
  age and, 198
  gender and, 197
  nationality and, 198
  social experience of, 203
visual anoneira, 98

waking consciousness. *See also*
  dreaming–waking continuities
  metaphors' role in, 131–32
  shift to, 47
  transitions and, 54
Walker, Matthew, 50, 81
Walsh, Mary, 193–94
Wang Ch'ung, 195
warm-blooded creatures, brains of, 22
Watson, James, 238

waves, dreams of, 185
wet dreams, 114, 168–69
whales, sleep of, 19–20
Whitehouse, Harvey, 222, 234–36
Whitley, David S., 83
Winget, Carolyn, 101
Winnicott, D. W., 136, 139
witchcraft, 218, 251
Wolman, Richard, 121
word search analysis, 101–5, 107–11,
  123–25, 135–36, 164–68, 199

yoga nidra, 265
Young, Serinity, 80
Yu, Calvin, 90

Zadra, Antonio, 93
zebra finch, cognitive abilities of, 22
zebra fish, sleep of, 18–19
Zen and the Brain (Austin), 264–65